THE *NEW* BOOK OF TRUSTS
"THE <u>WHOLE</u> TRUTH ABOUT TRUSTS
AFTER THE 1997 TAX ACT"

Stephan R. Leimberg, Esq.

Charles K. Plotnick, Esq.

Russell E. Miller

Daniel B. Evans

Leimberg Associates
Bryn Mawr, PA

Published by **Leimberg Associates Books**, a division **of Leimberg Associates, Inc**. (610-527-5216).

ISBN # 0-9644565-2-4   THE _NEW_ BOOK OF TRUSTS—2nd Edition

Copyright 1997. **Leimberg Associates, Inc**. P.O. Box 601, Bryn Mawr, Pa. 19010. Phone: 610-527-5216/FAX: 610-527-5226. Additional copies of this book can be obtained by calling 610-527-5216.

Printed in the United States of America

DEDICATION

To my best friend and wife, Jo-Ann, my daughters Charlee and Lara, my son-in-law Rob, and the most trusted member of our family, my new grandson, Max.

S.R.L.

To my wonderful family: My wife, Diane, my children Steven and Susan, Amy and Joshua, and my grandchildren Lisa, Benjamin, Lauren, Gregory and Ian.

C.K.P.

To my most sincere critic and loyal fan—my wife Winnie!

R.E.M.

To my wife, Storm, and my children, Merritt and Griffin, whose faith in me exceeds my grasp.

D.B.E.

CONTENTS

WHY WE NEED TRUSTS 1

HOW TRUSTS WORK 15

HOW TO CHOOSE THE BEST TRUSTEES 29

HOW TRUSTEES GET IN TROUBLE 45

RIGHTS OF BENEFICIARIES IN TRUSTS 55

ARE LAWYERS REALLY NECESSARY? 67

THE PROBLEM WITH TEAR-OUT TRUSTS 73

USING TRUSTS TO AVOID PROBATE 79

THE CASE FOR-AND AGAINST-REVOCABLE LIVING TRUSTS 103

HOW REVOCABLE LIVING TRUSTS ARE AFFECTED BY INCOME, GIFT,
AND ESTATE TAXES 141

WHAT ASSETS SHOULD NOT BE PLACED IN A REVOCABLE LIVING TRUST? 155

SHORT-FORM SECURITIES TRUSTS 171

MARITAL AND BY-PASS TRUSTS 181

JOINT TRUSTS 209

TRUSTS FOR MINORS 223

IRREVOCABLE TRUSTS 245

IRREVOCABLE LIFE INSURANCE TRUSTS 271

GENERATION-SKIPPING AND "DYNASTY" TRUSTS 317

TRUSTS FOR HANDICAPPED CHILDREN 331

HOW AND WHEN TO PUT YOUR HOUSE IN TRUST— THE HOUSE GRIT 339

TRUSTS FOR UNIQUE AND DIFFICULT SITUATIONS 349

GRATS AND GRUTS 357

THE USE OF TRUSTS IN MEDICAID PLANNING 371

TRUSTS FOR DISABILITY AND OLD AGE 377

CHARITABLE GIFTS AND PRIVATE FOUNDATIONS 389

CHARITABLE SPLIT-INTEREST TRUSTS 409

TRUSTS THAT PROTECT ASSETS FROM CREDITORS 441

IRREVOCABLE "SELF-SETTLED" TRUSTS 461

BUSINESS TRUSTS 465

TRUST FRAUDS, FANTASIES, AND ABUSES 475

APPENDIX:

      SAMPLE DEED PLACING REAL ESTATE IN TRUST 487

      SAMPLE REVOCABLE TRUST AGREEMENT 493

      CHECKLIST OF TRUSTEE'S DUTIES FOLLOWING DEATH OF
            GRANTOR/BENEFICIARY[*] 499

            WHAT ARE THE TRUSTEE'S DUTIES FOLLOWING
            THE DEATH OF THE GRANTOR/BENEFICIARY? 503

      IRS FORMS THAT MAY BE USEFUL IN PLANNING OR
            ADMINISTERING ESTATES OR TRUSTS[*] 507

      IRS ANNOUNCEMENT ON "ABUSIVE TRUSTS" 509

      GLOSSARY OF KEY TRUST PLANNING TERMS 515

FORWORD

Nationally known estate planning authorities, Professor Stephan R. Leimberg, attorney Charles K. Plotnick, radio commentator Russell E. Miller, and attorney Daniel B. Evans have teamed up to tell you everything you need to know about trusts—after the '97 Tax Act. You'll learn why a trust may be useful to you, how they work, how to select the best trustee, and the role of trusts in avoiding probate. Thirty chapters, a very useful appendix, and a thorough glossary put the subject of trusts at your fingertips.

There are three reasons **THE _NEW_ BOOK OF TRUSTS** is different than any other book on trusts:

First, as it's subtitle, "The Whole Truth About Trusts—after the 1997 Tax Act" implies, you'll learn the reality of the downsides, the costs, and the alternatives to trusts as well as the many advantages. This is a "no holds barred" honest look at trusts you may not have obtained before. Rather than the "panic and panacea" approach ("terrible things will happen if you don't have a living trust but buy this book, rip out and fill out the forms, and all your problems will disappear in an instant with no thinking or outside help required"), you'll find a solid consumers' objective view of the subject. Trusts aren't right for everyone. You'll find out if a trust is right for you and if so, what type of trust and trust provisions you should consider.

Second, rather than a quick "once over" treatment, this book will provide you with the detailed in-depth information to make a well-informed intelligent decision as to whether or not a trust is the appropriate vehicle for your personal planning and if so, how that trust can best be implemented and operated. Unlike "fine print" books which are difficult to read and are written to impress rather than inform or "picture" books which gloss over important details or don't cover Dynasty trusts, Alaska, Delaware, Massachusetts, offshore, or other key trusts used currently, this resource is both clear and comprehensive.

Third, rather than a "do-it-yourself" book, this is a "Think-for-Yourself" book. Rather than simplistic "ten minute mentality" ("read this book and in ten minutes you'll know everything you need to know"), this book will give you the questions you need to ask to be an informed and proactive trust grantor, trustee, or beneficiary.

THE _NEW_ BOOK OF TRUSTS is just that, a completely updated (Post TRA-'97) and expanded book about the many different types of trusts you can harness to save income, estate, generation-skipping, and other taxes at both the federal and state level. It is also a book that will give you many nontax reasons to protect yourself and those you love from both creditors and predators and provide security and management protection for generations.

We suggest you read **THE _NEW_ BOOK OF TRUSTS** slowly. Read the first five chapters in order. Then go through the Table of Contents and select the category that you are most interested in learning about or type of problem you'd like to solve. We're sure you'll find this an invaluable and frequently used reference tool.

Stephan R. Leimberg, JD, CLU
Editor and Publisher
Leimberg Associates, Inc.

ABOUT THE AUTHORS

STEPHAN R. LEIMBERG is Professor of Taxation and Estate Planning at the American College in Bryn Mawr, Pennsylvania. He is the author of over 40 books on estate, business, and retirement planning and is an adjunct professor at Temple University School of Law's Tax Masters program. Leimberg has been frequently quoted in *The Wall Street Journal, Kiplinger's Changing Times, Money Magazine, Standard and Poor's Outlook,* and *Business Week, was recently* honored by the American Bar Association's Probate and Property Section, and has appeared on numerous national TV and radio shows. Nationally syndicated columnist Sylvia Porter called Leimberg "a crusader for personal financial management."

CHARLES K. PLOTNICK is a practicing attorney specializing in estate planning and administration in Jenkintown, Pennsylvania and is listed in *Who's Who in American Law*. He is also an adjunct professor of estate planning at Temple University's Graduate School of Business. Plotnick is co-author, with Stephan R. Leimberg, of ***How To Settle An Estate, A Manual For Executors And Trustees***. He also co-authored with Leimberg ***Keeping Your Money*** published by John Wiley and Sons, ***Get Rich, Stay Rich***, and ***The Executor's Manual*** published by Doubleday. Mr. Plotnick's articles on estate planning have been selected for reprinting by the Judge Advocate General's School, U.S. Army. Plotnick is widely quoted in the *New York Times,* the *Philadelphia Inquirer,* the *Washington Post, Fortune Magazine,* by Standard and Poor's, and is a contributing author to the Dow Jones ***Handbook Of Estate Planning***. Plotnick has served as Director and President of the Montgomery County (PA) Estate Planning Council and was Regional Vice President of the National Association of Estate Planning Councils from 1974 to 1980.

RUSSELL E. MILLER is a REALTOR, radio talk show host, trust counselor and financial planner. Mr. Miller has hosted the "Russ Miller Show" featured as "Real Estate and Your Estate" on radio station WWDB in Philadelphia since 1974. He has also hosted several other such programs including NBC Talk Net from New York. Miller has written many pamphlets on real estate, financial and estate planing, including "A Millionaire's Secret," "The Revocable Trust Deed," "Joint Tenants with Rights of Survivorship," "Family Estate Plans," and "The Short-Form Securities Trust." He is the Past President and Founder of the Trust Counselors' Network, an estate planning organization for the development and use of trusts in estate planning.

Miller is the Past President of the Delaware County Association of REALTORS for 1969 and was awarded REALTOR of the Year in 1968. He originated and chaired the Standard Forms Committee for the Delaware County Association of REALTORS and Pennsylvania Association of REALTORS for 20 years.

DANIEL B. EVANS received his J.D. *cum laude* from the University of Pennsylvania and practices law in Wyndmoor, Pennsylvania, mainly in the areas of estate planning, estate and trust administration, and related tax planning for closely held businesses. e is active in the American, Pennsylvania, and Philadelphia Bar Associations, and has written and spoken extensively on estate planning and legal technology. In the ABA Section of Law Practice Management, Evans is (among other things) a member of the governing council and a member of the editorial board and New Products Co-Editor of *Law Practice Management* magazine. He is currently serving as the "Probate— Technology" Editor of *Probate and Property* magazine, published by the Section of Real Property, Probate and Trust Law of the American Bar Association. Evans is the author of a book, ***Wills, Trusts, and Technology: An Estate Lawyer's Guide to Automation***, published jointly by the Real Property, Probate and Trust Law and Law Practice Management Sections of the ABA. His complete resume, and many of his writings, can be found on the Internet at http://www.netaxs.com/~evansdb".

ACKNOWLEDGMENTS

The authors would like to express our particular thanks to Jenkintown, Pa. attorney Jonathan H. Ellis. Jon's careful examination of our text and helpful suggestions have added immeasurably to the quality of the book you have in your hands.

Stephan R. Leimberg
Editor/Publisher
Leimberg Associates Books

WHY WE NEED TRUSTS

Chapter 1 explains:

- Why so many of us need trusts

- How can a trust help you personally

- When you should set up a trust for your spouse

- When you should set up a trust for your children

- How trusts can provide for dependent parents

- How trusts can provide for other family members

- How trusts can provide for non-family members

- How trusts can save income taxes for your family

- How trusts can save gift and estate taxes

Q. Why do we need trusts?

    A. Because trusts are excellent solutions to many different kinds of problems. Trusts can:

- Protect against many of the legal and financial problems of disability and old age;

- Protect people from the financial consequences of bad marriages, bad business decisions, or other legal problems;

- Provide for children (or grandchildren) until they are mature enough to handle their own affairs;

- Avoid estate and inheritance taxes;

- Reduce income taxes;

- Provide professional investment and asset management;

- Prevent family assets like farms or businesses from being unnecessarily divided or sold; and

- Make sure that benefits go to the right people, at the right times, for the right purposes, and in the right amounts.

Properly structured, a trust can be one of the most beneficial methods of holding and transferring property. There are almost unlimited uses for trusts in today's complex society.

We therefore believe that anyone who cares enough to plan for the future must consider the many ways that trusts can benefit the people and institutions that are important to him or her.

Q. How can a trust help me personally?

A. By establishing a trust with yourself as beneficiary, you can make arrangements for your future care and comfort. Your trust can include provisions for future contingencies. For example, you may have just retired, have set aside money for yourself, and are receiving a pension. Though it appears you have financial security, you are concerned about managing your money, about disability, and about old age.

While you are well, you could be your own trustee. By establishing a trust with a bank or trust company or with a responsible individual as a "back-up" trustee, you could make arrangements to protect yourself from these potential future problems. If you became disabled or for whatever other reason could not or did not want to handle the assets in the trust, the back-up trustee would take your place. Alternatively, right now you could transfer your assets to a trustee, who would provide professional money management for you and relieve you of the everyday responsibility of handling your money. In the event of your future disability, the trustee would have funds available to use for your benefit, while at the same time continuing to manage the money. At your death, the trust would provide for the disposition of your funds to those persons or institutions whom you intend to benefit.

Q. Should I establish a trust for my spouse?

A. There are many specific situations in this book that explain the advantages of placing all or some of your assets in trust for your spouse at your death. If your spouse isn't accustomed to managing or handling large sums of money, is not a citizen of the United States, is not the parent of all of your children, or your total assets exceed the unified credit exclusion amount ($600,000 in 1997, but increasing by steps to $1,000,000 in 2006), a trust would almost certainly be the best method of providing for your spouse at your death. You should also consider a trust for your spouse in the event of his or her future disability. For example, as discussed more fully in chapter 13, if you are in a second marriage, have children from a prior marriage, and want to make provisions for your spouse at your death but still provide for your own children at your spouse's subsequent death, a *QTIP trust* is an excellent way to provide for both your spouse and your children. A *spendthrift trust,* discussed in chapter 27, is also an excellent way to protect your spouse from creditors.

Q. When should I set up trusts for children?

A. Although there are many ways to make provisions for minor children, such as custodial accounts and guardianship (both discussed in chapter 2), in many instances a trust will do a superior job for your children. A trust can provide professional money management for your children's funds, and distribute income to them in the manner and at the ages you select. This is preferable to a custodial account under which funds are distributed to them when the children reach the age specified under state law (usually either 18 or 21), because children often lack the emotional or intellectual maturity, physical capacity, or technical training to handle large sums of money at those ages. A trust can provide for your children's education and treat them equitably—but not necessarily equally—when appropriate.

For example, if one of your children has serious health problems, you may not want to leave your money equally to all of your children. If your daughter is a successful lawyer, and your son is partially handicapped, you might want to consider providing differently for them.

A discretionary trust may be the best means of providing for a handicapped child's needs and preserving his or her government entitlements, as discussed more fully in chapter 19. When a spendthrift provision is included in the trust document, trusts can also protect your children from claims of creditors (or their spouses).

Moreover, trusts for children can "sprinkle" the trust funds among them to meet their needs as they arise. In most families, the parents keep all of their money in one pot and use the funds for the children as expenses are incurred. For example, if you go into a shoe store with your young son and daughter, and your daughter needs corrective shoes that cost $25 more than the shoes you are buying for your son, you do not put an extra $25 in an envelope for your son. With a sprinkle trust, you can give your trustee the right to pay expenses as they are incurred without the requirement that all of the children receive exactly the same amounts.

Q. How can trusts provide for dependent parents?

A. In practically every instance where sufficient funds are available, a trust will be the best way to provide for dependent parents in the event of your death.

For example, if you have been helping to support your parents by giving them $5,000 a year and you want the payments to continue after your death, you could set up a trust for your parents and fund the trust with $100,000. These funds could be invested by the trustees, with the income (which you assume to be 5 percent or $5,000 a year) paid (and taxed) to your lower income tax bracket parents rather than to you at your higher tax bracket. At your parents' death, the balance remaining in the trust would be distributed to your children. This is preferable to giving the money directly to your parents, who may not be in a position to invest it properly, and whose estates could be required to pay additional death taxes on that $100,000, taxes that could have been avoided had a trust been set up. And something could happen to your parents or their estate plans that results in the entire $100,000 going to creditors or other family members instead of back to you or your children.

Q. How can trusts benefit other family members?

A. You should certainly consider trusts if you plan to leave money to grandchildren. Not only can trusts provide your grandchildren's educational needs, but they can also make provisions to distribute the remaining trust assets to the grandchildren at certain ages.

If you have a deceased child, you can set up a trust for your son-in-law or daughter-in-law during his or her lifetime, with the trust assets reverting to your grandchildren (or other family members) at your in-law's death.

Trusts can also be used to keep assets such as a home or a business in the family for many years or several generations.

If you have no immediate family, you might want to establish a trust to provide for a favorite niece or nephew, for example, or to provide a permanent source of income for a brother or sister who is not a good money manager.

Q. How can trusts provide for non-family members?

A. There may be certain people who are very important to you and for whom you would like to provide, although they are not related to you. Examples might be members of your church, synagogue, or fraternal order, or a close friend or live-in companion. Trusts can also offer the flexibility, reliability, and strict confidentiality in situations where publicity is not desired. Examples of such situations include making provisions for a child born out of wedlock, a close friend of the opposite sex who is not your spouse, or a lover.

Q. How can trusts save income taxes for my family?

A. It is important to understand our income tax rate structure and how trusts can help reduce the family's overall income tax bite. Income tax rates are progressive, which means that the rate of tax increases as your income increases. The more successful you become, the bigger the percentage of your income taken by the IRS. Trusts that can spread income among many family members can shift income to lower tax brackets and save income taxes. For example, if you set up a trust for your three children who are each age 14 or older, and in a 15 percent tax bracket while you are in a 33 percent tax bracket, your family will be paying 18 percent (33–15) less taxes on the income your children receive from the assets in the trust.

Trusts can also be used to defer income until after retirement, when your total income will probably be less, and your income tax rates should therefore be lower.

Since 1986, Congress has taken a number of steps to limit the benefits of income shifting, including the adoption of the so-called "kiddie tax" on the investment income of minors under 14, and the "flattening" of trust tax brackets to limit the amount of trust income that can be sheltered from the top income tax brackets. Because of the complexity of some of these rules, as well as the possibility of new limits in the future, this kind of tax planning will almost always require the assistance of a tax professional.

Q. How can trusts save gift and estate taxes?

A. As discussed much more thoroughly in chapters 10 and 16, the federal government imposes a considerable amount of taxes if you attempt to dispose of your assets either during your lifetime or following your death. These taxes—the federal gift tax, the federal estate tax, and the generation-skipping tax—are in addition to any death tax that your state may impose on your estate or its beneficiaries. In no other area can a properly drawn trust save more money for your intended beneficiaries than in the field of gift tax and estate tax planning.

Perhaps the most widely used tax shelter in the entire estate planning area is the credit shelter trust or, as it is often known, the *by-pass trust*. (See chapter 13.) Through the use of the credit shelter trust, a married couple can use both of their unified credit exclusion amounts ($600,000 in 1997, increasing by steps to $1,000,000 in 2006) from estate tax, or a total of $1,200,000 ($2,000,000 in 2006), even while the surviving spouse has the income and benefit from the entire estate during his or her lifetime. Used in this way, a credit shelter trust can save $330,000 or more in federal and state death taxes. It makes no sense for a married couple with children, whose total family assets exceed the unified credit exclusion amount ($600,000 in 1997, but increasing by steps to $1,000,000 in 2006), not to consider the use of a *by-pass* trust to save federal estate taxes for their children. Those persons with estates in excess of $1,000,000 should also have an understanding of how trusts can affect the onerous federal generation-skipping tax. (See chapter 18.)

The gift tax law allows every individual to give up to $10,000 (which may be adjusted for inflation after 1998) each year to as many beneficiaries as he or she wishes. Gifts that fall within this annual exclusion avoid both gift tax and estate tax, so for estates larger than the unified credit exclusion amount, each $10,000 gift saves at least $3,400 in federal estate tax. If your estate has the assets and you have the inclination, you may want to take maximum advantage of the $10,000 annual gift tax exclusion. For example, you may wish to use the $10,000 annual gift exclusion to give assets to each of your children. However, you may not want to make an outright gift to a young child, or even an older child inexperienced with handling money. A trust can be the logical vehicle to use to implement your gift. Once the gift qualifies for the annual exclusion, the terms of the trust are limited only by your imagination. You could set up a minor's trust as described more fully in chapter 15, under which the money will be held in trust for your child and made available to him or her at age 21. Or you could set up an irrevocable trust under which your child would receive the income for the rest of his or her lifetime, with allowances made for educational needs, a wedding, or to purchase a business, and the child could be given the right to withdraw certain amounts of principal at stated ages. Gifts with trusts to utilize the $10,000 annual exclusion can also be made to other family members such as nieces or nephews.

If you wish to make even larger gifts, you might want to use a special trust designed to reduce the amount of gift taxes to be paid when making a gift. Through the use of a *grantor-retained annuity trust* (GRAT) or a *grantor-retained unitrust* (GRUT), both explained in chapter 22, you can make larger gifts to obtain the maximum benefit from your $10,000 annual exclusion and your lifetime unified credit exclusion. There is also a trust called a *personal residence trust* (PRT) that can be used to maximize gift tax savings by transferring your home to a trust and reserving the right to live there for a specific period of time. The personal residence trust is described more fully in chapter 20.

There is a $1,000,000 exemption that each person has that can be used to eliminate the draconian generation-skipping tax. (That $1,000,000 exemption may also be adjusted for inflation after 1998.) In order to get the greatest benefit from that exemption, it is usually best to apply the exemption to a separate trust, created either during lifetime or at death, for the benefit of your children or grandchildren.

Q. When should a trust be used for making gifts to charity?

A. Trusts can enable you to make larger gifts to charity, while saving income taxes and estate taxes at the same time. Instead of an outright gift or bequest to your favorite charity, you could spell out in a trust document the exact way that you would like your funds to be handled. For example, instead of an outright gift of $50,000 to the United Way, you might want to have that money invested and the proceeds used for needy children in your hometown. An outright bequest of funds to your college could be individualized to include setting up a trust to establish a scholarship fund for students in your particular area of expertise.

Through the use of a charitable remainder trust, you could make a gift to charity but reserve a specific amount of income for yourself during your lifetime. For example, you could make a gift in trust of $75,000 but retain the right to receive $6,000 each year for the rest of your life. Upon making that gift, you would receive a charitable deduction on your income tax return for the value of the gift, less the value of your retained interest in the trust. There are many other benefits—to you and to the charity—to making gifts in trust which benefit charity, either during your life or at your death, as explained in chapters 25 and 26.

Q. Are there trusts designed to be used with specific assets?

A. There are trusts specifically designed to purchase and own *life insurance.* As discussed in chapter 17, life insurance that you own is includible in your estate for federal estate tax purposes, so you can in effect double the value of your insurance to your beneficiaries by removing the life insurance from your taxable estate through an irrevocable life insurance trust.

There are also revocable insurance trusts, whose primary purpose is to receive the proceeds from your life insurance policies at your death and hold and invest the proceeds for your beneficiaries on the terms and conditions that you spell out in the trust document. A *pourover* life insurance trust frequently contains the *credit shelter trust* and marital trust.

Trusts can also be valuable tools in the administration or distribution of your *business.* You can use trusts to specify how to operate your business. A trust can also be used as a vehicle for you to make gifts of your corporation's stock with a minimal loss of control. Trusts can help keep the family business in the family after death, and they can establish the machinery to provide for continuity of management and ownership for future generations. (See chapter 21.)

Real estate can often be best handled through a trust. A trust can be used in situations where the real estate in question does not lend itself to fragmentation, but the person establishing the trust desires to spread beneficial ownership among a number of people. For example, land is often more valuable if it is not divided; a 10-acre tract of land may be worth substantially more than 10 one-acre tracts. If a trust is used as a receptacle for the gift, 10 beneficiaries could share in the growth and income from the land without necessitating an actual division of the property itself.

If you own several pieces of property of equal value, you could make outright gifts of Parcel A to your son and Parcel B to your daughter. However, you may be treating the children unequally since one property could increase in value, while the other could fall, or the properties could increase or decrease in value at different rates. By placing both properties in trust and giving both children equal shares in the trust property, you could equalize benefits between the children.

Q. Can a trust protect assets from creditors?

A. As discussed more fully in chapter 27, in most states you can set up a *spendthrift trust* to protect your family's assets from creditors. These trusts can also help protect your children's assets in the event of marital difficulties, and they can protect a professional person's assets from a malpractice lawsuit. For even greater protection, some lawyers are now advocating the establishment of an *asset protection trust,* which permits the grantor of the trust to safeguard his or her assets by placing them in an overseas trust. (See chapter 27.)

Q. Can I place my home in a trust?

A. If your home has strong sentimental value to you and your family, you might want to consider placing it in trust and reserving the right to live in it for the rest of your life. At your death, a trust could give your spouse or dependent child the right to live in the home for his or her lifetime, with provisions for the trustee to pay the cost of maintaining the home.

Your family might also your family may save considerable gift taxes through the use of a personal residence trust as discussed in chapter 20, placing the home in trust and reserving your right to live in the home for a certain period of years.

Q. Why are trusts more flexible than other methods of transferring property?

A. Most forms of ownership are very simple, and can deal with only a limited range of possible future circumstances. Also, the rules governing most forms of ownership are fixed by formulas or specific dates or ages, while a trustee can have the flexibility to deal with a variety of changing conditions.

For example, if you want to make a gift to your grandchild, you could simply place money into a bank account or purchase a certificate of deposit or a stock or mutual fund, and title it in the name of your child as custodian for your grandchild under the Uniform Gifts to Minors Act (or Uniform Transfers to Minors Act, whichever is in force in your state). Only one beneficiary is permitted for each account, and the funds must be turned over to your grandchild no later than an age specified by the statute in your state (usually either 18 or 21). Your state also imposes specific regulations on how the money should be titled and invested, and for what purposes the money can be spent.

On the other hand, you could establish a trust for your grandchild or grandchildren, and set up flexible provisions for their future care. All of the money could be placed in one trust, and the trustee could be authorized to use funds for each grandchild's college education, for example. The funds could be held in trust until the youngest grandchild is 25, at which time, regardless of prior distributions, the money would then be divided equally among all of the grandchildren. If a child was disabled or preferred to have the money remain in the trust because of creditor problems, domestic problems, or lack of money-managing experience, the grandchild (or the trustee) would have that option available to him or her at that time.

Since none of us can foresee the future, the flexibility that a trust provides is often its most valuable feature.

Q. How can trusts be used to solve unusual problems?

A. In many instances, a finely tuned trust instrument may be not only the best, but also the only vehicle to deal with unusual situations. Suppose, for example, you want to make provisions for an individual who because of age, health, location, or relationship with you makes providing for him or her extremely difficult. These situations could include providing for a handicapped person, relatives who live outside of the country, a child born out of wedlock, a friend of the same or opposite sex, and even the care and maintenance of pets. Trusts can contain the provisions necessary to provide for such beneficiaries, and also give a considerable degree of comfort to the person setting up the trust. There are countless other examples of the many and varied special uses for trusts, as a review of this and the following chapters will indicate.

Q. How can a trust assure me of privacy?

A. Trusts offer flexibility, reliability, and confidentiality in situations where publicity is not desired. You can attain your goal with just you and the trustee aware of the nature of your gift and the specific terms of the trust. Most trusts are not accessible by the public during your lifetime, and they are not filed in a probate proceeding at your death. Therefore, it may be possible for you to make whatever arrangements you wish without unwanted publicity.

Here are two examples of situations in which privacy is often desired:

- Gifts in trust in which the grantor does not want the beneficiary to know the identity of the grantor. (Examples include anonymous gifts to a college or institution or providing for a child born out of wedlock where the grantor desires to remain in the background.)

- Trusts set up for a particular beneficiary of whom the grantor's family is not aware, or with whom the grantor does not wish to be publicly associated. (These could include a trust for another woman or man in your life, a trust for an illegitimate child, or a trust to help a friend or relative pay for a criminal lawyer.)

Q. Why should I make gifts in trust rather than outright?

A. There are many reasons other than estate or income tax savings for making gifts in trust rather than outright. We call these people-oriented goals. If you examine the list below, you'll find that most of the reasons for making gifts in trust fall into one of these three categories:

- You want to guarantee proper management for the assets.

- You want to conserve principal for as long as possible.

- You want income and principal paid out in the time and manner and to the persons of your choice.

See if any of the following situations apply to you or your beneficiaries:

- You are afraid that your beneficiary is unable to handle the asset. If you feel that your spouse, friend, children, grandchildren, niece, nephew, parent, or other beneficiary is unwilling or unable to invest, manage, or handle the responsibility of an outright gift, you should consider making a gift in trust. Minors and legal incompetents are obvious members of this class. So are adults who lack the emotional or intellectual maturity or who do not have the physical capacity or technical training to handle large sums of money or assets that require constant, high-level decision-making capacity such as a family business.

  Legally, a minor cannot buy or sell assets or enter into binding contracts. This means that if property is given to a minor, the property cannot be purchased, sold, exchanged, or mortgaged without the appointment of a guardian by a court and the accounting to the court for every dollar spent on behalf of the minor. Using an irrevocable trust could minimize or avoid that often expensive, troublesome, and inflexible process.

- You fear that your beneficiary will not feel dependent on you. You may want the income and estate tax advantages (which we'll describe shortly), but you don't want to put all of the ownership rights in your child or other beneficiary's hands. Suppose you want to start a gift program but you are afraid that if you make no-strings-attached-gifts, your child will no longer feel dependent on you. Unlike an outright gift, an irrevocable trust will *not* allow a beneficiary to "take the money and run" because he or she will not receive it all at one time.

- The property is not fragmentable. Perhaps the property doesn't lend itself to fragmentation, but you still want to spread the benefits among a number of people. (For example, a large life insurance policy and its eventual proceeds may be best held by a single trustee, rather than jointly by a half a dozen individuals.)

    Say you have 10 children and grandchildren. You also have 10 acres of real estate, which may be more valuable to them if it is not subdivided into 10 one-acre plots. If you placed the real estate into an irrevocable trust, all 10 of your children and grandchildren could enjoy the property's growth and income without the need to subdivide it. Upon the occurrence of a specified event (for instance, when the youngest of them reaches age 25 or when the property can be sold for an amount in excess of $100,000 an acre), your trustee could sell the property and divide the proceeds or hold the money for the trust's beneficiaries.

- You want to limit ownership. Consider an irrevocable trust in place of an outright gift if you want to limit the class of beneficiaries. For instance, suppose you want to be sure that stock in your family business, the family vacation home, or Grandpop's pocket watch don't end up outside the family. With an irrevocable trust you can make sure that doesn't happen. You can set up a trust that will retain family control and provide protection against the fallout from a beneficiary's unsuccessful marriage, for example, and thus prevent his or her spouse from acquiring that asset. Such ownership restriction is not possible if you make an outright gift.

- You don't want the property to return to you once you have given it away. If a parent makes a direct gift to a child and the child predeceases the parent, absent a valid will, the property may return to the parent rather than pass directly to another child under state intestacy laws. To then remove the asset from the parent's estate, he or she would have to make another taxable gift. This second gift may be even more expensive than the first because the asset may have appreciated in the hands of the deceased child. Placing the gift in an irrevocable trust, however, can ensure that it doesn't end up back in your estate.

- You'd like to familiarize your trustee with managing your trust. Initially, your irrevocable trust may have only a life insurance policy and a relatively small amount of investable assets in it. You may plan to "pour over" other assets from your probate estate (assets you own in your own name when you die), from a revocable trust you've established during your lifetime, or from a group life insurance plan into the trust. In other words, your trust may be relatively small now but at your death contain a sizable sum of money and other assets. You may want to know now how well your trustee will perform and so you need to familiarize the trustee with your assets, your family, your plans, and the relationship of each to the other. Even though the trust is irrevocable, you can give the trustee suggestions as to property investment and management.

- You desire to protect assets from creditors and predators. You may want to ensure your beneficiary's financial security, yet not make him or her the target of a fortune hunter. You can do this—create significant economic security but protect the beneficiary from himself and others—by using a trust that provides only income, with additional amounts of principal—at the trustee's sole discretion—for the beneficiary's health, education, maintenance, and support. Alternatively, you could give the beneficiary the right to demand certain amounts for specific needs but stipulate that amounts above those levels or beyond those categories of need would be paid out only if the trustee deemed it desirable.

HOW TRUSTS WORK

Chapter 2 explains:

- What a trust is

- How a trust works

- The relationship between a grantor, trustee, and beneficiaries

- What laws affect trusts

- The definition and advantage of a living trust

- The definition and advantage and disadvantage of a testamentary trust

- The definition and advantages of a revocable trust

- The definition and advantages of an irrevocable trust

- How trusts differ from powers of attorney, wills, custodial accounts, guardianships, corporations, and family limited partnerships

- How a typical family trust works

Q. *What is a trust?*

A. A trust is a legal relationship in which the legal ownership of property is separated from the beneficial ownership of the property. In a trust, one person or group of persons (the *trustee*) holds money or other property (the trust *principal* or *corpus*) for the benefit of another person or group of persons (the *beneficiaries*).

The person who creates the trust, by transferring the money or property to the trustee, is called the *grantor* or *settlor* or *trustor*. The terms and conditions are usually stated in a written document called a *deed of trust* or *agreement of trust*. (In this book, we will usually refer to the creator of the trust as the *grantor* and the document creating the trust as the *trust document.*)

As will be discussed in other chapters of this book, it is possible for the grantor to be the trustee, for the grantor to be a beneficiary, and for a beneficiary to be a trustee. The only thing that is usually not possible is for the sole trustee to be the sole beneficiary (with no future beneficiaries). In that case, the legal and beneficial interests are said to *merge*, and the trust is no longer valid.

It is also possible for a trust to exist without a trust document. A trust can be created accidentally, which is sometimes called a *resulting* or *constructive* trust. It is also possible in some states to create an *oral* trust, by a conversation between the grantor and the trustee, with nothing in writing. In this book, we will be describing trusts created intentionally (sometimes called *express* trusts), and we will hope that the grantor has had the sense to put the terms of the trust in writing, and not merely depend on the memory (and honesty) of the trustee.

A trust document will usually spell out the following:

- how the assets of the trust are to be managed and invested

- who will receive the money and assets from the trust

- how and under what terms and conditions that money is to be paid out (for example, whether money is paid directly to the beneficiary for any purpose, or only paid to a school for the educational expenses of the beneficiary)

- when money is to be paid (for example, at what ages or in what circumstances the beneficiaries will receive their shares)

In directing how and when money will be distributed, a trust document will usually have different directions for the *principal* placed in the trust and the *income* from that principal, such as interest, dividends, or rents. (Capital gains, representing the increase in the value of the property in the trust, are usually considered to be part of the principal even though they are taxable income for tax purposes.) For example, a common arrangement is for one beneficiary to get the income from the trust during his or her lifetime, and principal if the trustee decides it is needed for some purpose specified in the trust document, but the remaining principal will be distributed to someone else after the death of the original beneficiary.

Q. How does a trust work?

A. Picture in your mind a box. Let's call that box a *trust*.

Into that box you can put cash, stocks, bonds, mutual funds, the deed to your home, or even life insurance. When you put property into the box, you are "funding" the trust. You can put almost any asset into a trust, at any time. You can name a trust as the beneficiary of your personal or group life insurance, pension plan, IRA or other work-related benefits, and you can determine how the proceeds should be administered and distributed at your death.

Once property is put into the trust, it is the responsibility of the trustee to administer the property in accordance with the trust document. For this purpose, "administer" means holding the property and collecting the income, distributing or reinvesting the income, selling the property and reinvesting the proceeds, and making other decisions regarding the investments of the trust, subject always to the instructions in the trust document (which can be very flexible or very restrictive). The trustee must also make the distributions to the beneficiaries required by the trust document and, if the distributions are "as needed" for specific purposes, such as support or education, the trustee may need to decide when the distribution is needed.

For example, Grandfather wishes to set aside $10,000 for his granddaughter, age six, to be used for her college education. Grandfather (the grantor) can give $10,000 to Father (the trustee) to hold in trust for Granddaughter (the beneficiary). Under the terms of the trust, the money is invested as Father decides, and the income and principal may be used for Granddaughter's education as Father decides is appropriate. Any money not spent for education will be paid to Granddaughter at age 25.

Q. Explain the relationship between the grantor, trustee and beneficiaries.

A. In establishing a trust, the *grantor* decides

- what goes into the trust
- who benefits from the trust

- the terms and conditions of the trust

- who administers the trust

Someone is needed to safeguard, invest, and then pay out the assets, or the income from the assets, to the beneficiaries. This someone is the *trustee* whose obligation may last only a few years or it may run for generations. There can be more than one trustee, and there can be individuals or corporate trustees such as banks. When several parties are named, they are *co-trustees* and make decisions jointly (and are jointly liable for mistakes).

The people for whom the grantor set up the trust are the *beneficiaries,* who receive income from the trust assets, and perhaps also principal, at the age or ages and under the terms and conditions the grantor has specified. The person who is entitled to all of the income from a trust is sometimes called an *income beneficiary* or *life tenant.* For example, if the trust instrument says that the grantor is to be paid the income for as long as he or she lives, he or she is the life tenant. If a child is to receive what remains in the trust at a mother's or father's death, he or she is the *remainderman.*

Because the trust is for the benefit of the beneficiaries, not the trustee, the trustee has a legal obligation to act for the benefit of the beneficiaries (consistent with the trust document) and not for the trustee's own benefit. This is often called a *fiduciary obligation* (from the Latin word for "trust") and a trustee is often referred to as a *fiduciary.*

Q. What laws affect trusts?

A. There are a number of different laws that affect trusts (which is one of the reasons a lawyer is usually needed to decide when and how to set up a trust).

- *State trust law.* The rules that govern how trusts are created, and the rights and obligations of trustees and beneficiaries, are determined by state law, not federal law, and can vary greatly from state to state. (Residents of Louisiana should be especially careful, because the many Louisiana law is derived from French law, not English law like the other 49 states.)

    The explanations provided by this book are the general rules that apply in most states, but may not be true in every state.

- *Federal gift and estate tax.* The federal gift and estate tax consequences of a trust, such as whether a gift to a trust qualifies for the annual gift tax exclusion (presently $10,000, but may be adjusted for inflation after 1998), or whether the trust is subject to estate tax on the death of the grantor, is governed by federal law, not state law.

- *State gift and estate tax.* Several states have gift taxes or death taxes that are independent of the federal gift and estate tax, and those laws can apply to trusts in ways that are different from the way federal taxes are applied.

- *Federal income tax.* The income received by trusts is subject to federal income tax, and federal law determines what income might be taxable to the grantor and the beneficiaries.

- *State income tax.* States with income taxes will also have rules governing how those taxes apply to trusts, and the results may be different than the results under federal law.

In addition to these laws, a trustee is subject to the same laws and rules that apply to individuals when it comes to entering into contracts to buy or sell property, local property taxes, and other laws of general application.

Q. What is a living trust?

A. A trust set up during the grantor's lifetime is an *inter vivos trust* (from the Latin meaning "between living persons) or a *living trust.* A trust is considered to be a living trust even if the trust receives assets after the death of the grantor, so the grantor's will could "pour over" assets into a previously established living trust just like a funnel could channel assets into a box.

For example, while he was alive, Grandfather could establish a living trust and put cash, real estate, mutual funds, or other assets into that "box." He could name his daughter, a bank or trust company, or himself as the initial trustee of the trust, and he could spell out in detail the duties of the trustee during his (Grandfather's) lifetime. The trustee could be authorized to use Grandfather's assets for Grandfather's care and support, or for the care and support of Grandmother and Grandfather's children and grandchildren. The trust could provide for the disposition of Grandfather's assets following his death. Grandfather could revoke the trust at any time while he was alive. When he died,

Grandfather's will could provide that some or all of his assets were to pass through the "funnel" into the trust.

Q. What is a testamentary trust?

A. If a trust is created by your will, it is a *testamentary trust.* Assets owned in your name at death pass by your will into the trust. Why use a testamentary trust? Attorneys use a testamentary trust to save you costs in two ways. First, a testamentary trust reduces the number of documents. A testamentary trust is part of the will itself, so there is only one document, but a living trust and a will require two separate documents. Second, a living trust must have assets transferred to it during your lifetime in order to have any effect. That can means spending time (and perhaps money) transferring the assets into the trust, and it can also mean other administrative expenses during your lifetime if you are not the trustee. A testamentary trust requires no effort during lifetime (other than signing the will), because the trust will not be funded until after your death.

One drawback of the testamentary trust is that if the will is revoked, lost, or otherwise not probated for any reason, the testamentary trust may never come into existence.

Q. What is a revocable trust?

A. Remember the trust box we discussed earlier? Now picture a string on the box. That string enables you to pull the box back and reach in. You can revoke the trust, take back what you have transferred to it, alter it, amend it, or terminate it. This is a *revocable trust.* Its advantages of control, flexibility, and psychological comfort are obvious.

Q. What is an irrevocable trust?

A. Cut the string you hold to the trust box and you have an *irrevocable trust.* No property can be removed from the trust and nothing can be changed. Once the terms and conditions of the trust are written down and the trust is signed, those provisions are fixed.

Why would anyone give up the control, flexibility, and psychological comfort of a revocable trust to create an irrevocable trust? The problem with a revocable trust is that, as

Trusts/Leimberg Associates Books: 610-527-5216

long as the grantor retains the revocation "string," the assets in the trust are still considered to be owned by the grantor for income tax and estate tax purposes (and are still subject to claims of the grantor's creditors). If you can pull on the string and get the property back, the IRS can pull the property in the trust back into your estate and pull the income trust assets earn into your taxable income. Irrevocable trusts are usually created to save income tax or estate taxes (see chapter 16), and sometimes to protect assets from creditors (see chapter 27).

Q. How are trusts different from other methods of administering or transferring property?

A. In deciding whether or not to use a trust, you should consider the other transfer devices available to accomplish your goals. These other methods of administering or transferring property include powers of attorney, wills, custodial accounts under the Uniform Gifts or Transfers to Minors Act, guardianships, corporations, and family limited partnerships. (More information on these estate planning devices can be found in *Tools And Techniques Of Estate Planning*, which can be obtained by calling 800-543-0874.) Let's look at each of them in greater detail.

- *Power of Attorney.* Under a power of attorney, an individual (usually known as the *principal*) can designate another person or persons as his or her *agent* or *attorney-in-fact* to act on behalf of the principal. The power of attorney can be as broad as the principal wishes, and can usually include the powers to buy and sell investments for the principal, file tax returns, make gifts, and even make medical decisions.

  A *durable power of attorney* is a power of attorney that will remain valid even if the principal should become disabled or even legally incompetent. A power of attorney can become effective immediately after being signed by the principal, or it can take the form of a *springing power of attorney,* under which the attorney-in-fact can act only after furnishing proof of the principal's disability or incapacity.

  Compared to a guardianship or other procedure under state law for the management of the assets of an incapacitated person, a power of attorney is an inexpensive way to arrange for the care and management of an individual's affairs if he or she is unable to manage them because of age, illness, or any other reason. For example, suppose Grandfather was worried that he might become sick or disabled and there would be no one available to handle his money and other assets for him. Grandfather could prepare a durable power of attorney under which he could give his daughter the power to act for him. The power of attorney could spell out all of the circumstances under which Grandfather would want Daughter to act for him, it could indicate the assets that Daughter was permitted to handle for Grandfather, and if it was a durable power of attorney, it would allow Daughter to act even if Grandfather became physically or mentally disabled. (However, the power of attorney would still have to terminate at Grandfather's death.)

These same asset management goals can also be achieved with a revocable living trust, under which the grantor (or principal) can establish a trust for himself or herself and name a trustee with specific provisions on how that trustee is to act on the grantor's behalf. Compared to a durable power of attorney, which terminates at the death of the principal, the trust vehicle is usually much more flexible, and it can make provisions for the distribution of the grantor's assets following his or her death. (See chapter 9 on revocable trusts.) However, it may be possible to give an attorney-in-fact powers that cannot be given to a trustee, such as the power to file tax returns for the principal, or the power to make medical decisions. For that reason, it is often advisable to have both a revocable trust and a power of attorney.

- *Will.* A will disposes of property at death, and a revocable living trust can achieve the same results. (A revocable living trust is sometimes referred to as a "will substitute." For more details, see chapter 9.) However, living trusts have at least two advantages over wills:

  A revocable living trust can provide for the management of assets during lifetime, providing protection in the event of disability due to accident, illness, or old age.

  An irrevocable living trust can receive gifts during lifetime and save estate taxes.

- *Custodial Accounts under the Uniform Transfers to Minors Act.* Gifts may be made to minors without giving them outright possession of the property and without establishing a trust. Under the Uniform Transfers to Minors Act, as adopted in most states, property must be transferred to a custodian who holds it as "custodian for the minor under the (name of the state) Transfers to Minors Act."

For example, Grandpa Charlie would like to make a gift of $10,000 to his granddaughter, Lisa, who is 6 years old. Grandpa Charlie could set up a bank account or purchase securities and title the account with Lisa's mother, Amy, as custodian. The account could be titled "Amy Brody, Custodian for Lisa Brody, under the Uniform Transfers to Minors Act."

The Uniform Transfers to Minors Act has been enacted by practically every state, and the Act sets forth the terms and conditions under which property can be held for a minor child. According to the act, a separate custodian must be appointed for each child, and the age of distribution is usually either 18 or 21. The cost of setting up the account is negligible, and in many instances where the amount of property in the trust is small and the beneficiary is emotionally mature, this might be preferable to setting up a trust.

There are, however, several advantages that a trust would have over the custodial account. A trust for minors could have more than one beneficiary and trustee, the provisions could be much more flexible, the trust could continue past the age specified by the act (usually 18 or 21), and it could also include provisions for a successor trustee and for the disposition of the assets at the minor's death.

- *Guardianships.* A guardian is usually appointed by the court for a person who is under a disability, either because of age or mental or physical incapacity. The guardian's duties are established by law and not by the person under the disability. A guardian's actions are usually controlled by the courts very closely, and therefore guardianships provide much less flexibility than trusts. A guardian does not take title to property in his or her name and serves only during the incapacity of the beneficiary. A guardianship is not an alternative that one selects. Rather, it is one that is imposed by state law because of the failure to set up a custodial account or trust for the minor, a power of attorney, or a trust for the incapacitated individual.

For example, if Grandfather names his 6-year-old granddaughter the beneficiary of a $100,000 life insurance policy, the insurance company would refuse to pay the money directly to Granddaughter at Grandfather's death. It would be necessary for Granddaughter's parents to go to court and have the court appoint a guardian to handle Granddaughter's money until she attains her majority (age 18 in most states). Had Grandfather established a trust for Granddaughter and named the trust the beneficiary of the policy, the court proceedings could have been avoided, and Grandfather could have spelled out how and when Granddaughter would receive the money.

- *Joint Ownership.* Many people consider joint ownership of property to be a good way of managing property during their lifetimes and as a good way of transferring property at death. However, joint ownership frequently results in disasters.

For example, suppose that Father has died and Mother is getting on in years and is concerned about failing health. She puts her assets in joint names with Son with the expectation that Son will then be able to pay her bills and take care of her assets, but will divide her estate with his sisters after she dies. Mother may even believe that putting the assets in joint names with Son will reduce death taxes. After Mother dies, Son discovers that all of the assets are subject to federal estate tax. He also discovers that he is the owner of the assets under state law, which tempts him to keep the assets for himself, regardless of what his mother intended or his sisters expect. After some bitter arguments with his sisters, he relents and agrees to give them their shares of the assets. Unfortunately, it is too late, because his ex-wife has claimed all of the assets to satisfy his support obligations. If Mother had created a revocable trust, naming Son as trustee, the assets would not have been subject to the claims of Son's creditors, and the sisters would have been assured of getting the shares Mother intended.

There can be problems even when husbands and wives set up joint checking accounts and brokerage accounts so that both can make deposits and withdrawals during lifetime. There is no federal estate tax at the first death, because the survivor will become the sole owner and the amounts passing to the survivor will qualify for the federal estate marital deduction. However, there could be unnecessary tax at the second death if the assets exceed the unified credit applicable exclusion amount ($600,000 in 1997, but increasing by steps to $1,000,000 in 2006), because the unified credit in the first estate was not used. (See chapter 13 for additional information on tax planning for the unified credit.) A better alternative might be separate revocable trusts (see chapter 9) or even a joint revocable trust (see chapter 14).

- *Corporations.* There may be estate tax planning advantages, as well as business advantages, in deciding to set up a business as a corporation.

  Because a corporation is a separate taxable entity, as an employee of the corporation you will be entitled to the same fringe benefits as any other employee. Incorporating gives you a relatively simple and inexpensive way to transfer ownership of corporate assets. Gifts can be made by endorsing shares of stock to your donees or intended beneficiaries, and gifts can be made to children, friends, relatives and charities quickly and easily. Through gifts of stock, family members can be given an interest in the business, but you can keep control. You can also shift the growth in the business to children, and by dividing shares among family members, shift a portion of your estate to your children's lower estate tax brackets. You can also maintain privacy because the transfer of stock in a closely held corporation is not public information.

  Whenever the management and disposition of a family business is involved, an attorney should always be consulted about the advisability of incorporating the business. However, a corporation is not a substitute for a trust. In order to control a corporation, you must still own stock, and that stock must be managed during your lifetime and following your death. If you own that stock directly, and not in a trust, you may not be able to control the corporation as you would wish during your lifetime and following your death. Trust arrangements must therefore still be considered along with a corporation.

- *Family Limited Partnership.* Another planning device whose goal is the maintenance and distribution of business and non-business assets is the family limited partnership. A limited partnership has two classes of partners—the general partner, who manages and controls the partnership, and the limited partner, whose rights and obligations are similar to those of *investors* in a partnership. By setting up a family limited partnership, a parent or parents can maintain control of the assets in the partnership, while at the same time gifting limited partnership interests to their children and reducing the size of the parents' estate. Limited partners are considered less vulnerable to the creditors of a limited partnership, and because of the limitations on transferability, limited partnership interests are considered to be of less value than the underlying obligations represented by the interest. That "reduced value" may lead to very advantageous gift or estate tax discounts.

  For example, suppose that the limited partnership owned 500 shares of General Motors and 500 shares of IBM stock, and a third party had the choice of either buying the stock directly from a stockbroker or buying the limited partnership's share that owned the stock. Which would have a higher value? The limited partnership interest should be worth less than the stock itself. Because it would actually be only a non-controlling interest in a partnership that owned General Motors and IBM stock, the owner of the limited partnership interest might be able to obtain a valuation discount, which would be useful in lowering the value of the limited partnership interest for estate and gift tax purposes.

  For example, Grandfather has over $1,000,000 in closely held stock and would like to set up a gift-giving program to benefit his children and grandchildren. His lawyer tells him that he could set up a family limited partnership under which he could keep control by making himself or Grandmother a general partner and also limited partners. He and Grandmother could then give their limited partnership interest to their children and grandchildren and still keep control of their assets because they would be general (that is, controlling) partners. There is also a possibility that when they die, their limited partnership interest could be discounted for death tax purposes.

Although the limited partnership form of owning assets and doing business would, in many instances, be more costly than a trust, individuals with larger estates should consider the use of limited partnerships in their overall estate plans. However, a limited partnership is not a substitute for a trust, any more than a corporation could be a substitute for a trust. In order to control a partnership, you must still own a partnership interest, and that interest must be managed during your lifetime and following your death. If you own that partnership directly, and not in a trust, you may not be able to control the partnership as you would wish during your lifetime and following your death. Many sophisticated attorneys will suggest a marriage of one or more trusts and a family limited partnership.

Q. How does a typical family trust work?

A. The following is an illustration of a family trust without considering any tax implications. Jim and Helen have two children, Greg and Lauren, who are 12 and 10 years old respectively. They plan to have Jim's sister, Mona, act as guardian for the children if both of them die. However, their assets plus Jim's life insurance will be approximately $500,000 and they feel this would be too much for Mona to handle on her own.

Jim and Helen could set up a trust that would go into effect only at the death of the survivor of both of them. This could be done in their wills or in a separate trust document. The trust would provide that at the death of both Jim and Helen, all of their money, including Jim's life insurance, would be payable to the Very Secure Bank and Trust Company, who would act as trustee for the children and invest the money for them. The trust could provide that until their younger child is 22 years old and finished with his basic college education, all the money would be held for the children in one trust and would be used for them according to their needs, which Mona could determine, and also for their education. When the younger child is 22, the balance then remaining in the trust could be divided into equal shares, and each child would then receive all of the income from his or her share of the trust. Each child would have the right to withdraw one-half of the principal in his or her trust at age 25, and the balance at age 30, with the trustee able to use the principal for each child's support, maintenance, health, and education, until his or her 30th birthday.

If a child should die before receiving the entire balance in his or her trust, such child's share would go to his or her children, and if he or she had no children, the share would be distributed equally to his or her then-surviving brother or sister. The trust could also have a catastrophe clause that would provide that if something should happen to the entire family, one-half of the balance would go to Jim's family and the remaining one-half to Helen's family.

Through this trust, Jim and Helen could provide professional money management for their children, while at the same time having a trusted family member taking care of their children's every-day needs. The trust could also give Mona the right to replace the bank in the future if she and the children moved to a different area or she was dissatisfied with the way the bank was managing the children's funds.

HOW TO CHOOSE THE BEST TRUSTEES

Chapter 3 explains:

- Why your choice of trustee is important

- Eight qualifications of a good trustee

- Factors you should consider in choosing a trustee for a particular trust

- Nine potential candidates to serve as trustee

- The five factors to consider in deciding where your trust should be located

Q. Why is a good trustee important?

A. The selection of the trustee is one of the most important decisions in establishing a trust. It doesn't make any difference how carefully the trust document is prepared or how clear your intentions are expressed if the trustee that is appointed is not a good choice. A trustee who chooses poor advisors, is careless about taxes, makes poor investment decisions, or is not sensitive to the needs of the beneficiaries can create a nightmare of conflicts, unnecessary expenses, unnecessary taxes, and losses on investments. A good trustee, on the other hand, often will be able to find a way to carry out your wishes with the least costs and conflicts even if mistakes are made in creating the trust, or unforeseen problems arise.

Q. What are the qualifications of a good trustee?

A. A good trustee should have the following eight characteristics:

1. *Competence.* Although it would seem unnecessary even to list competence as a qualification, in many instances grantors, when setting up trusts, allow personal or emotional considerations to govern their thinking in the selection of a

trustee. A child who lives near you or your beneficiaries may be a convenient choice as a trustee but not a wise choice when the subject matter of the trust is the family business of which he or she has no personal knowledge. Competence does not necessarily have to be measured by knowledge of all of the trust assets, but a competent trustee should be able to understand the nature of his or her specific duties, select a course of action to take, recognize the limits of his or her knowledge and capabilities, and have the maturity to secure professional assistance where and when needed.

2. *The ability to act in the best interest of the beneficiaries.* While the trustee is charged with carrying out the provisions of the trust as dictated by the trust instrument, the overriding consideration is the fact that he or she is acting in a fiduciary capacity in handling assets for the trust beneficiaries. A fiduciary capacity means that all short- and long-range decisions should be in the best interests of the beneficiaries and even the appearance of a conflict of interest must be avoided. Selling a home or business or allocating trust funds for the purchase of a home or business, are examples of the types of serious considerations that trustees must deal with regularly. It is often necessary to make long-term decisions that are not necessarily popular with the beneficiaries. In addition to following the terms of the trust and absolute loyalty to the trust's beneficiaries, the trustee must have the objectivity and intestinal fortitude to make difficult and sometimes unpopular decisions.

For example, if a trust is set up to hold assets for the grantor's son after the grantor's death until the son reaches age 40, how should the trustee react to a request by the son to invest $100,000, or 20 percent of his trust, in a take-out pizza restaurant suggested by a couple of the son's high school friends (who themselves have no money to invest)? The trustee must consider whether the investment itself is worthwhile, what funds will be available after the investment, whether the investment will require the allocation of additional funds, whether the beneficiary is really capable of running the business, whether it is the type of business in which the beneficiary should invest, and what the effect of saying "no" will have on the beneficiary. In many instances, what is really in the best interest of the beneficiary is a subjective and extremely difficult decision for a trustee to make.

3. *Knowledge of the beneficiary's needs.* Before making any important decisions, the trustee must have a good understanding of the needs of the beneficiaries. If a husband has set up a trust for his wife and children, for example, the trustee must have accurate knowledge of all of the family assets, both outside and inside the trust. An income and expense statement must be worked out so that the trust will fit into the overall family plan and meet the needs of the beneficiaries.

   The trustee must also be aware of any special needs of a beneficiary. For example, a child might have a physical or mental handicap that would require special care and treatment. These considerations must also be worked into the overall financial trust plan.

4. *Knowledge of the subject matter of the trust.* If the bulk of the trust assets consist of listed securities, a trustee with a good investment adviser, or a bank or trust company with a good investment department can usually handle the trust effectively. If most of the trust's assets consist of mutual funds, little day-to-day management may be necessary.

   However, if the bulk of the trust assets consist of a family-owned business or a unique piece of real estate, it would be helpful if the trustee were familiar with the assets in question. Examples of such trustee choices include a brother who knows and cares about your children and is also active in the business with you (unless this could create a conflict of interest in regard to the business following your death). Someone who has worked with you to handle and manage the real estate to be placed in the trust and is aware of any particular problems such as past history, zoning regulations, environmental matters, and the like would certainly be an excellent choice as a trustee or co-trustee to administer the real estate in the trust.

5. *Experience.* The job of a trustee is a difficult, time-consuming and multifaceted one. Selecting someone who has no experience or background in handling the duties that the trustee will be called upon to perform, may not be advisable. While it is not necessary that the grantor choose someone who has acted as a trustee before, it is wise for the grantor to select someone who, because of background and experience, will be familiar with the responsibilities that he or she will be asked to undertake.

   In this regard, consider choosing professionals to act as the sole trustees or as co-trustees. These persons or an institution such as a trust company could serve together with family members or other persons who might have a close and caring relationship to the beneficiaries but do not have the background and experience to perform the important functions of the trustee. These professionals include investment advisers; lawyers or accountants who are familiar with the grantor's needs, assets, business, and family members; and especially banks and trust companies who have years of experience and expertise in handling and managing other people's assets (and who are accountable to state auditing teams).

6. *Availability to serve.* Not only are a trustee's duties difficult and time consuming, but in many instances they can also extend over long periods of time. A trust set up by a mother for her daughter until her daughter is 35 can last for 30 years if her daughter is only 5 years old when the trust is established. As grantor, you are imposing a tremendous obligation when you appoint someone as a trustee to handle, supervise, and manage the trust assets for the beneficiary over such an extended period of time.

You might have selected an ideal candidate, extremely qualified because of his or her personal attributes and affection for the trust beneficiaries. However, despite good intentions, his or her own personal situation might prevent that person from performing all the necessary tasks and taking the time to handle the day-to-day functions necessary to adequately manage the trust investments for the beneficiaries. In these situations, consider the selection of a bank or trust company to serve as a co-trustee. Under this arrangement, the trust company could perform day-to-day trust functions and the individual you selected as co-trustee could act as a liaison between the bank and the beneficiary and therefore have the time to make certain that the beneficiary's needs are being properly met. If you wish, provisions could be made in the trust instrument for the individual trustee to replace the corporate trustee with another corporate trustee if he or she is not satisfied with the trustee's performance.

7. *Proximity to beneficiary.* Your sister in California might otherwise be an excellent choice as trustee if your grandson did not live in Florida and have needs that must be attended to on a regular basis. In that case, it might be beneficial to have a local trustee, perhaps to serve with your sister as a co-

trustee, so that there will always be someone present to make sure that the beneficiary's needs are being met.

8. *Lack of conflict.* One element that grantors often do not consider when selecting a trustee (or trustees) is the potential conflict that may arise between the trustees and the beneficiaries of the trust. Your business partner of 30 years would make an ideal trustee to handle your share of the business for your children following your death, were it not for the fact that, as trustee, he will in effect be his own partner. In other words, an unavoidable conflict will be created because every decision that the trustee makes concerning the business will affect him and his family as well as your family.

The trust and confidence that you and he built up over a lifetime as business partners do not necessarily extend to your family after your death. Instead of two people making business decisions objectively, one person is now forced to make those decisions for two distinct (and possibly opposing) groups of people with different needs, objectives, and agendas. For example, as trustee he may have to sell your business and attempt to obtain the highest possible price. But as an owner himself, that action may not be in his best interest. You must therefore consider what other alternatives are available such as an outside trustee or a family member (if someone in the grantor's family is familiar with the business).

The preferred solution in the business context is a buy/sell agreement drafted during your lifetime with your business partner. Under the terms of such a buy/sell agreement, you can agree, for example, that at your death, your business partner will buy your share of the business for $250,000, and the partner will have purchased an insurance policy in that amount on your life. At your death, instead of an unwieldy business interest being placed in a trust for your family, the $250,000 will be put in a trust, which can be invested in a diversified manner and utilized for the family's benefit in a much more efficient manner.

Other conflicts can arise when one child is chosen as a trustee to manage assets for your spouse or for your other children. A child who is a trustee for a parent usually has a conflict of interest because the child is also a remainderman, and any money distributed to the parent or spent on the parent may mean less for the child upon the death of the parent. A child might therefore be inclined to make investment decisions, and spending decisions, that give your spouse less current income and financial security than you intended. Even if the child is perfectly fair about carrying out your wishes, the suspicion that the child might be motivated by greed and not love could poison the relationship between your child and your spouse (who may also resent having his or her life controlled—even in some small way—by a child). For these reasons, it may be better to have an independent trustee (individual or corporate) than have children serve as trustees for a parent.

Similarly, giving one child the responsibility for the management of funds and family assets for the benefit of his or her siblings can divide families that may have gotten along well during the grantor's lifetime. Possible solutions include appointing all of the children as co-trustees—which may or may not result in the same problem—or appointing an independent trustee to act as tie breaker or sole trustee.

Q. What factors should I consider when choosing a trustee for a particular trust?

A. Even if you know a number of persons whom you believe are qualified to serve as trustee of a trust you create, you should carefully consider the following seven considerations for selecting trustees for a particular trust:

1. *The nature and purpose of the trust.* If you are setting up a revocable living trust to manage your own assets during lifetime and to avoid probate at death, with ultimate distribution of assets to your children, you could name yourself as initial trustee. It would not be necessary to review other potential candidates (although we suggest you name at least two backup trustees). On the other hand, if the purpose of the trust was to hold and invest $1,000,000 for your grandchildren, you should consider a corporate trustee or a professional money manager in addition to one or more personally named co-trustees who know your grandchildren.

2. *The size of the trust.* If you wanted to place $10,000 in a trust account for a niece, the small size of the trust alone would not warrant the consideration of a corporate or professional trustee. However, if the trust assets were considerable, managing the trust might be too great a responsibility for an individual trustee without a strong background in money management and taxation.

3. *The duration of the trust.* A trust established for your children and young grandchildren could last for a very long time. This should rule out using a contemporary to serve as the sole trustee, pointing instead to a younger trustee or, preferably, a corporate trustee that could serve for an indefinite period of time.

4. *The nature of the trust assets.* You will want a trustee with the ability to manage the type of asset held in the trust. For example, if you were to place a business interest or complex real estate portfolio in trust, the trustee should be someone with sufficient experience to manage the business for the beneficiaries.

5. *The location of the assets and the beneficiaries.* If the major asset in a trust is a home in suburban Philadelphia, a corporate trustee in California might not be the best choice. Similarly, if all your children live in the New York City area, an uncle in Florida may not be the best possible choice as trustee of the children's trust.

6. *Tax considerations.* There are a number of situations in which tax considerations make it inadvisable to use either the grantor or the beneficiary of the trust as a trustee. For example, if a father sets up a trust for a child and names himself as trustee of that trust, the powers of the father as trustee could cause the trust to be a part of his taxable estate at his death, even though the trust is irrevocable. Similarly, it may not be advisable to name the grantor's spouse as the sole trustee of a trust which is designed to avoid death taxes at the spouse's death. Unless the trust is properly drafted, the assets in the trust might be included in the spouse's estate and the children would have to pay death taxes unnecessarily. And there are situations in which children who are trustees for themselves or their own children would have to pay income taxes on trust income or gains that are not distributed to them. If tax considerations are important, we usually suggest that an independent trustee should be used to avoid adverse estate and income tax consequences.

7. *Fees and costs.* Although fees and costs are always a consideration in the selection of a trustee, this is especially true in the case of smaller trusts. Even though a parent might want to use a corporate trustee to handle money in the event of his or her death, if the trust is under $100,000, the corporate trustee's minimum fee schedule might make selecting a corporate trustee economically unwise. Before considering a professional trustee or attorney, you should

find out the fee to be charged for acting as trustee. In fact, it's always a good idea to discuss fees with anyone being considered as trustee and to stipulate in the trust whether and how much family members or friends are to be paid for acting as trustees.

Q. Who are the potential candidates to serve as a trustee?

A. In most states any individual of legal age (i.e., over eighteen) can serve as trustee. There are trust departments of commercial banks and a growing number of trust companies not affiliated with commercial banks that serve as professional trustees. It is also possible to name a group of individuals to serve together or to serve with a corporate trustee. The following list summarizes the available choices and gives the advantages and disadvantages of each:

1. *The grantor.* It is almost always possible under state law for the person establishing the trust to name himself or herself as trustee. If two people - a married couple for example - set up a trust, they can name themselves as the initial trustees of the trust. The obvious advantage of naming yourself as the trustee is that you can utilize many of the advantages of a trust, while keeping absolute control. One of the principal uses for setting up a trust and naming yourself as the trustee is to avoid probate. If all of the grantor's assets are held in trust by the grantor during his or her lifetime, at death these assets can pass directly to the beneficiaries without the necessity of going through probate. (For a realistic examination of the advantages and disadvantages of revocable trusts to avoid probate, see chapters 8 and 9.) Even though the grantor of a trust can name himself or herself as the initial trustee, the trust document should make provisions for a successor trustee in the event of the grantor's disability or death. Then, once the trust is established, it can continue uninterrupted despite the disability or death of the grantor.

   On the other hand, there are many reasons for not naming the grantor as trustee. Obviously, the grantor cannot act as a trustee after his or her death. By naming yourself trustee of your own trust, you may destroy some or all of the income, gift, and death tax advantage that may have been the motivating factor in establishing the trust. While control is always desirable, the IRS will not permit a gift in trust to remove assets from your taxable estate when you name yourself as sole trustee, and it may also require you to include the income from the trust in your personal tax return. In most instances, if the purpose of the trust is to remove assets from your estate, you should not name yourself as sole trustee. We also suggest that if estate tax savings are important that you name someone other than your spouse as trustee.

2. *Family members.* Probably the most frequently named trustees are members of the grantor's family. There are many obvious reasons for a grantor to choose his or her spouse and children as trustees to serve either as co-trustees with the grantor or as backup trustees in case of the grantor's disability and following the grantor's death. A very real benefit in selecting a family member as trustee is the ability to maintain family control of the trust. Many people are much more comfortable if they know that trust assets will be managed for them and their family by other members of their immediate family in the event of their disability or death. Not only are the family members the most familiar with the grantor, but they also have a much better understanding of the grantor's method of handling his or her assets, and they are aware of the grantor's plans for the future. Another advantage is the elimination of fees that would otherwise be charged by a professional trustee. Since the family members might very well be the beneficiaries as well as the trustees, this should result in reducing the administrative costs of the trust.

Of course, the selection of a family member as a trustee must be consistent with the purposes of the trust. It would make no sense to create a trust for a child because of concerns about the child's maturity and then appoint the child as trustee. Similarly, it makes no sense to create a trust in order to avoid taxes and then name a related trustee that recreates or aggravates the tax problem, because of the possible adverse estate and income tax consequences described above.

Earlier in this chapter, we discussed the financial conflicts of interest that a family member may have if appointed to serve as a trustee. Another disadvantage of choosing family members as trustees are the potential emotional conflicts, intra-family communication problems, and other personality-related issues that could arise. A potential conflict may arise between the surviving spouse as trustee and a difficult child. Even worse, if the grantor's children have been appointed as trustees to manage funds for the surviving spouse, the surviving spouse may resent having to come to his or her children for money.

3. *Friends.* In many instances, a close and trusted friend can be an excellent choice as a trustee. A close friend might very well have a good understanding of what the grantor wishes to accomplish under the trust and a close relationship with the proposed beneficiaries. Fees, which should always be arranged in advance, can often be lower than those of a professional trustee. The disadvantages of using friends as trustees include the friend's lack of experience, inability to devote sufficient time to the trustee's duties, advanced age, possible conflicts with the beneficiaries and their resentment at having the grantor's friend (an outsider no matter how close to the family) chosen to make decisions for family members.

4. *Business associates.* Long-term business associates are often selected to act as trustees because the grantor has confidence in their business and managerial experience, and there is an underlying comfort level built on their long-term relationship. The downside risks include potential conflict when the business interest is an asset of the trust and, if the business associate is a contemporary of the grantor, the fact that he or she might not be able to serve over the lifetime of the trust. Often, these problems can be solved by a properly funded buy-sell agreement.

5. *Private investment advisers.* When the bulk of the trust assets consist of cash and listed securities, one obvious potential candidate for trustee is an investment adviser: a stockbroker, financial planner, or other type of professional money manager. Clearly, the major advantage in this area is the benefit of having people who are supposedly skilled in handling and investing other people's money. If the investment advisers also have the time and ability to stay in close contact with the beneficiaries to determine their constantly changing needs, they deserve serious consideration as candidates for trustee. If they have a close relationship with the beneficiaries, too, that's still another plus.

One disadvantage of using private investment advisers as trustees is that their major emphasis is on handling and investing money, not on keeping in constant touch with trust beneficiaries. Another is the obvious and almost certain conflict of interest and ethical problem, a lack of checks and balances where the person responsible for investing trust assets receives a commission on each sale.

6. *Lawyers as trustees.* In many cases, grantors turn to the lawyers drafting their trust documents as their choice to act as trustee. Lawyers who are familiar with the grantor's assets and beneficiaries, have investment experience or are in a position to hire qualified investment advisers, and have the time to devote to the administration of the trust and the welfare of the beneficiaries make good trustees. One major advantage of any professional as a trustee is that he or she is more likely to carry professional liability insurance than would a family member or friend of the grantor. Therefore, if trust assets are handled improperly, the trust beneficiaries may be in a better position to be compensated for any loss incurred in managing the trust. If the grantor of the trust has confidence in the lawyer's ability to serve, and the lawyer has the characteristics and qualifications listed earlier in this chapter, the lawyer may be a good choice as trustee.

When a lawyer is chosen as a trustee, there is always the possibility of a conflict of interest: Does the lawyer, in fact, represent the grantor who set up the trust, the trustees, or the beneficiaries? If the lawyer represents the family business, who does the lawyer represent after the grantor's death? If the trust beneficiaries are dissatisfied with the trust and the trustee, the attorney as the person who prepared the trust document, clearly has a conflict that is difficult—if not impossible—to resolve. Also, few lawyers have the time or skill to properly administer a trust, and there is the possibility that the administration of the trust will not receive the attention it deserves when the lawyer has a demanding, time-consuming practice.

Finally, the ethics rules of many states prohibit a lawyer from recommending himself or herself as a trustee or other fiduciary. If your lawyer has suggested himself as trustee, or drafted a trust document with her name included as a trustee, your lawyer may have demonstrated a lack of sensitivity to the kind of fiduciary obligations good trustees must and should observe.

7. *Accountants.* If the grantor has utilized the services of a CPA or an accountant over an extended period of time and has confidence in the accountant's ability, the accountant could be a good choice as a trustee or a co-trustee. Accountants, even more so than lawyers in many instances, have a broad and current picture of a client's financial

situation. In some cases, this also includes a personal acquaintance with the family members and a knowledge of their various needs. Because many people rely on their accountant's advice in making major financial decisions throughout their lifetime, they hope to have their accountant continue to advise their family following their death. However, in many cases, a grantor's accountant is a contemporary of the grantor and therefore may not be able to serve throughout the lifetime of the trust. There could also be conflicts between the accountant and other family members, and because of other business commitments, the accountant might not have sufficient time to devote to the administration of the trust.

8. *The corporate trustee.* Commercial banks with trust departments and independent trust companies are in the business of acting as professional trustees. They have the experience, the investment expertise and a diversified staff–including lawyers and investment, business, and real estate specialists–to be able to administer most trusts adequately. They can also take care of the routine but very important bookkeeping that is essential to proper trust administration and is often severely lacking when a trust is administered by a nonprofessional. Unfortunately, when handling a trust for the beneficiaries, a large bank or trust company is only as good as the people administering the trust in question. While size and experience are excellent attributes, they cannot guarantee perfect results.

Often, a trust officer assigned to a particular trust has the personality and qualifications to make certain that the trust is administered properly, following the grantor's wishes and in the best interests of the beneficiaries. Unfortunately, however, this may not always be the case. Personnel of a trust company change. In deciding to utilize the services of a corporate trustee, therefore, you must consider the disadvantages, as well as the advantages.

One negative factor is the fee charged by corporate fiduciaries. There is typically a fee schedule that includes a minimum fee, regardless of the size of the trust. For that reason it may not be economically feasible to choose a corporate trustee if the assets in the trust are less than several hundred thousand dollars.

Corporate trustees may also lack the knowledge or experience to administer a family business. In addition, corporate trustees do not have the personal knowledge and interest that a family member, friend, or long-time professional adviser can bring to the trust administration. Therefore, the corporate trustee, while highly qualified in many respects, may not always be the right choice as trustee.

9. *A combination of family, friends and professionals.* If the size of the estate warrants it, a combination of two or more of the above potential candidates may be the best solution. If you want professional money management but also want to make certain that the trustees keep close watch over the beneficiaries to see that their needs are being regularly met, then the combination of a corporate trustee and a friend or family member as co-trustee may be the preferable choice. The corporate trustee can manage the assets of the estate, and the individual can ensure that these assets are being used properly for the beneficiaries. The individual trustees can keep in close contact with the beneficiaries and see that their day-to-day requirements are being met, and the professionals can make the investment decisions. It is also possible to separate the trustees' functions. A child active in the business can be placed in charge of it, for example, while a professional money manager can manage the other investments.

It is often wise to build safeguards into the trust to handle future contingencies regarding the trustees. For example, there is no guarantee that a strong locally based friendly financial institution will continue to be either strong or locally based and friendly indefinitely. It is often advisable, therefore, to appoint an individual trustee who has the right in the future to replace the bank or trust company with another corporate trustee of comparable size and investment expertise. The decision to replace the corporate trustee might be motivated by a change in the corporate trustee's financial position, a personality conflict with the trust officer handling the trust, or a decision by the trust beneficiaries to move to a different area. It is always advisable to include backups in the trust documents for a trustee unable to continue to act as such (we recommend naming at least two successors) and to provide the machinery to replace a corporate trustee.

Q. What are the five factors that should be considered in choosing a "home" (attorneys call this a "situs") for my trust?

A. Most times, the situs of a trust is decided by the most obvious factors, where the creator lives, where the trustee is located, where the assets are—or are to be administered—where the beneficiaries live, where income producing property is located, and the trust laws of the state involved. But according to an excellent article by Carolyn Geer in Forbes Magazine (June 16, 1997) starting on page 190, five additional factors that should be considered when deciding where a trust with significant assets should be located are

(1) local income taxes (Although situs has no impact on federal income tax, some states have more or less income taxes than others. A move to a state income tax free state could save thousands in income or capital gains taxes. Beware, it is possible for more than one state to attempt to tax a trust's revenue where the trustee and the trust and its beneficiaries are all in different states)

(2) creditor protection (Almost all states provide protection from the creditors of a trust's beneficiaries through what are called "spendthrift" provisions. Illinois, New York, Washington, and Delaware provide significant protection in this regard. Some states also offer more or less protection from the creator's creditors. Alaska, for example, now provides that you can create your own trust, give the trustee discretion to return income or principal to you, and be protected from "unknown future creditors", i.e., you are protected as long as you are not trying to defraud known creditors. See the chapter 27 discussion of Delaware and Alaska trusts)

(3) protection of privacy (A living trust, one you create during lifetime, does not become a public document. So the terms, conditions, parties, and the amount of assets placed into the trust while you are alive do not become public knowledge. This is important in achieving the objective of protecting trust assets against both creditors as well as predators. A trust created in your will becomes a public document when it is probated. Additionally, states that have enacted the Uniform Probate Code require that you register names and dates—but not dollar amounts—in state court)

(4) ability to continue the trust perpetually (Many states limit the duration of a trust to 90 years. But a number of states, including Idaho, South Dakota, Wisconsin, Delaware, and Alaska, allow a trust to continue in perpetuity. This extended duration is essential to the success of the control and tax device for ultra wealthy families called the "Dynasty Trust" discussed in Chapter 18)

(5) convenience and expense (A trustee is given significant investment flexibility in states that have adopted the UPIA, the Uniform Prudent Investor Act. The trustee can invest assets or select or fire a money manager with great freedom. Keep in mind that a trust in a state with numerous reporting requirements or that is far away and which will require extensive correspondence and telephone calls may result in expenses and inconvenience not considered when other advantages were.

The selection of situs is exceptionally important and may have dramatic implications. Here are some thoughts to consider before pondering the five points listed above:

- Remember that you don't have to locate the trust's situs where either you or the beneficiary live.

- An attorney will tend to locate a trust in a state where he or she knows the law, works with and retains referrals from local trust companies, and finds it convenient to work.

- A money manager will tend to favor states where he, she, or it has a local office.

- A state whose law's appear to be the most favorable today may not be the state of choice at some future date. So the ability for the grantor and/or the beneficiaries of the trust to change the jurisdiction is important.

HOW TRUSTEES GET IN TROUBLE

Chapter 4 explains:

- Why it is dangerous to accept the position of trustee

- The duties of a trustee

- Guidelines a trustee must follow

- The "Prudent Man" rule

- The "Prudent Investor" rule

- The implications of a trustee's breach of fiduciary duty

- Trustee liability in managing a family business

- Why constant communication with trust beneficiaries is essential

- The importance of acting in a timely manner

- A trustee's potential personal liability to third parties

- Joint liability in the case of multiple trustees

- Environmental liability as a concern to trustees

- Ways a trustee can avoid or reduce the threat of personal liability

Q. Why is it dangerous to be a trustee?

A. Trustees assume tremendous responsibility. Many people agree to serve as trustees without appreciating the nature of the work they are to perform or understanding that they can become subject to personal liability. In certain instances, trustees' personal funds may be at risk because of actions (or inactions) on their part, and even if their actions prove correct, their right to reimbursement for the cost of defending themselves may be limited.

If the trustee does something that is improper, or fails to do something the trustee is properly required to do, and the action (or inaction) causes the beneficiaries of the trust to lose money or suffer damages, the trustee can be "surcharged." That means that the trustee is required to make up the loss to the beneficiary out of the trustee's own assets. This chapter explores the area of trustee liability, and it suggests ways to eliminate—or at least reduce—such liability.

Q. What are the duties of a trustee?

A. The duties of a trustee can be summarized as follows:

- Assemble the assets of the trust. This is obviously no problem if the trust consists of a bank account or the proceeds of a mutual fund. But it can be extremely difficult if the trust assets are a business or widely scattered real estate investments.

- Make certain that the assets are protected. Are the locks changed on the house? Are there adequate amounts of fire and casualty insurance on property? Are valuable collectibles or gun collections under lock and key?

- Make sure that the assets are properly invested. Are the trust assets being invested and used in the best interest of the beneficiaries and in the manner that the grantor of the trust intended they be used? Are they invested in risky stocks that should be sold? Is all or a substantial portion of the money in a non-interest-bearing checking account?

- Determine who the trust beneficiaries are (a child born out of wedlock, the child of deceased sister, and so on).

- Communicate regularly with the beneficiaries, and ensure that their needs are met.

- Comply in a timely manner with the necessary administration and recording procedures.

- Make certain that income and other tax returns are timely filed.

- Keep careful records.

- At the end of the trust, prepare a final accounting and make final distribution to the beneficiaries.

(For a detailed list of the duties of the trustee of a revocable living trust following the death of the grantor/beneficiary of a trust, see "Duties of the Trustee" and "The Trustee's Checklist" in the Appendix.

Q. What personal guidelines must a trustee follow?

A. As a trustee, your fundamental duty is loyalty. Every action you take should be for the benefit of the beneficiaries of the trust and not for yourself. Confidentiality is an inherent part of loyalty; therefore, you should never disclose information concerning the trust or its beneficiaries to unauthorized persons. You should never buy any assets from the trust for your own benefit, sell any of your own assets to the trust, or engage in any other act of "self-dealing" without the full knowledge and informed consent of all of the beneficiaries.

Moreover, you should avoid conflicts of interest and never put yourself in a position that might favor your interest over the beneficiaries' or favor one beneficiary over another. In addition, generally you should not receive any fee for services (other than your fee as trustee), and you should not derive any personal advantage from or realize a profit in dealing with the trust. Attorneys and accountants who serve both as trustees and as professionals who bill the trust for services must be particularly careful to avoid a conflict of interest and scrupulously document their time and charges.

Q. What is the "prudent man" rule?

A. As a trustee, you have a duty to exercise care, diligence, and prudence in handling the trust property. Your conduct will be considered to meet the these standards if you act with the care and skill that a prudent man or woman would exercise in his or her own affairs. However, because professional trustees such as banks, trust companies, and attorneys are often deemed to have special skills or superior expertise, they are often held by courts to a higher standard.

Unlike an executor—whose principal duties are to gather up the assets of an estate, pay the outstanding obligations, and make distributions to the beneficiaries—the trustee's duties are much more complex, and they can often extend over a considerable period of time. In deciding how to invest trust assets, as opposed to estate assets, therefore, the trustee must consider all of the different facts that affect the trust and its beneficiaries.

For example, if Zeda Steve wants to leave $250,000 in trust for his daughter, Charlee, for Charlee's lifetime and then distribute the balance in the trust to Charlee's son Max after Charlee's death, the trustee has to have an investment plan that can satisfy the needs of the different classes of beneficiaries. Charlee will want an investment that will produce high income for her during her lifetime, but the trustee must also consider building up the trust assets for Max, the grandson. Investing the funds in a 100 percent safe certificate of deposit paying 3 percent interest might be the safest way to proceed, but it would not be in keeping with Zeda Steve's wishes for his daughter, Charlee and grandson, Max.

As a trustee, therefore, you have a duty to make the trust assets productive within the guidelines of the trust instrument and in accordance with the prudent man rule. In most cases, it is your conduct, rather than the investment performance, that is judged by the courts. You will be held personally liable only when lawsuits result from imprudent conduct, not when investment performance has not been as good as possible. (But typically it is when investment performance is poor that trust beneficiaries sue.)

Q. What is the "prudent investor" rule?

A. There have been several problems with the traditional "prudent man" rule when applied to trust investments.

One problem is that courts have tended to look at the wisdom of particular investments, rather than the over-all performance of all investments held by the trustee. This has encouraged trustees to make "middle of the road" investments, neither too safe (beneficiaries complain because there is not enough income, or the trust is not growing fast enough) nor too risky (beneficiaries complain when the risks do not pay off and the investments lose money). Meanwhile, modern investment practices are to try to maintain a "balanced" portfolio, with some dependable, low-risk investments and some higher-return, higher-risk investments, the exact mix depending on the goals and needs of the investor.

Another problem with traditional measures of trustee responsibility is the principle that the investment decisions of the trustee cannot be delegated. If the investment decisions result in

Trusts/Leimberg Associates Books: 610-527-5216

loses, it is no excuse that the trustee was following the advice of respected investment advisors. In fact, reliance on investment advisors might be used as evidence that the trustee had failed to exercise independent judgment on behalf of the beneficiaries!

Finally, many states have statutory lists of "fiduciary investments," sometimes limited to bonds backed by the full faith and credit of the United States or the particular state. These "fiduciary investments" are often considered to be too conservative for modern investors used to the historically large yields on common stocks, and yet trustees risk litigation with beneficiaries anytime they depart from those approved investments.

In response to these and other problems with the traditional "prudent man" rule, the American Law Institute formulated a "prudent investor" rule as part of the *Restatement of Trusts (Third)* in 1990 and, in 1994, the Commissioners on Uniform State Laws recommended that each state adopt the Uniform Prudent Investor Act. The changes made by the Uniform Prudent Investor Act can be summarized as follows:

- The performance of the trustee is measured by all of the trust investments, taken as a whole, and not by the performance of any one investment.

- It is expressly recognized that the trustee must choose between risk and return in selecting investments, so that a risky investment can be justified by a higher expected return.

- No investment is automatically prohibited. Any investment can be defended as long as it is consistent with the over-all investment risks and returns appropriate to the trust.

- It is clearly stated that trustees should diversify their investments. So investing in nothing but federal securities can be criticized as much as investing in nothing but the stock of one corporation (a frequent subject of litigation with beneficiaries).

- Delegation of investment decisions is allowed, as long as the trustee selects the investment advisor carefully, provides guidance to the advisor in setting the investment goals for the trust, and monitors the performance of the advisor.

The Uniform Prudent Investor Act has been enacted in a number of states, and the courts in several other states have adopted the "prudent investor rule" of the *Restatement of Trusts (Third)*. If you are a trustee and you want to comply with the law and minimize potential conflicts with beneficiaries, you must consult a lawyer to find out what laws apply to your trust and what you can (and can't) do with the investments of the trust.

Q. What happens if a trustee breaches his or her duty?

A. If you violate or fail to perform any duty that you owe to the beneficiaries of the estate, you are liable for resulting damages. In other words, a beneficiary can recover in a lawsuit those values that he or she would have enjoyed had there been no breach. For example, if the trustee sold a trust asset to himself or a close member of his or her family for less than the fair market value of that asset, the trustee would be personally liable to the trust for the difference. If the trustee permitted a large sum of money to remain uninvested or invested it at 2 percent in a bank account, the trustee could be held liable for the loss of income to the beneficiaries when compared to a more productive—but still conservative—investment, such as certificates of deposit, Treasury notes, or even a conservative investment in securities if such investment is permitted under the terms of the trust agreement.

Q. How can a trustee be held liable for managing a family business?

A. As a trust asset, a family business can cause considerable problems for the trustee. A family business is often the largest asset of a trust, and a closely-held business is usually one of the riskiest investments possible. Continuing to operate the business through the trust, and thereby putting all of the financial "eggs" of the trust in one "basket," is a strategy often criticized by courts, and one that exposes the trustee to a significant risk of legal action by the beneficiaries if the business fails or is less profitable than expected. And quite often, the grantor's death causes considerable harm to the continued success of the business, and the business can fail despite all of the trustee's good intentions and hard work. Furthermore, there are often family members who are active in the business, and this can create tension and conflict with the trustee.

The terms of the trust must be carefully examined. If the trust document directs that the business be continued, or shows that the grantor clearly intended that the business be continued, the trustee is less likely to be liable for business losses.

To avoid being held liable for business losses, the trustee should regularly communicate with the beneficiaries of the trust and whenever possible secure their written permission before making any major decisions about managing or continuing the business.

Q. Why is it important to communicate with the beneficiaries?

A. In a great many instances, the underlying causes for lawsuits against trustees arise because of the trustee's failure to properly communicate with the beneficiaries. Beneficiaries who seek—but are unable to obtain—information about the assets and the management of the trust, whose needs are ignored, and whose telephone calls are not answered, are obvious candidates for instituting a lawsuit against the trustee.

If the trustee keeps the beneficiaries aware of the day-to-day management and treatment of the trust assets, they are more likely to understand and feel a part of the entire trust process, and their predominant fear of having their interest from the trust reduced or eliminated can be avoided (or at least greatly alleviated). If the beneficiaries are kept informed of the administration of the trust and fail to object to investment decisions or other actions of the trustee until a loss occurs, it is possible that the court will find that they effectively consented to the actions of the trustee by failing to object in a timely fashion.

In those instances where the beneficiaries are capable of making decisions, trustees would be well advised—even if the trust instrument does not call for it—to consult with the beneficiaries and, where appropriate, obtain their permission or at least inform them before making any major investment and other trust decisions.

Q. Why is it important to act in a timely manner?

A. Trusts, even more so than other legal entities in many cases, have certain deadlines to meet. Depending on how the trust is structured, there can be several income tax returns to be prepared. The trust may have its own state and federal income tax returns, informational returns may have to be prepared for the beneficiaries for use in computing their tax returns, and accountings may be required for the beneficiaries and the court. In addition, there are always decisions to be made when handling investments or other assets, such as exercising certain stock options or filing tax returns for different businesses that are part of the trust. In many instances, failure to act timely can result in added interest and penalties, all of which can be surcharged to the trustee.

Q. Can a trustee be sued by a third party who is not a beneficiary of the trust?

A. While many trustees understand that they can be personally liable to the beneficiaries of the trust for violating their fiduciary relationship, they are not aware that they also face personal liability for injuries or damage to third parties and also for contract claims of third parties that occur during the administration of the trust. The trustee's individual assets may also be at risk for payment of the injury or claim if the damage exceeds the assets of the estate or trust. For example, if the trustee is running an unincorporated pizza business as an asset of the trust, the driver of the pizza delivery truck strikes and seriously injures someone, and the trustee had failed to pay the automobile insurance premiums, he or she could be held personally liable for the injuries to the injured person.

Q. What happens in the case of multiple trustees?

A. In most instances, trustees all share in the management of the trust assets and are responsible for all of their actions. If one trustee does something improper, all of the trustees can be subject to liability, particularly if they failed to supervise the other trustee. If the trust document gives any of the trustees the right to make independent decisions, it is still possible for a co-trustee to be held jointly responsible for that decision.

Q. Why is environmental liability a serious concern for all trustees?

A. Trustees have potential liability for environmental damages, cleanup costs, and penalties for properties which they hold as trustees.

The Comprehensive Environmental Response Compensation and Liability Act of 1980 (CERCLA), also known as the Superfund Act, was enacted by Congress in 1980 to provide a response system for cleaning up hazardous waste sites. Under CERCLA, the "owner" of a property can be liable for the clean-up costs of environmentally polluted property, and trustees have been ruled to be "owners" for the purpose of the Act. If the trust assets are insufficient to pay for the costs of clean-up (which can be tens or hundreds of thousands of dollars, if not millions of dollars, for spills or leakage of chemicals as common as fuel oil, lubricants, or even ink), the trustee must make up the difference out of his or her own pocket.

Recent legislation has limited the liability of trustees and other fiduciaries for personal liability relating to contamination that occurred before the property was placed in trust, or before the trustee became trustee. However, trustees still face almost unlimited personal liability for contamination that occurs while the property is controlled by their trust, and the liability can be strict, without regard to any negligence or other fault of the trustee. For example, if a commercial property is an asset of a trust, there are storage tanks on the commercial property, and those storage tanks should leak, the potential liability can be enormous. Trustees must therefore be extremely careful of accepting responsibility for any property without thoroughly investigating the history of the property, how it is being currently used, and whether there are any possible problem under any environmental law.

Q. How can trustees protect themselves from liability?

A. There are several ways to protect yourself from liability as a trustee:

- Before agreeing to act as trustee, review the terms of the trust agreement and recommend any changes that might be needed to clarify your duties and liabilities.

- Make certain that the trust document allows you to resign as trustee if future contingencies warrant your doing so.

- Clarify your responsibilities with other co-trustees (if there are co-trustees).

- Familiarize yourself to the greatest extent possible with the nature of the assets and the trust beneficiaries.

- If there is potential environmental liability, have the agreement drafted to protect the trustees to the extent that can be done under federal or state law.

- Keep careful records of every receipt and disbursement of the trust.

- Keep all trust assets separate from your personal assets, and be sure that trust assets are always registered in the name of the trust or in your name as trustee, but never in your own name without disclosing your position as trustee.

- Obtain competent tax advice and be sure all necessary tax returns are filed when due.

- Document your actions and decisions. If you give money to a beneficiary, use a check or get a receipt. If a timely response is required, send it by certified mail. If you exercise your discretion under the trust document to make an extraordinary distribution, explain the reasons for the distribution in a letter to the beneficiaries.

- Do not buy or sell any asset from or to the trust, or allow any other transaction between the trust and yourself, your family or friends, or any business in which you are interested. Avoid entering into any other transaction that might suggest a conflict of interest or an attempt to make a personal gain at the beneficiaries' expense.

- If possible, obtain the written consent of all competent beneficiaries whenever you are making any major investment decision or when you are selling or changing the status of a major trust asset.

- When your duties are finished, obtain a written release from the beneficiaries. If there is any danger of any liability to any potential beneficiary, creditor, or any other person, file a formal accounting with the court and receive a formal discharge.

RIGHTS OF BENEFICIARIES IN TRUSTS

Chapter 5 explains:

- Who are considered "beneficiaries" of a trust

- The different possible interests of beneficiaries

- How to obtain a copy of the trust document and find out if you are a beneficiary

- How to find out what the trustee is doing

- What a fiduciary account is

- What your legal remedies might be if the trustee has done something wrong

- Who pays the legal expenses of the trustee

Q. *Who is a beneficiary?*

A. Generally speaking, a beneficiary of a trust is anyone to whom (or for whose benefit) money or other property might be distributed from a trust.

The phrase "for whose benefit" means that money could be paid to someone else for the beneficiary. For example, a trust might direct that the trustee pay the educational expenses of a minor child. In most cases, the trustee would send checks for tuition, room, and board directly to the school or to the parent or guardian of the child, but not to the minor child. The minor child is still considered to be the beneficiary, and the payments for the child will carry out the taxable income of the trust to the child. (See chapter 15.)

Q. Who can be a beneficiary of a trust?

A. Just about any individual now living or who might be born in the future, and any organization that can own property, can be a beneficiary of a trust.

Any individual can be a beneficiary—even a minor or an adult who is legally incompetent—because the beneficiary does not need to manage any property, only receive the benefits from the trust. (Of course, if the beneficiary is a minor or legally incompetent, it may be necessary to have a guardian appointed to receive the income or principal if the trustee does not have the power to hold the income or principal for the beneficiary and apply it for his or her benefit. In order to avoid the need for guardians, most trusts have provisions for minor or disabled beneficiaries.)

You don't have to identify any of your beneficiaries by name. You can specify, for example, that "income is to be paid annually or more frequently to my children." In fact, beneficiaries don't even have to be alive when you create the trust. The law requires only that beneficiaries be an identifiable and definite class or group, such as spouse, children, grandchildren, nieces, or nephews. You could, therefore, include children or grandchildren not yet born as beneficiaries—even if you have no children at the time you set up and fund your trust.

Beneficiaries do not have to be related to you. For example, you can name a friend or employee as the beneficiary of your trust. (You could even name the authors of this book as beneficiaries!)

Charities and other organizations can also be named as beneficiaries, including corporations, other trusts, partnerships, federal, state, and local governments, and even foreign governments. However, complications can arise if the beneficiary is an unincorporated association or other organization unable to hold legal title to property. There are also strict rules regarding the types of organizations, and the types of interests, that will qualify for charitable deductions for gift or estate tax purposes. (See chapter 25 for details.)

You cannot name a dog, cat, or other pet as a beneficiary of your trust (although you can name an individual as a beneficiary with the request that he or she take care of a specified animal or that trust funds be used to care for your pets during their lifetime). (See Chapter 21).

Trusts/Leimberg Associates Books: 610-527-5216

Q. Must all beneficiaries be named in the trust document?

A. The trust document does not need to include the name of the beneficiary, but the beneficiary can be described by a relationship to the grantor or another person. For example, if a grantor establishes a trust for the benefit of "my grandchildren," all of the grandchildren of the grantor are beneficiaries, even though their names are not in the trust document. However, there is sometimes a problem if a new grandchild is born, because there can be a question as to whether the grantor intended to benefit grandchildren born in the future (i.e., the class of beneficiaries is "open") or whether the grantor intended to benefit only those grandchildren living when the trust was created (i.e., the class of beneficiaries is "closed").

One note of caution: If you name a class of beneficiaries that is too vague, the provision might be held invalid because of its indefiniteness. For instance, if you provided "income to my friends for life" without specifying which friends you mean, the class "friends" would create problems because of its vagueness. (Even the term "my relatives" might cause litigation.)

You must therefore be careful in identifying your beneficiaries. Even when identifying beneficiaries by name, make sure that there is no confusion or possibility of error. So, for example, when a parent and child carry the same name, be sure to include the beneficiary's middle initials and his or her exact relation to you.

Q. What are the possible interests of a beneficiary?

A. There are many different types of interests that can be created in a trust, and many different ways in which beneficiaries can be classified.

Most beneficial interests are divided between "income" and "principal" (also sometimes called "corpus", the body of the trust). Generally speaking, "principal" is what is paid into the trust when it is created, while income is what is earned by the principal. Interest, dividends, rent, and royalties are all examples of income. Capital gains (such as the profit earned on the sale of a stock or a sale of real estate) are usually considered part of the principal, and not income, because they represent increases in the value of the principal. A trust will typically direct that income be distributed in one way and that the principal be distributed in another way.

One of the simplest kinds of trusts pays all of the income to one beneficiary for his or her life, then pays the principal of the trust to someone else upon the death of the income beneficiary. The income beneficiary may be called a "life tenant" and the future beneficiary of the principal may be called a "remainderman," because he or she receives only what is left after the life tenant dies.

Trust distributions can be "mandatory" or "discretionary". If the trust document states that all of the income must be distributed to the current beneficiary, then the distributions are mandatory. If the trust document states that the trustee "may" distribute income for the "support" or "maintenance" of the beneficiary, or in the discretion of the trustee, then the trust is discretionary, and the trustee must decide whether all, some, or none of the income should be distributed. If the beneficiaries believe that the trustee has distributed too little (or too much), the beneficiaries must usually show that the trustee has "abused" his or her discretion, and failed to act within the bounds intended by the grantor.

A "current interest" is one in which the beneficiary has an immediate, unfettered, and ascertainable right to use, possess, or enjoy property in or income from the trust. For example, an income beneficiary has the immediate right to the trust's income. A future interest is one which is not current, i.e., the beneficiary must wait for some period of time or event (such as the death of the income beneficiary or the expiration of a period of time or the attainment of a certain age) to have the right to receive his or her interest.

Future interests in a trust can be "vested" or "contingent." A "vested" interest is one that is not dependent on the beneficiary being alive, or on any other similar condition. (If the beneficiary is not alive when the trust is distributed, then the estate of the beneficiary receives the distribution and it is disposed of according to the beneficiary's will.) A "contingent" interest is one that is dependent on the beneficiary surviving some other person or upon another similar condition. If the beneficiary is not alive when the trust is distributed, or otherwise fails to fulfill the conditions of the trust, the trust document should state what should happen to the property in the trust.

The difference between current interests and future interests is important, because current bencficiaries may be entitled to regular accountings by the trustee, and have greater rights in enforcing the trust, than a beneficiary whose rights only arise in the future.

Trust beneficiaries can also have different priorities. If you create a trust for your wife and your adult children, you might be concerned that your wife have enough money to provide for her support for her entire life, but still want to include provisions for your children in case they have medical or other emergency needs, or in case it turns out that there is more money in the trust than your wife will ever need. In that case, you might want to include language in the trust to make it clear that your wife is the *primary* beneficiary and that your children are only secondary beneficiaries, whose interests are less important than your wife's welfare.

Q. How can I find out if I am a beneficiary of a trust and get a copy of the trust document?

A. The easiest way to find out if you are a beneficiary is to ask the grantor (if living) or the trustee. However, many trusts are created with the intention that they remain private, which means that the trustee is not likely to want to show you a copy of the trust document if the trustee believes that you are not a beneficiary. The trustee is then in a dilemma, because the only way to prove to you that you are not entitled to the information you have asked for is to give you the information you have asked for.

If the grantor is living and the trust is revocable, you may have no enforceable right to obtain a copy of the trust. Although you may be a beneficiary, you are probably only a future beneficiary, the grantor being the primary beneficiary during his or her lifetime. You therefore have no current rights that can be enforced. More importantly, if the grantor is living and the trust is revocable, any legal action to obtain a copy of the trust will probably just annoy the grantor and result in an amendment to the trust that eliminates your beneficial interest and makes your request irrelevant. (This is therefore one case in which it may be better not to look a gift horse in the mouth.)

If you are a beneficiary of a testamentary trust (a trust created by a will), you can obtain a copy of the will, and perhaps other documents showing the size of the estate and what went into the trust, from the probate court (or "Register of Wills" or "Surrogate's Court" or "Orphans' Court," the name varies from state to state). If you know the name of the decedent, in what county or state the decedent resided before his or her death, and the year of death, send a letter to the probate court in that county and request copies of all of the relevant documents.

The more difficult case is an irrevocable living trust, because it is quite possible that the trust document has never been filed in any court. However, it is also possible that it was, so you might want to check with the officials of the county in which the grantor resided at death (or still resides, if still alive) to see if there have been any court proceedings involving a trust by that grantor. If there has been a court proceeding, it will be a public record and you should be able to obtain a copy of the documents.

If you believe that you are a beneficiary of a living trust but can't find any public record of the trust and can't get the grantor or the trustee to give you any information, you will ultimately have to decide whether to believe the person you think is the trustee or take legal action to try to force that person to disclose the existence of the trust. Any legal action will require a lawyer. (See the question on legal enforcement of trusts at the end of this chapter.)

Q. How can I find out what the trustee is doing?

A. In many states, a trustee is required to account annually to the court or the beneficiaries. Even if it is not required by law, a sensible trustee will provide copies of tax returns, brokerage statements, or other information to a beneficiary to enable the beneficiary to see that the trust is being administered conscientiously and competently. Bear in mind, however, that a trustee (and perhaps also a court) is more likely to be responsive to a beneficiary with a current interest in the trust (such as a beneficiary entitled to all of the income) than a beneficiary who has only a contingent future interest, and who may be viewed more as a busybody than a real party in interest.

If the trustee refuses to provide the information you want, you might be able to obtain at least copies of the tax returns of the trust from the Internal Revenue Service if you know the trust's employer identification number (It's like a Social Security number for a trust). Those returns would show the income and expenses of the trust, and how much was distributed to each beneficiary. If the sources of income are listed, the returns could help determine the size of the trust and how it is invested. To obtain copies of the trust's tax returns, contact your local IRS

District Director to find out what forms you must file, what information you must provide, and what fees you must pay.

If all else fails, and the trustee refuses to provide you with adequate information about the investments, expenses, and distributions, you will have to ask a court to order the trustee to "account". (See questions below.)

Q. What is a fiduciary account?

A. A fiduciary account is a statement of all of the receipts and disbursements of an executor, trustee, or other fiduciary. Fiduciary accounts are often filed with a court in order to obtain court approval of the actions of the fiduciary. So the specific content and format of the account is determined by rules of the court in your jurisdiction. However, an account can be understood by anyone willing to take the time to learn some of the concepts and conventions.

A beneficiary should take the time to read and understand a fiduciary account, because an account can answer the following questions:

- What assets were placed into the trust—and when—and by whom?

- What debts, taxes, and expenses were paid?

- What assets were sold by the trust—and for how much?

- Was the money reinvested? If so, did the investments increase or decrease in value?

- How much income was received by the trust, and on which investments?

- What was (or will be) distributed, and to whom?

Because income and principal are often distributed separately, to different beneficiaries, a trust must account separately for income and principal. After dividing all receipts and disbursements between income and principal, the account proceeds fairly logically. It shows the cash inflows and outflows, i.e., what the trustee received, what was sold, what was spent, what was distributed, and what is left in the trust. While there can be variations from state to state, the account of a trustee will usually consists of the following sections or schedules:

Summary. The first page is usually a summary page that also serves as a table of contents. It shows the totals for each schedule, and the page number on which the details can be found for that schedule.

Principal Receipts. After the summary page, the first schedule is a schedule of principal receipts. In the case of a trust, the principal receipts are the distributions from the estate to the trust (in the case of a trust under a will) or the contributions to the trust (in the case of a lifetime trust).

Sales or Other Dispositions. If an asset is sold, the difference between the net proceeds of sale and the "fiduciary acquisition value" (which is the value of the asset when received or the cost of the asset if purchased) is shown on a schedule of gains and losses.

Principal Disbursements. Principal disbursements are expenses of the trust which are charged to principal, the most common of which are income taxes on capital gains (because the capital gains are charged to principal, not income). Some (but not all) trustees' commissions and some (but not all) legal and accounting fees may also be charged to principal, depending on the nature of the commissions and fees. It is often difficult to draw a line between principal expenses and income expenses, but income expenses are usually recurring expenses required by the ongoing administration of the trust, while principal expenses are usually non-recurring (i.e., one-time-only) charges relating to the start of the trust or the termination or distribution of the trust.

Principal Distributions to Beneficiaries. Each distribution of principal to a beneficiary is listed with the name of the beneficiary and the value of what was distributed.

Principal Balance on Hand. This is a list of all assets still held by the trustee, after all disbursements and distributions. This list normally shows the "fiduciary acquisition value," which is the value of the asset when received (or the cost of the asset if purchased by the trustee), but may include the fair market value of the assets as of the date of the account. The assets comprising undistributed income may be shown separately, or the net undistributed income could be subtracted from the value of the assets in order to show the value of the principal on hand.

Information Schedules. There are a variety of transactions which do not increase or decrease the account value of the trust, but which should be disclosed. These include sales of assets without gain or loss, reorganizations (such as stock splits or mergers), and purchases of new investments. These transactions are usually shown on informational schedules which follow all of the principal schedules.

Income Receipts. Income receipts are normally grouped by type of income (dividends, interest, rents, etc.), then grouped by the stock, bond, or other asset generating the income, then by date. For example, the dividends received on AT&T stock would normally be shown chronologically among the other dividend receipts.

Income Disbursements. The income disbursements are the regularly occurring operating expenses of the estate or trust, and would include income taxes, property taxes, interest expenses, income commissions paid to the trustees, and any other expenses of earning, collecting, or distributing income.

Income Distributions. The dates and amounts of any income that has been distributed is shown, along with the names of the beneficiaries receiving the income.

Proposed Distributions. If the account is a final account before the final distribution of a trust, a schedule may be attached at the end of the account, showing the proposed distribution of all of the assets, both principal and income.

Q. What if the trustee has done something wrong?

A. If the trustee has done something wrong, there should be a remedy under state law. But whether the trustee has really done anything wrong, and the way in which the wrong might be remedied, can vary greatly from state to state. (Many times the real problem is the trustee's failure to continually and adequately communicate properly with trust beneficiaries).

The most common complaints against a trustee for which there may be a legal remedy include the following:

- Investment losses due to the negligence of the trustee

- Payment of excessive or unnecessary expenses (of which the most common complaint is excessive legal fees or trustee commissions)

- Losses due to acts of self-dealing between the trust and the trustee, such as the purchase of trust assets by the trustee at less than fair market value, or leases or other transactions that are more favorable to the trust than the trustee

- Failing to make distributions to the beneficiaries, or distributing too much money to some beneficiaries at the expense of other beneficiaries

- Investments that favor one beneficiary over another (such as investments in capital growth stocks that favor the remaindermen and pay very little in dividends to the income beneficiary)

- In rare cases, embezzlement or theft by the trustee

While procedures can vary greatly from state to state, correcting what a trustee has done wrong usually requires that you hire a lawyer. Typically, the lawyer will advise you that:

1. You must prove that a trust exists, that the person you believe is the trustee is in fact the trustee, and that you are a beneficiary. This is usually not a problem, because you usually have a copy of the trust document and the trustee has never denied being the trustee. It is a problem only when you do not have the trust document and the trustee has denied that a trust exists. Exactly how to prove that a trust exists is obviously a problem for which you will need a lawyer, and is beyond the scope of this book.

2. You must compel the trustee to file an account of his or her administration of the trust. Once you have proven that there is a trust, and you are a beneficiary, a court will usually order the trustee to account, but some states may require you to show a good reason why the trustee should account. The fact that the trustee has failed to provide you information about the trust, or the fact that the information you have shows that something may be wrong, should be sufficient reason to order an accounting.

3. Once an account has been filed, you will have an opportunity to examine the account and decide whether you agree with it. In most cases, an account prepared by an honest trustee will be an accurate record of the trustee's administration, and your objections will go to whether or not the trustee should have done the things that he, she, it, or they admit(s) has been done. For example, if the account shows that the trustee has accumulated income, you might object to the accumulation of the income, which you believe should have been distributed to you or other beneficiaries. In rare cases, beneficiaries must object that the account does not disclose assets or transactions, in which case the trustee is really being accused of fraud or theft.

4. If your objections raise "issues of fact" (i.e., if the parties dispute what actually happened), the court may hold a hearing and take the testimony of witnesses as to what actually occurred or what the grantor of the trust really intended. For historical reasons, most trust disputes are tried before a judge without a jury.

5. If the court agrees with your objections, it may "surcharge" the trustee and order him (her, it, or them) to pay money into the trust to make it whole (as it would have been if the trustee had not made a mistake). In extreme cases involving dishonesty or gross negligence, the court might also remove the trustee and appoint a new trustee to complete the administration of the trust. If the trustee fails to pay the money to the trust as ordered, the court might hold the trustee in contempt, or might enter a money judgment against the trustee that could be enforced like any other debt. If the trustee distributed too much money to some beneficiaries (or to the wrong beneficiaries), the court might order those beneficiaries to return the money to the trust.

Q. Who pays the legal fees of the trustee?

A. A trustee is ordinarily entitled to be reimbursed by the trust for the routine legal expenses paid for the administration of the trust. So if you force a trustee to file an account with the court, the costs of preparing and filing the account (which can be significant) will be paid by the trust fund, not the trustee. In addition, many states allow a trustee to pay from the trust any legal fees incurred defending the trustee against charges of wrongdoing—if the charges against the trustee are not proven. This could become an important consideration in deciding whether to bring a legal action against a trustee, because if you sue the trustee and lose, you will not only have paid significant fees to your own lawyer, but the legal fees of the trustee will be paid out of the trust fund and will undoubtedly reduce the amounts you receive from the trust in the future. This "Catch 22" for the beneficiaries also illustrates the importance of choosing a trustee who will work with the beneficiaries, and not against them. (See chapter 3.)

6

ARE LAWYERS REALLY NECESSARY?

Chapter 6 explains:

• The need for a lawyer in setting up a trust

• The qualifications of a good trust lawyer

• How you can find a competent and caring lawyer

• How to handle legal fees

• Factors to consider in determining the fairness of legal fees

• Criteria courts often use in limiting legal fees for trust work

Q. Do you need a lawyer to set up a trust?

A. We feel that it is absolutely essential to use the services of a lawyer both in the preparation of the trust document and in assisting the trustee in administering the trust. In our opinion, if what you wish to accomplish could best be done through a trust, then, just like your mother told you, if it's worth doing, it's worth doing it right. And that means utilizing the services of an experienced estate planning lawyer. When you realize the many advantages that trusts have over other methods of handling and transferring property, you can understand why you should retain the services of an experienced professional to make sure that your trust meets your estate planning goals. As you can see from reading this book, there are a great many decisions to make when you establish a trust, and you should have someone who understands the complexities of the law to advise you—objectively—of the available options and the effect of each option on your overall estate plan.

For example, should your trust be revocable (as discussed in chapter 8) or irrevocable (as discussed in chapter 15)? Is it more advantageous to locate the trust in a particular state, and are there certain administrative procedures or even substantive legal decisions that change as the situs (location) of the trust changes?

Suppose Grandfather wishes to set up a trust for his grandchildren and fund the trust (place assets in the trust) with stock in Grandfather's corporation. These are some of the decisions that grandfather must make:

- What is the best way to place the stock in the trust for state and federal income tax purposes, state inheritance tax purposes, federal estate tax purposes, and generation-skipping transfer tax purposes?

- Will the trust be treated differently if Grandfather's corporation is a C corporation or an S corporation?

- Is it more advantageous to establish the trust in the state where Grandfather lives or in the state where the grandchildren live?

- Should the trustees be Grandfather's children, Grandfather's contemporaries, contemporaries of Grandfather's children, professional individual trustees (an accountant or lawyer for example), or a corporate trustee such as a bank or trust company?

- Should the income from the trust be paid out to the children, or should it be accumulated for their future use?

- Should the trustees be empowered to use trust principal for the health, maintenance, support, and education of the grandchildren, or only for their education? Or should their parents be responsible for the above needs so that all of the trust money will be available for the grandchildren's future use?

- How long should the grandchildren's money be held in trust–until they reach the age of majority (which is from 18 to 21, depending on the state in which they live) or until they are 25, 30, 35, or 40? Or should it be held in trust for their entire life and paid to their children at their death?

- Should all grandchildren be treated equally, or should each family be treated equally? For example, if Grandfather's son has one child and his daughter has two children, should his son's child receive one-half of the trust and each of his daughter's children receive one-quarter, or should each grandchild receive an equal one-third? What happens if grandchildren are born after Grandfather's death?

- What happens if a grandchild dies? Do his or her children receive a share, or does it go back to the other grandchildren or to Grandfather's child?

It certainly is difficult to imagine anyone, besides an experienced lawyer even being aware of all these and dozens of other issues, let alone being able effectively to capture your thoughts about each in a written trust instrument. Generally, the old adage, "He who has self for an attorney has a fool for a client" applies in the area of trusts.

Q. What are the qualifications of a good trust lawyer?

A. A good trust lawyer must be able to demonstrate to you that he or she has both the educational background and training in this particular area of the law and the experience in handling and administering the type of trust that meets your specific needs. In this age of specialization—when doctors are not simply surgeons but hand specialists and foot specialists—it just does not make sense to have a lawyer who primarily does criminal or accident work prepare trust documents for you.

As an educated consumer, you are certainly within your rights to question the lawyer about his or her educational background. Ask whether he or she has received any specific training in estate planning or preparing trusts, taken any special courses, received any advanced degrees such as a master's degree in law or taxation, taught courses, or written any articles or books on trusts and estate planning.

A good trust lawyer must not only have the background and experience to do trust work but must also makes you feel comfortable in his or her presence. Does he or she patiently answer your questions in an understandable manner? In order to make proper recommendations, the lawyer must have a thorough knowledge of your personal finances, your family, and your hopes and plans for your family's future. It's often difficult to express private feelings to a stranger, especially if you are not comfortable with that person. Therefore, the very best lawyer is one who, in addition to having the necessary background and qualifications, clearly indicates by words and conduct that he or she cares about you and your family and will work with you to help you achieve your planning goals.

Q. How do you find the right lawyer?

A. When you want a specialist, it is often wise to ask another specialist. To find a good trust lawyer, therefore, contact other estate planning specialists. Chances are, they will have worked with many lawyers as a member of the estate planning team and could probably give you good advice. These professionals include trust officers of banks and trust companies, experienced insurance and investment people such as those holding the CLU/ChFC or CFP designations, and CPAs.

Many qualified lawyers are members of estate planning councils. So contact your local estate planning council for a free list of its members who live in your area. Your local bar association also should have lawyers listed by their specialties, and a personal referral by a satisfied client is always a good source. If you have a close working relationship with the lawyer who handles your business or other work, he or she might be able to refer you to a lawyer who specializes in estate planning.

Q. How do I handle the question of legal fees?

A. First and most important, always demand that the fee arrangement be in writing. There are enough unpleasant surprises in life without having a large and unexpected bill presented after all of the work on that trust has been completed. It is always proper for you to bring up the subject of fees at your first meeting with the lawyer. But as with any other service or product, remember that you get what you pay for. What appears to be the cheapest lawyer may not be, and may certainly not be the best choice. Instead, the lawyer whose fee is reasonable in light of the lawyer's professional skill and standing might in the end turn out to be a much better bargain.

Q. What are reasonable lawyer's fees?

A. There are many factors to consider in determining the fairness or reasonableness of the fees that a lawyer will charge you for the preparation of the trust and for assisting in its administration. If the trust document is one that a specialist should be preparing quite often, such as a Marital and Credit Shelter Trust, the lawyer might be able to quote a flat fee for his or her services. If, on the other hand, your situation requires a much more detailed and individual approach, then services can be billed on an hourly basis.

For trust administration purposes, the trend today is to charge on an hourly basis for services rendered. In most instances, we urge you not to agree to a fee based on a percentage of the assets in the trust, since this may not be an indication of the work required to be performed. For example, a trust designed to make funds available for a handicapped child while not disqualifying that child from government benefits would have the same detail and legal consequence if the trust contained $50,000 or $500,000. It, therefore, would not seem reasonable for the client with the larger trust to pay 10 times as much for the identical work. On the other hand, because of the desire to perform a service for the client, the lawyer might charge less for the smaller trust if the client were not in a position to pay the normal fee for such services.

Q. What are the criteria that lawyers and courts use in setting legal fees?

A. Lawyers and courts consider the following factors in determining the amount and reasonableness of legal fees (and you should consider them also):

- the amount of work to be performed

- the character of the services rendered

- the difficulty of the problems involved

- the amount of money or the value in question

- the degree of responsibility incurred

- whether the fund in question was "created" by the lawyer

- the professional skill and standing of the lawyer

- the results that the lawyer was able to obtain

- the ability of the client to pay a reasonable fee

THE PROBLEM WITH TEAR-OUT TRUSTS

Chapter 7 explains:

- Why using "ready-made" trusts from "living trust" books is dangerous

- Why "packaged trusts" are unreliable

- The hidden agenda behind some of the living trust books

- Why people need tailored trusts

- Is a "tear-out" trust better than no trust at all?

Q. Should I hesitate about using ready-made trusts from "living trust books"?

A. There is a thick, not a thin, line between giving consumers advice and information on trusts and giving them the actual trust documents. While there are extensive legal treatises, such as the *Restatement of Trusts,* written specifically for lawyers, we have attempted to make this one of the most comprehensive books about trusts ever written for the consumer, so that you can decide whether trusts should play a role in your future planning. However, this book does not include a variety of "do-it-yourself" forms.

There are some consumer-oriented books that give readers choices of different forms to use under different circumstances, but our experience has been that those forms can lead to a number of different problems, including the following:

- It is almost impossible for a "form" trust to adequately satisfy everyone's individual needs. (Do you wear "one size fits all" clothing?)

- If a variety of forms are offered, in order to cover different situations, there is the very great danger that the reader will select the wrong form for his or her situation. (Even if the form is a good form under state law and local practice, it may be the wrong form for that individual.)

- Local court officials are often reluctant to accept forms that do not comply with local practice in appearance or terminology, even if the forms technically comply with the laws of that state.

- Finally, forming a trust involve a number of important decisions regarding the selection of trustees, tax planning, the selection of beneficiaries, the timing or conditions for distributions to beneficiaries, and other important issues, all of which may require the advice of a professional. (Do you also believe in "Do it yourself brain surgery"?)

It's our hope that the knowledge you gain after reading this book will help guide you in your future planning decisions. The sample forms and letters should also give you a more exact understanding of how a trust should be prepared and later administered.

However, the tax-planning, investment planning, and people-planning variables are so many and so complex that it would take a form book 12 inches thick even to attempt to cover every possible situation. That, as we see it, is the problem with "tear-out" trusts. We have never seen a tear-out trust that completely protects a handicapped child or that takes into consideration state and federal income, inheritance, and death taxes—many of which will change before the book is even published. Granted, in a very simple situation, a very simple trust may, in fact, produce the desired results, but in our opinion, the dangers far outweighs the benefits.

Q. How reliable are "packaged trusts"?

A. The public's increasing interest in living trusts as a method of passing assets to heirs in a less expensive and more efficient manner has spawned a new product with a new sales force. The product is the *revocable living trust,* and the salespeople range from lawyers, insurance representatives, and investment personnel to salespeople with little or no professional background. Often, revocable trust kits or packages are sold door-to-door or advertised on the radio, on television, or through the mail. Prices for these packaged trusts can range from $50 for a mail-order kit to $5,000 for a complete package, and even the most expensive package may fail to meet some of the major needs of you and your family. We sincerely doubt that anyone who is familiar with the information in this book will feel comfortable with the type of packaged product we just described. We reiterate—a good plan requires the services of a good lawyer.

Q. Is there a "hidden agenda" behind the proliferation of books on revocable living trusts?

A. Unquestionably, there is often a hidden agenda that goes beyond the sometimes actual, and sometimes exaggerated, fear of probate. Since in most cases, there is absolutely no death tax advantage to a revocable living trust over a testamentary trust (a trust that goes into effect at death), the real reason, sometimes stated but often unstated, is the attempt to reduce or eliminate large legal fees. As lawyers, we must acknowledge the fact that, as in every system, there are those who might abuse the probate process. There are lawyers who charge fees based on percentages of the estate or based on archaic fee schedules that bear no reasonable resemblance to what a fair fee should be. In chapter 6, we review the subject of lawyer's fees in detail, but we should make three specific statements at this point:

1. As the consumer, you have the absolute right to choose your own lawyer and to have a written fee agreement from that lawyer *before* any legal services are performed. This applies to both estate planning services and estate (or trust) administration services. An executor always has the right to negotiate fees for legal services to be performed for an estate.

2. You *always* retain the right to dismiss the lawyer if you are unsatisfied with the services performed, upon paying the agreed-upon fee for the services performed to that time.

3. You have the *absolute* right to question the lawyer about his or her education, background, experience, and expertise in establishing and administering your trust.

Excessive legal fees for estates are often caused by the ignorance or poor judgment of the executor, or by the selection of the wrong person as executor, not by the absence of a revocable living trust. Large legal fees can also be caused by legal problems left behind by the decedent, such as unresolved tax liabilities or other debts, complex business arrangements, or unsaleable assets. Transferring the decedent's problems to a revocable trust will not make those problems go away or reduce the costs of resolving them after death.

Proper estate planning, and the proper use of trusts, can help reduce legal fees and other costs of transferring and administering assets, but tearing a form out of a book can actually result in more legal fees, not less, if the trust is the wrong form of trust, is not a form appropriate to your state, is not properly customized to your situation, is not properly executed, or is not properly funded.

Q. Why do people need tailored trusts?

A. Every one of us is special. Regardless of our many similarities, we are all in our own way unique and different from our neighbors. Our incomes are different, our personal needs and goals, hopes and fears are different, and what we require for our future security will differ based on our present economic situation. We differ in our present conditions of our health, as well as in our future earning capacity. We may or may not have a spouse, one or two parents, and one or more children, and their ages, needs, and health will vary considerably. Our current financial conditions and our future potential will also affect the tax consequence of our plans for the future. How, then, can a packaged trust from a nonprofessional salesperson, even begin to meet our own distinctly individual needs?

Q. Isn't a "tear-out" trust better than no trust at all?

A. It may in some circumstances be better, but in many circumstances it can make matters worse. Remember, you get what you pay for. It is your family who may have to pay for the fact that not only did your plan not meet your needs, but by adopting that plan, you also paid an "opportunity cost" because you gave up the opportunity to establish the proper estate plan. For example, if the total assets of you and your spouse, including the equity in your home, your personal and business life insurance, the present values of your pension plans, and your personal investments, exceed the federal estate tax unified credit applicable exclusion amount ($600,000 in 1997, but increasing by steps to $1,000,000 in 2006), and the packaged plan you purchased did not contain a properly drafted *credit shelter trust*, the trust you selected could eventually cost your children a quarter of a million dollars or more! If you had consulted an experienced estate planning lawyer, the trust that he or she prepared, together with the proper titling of your assets, would have saved your children a substantial amount of money.

If your form trust provided that at the death of you and your spouse, everything went equally to your children, and one of your children was handicapped and receiving government benefits, your trust could disqualify that child from receiving those benefits. A properly drawn *discretionary trust* could have preserved the lost one-third of your assets for your family. In other words, what you don't know can sometimes really hurt you (and your family). It took you a lifetime to build an estate. Doesn't it make sense to take a few hours—and spend a relatively few dollars—to preserve that lifetime of effort?

USING TRUSTS TO AVOID PROBATE

Chapter 8 explains:

- The probate avoidance advantage of the revocable living trust

- The reasons for the probate system

- Advantages of probate

- Why a revocable living trust will not necessarily not save any taxes

- The privacy factor in avoiding probate

- The real costs of probate

- Why a revocable living trust cannot assure that your estate will totally avoid probate

- Legal fees likely in the probate process

- What is really saved by using a revocable trust to avoid probate

- The relative costs of a will and revocable living trust

- Costs of creating and maintaining a revocable living trust

- Tools or techniques other than trusts to avoid probate (and their advantages and disadvantages)

- Advantages and disadvantages of payment of life insurance to your estate

- Questions that will help assure the selection of the most appropriate estate planning tools or techniques

- Dangers of a revocable living trust

- The dangers of "trust mills" and trust promoters

Q. Isn't avoidance of probate the most important advantage of a revocable living trust?

A. Typically, in our books and lectures, when we use a term such as "revocable living trust," we'll define it first and then explain its advantages and disadvantages. But because a discussion of these trusts is so emotionally charged, we're going to dispose of the "how to avoid probate through revocable living trusts" issues first. For a more detailed look at the revocable living trust as an important estate planning tool, see chapter 9.

Technically speaking, "probate" is the process of proving that a will was the valid last will of a decedent. In some states, the probate of a will takes 15 or 20 minutes at the local courthouse and may not even require a lawyer. In other states, the probate of a will can require a lawyer, advance notice to heirs, a court hearing, and 30 days or more to complete.

The term "probate" is also sometimes used to describe the entire process of the court-supervised administration of an estate, from the initial probate of the will to the distribution of the estate and the discharge of the personal representative (the executor named in the will or administrator appointed by the court if there is no will or no executor named in the will). Once again, the complexity of the court supervision (or whether there is any court supervision at all) varies greatly from state to state.

In some states, routine estate administrations may require no court supervision at all, and the personal representative can collect the assets of the estate, pay the debts and taxes, and distribute the estate without court approval. In those states, the parties go to court only if there is a question or dispute that the court must resolve. In other states, the personal representative of the estate (the executor or administrator) cannot sell assets or even pay debts without prior court approval. This is where the administration of an estate can be a slow, complex process of seemingly endless court pleadings and court proceedings.

The probate process can also result in complications and consequent expense and delay if you own property in several states, assets in a foreign country, or if you have heirs or relatives overseas. (One state, New York, will not conclude probate until all those who could take a share of the estate if there were no will have "signed off"—the technical term is "waive citation"—even if they have absolutely no right under the will. In other words, if you lived in New York State and had relatives in England, Italy, and France, they would all have to be located and contacted, and they would have to return documents to the court—even if they were not beneficiaries under your will.)

Whether or not there is an advantage to "avoiding probate" therefore depends to a great extent on the laws of the state in which you live. If you live in a state in which probate procedures are simple and inexpensive, it may not be worthwhile to spend the time and money to create and administer a trust during your lifetime. However, if you live in one of the few remaining states in which probate procedures can be complicated and expensive, a revocable living trust might benefit your family. (Our book, *How To Settle An Estate*, which you can obtain by calling 610-527-5216, can be incredibly helpful if you are named executor or administrator of an estate).

And a revocable living trust can have advantages that are totally unrelated to the probate process. For example, an elderly person might want a bank or trusted friend or relative to manage his or her investments during lifetime and administer his or her estate at death. Under those circumstances, the most important advantage of a revocable living trust is that it would allow the selected trustee to both manage the investments during lifetime and distribute them after death with the least number of complications when buying, selling, or distributing the assets.

Q. What are the reasons for probate in the first place?

A. In spite of what you may have been led to believe by those who pander to your fear of probate to sell their probate-avoidance books or to market their services, the process of probate as it exists today is neither a state-designed form of punishment nor a form of indirect tax. There are, in fact, a number of legitimate reasons for the probate process. Knowing those reasons may help you to understand why—believe it or not—the probate process is not necessarily something you want to avoid. (Even with a revocable trust, it may not be possible to avoid completely all possible court proceedings).

The most important reason for the probate process is so that people who have possession of the decedent's assets, or who owe the decedent money, know to whom to deliver the assets or payments. Imagine you are a stock broker and one of your clients has died. After a few days, a man comes into your office and says that he is the only son of the decedent. Please give him a check for balance of the decedent's account. What do you do? Do you check his story? Find out if the decedent had any other children? Search for a will?

Fortunately, you don't need to do any of those things. You can offer your condolences on the man's loss of his father and tell him to come back when he has a "short certificate" or other evidence of his authority as personal representative of his father's estate. As soon as someone comes to you with a document from the proper court official, certifying that the holder of the document is the "personal representative" (i.e., executor or administrator) of a decedent's estate, you can turn over the decedent's assets to that person and be completely released, without any fear that some other relative might come out of the woodwork with some other will. So the probate process identifies the person with whom third parties can—and must—deal in order to settle the decedent's financial affairs.

The probate process also serves to consolidate the process of settling the decedent's estate, so that conflicting claims can be sorted out in an orderly fashion. Imagine again that you are the stock broker whose client has died. After the man comes into your office claiming to be the decedent's only son, a young woman walks into your office and says that she is the decedent's granddaughter and a beneficiary under his will. She asks that you distribute her share of the decedent's estate directly to her, because her father (the executor you have met) is an embezzler and she fears she will never see her share of the estate. Finally, another woman comes into your office and says that she is the decedent's widow, and the will is irrelevant because she is still entitled to one third of the assets under state law. While the three of them are sitting there, the bank calls and asks you to pay off the decedent's mortgage. All of them threaten to sue you if you don't pay them. What do you do? You tell them all to go away. Your only responsibility is to deliver the decedent's assets to the duly appointed personal representative of his estate. After you have done that, you have no responsibility to anyone else. If they have claims against the estate, they should file them with the personal representative and the probate court, and the probate court will decide among the conflicting claims.

In some states, the probate court not only serves as a forum to resolve disputes, but also serves as a watchdog for the beneficiaries of the estate and looks over the shoulders of those who will be handling your affairs when you cannot. The probate court is meant to serve as an objective, disinterested party that oversees and safeguards the interests of your estate's beneficiaries. Many courts require a full accounting of fees charged by lawyers and executors. In many cases courts will strike down exorbitant fees even if there is no objection by any beneficiary. If you "avoid probate" through a revocable living trust, you also avoid the protection that a court might provide to your beneficiaries to look after their interests even if they cannot or are not sophisticated or diligent enough.

The probate process can therefore serve to protect both the executors of the estate and the beneficiaries. If you "avoid probate" through a revocable trust, your trustee will also not have the same protection from conflicting claims of creditors and beneficiaries, your beneficiaries will not have the protection of a readily available forum to present their claims, and your beneficiaries will not have the protection of court oversight to safeguard their interests.

If you nevertheless decide to "avoid probate," we still suggest that you specify in your trust document that the trustees must account annually (or more frequently) to beneficiaries for all income, expenses, and other disbursements, so that the beneficiaries will have an opportunity to review the actions of the trustees, and that you specify that your beneficiaries can require the trustees to account to the court if the beneficiaries suspect that the trustees are not carrying out their duties properly.

Another purpose of probate is to protect the interests of creditors, and make sure that beneficiaries cannot take assets out of the state without first paying the lawful debts of the decedent. The beneficiary designations for life insurance policies and retirement benefits have not been a concern to creditors, because those assets are not normally subject to the claims of creditors. However, the increasing use of revocable living trusts has lead many states to consider, and some states to adopt, new probate-like procedures to protect the rights of creditors in the assets of revocable trusts.

Legal systems evolve in response to perceived problems. The perceived problems in the probate system have led many people to avoid probate through revocable trusts. But many courts and legislatures now see the same problems in revocable trusts that led to the creation of probate systems. As result, many states now require court supervision or other probate-like procedures for living trusts regardless of the terms of the trust. We predict that more states will do so. Once a trustee comes under the supervision of a court, there is little (if any) difference between probate and "avoiding probate."

Q. Does probate have any advantages?

A. One major advantage of the probate process is that possible claims of creditors are usually cut off after a stated period (from six months to one year) following the advertisement of the probate process. Executors must usually notify known creditors directly and must notify unknown creditors by advertising the fact of the decedent's death, typically in one legal newspaper and one local newspaper. If creditors don't make their claims within the statutory time limit (called a "statute of limitations"), they lose all rights.

The assets of a revocable living are subject to the claims of the decedent's creditors (including lifetime income taxes), just like the assets that are owned by the decedent and are administered through a probate proceeding. The trustee may become personally liable to the decedent's creditors if the trustee makes distributions to beneficiaries before paying taxes and debts.

Without the legally required notice to debtors, the "clock" on the statute of limitations on debts may not run out for many years. For example, the statute of limitations on a debt might be six years without probate and notice to creditors, but only six months with probate and notice to creditors. The trust (and in some cases the trustee) could therefore be liable for many years longer than necessary. (Some states may have procedures to cut off the claims of creditors even if there is no probate. Ask a local lawyer if your state might have that kind of procedure available.)

Court supervision of an executor also protects the executor from the claims of beneficiaries. Adult beneficiaries can review the actions of an executor and then sign "receipts and releases" that approve the accounts of the executor and release the executor from any further liability to them. However, minor beneficiaries of a trust (and beneficiaries that might be born in the future) cannot review the actions of the executor and cannot sign legally binding receipts and releases. The probate court can act for the minor beneficiaries (or appoint someone to represent them, usually called a guardian or trustee "ad litem") so that the administration of the executor can be terminated and the executor can be released from any further liability to any beneficiary. In the absence of a court proceeding, the trustee of a revocable living trust may have to wait for years to know whether the minor beneficiaries of a trust have any objections to investments, disbursements, or distributions. A trustee might therefore choose to go into court, even if it is not required by law.

Q. Will a revocable living trust save me taxes?

A. A revocable living trust does not—by itself—save any income, estate, or generation-skipping transfer taxes. Any estate or generation-skipping tax that can be saved through a well-drafted revocable living trust can also be saved through a well-drafted will.

A revocable trust is "transparent" for income tax purposes during your lifetime. Any assets transferred to the trust during your lifetime will still be considered to be yours for income tax purposes. Any income earned by the trust must be reported on your personal income tax return.

Similarly, each and every asset in the revocable trust at your death will be part of your "gross estate" for federal estate tax purposes (and for the purpose of any state death tax that might apply to your estate). Any tax savings that might be generated through a revocable living trust will be the result of a marital deduction formula, credit shelter trust, marital trust, generation-skipping trust, or charitable split-interest trust that takes effect only after your death. And a will can contain the same kind of marital deduction formula and the same kinds of trusts (through "testamentary" trusts, which are trusts created by your will after your death). Therefore, the property subject to death taxes will be the same whether or not you avoid probate and whether or not you set up a revocable living trust.

Q. Can a revocable living trust avoid probate entirely?

A. Your living trust will avoid probate only if you have transferred to it the full legal title to all of your assets. If you don't transfer title to all of your assets, keep title in the trust, and continue to title new assets to the trust, you won't avoid probate with respect to assets outside the trust. So to that extent, you've wasted the time and expense of creating the trust (if probate avoidance was your goal). In calculating the costs of a revocable living trust, you must therefore factor into your computation the time, cost, and aggravation of titling and retitling property you might now own (or might acquire in the future) in your sole name, your spouse's name, or joint names. In some cases, you may be required to pay state real estate transfer taxes for transferring your home or other real estate into your trust—even though it is revocable—and even though federal income tax law treats you as the owner of trust assets.

Even if you put every asset you presently own into a revocable living trust and keep all of your assets titled in the name of the trust, you may still own assets at your death that you do not own now and could not have transferred. For example, you might have claims for wages or personal injuries that arose immediately before (or at) death and could not have been transferred to the trust. So no matter what you do, the possibility of a probate proceeding cannot be entirely avoided.

Another reason you might not be able to avoid all court proceedings is because of the uncertainties that can arise when a successor trustee must take over. If you are serving as the trustee of your own revocable trust (as many advocates of living trusts will recommend), then another trustee must take over after your death to pay any death taxes and distribute the assets in accordance with the terms of your trust.

How will banks, stock brokers, and other third parties know that the person who claims to be your successor trustee is really the person entitled to take over administration of the trust? If the bank or broker does not have a copy of the trust, how will they know that the trust document that is shown to them is really the trust document? Even if they have had a copy of the trust, how will they know it was not revoked or amended before death? In a probate proceeding, the court issues a document (called "letters testamentary," "letters of administration," or a "short certificate" that identifies the person who is legally entitled to take over the property of the decedent, and banks and stock brokers can rely on those documents. Some banks and brokers have gotten into conflicts or problems after delivering trust property to the person they thought was the successor trustee without any court certification and, as a result, many banks and brokers are starting to require court certification of successor trustees before delivering any trust property to them. Court certification of a trustee means that the trust document must be filed in court and proven to be valid, a process that is almost identical to the probate of a will. A revocable living trust therefore "avoids probate" only as long as banks, stock brokers, title insurance agents, and others concerned with the title to property are willing to accept the authority of the successor trustee without any approval by any court.

Trusts/Leimberg Associates Books: 610-527-5216

Q. What about privacy—isn't it one of the biggest advantages of avoiding probate?

A. Privacy is important and can be a bona fide reason to avoid probate. Once a will is probated, it becomes a public record. Furthermore, any inventory that is filed or account that is filed may also become a public record. So both the identity of the beneficiaries and the assets passing under the will can be known to anyone who goes to the courthouse and requests that information.

However, as an advantage of a revocable living trust, privacy may be overstated. If real estate is transferred to or from the trust, a copy of the trust may have to be recorded among the deeds at the local courthouse, so the trust document becomes a public record and the much-touted privacy advantage may not exist. (One possible solution is to create a partnership that will operate as the agent and nominee of the trust. The partnership could hold title to the real estate, and title could be recorded in the partnership's name. This puts a layer of privacy between the partnership and the trust itself.)

Banks, stock brokerage firms, life insurance companies, retirement plan administrators, and other financial institutions dealing with the trustees may also demand a copy of the trust. Paradoxically, a trust intended to provide more privacy after death may provide less privacy before death, because the grantor of the trust may have to provide copies of the trust to many different people and institutions during his lifetime, but could have kept his will a secret until his death.

Another problem is that if a trustee wants to resign and is unable to get (or is unwilling to accept) releases from all beneficiaries, the trustee might file a formal accounting in court in order to get a complete release from all liability. In that case, both the terms of the trust and the assets and liabilities of the trust become a matter of public record. Similarly, if there is any dispute between the trustees and beneficiaries, or among the beneficiaries, the trust and its financial history may become part of a court record and open to public disclosure.

You can also no longer assume that all probate records are public while all trust records are private. Some states have begun sealing inventories and other parts of probate records so that they are not available to the general public. Some other states have begun requiring court filings for revocable trusts, with the result that the records of the administration of a trust may become as public as the records of the administration of a will.

In some states, inheritance tax returns may be a matter of public record, and the assets of a revocable trust and terms of the trust must be disclosed as part of the inheritance tax return. In those states, a revocable trust is completely useless as a technique to maintain privacy.

Finally, the entire issue of privacy may be overstated because, as a practical matter, the general public doesn't take much interest in probate records unless the decedent was a movie star, politician, or was known to be wealthy or notorious. You might therefore be disappointed to find that the disposition of your estate is not really of much interest to anyone outside of your family.

Q. What are the real costs of probate?

A. The biggest "bogeyman" of probate is the purported cost. Here are the costs you can expect if you are probating an estate:

- Filing fees for the petition for probate. These fees vary greatly from state to state (or even county to county), but are rarely large enough to be a significant cost in the administration of an estate. We suggest you call your local probate court and request a schedule of fees to find out.

- Bonding the executor. Most states require that personal representatives be bonded by an insurance company against mistakes or dishonesty by the personal representative. However, it is usually possible for your will to waive the requirement that the executor post a bond.

- Filing fees for the inventory of estate assets. In almost all states, the personal representative (executor or administrator of the estate) must file a list of probate assets and their values. There is often a fee for filing this inventory with the court (although the fee is usually small, or is included in the probate fee).

- Advertising the grant of letters. The personal representative must publicly advertise that "letters testamentary" or "letters of administration" have been issued, so that any outstanding creditors can file their claims against the estate—and so that the statute of limitations against creditors' claims begins to run. The cost of advertising is almost never more than a few hundred dollars, regardless of the size of estate.

- Executor's commissions. By law, an executor is allowed a fee or commission for his or her services. These fees may be set by statute or rule of court, or may be subject only to a standard of "reasonableness." Usually, an executor's fees are based on the value of the estate and the nature of the services rendered by the executor. However, there is often no fee paid when the executor is a surviving spouse, child, or other beneficiary of the estate, so most estates pay no executor's commissions at all. When compensation is paid to an executor (or trustee), the compensation is always subject to the review of a court if any beneficiary objects to the amount of the compensation.

- Legal fees. These fees will also vary from state to state and from estate to estate. Like executor commissions, legal fees are also subject to review by a court if any beneficiary objects to the amount of the fees. In a few states, the maximum amount of legal fees payable by an estate is fixed by statute, but most states tend to limit lawyers to what is "reasonable," based on the time spent by the lawyer, the nature of the services rendered, and other factors. (For a review of the factors that courts typically consider in determining what is reasonable, see chapter 6.) Although it is usually not possible to administer an estate without an executor, it is often possible for an executor to administer a very small and simple estate without a lawyer.

- Accountant's fees. If an accountant is needed to prepare tax returns, prepare financial reports, or other tasks, the accountant's fees will be paid from the estate. The fees will obviously vary, depending on the tasks to be performed by the accountant and the size and complexity of the estate.

- Other expenses may include appraisal fees needed for inventories or tax returns, broker's commissions, and other expenses of selling real estate or other assets, investment advisory fees, the expenses of operating any business owned by the decedent, casualty insurance and property taxes, and other expenses of preserving, maintaining, and investing assets.

In some states, an executor may be able to obtain what is called "independent" or unsupervised probate. This would, of course, reduce the costs compared to a trust.

The biggest expenses in the total probate cost are typically the fees charged by the estate's executor and the executor's lawyer. If your executor is also the sole (or primary) beneficiary of your estate, then the issue of executor's commission is not important, because the money goes to the same person regardless of whether it is in the form of an executor's commission or part of the estate. (Although it rarely makes sense for a beneficiary to take a commission, which is taxable income, unless the commission somehow saves more in taxes than it costs in taxes.) Even when the executor is only one of the beneficiaries (such as one of three children serving as executor), there are rarely disputes, because the executor either serves without compensation or the family is able to agree on a reasonable fee (although you might want to avoid any possible dispute by directing that your executor should serve without compensation).

It is only when the executor is a bank or other third party that careful consideration must be given to providing that the commission will fairly compensate the executor without undue cost to the beneficiaries. If your estate is complex and will require the executor to devote hundreds of hours of time and make difficult or potentially dangerous financial decisions, we suggest that you set a reasonable hourly fee based on the services to be rendered and the expertise of the person you have selected. If your executor is to be a corporate fiduciary such as a bank, you can obtain a written contract with the bank for handling your estate, and that fee schedule can even be incorporated into your will. (In very large estates, you may be able to negotiate the fee).

Although many people believe that legal fees are always a fixed percentage of the estate, the nature of the services to be performed by a lawyer, and the fees to be charged for those services, can always be negotiated between the executor and the lawyer. Therefore, if you have chosen wisely in your selection of an executor, your executor should be able to minimize the legal fees to the estate. For example, the largest legal fees result when the executor simply turns over the administration of the estate to the lawyer, letting the lawyer (or paralegal working for the lawyer) collect the assets, do the bookkeeping, prepare all the tax returns, and handle all correspondence with beneficiaries.

If the executor is willing to spend the time necessary to take care of many of the time-consuming (but routine) aspects of estate administration, such as confirming date of death bank balances, transferring assets from the decedent's name to the estate, paying debts, and keeping the books and records for the estate, the lawyer's services can be limited to those for which a lawyer is really needed (such as minimizing death taxes and complying with state laws for opening and closing estates). In that way, an able and willing executor can greatly reduce the legal fees otherwise payable.

Many of the time-consuming duties of the executor and the executor's lawyer (such as collecting the assets of the estate, settling the debts and taxes, selling the assets that need to be sold, and distributing the assets of the estate) will be the same regardless of whether the assets pass by a will or through a revocable trust. Switching from a will to a revocable living trust might change the name given to those expenses ("executor's commissions" become "trustee commissions"), but will not necessarily reduce the amount of the expenses.

Q. What legal fees should I expect to incur?

A. The bitter truth is that if your estate is large or complex some legal fees *must* be paid—both in planning and administering your estate—whether or not you are avoiding probate. There are costs attached to the difficult and time-consuming process of valuing property and filing federal and state death tax returns. These costs are present whether or not a will or trust is used, and typically an untrained person should not even attempt them. (See our book for executors and trustees entitled, *How to Settle an Estate, 610-527-5216*, for a complete explanation of estate administration.) Likewise, whether it is your accountant or lawyer who prepares income tax returns, returns must be prepared and filed for your last year of life and for your estate (or trust, as the case may be). Someone must be paid for these tasks, whether or not you have a trust.

You can set up an agreement in advance with the lawyer who prepared the will to administer your estate for a set hourly fee or a specified amount. However, you cannot require your executor to employ your lawyer. Although the lawyer who drafts your will may be the most appropriate person to advise your executor through the administration of your estate, we suggest that you not try to prevent your executor from choosing his or her own legal advisor. It is important that your executor (who typically should not be your lawyer, in order to avoid conflicts of interest) be able to negotiate for services and fees with the lawyer he or she feels will follow the "3 Cs", that is, combine competence with consideration and compassion. (If a lawyer serves as your executor, most states will allow either lawyer's fees or executor's fees, but not both.)

We also suggest that if you are an executor that you demand a written fee agreement from your lawyer that sets either a fixed fee (if possible) for the expected estate administration services or a fee based on a fair hourly rate, with a lower rate for routine bookkeeping services that can be performed by a non-professional (para-legal). Keep in mind that selecting the lawyer to administer an estate is a lot like choosing a brain surgeon: The least expensive is not usually the best choice. Experience and performance are what count.

Q. Do I really save anything by using a revocable living trust to avoid probate?

A. As explained above, "probate" may not be nearly the expensive process you have been led to believe. The actual court costs vary from state to state. Expect the costs in Florida, California, New York, and Delaware to be higher (in some comparisons substantially more) than in most other states. The reason is that in those states probate requires a formal court procedure. In most other states, the filing fees and court costs are significantly lower.

But rather than believe any author or lecturer, find out for yourself. Call your local Register of Wills (or Surrogate or Probate Court or Orphans' Court) and ask them to send you a copy of the schedule of probate fees. Visit their office and ask them to explain what filings are required to administer an estate (such as petition for probate, inventory, and final accounting) and the costs of filing those documents.

Many states also have a streamlined process for "small estates" that is not only very inexpensive (perhaps far less than the cost of drafting a revocable living trust) but also very simple. In fact, many states allow an executor to avoid accounting to the court altogether. This process, called "receipt and release," provides beneficiaries with an informal documentation of what came into the estate, what went out, and to whom, and shows the distributable assets and the proportion going to each beneficiary. If the beneficiaries agree to this process and accept the executor's informal accounting, they sign a receipt acknowledging their acceptance and release the executor from liability. This process may also be significantly less expensive than the cost of a well-drafted revocable living trust.

The actual cost and speed of probate depends mainly on the size of the estate and complexity of asset ownership (which has an impact on asset valuations and taxes). Distribution of probate assets can be made very quickly if the executor isn't concerned about personal liability for your estate's ability to pay taxes and creditors' claims.

Another factor to consider is the nature of your estate plan, because your executors or trustees may wind up in court regardless of whether you use a will or a revocable living trust for your estate plan. For example, if you have minor children and there will be trusts for your children that will begin at your death, your trustees may *want* to go to court to get approval for their administration of your assets, even though they are not required to by law, to make sure that your children cannot sue them years later, when your children become adults and it is too late for the trustees to correct any mistakes your children claim were made. If the people who administer your assets after your death are going to go into court to get court approval for their administration, then having a revocable living trust will not avoid court supervision of your estate and will not save your children any money.

Certain administration expenses costs will be incurred whether or not you use a revocable living trust. Your heirs will directly or indirectly have to pay for the valuation for death tax purposes of real estate, collectibles, closely held stock or other business interests, and other assets. Likewise, the costs of hiring a lawyer or accountant to file federal and state death tax returns and federal and state income tax returns will also be incurred—whether or not your assets are subject to probate and whether or not you've used a revocable living trust. Similarly, you or your beneficiaries may have to pay some trustee fees even if you have avoided executor's fees, and the trustee's fees might not be much less than the executor's fees otherwise payable.

In many cases, a revocable living trust is preferable to a will if (and only if) you are willing to incur certain costs and take certain steps which themselves may involve costs (such as transferring the title to each and every one of your assets continually for the rest of your life). Doing so may result in some savings to your heirs—mainly because during your lifetime you or your lawyer has already performed a lot of the work that would otherwise have to be done at your death. Setting up a revocable living trust implies that you have already paid a lawyer for drafting the document (figure from $1,000 to $5,000, depending on the complexity of your situation) and taken the time to organize your affairs and do many of the tasks that your executor or estate's lawyer would otherwise have to perform (and charge for).

Q. How do I compare the relative costs of a will and a revocable living trust?

A. Relative cost has always been cited as an advantage of revocable living trusts over wills. Yet the day-to-day investment and management of a "funded" trust (one into which you've placed cash or other assets) and the communication and correspondence with banks, transfer agents, title companies, and others require time and effort. And if you are not the trustee, you will have to pay someone to assume the duties and responsibilities of trustee.

A funded trust may be more difficult and more expensive to change than a will because, if you revoke the trust or change the trustee at any time before death, you will have to go through the expense and aggravation of retitling assets—again! And a bank or other third party trustee may charge a termination fee if the trust is revoked or the trustee is removed or replaced before your death.

Finally, you (or any other nonprofessional trustee) will find that you need to know more about the law to properly administer the trust than you will find in this or any other book. Mistakes can be costly. A corporate or other professional trustee's experience may help avoid mistakes, but experience—like time and knowledge—also comes at a price that you or your trust's beneficiaries must be willing to pay.

Q. What costs are involved in setting up and maintaining a revocable living trust?

A. You should expect a number of costs or fees with the creation and ongoing operation of a revocable living trust. First, there are legal fees incurred in setting up the trust. (Your overall cost will be higher for a trust than for a will because you will need a will even when you have a trust. Furthermore, a trust must build in all the flexibility you will need for an entire lifetime, then well beyond your life if the trust will continue to serve other beneficiaries.)

The amount you'll pay to have a revocable living trust drafted depends on a number of factors, but the normal hourly (or set) fee of the lawyer is usually the single largest determinate. Here again, the lowest charge may not actually turn out to be the least expensive or the best value in the long run. Your overall cost should depend on the degree of complexity involved, the lawyer's level of expertise, and the prevailing legal fees in the area.

It is very possible that certain (sometimes unexpected) costs will be incurred in transferring title to various assets. Retitling real estate and partnership interests may require the services of a lawyer or professional conveyancer. Conveyance of real estate to a trust, even if it is revocable, may trigger real estate transfer taxes. In any case involving real estate, a deed will be required. Marketable securities held in "street name" will be relatively inexpensive to transfer to the trust (assume a $25 per security reregistration fee), but reregistering securities titled in your own name will require more paperwork, more time, and (as a result) more costs and aggravation.

A third cost of a revocable living trust is the payment that must be made to a trustee (other than yourself) for the services that the trustee renders. Even if your trust has little or no assets, bookkeeping and internal accounting costs may run annual trustee fees up to as much as 1.5 to 2 percent of trust assets. These annually recurring costs can mount up over a number of years. In many cases it will not be economically feasible to operate a trust with few income-producing assets (even if it's a family business or an art collection worth millions). In comparing revocable living trusts (where current out-of-pocket costs must be considered) to passing property by will (where most costs are incurred after death), be sure to take the time value of money into account.

Another cost that must be factored into the living trust-versus-will equation is what we call "hidden obstacles." An example of a hidden obstacle is when a bank holds a mortgage on your property and refuses to allow you to transfer the mortgage to the trust. One reason a bank might refuse to do this is because a lender might have difficulty selling the mortgage on the secondary market if title is held by a trust (or the mortgage may have already been sold and the transfer of the title would have adverse consequences for the lender or the present holder).

Yet another cost (and aggravation) is insurance. You'll have to check to see if your property and casualty insurance company will insure a car, home, or otherwise insurable asset if legal title is held by a trust. Why would this even be an issue? It may not be clear who has the right to drive cars owned by a trust. In some cases, the casualty insurance company may increase premiums on cars held by a trust because of a business rather than a personal rating. We would therefore suggest that you continue to hold the title to your cars jointly with your spouse or another co-owner, rather than placing title in the trust. (Some state laws do not even permit automobiles to be owned by a trust.)

Finally, you'll have to be willing to complete special forms at banks and brokerage houses because titling assets in a trust's name may not be an everyday occurrence with your broker. Likewise, you must be willing to hire a conveyancer to prepare and record new deeds. (In states such as Pennsylvania, also be prepared in some instances to pay real estate transfer taxes even if you transfer assets from you to yourself as trustee, because of the nonexempt status of your beneficiaries.)

Moreover, you must be willing not only to make these reregistering and title transfers for all your currently owned assets, but also to transfer title to all of those you intend to purchase in the future. To the extent that you don't continue to title assets for the rest of your life in the name of the trustee, to that extent, you'll forfeit the benefits for which you set up the trust.

Q. Are there ways other than a revocable living trust to avoid probate?

A. There are many ways to avoid probate besides revocable living trusts. These include the following:

1. Title property jointly with your spouse or other heir. Titling property jointly, with right of survivorship or as tenants by the entireties, will make your will irrelevant. The property automatically and immediately passes at death to the surviving spouse and does not become part of your probate estate. That way, you will avoid probate at the first death, although not at the second death. For instance, if you and your spouse own your home jointly with right of survivorship or as tenants by the entirety, at either spouse's death, the survivor will receive the home without having it pass through probate. Just as a revocable trust is not a panacea, however, neither is jointly held property. Consider the following, for example:

- If you put real estate into joint names with your beneficiaries, you won't be able to sell the property, or even change your mind about the division or disposition of the property, without the consent of every person named as a joint owner. You, the original owner, may have lost control over who will eventually receive the property because it will pass outright to the surviving joint tenant.

- Although you may still be able to change the joint ownership of bank accounts or brokerage accounts at any time, your joint owners may have the same power to take the property from you. Once you name a child as joint owner of an account, there may be nothing you can do to stop a child from withdrawing money from the account at any time.

- If your joint tenancy involves someone other than your spouse, you may be making a taxable gift when you create or when you divide up the joint tenancy.

- If you have many children or other intended beneficiaries, you'll find it cumbersome to list each beneficiary on each asset as a joint owner.

- In some states, an inventory of joint accounts must be publicly recorded, so you will not necessarily achieve any privacy.

- In some states, a joint account is "frozen" when you die until the issuance of a tax waiver certificate.

- In some states, you might be required to pay a state death tax if one of the joint owners predeceases you, even though the property was originally yours. (There should be no federal estate tax as long as you can prove that you paid for the property.)

- As a practical matter, it is more difficult to plan an equal distribution of assets when jointly held property is involved.

- Too much jointly held property with your spouse will result in what estate planners call "overqualifying the marital deduction." Stated another way, joint ownership with your spouse may waste your federal estate tax unified credit, needlessly adding assets to your spouse's taxable estate and resulting in excessive estate tax (or higher estate tax brackets).

2. Life insurance that is payable to a named beneficiary (including a trust), and not to your estate, will not be subject to the probate process. To guard against the possibility that your beneficiary may predecease you, you should also always name a secondary (backup) beneficiary, or else the insurance proceeds might still be paid to your estate.

3. The proceeds of a qualified retirement plan, such as a pension plan, profit-sharing plan, Keogh plan (HR-10), simplified employee pension (SEP) plan, 401(k) plan, or stock bonus plan, as well as an individual retirement account (IRA), tax-deferred annuity, and other forms of contractual benefits can be made payable to a named beneficiary (including a trust), and so avoid administration by a court-supervised executor.

4. Some states recognize "Totten" (or "tentative") trusts for bank accounts and brokerage accounts, or accounts "payable on death" to a named beneficiary. Under each arrangement, you are still considered the sole owner during your lifetime. But your named beneficiary automatically becomes the owner of the account upon your death, without any probate or other court proceedings.

5. You can sell property during your lifetime to an intended beneficiary under an installment sale (a sale in return for which the buyer pays the seller a fixed amount for a specified number of years), a self-canceling installment note (an installment sale in which the debtor's obligation is canceled if the borrower dies before paying off the entire loan), or a private annuity (a sale in return for which the buyer pays the seller a fixed annuity for life). In each case, the property will be owned by the buyer, without any probate process, and the only assets that might be subject to probate are the payments owed at death (or accumulated during lifetime).

6. Gifts you make while you are alive will not be part of your probate estate because you no longer own the asset at your death. This is true even if you make those gifts minutes before your death. (However, a gift of appreciated property immediately before death can have adverse income tax consequences, because the recipient of the gift will have your income tax basis, and will not receive a "stepped-up" basis at death. This can result in unnecessary income taxes on capital gains.)

Q. Is paying a small amount of life insurance to the executor of the estate a good idea?

A. Some authorities have suggested paying a small amount of life insurance directly to the executor of an estate. Why, with so much talk about the advantages of avoiding probate would an expert make such a recommendation—especially when life insurance is by contract a nonprobate asset? The answer is to achieve these three goals:

- To provide cash for the estate to pay taxes and other expenses it must meet;

- To ensure that there is no question that the estate can meet its financial obligations; and

- To achieve administrative simplicity in dealing with the estate's creditors.

Paying a relatively small amount of life insurance to the executor is in recognition of the fact that creditors' ability to reach nonprobate assets (such as those in a revocable living trust) is expanding steadily and significantly. Paying a small amount of life insurance to the probate estate deals with the issue efficiently and directly rather than exhausting the estate in an attempt to sidestep it. However, we suggest this technique be used sparingly and only with the advice of a competent lawyer or tax accountant working together with your CLU (Chartered Life Underwriter), ChFC (Chartered Financial Consultant, or CFP (Certified Financial Planner).

Q. What should I ask to make sure I select the right estate planning technique(s)?

A. Here are some questions to ask yourself and your estate counselors about your estate plan. Will the tool or technique (or combination of tools and techniques):

- accomplish my (our) personal ("people-planning") objectives?

- eliminate or substantially reduce federal and state death taxes?

- reduce income taxes?

- minimize administration expenses in my estate and my spouse's estate (avoiding probate, if necessary)?

- provide management and investment expertise?

- help to unify my assets or coordinate them with the dispositive provisions of my employee benefit plans?

- add to my peace of mind?

Q. What is a "trust mill" and what are the dangers posed by trust promoters?

A. Selling revocable trusts to the public is to the legal profession what selling aluminum siding is to the home improvement industry. First, the aluminum siding salesman points out real or imagined problems with your house, including cracked paint, rot, and termites, and then promises to solve all your home maintenance problems forever through the installation of over-priced aluminum siding that covers up your house's problems but does not solve them. Similarly, trust promoters lure you to "estate planning seminars" and then predict incredible expenses, delays, and frustration for your heirs. The trust promoter then promises that all of your problems will be solved if you purchase their package of forms or services. It's the classic "panic them and then sell them the panacea" routine.

What are the problems with these "trust mills"?

- The trusts that are sold are usually not tailored to the specific needs of the individual client, but are mass produced from standard forms.

- Signing a trust document is only part of the solution. If the purpose of the trust is to avoid the probate process, then the assets of the grantor must be transferred to the trust. Otherwise, the trust is worthless as a probate avoidance device. And yet most trust promoters do not take responsibility for the transfer of assets, and do not adequately explain the problem to the client.

- The generic trusts that are sold are frequently over-priced, the trust promoter charging a fee for what amounts to a pre-printed form. Often, the size of that fee is higher than what would have been charged by a qualified lawyer for a customized document and individual and highly specific tax advice.

- The sale of a trust package, where the product precedes the problem, is the antithesis of good planning, a process which starts with an investigation of your problems and goals and ends with the implementation of one or more appropriate tools or techniques. When the promoter of a trust has only that to sell, the investigation into many important but unaddressed estate issues or a search for viable alternatives or a more efficient mix of answers is foreclosed.

A typical trust promotion scheme is described in a complaint settled by the Federal Trade Commission in 1997 against two companies that had sold more than 3,000 revocable trusts to elderly consumers in 43 states. According to the FTC, the companies falsely claimed that the trusts would avoid all probate and administrative costs, allow assets to be administered immediately upon death, and protect against catastrophic medical costs. The companies also falsely represented that the trusts were appropriate estate planning devices for every consumer and that the trusts were prepared by local lawyers. (In fact, the trusts for almost all 43 states were prepared by one lawyer in Arizona.) More importantly, the companies charged $2,000 to $3,000 for preparing the trusts and took no responsibility for seeing that assets were transferred into the trusts. According to a representative of the FTC, *"The practices we challenge in this case are particularly contemptible because they were designed to prey upon the financial fears of the elderly."*

Q. *How can a revocable living trust be a dangerous estate planning tool?*

A. A revocable living trust is one of many available estate planning tools. It is an excellent and highly flexible tool when drafted by a knowledgeable, competent estate planning lawyer and coordinated with other estate planning tools and techniques. But a revocable living trust is a potentially dangerous and harmful device when used as a one-size-fits-all, "do-it-yourself" panacea in isolation and without regard to an effective, over-all estate plan.

As explained above, fear mongers have used (abused) the revocable living trust to sell their books or some other product or service without regard to the individual's tax and non-tax objectives. First, they instill panic at the prospect of probate as an overly complex and expensive process (which it generally is not). Then they tell you or imply, "If you buy my book or set up this trust, all your estate planning problems are solved."

Nothing could be further from the truth. As noted above, used alone and without due regard to a multiplicity of other factors, the revocable living trust can fool you into a false sense of security. Through the choice of the wrong trust form, the failure to customize the form of trust to your particular circumstances, failing to transfer assets to the trust, or ignoring your overall real planning needs, the adoption of a trust can actually lead to a more complicated, time-consuming, and expensive estate "plan" than the probate process could ever have created. The revocable trust (or, more accurately, the lack of an estate planning process that lead to the revocable trust) did not make matters better, but worse, just like the wrong surgery, the wrong drugs, or the right drugs in the wrong dosage, can make a patient worse, not better.

Whatever your view on avoiding probate, and no matter how appropriate you feel a revocable living trust might be for your situation, don't think you can purchase a book, fill out the forms, pull them out, sign them, and then expect to "beat the system." (See Tear-Out Trusts, chapter 7.) This is foolish and simplistic thinking, and is as dangerous as treating a life threatening medical problem with a home remedy.

Your whole family's financial future is at stake. Do you want to entrust their future to a patent medicine solution?

We suggest that you view probate avoidance as one of many possible estate planning objectives, and the *revocable living trust* not as an "either-or" alternative to a will, but rather as another highly useful tool that in many cases may (and, in our opinion, should) be used in conjunction with a will and one or more other estate planning tools and techniques.

Revocable Trust

Revocable Trust

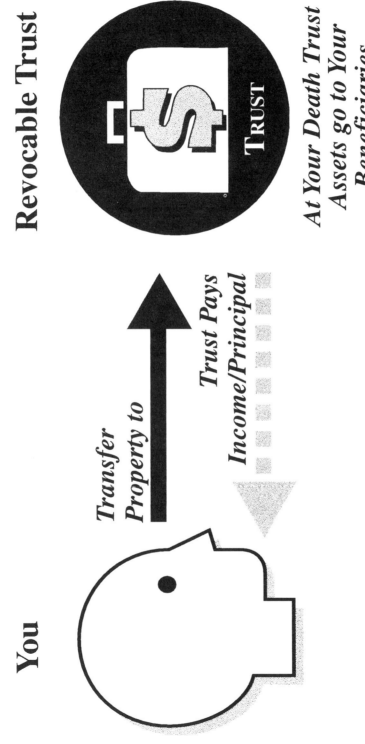

You

Transfer Property to

Trust Pays Income/Principal

TRUST

At Your Death Trust Assets go to Your Beneficiaries

Avoid probate but not Income or Estate tax

THE CASE FOR-AND AGAINST-
REVOCABLE LIVING TRUSTS

Chapter 9 explains:

- What a revocable trust is and how it works

- Why you might want to create a revocable living trust

- How to set up a revocable living trust

- How a living trust operates while you are alive

- How a living trust operates after your death

- The difference between a living trust and a revocable trust

- The rights you have after you create a revocable living trust

- Types of property that should be placed into a revocable trust

- How you terminate a revocable trust

- How a trust may be revoked by someone else on your behalf in the event of your disability

- How you can be the trustee of your own trust

- Why a trust document is needed even if you are the trustee

- Who you can name as beneficiaries of your trust

- Why you should have the trustee you have named acknowledge acceptance in writing

- You don't need to tell the beneficiaries of the trust that you've named them

- Why beneficiaries do not have to accept either income or principal from the trust

- Why unmarried and often-married individuals find revocable trusts appealing

- How revocable living trusts can be used to make gifts to charity

- The potential FDIC problem with revocable living trusts

- The liability of revocable trust assets to creditors' claims

- The limitation on protection against disgruntled heirs

- The impact of divorce on a revocable living trust

- How your trust can be coordinated with your overall estate plan

- The legal capacity to create a revocable living trust

- Duties of the trustee of a revocable living trust at the grantor's death

- How to transfer title to bank and stock accounts to the trust

Q. What is a revocable living trust?

A. Picture in your mind a box into which you can place assets. Imagine that someone, perhaps yourself or someone else, will manage and invest the assets in that box and pay the income and capital to anyone you want, including yourself or your husband or wife. Now think of your fear that you might not be able to get those assets back or that you might change your mind about who receives what's in the box or how, when, or under what terms they'll get it. So you attach a string to that box. What you've just described is a revocable trust. Just like when you were a kid, you've got a yo-yo on a string, and any time you want to make it come back to you, you can.

Technically, a revocable trust is a trust to which you, the *grantor*, transfer all or part of your assets during your lifetime, while retaining for as long as you live the right to the trust's income, the right to withdraw (or add to the trust) assets, and the right to end the trust and recover all your assets. You may (or may not) choose to be the sole trustee or a co-trustee of a revocable living trust. You can retain the right to revoke the trust by yourself, share the right with someone else, or give someone such as your spouse or child that power.

The most important point is that, as its name implies, a revocable trust is one that can be revoked at the whim of the grantor (sometimes called the "settlor" or "trustor"). You can end your trust and recover assets you've placed into the trust, or you can change the terms at your discretion at any time you choose.

When you set up a revocable trust, you should specifically reserve the right to alter or amend its terms, or terminate the trust and recover its assets, at any time. However, your death or legal incompetence will automatically make your revocable trust irrevocable. At either of those two events, no one can alter, amend, revoke, or terminate your trust.

To be revocable, a trust must state just that. It is extremely important that you specifically state, "I reserve the right to revoke this trust" (or words to that effect). Otherwise, you will *not* have the right to alter, amend, revoke, or terminate the trust in most states, and the trust will be *irrevocable* once it is set up and *funded* (i.e., once assets have been placed into it). This is very important: In most states a trust is irrevocable unless it clearly states that it is revocable!

If you and your spouse will both contribute property to the trust, you should specifically state whether the right to amend or revoke can be exercised by either of you, or if you both must sign any amendment or revocation. You should also state whether the power to revoke extends only to what you have contributed or if it applies to both contributors' portions, and whether the power to revoke continues after one of you has died. (A joint revocable trust can have complex tax consequences, and should never be created without the advice of an experienced lawyer. See chapter 14 for details.)

For reasons we'll explain below, *it is a foolish—and financially dangerous—act to retype specimen documents you find in a book, in software, or on the Internet and use such a sample as your trust.* Why? It is impossible in any book to create a document that serves everyone's needs appropriately, and no single book—not even this one—can possibly begin to give you all the insight you need to properly adapt this general form to your personal situation and your own state's laws.

If you have any questions about this, think of how you'd feel about someone who found a bottle of antibiotics on a pharmacy shelf and then took the pills so that he'd feel better. Only a lawyer who specializes in estate planning is really qualified to know if the revocable living trust is the right "antibiotic," whether you even need an antibiotic, if you need some other medicine besides the antibiotic, and what the proper dose is. As we have throughout this book, we urge you to use the information in our book to become a better-informed consumer and to know what to demand from financial services professionals—not to "self-prescribe."

Q. *Why might I want to set up a revocable living trust?*

A. Writing a will conjures up old fears in many people that to talk about death is to invite it. A revocable trust might be a solution to the psychological barrier of signing a will. Because it is not as threatening as a will, a revocable trust can overcome the mental blocks often associated with wills.

Moreover, there are many legitimate reasons why you may want to consider placing some of your assets in a revocable living trust. Through a revocable trust, you could accomplish one or more of these major goals: You want someone else to manage and invest your assets. You want someone to take care of your assets if you can't or don't want to. You want to be sure the income and principal from your assets will be distributed to the persons (including yourself) you select in the time and manner and under the terms of your choice. And you would like to accomplish these three goals in the most effective and efficient manner possible.

Now let's look at each of these goals, along with some specific situations in which you should strongly consider a revocable living trust:

- *Management and investment of assets.* You may want to relieve yourself of the burden of managing or investing stocks, bonds, real estate, or other assets. You may be too busy and not want to be bothered paying bills, filing tax returns, or keeping voluminous records. You may feel that someone else can do these things for you more efficiently or more successfully than you could. Perhaps you are entering public service and would like to avoid any appearance of a conflict of interest regarding investments. Maybe you recently inherited a large sum of money or assets requiring considerable time or special management. A corporate or other professional trustee may be a viable solution.

  Perhaps, on the other hand, you are confident about your management and investment ability as long as you remain healthy. But you are very worried that if you get sick or become disabled because of an accident, you'll need to find a competent management and investment person to handle your financial affairs on your behalf. If you are not married and you care for yourself, the revocable living trust is especially appropriate. A revocable living trust allows you to select a capable and trustworthy individual or bank (or combination of them) to deal with your property if and when you can't (or no longer choose to). It makes sense to set that mechanism in place while you are well and before you are forced to make major decisions under stress. If you are old, ill, or single, a revocable living trust can serve as a particularly useful financial management safety net.

Without a trust, your family might have to suffer the expenses, delays, and restrictions of going to court and obtaining a court-appointed conservator to hold your assets and manage your affairs. A revocable trust can help avoid the expensive, complex, aggravating, and in some cases embarrassing court process if your family has to request that a court declare you legally incompetent. Nor will your investments be restricted to the usually very conservative types of allowable investments that are forced upon an conservator by state law. By coordinating a well-drawn durable power of attorney with a revocable trust and a *step-up* trustee (who will "step up" and take over if necessary), you can assure yourself that your financial matters will be handled carefully if you are disabled.

If your disability ends, you can resume trusteeship over the assets in the trust. The combination of durable power of attorney and revocable living trust offers much more flexibility than a power of attorney alone, and it eliminates the difficulty that attorneys-in-fact sometimes encounter when dealing with banks and stock brokerage firms.

Perhaps you travel overseas and would like someone to make investment decisions only while you are not able to. A revocable living trust, coupled with a corporate or other professional trustee, can provide continuity to your investment planning even when you are out of the country for extended periods of time.

You may be willing and able to control all management and investment decisions, but you may be worried (or certain) that your beneficiaries don't have the experience, inclination, and time, or the legal, mental, or emotional capacity, to handle these responsibilities. Gifts to minors and mental incompetents can fall into this category. Under law (and as a practical matter) a minor cannot make decisions or take actions regarding stocks, bonds, real estate, or other property. Appropriate actions can be taken, however, if that same property is placed in trust for the minor. This allows the sale, exchange, or mortgage of property you give to a minor child or other relative without the expensive, inflexible, and troublesome process involved when a guardian must be appointed. Through a revocable trust, you can give a successor trustee the discretionary power on behalf of a beneficiary who is ill or for any other reason is not capable of handling the assets and income you'd like to provide.

By setting up and funding a trust while you are alive, rather than waiting until you die or become disabled, you can give yourself the opportunity for a "trial run." You can watch and see how well your trustee manages the property you have placed into the trust and how well your beneficiaries handle the income or other rights given to them. A living trust also makes it possible for your trustee to become familiar with your assets, beneficiaries, and the terms and conditions of your trust. The beauty of the situation is that if you don't like what happens or how the assets are invested, you can make the changes you want.

- *Distribution and control of assets.* The single most important reason many people choose a revocable living trust over other alternatives is that it accomplishes all their other objectives, yet it enables them to retain almost total control of the assets they place into the trust. If retention of lifetime control is essential to you, and you want the continuing flexibility to meet unknown future contingencies but still accomplish other non-tax savings goals that are best met through a trust, the revocable living trust may be the appropriate solution.

What are some of these distribution and control goals? Perhaps you'd like to limit the class of beneficiaries (for example, no in-laws) that will or can receive your company's stock or your family's summer home. If it is important to you to be sure your property doesn't go to persons outside the family, you should definitely consider a revocable living trust. Perhaps you are an aunt or uncle who wants to benefit a nephew or niece but for whatever reason do not want that child's parents to obtain the cash or other asset. An outright gift to the child is highly likely to end up in the hands of the child's parents (or the child's spouse or someone other than the party to whom you'd want it to go) if the child predeceases you after receiving your outright gift. Placing the same property into a revocable living trust, however, offers much greater assurance that it will eventually end up where you wanted it to go.

Living trusts enable you to control the manner and timing of asset distributions. You may want to consider a revocable living trust to postpone full ownership until the donees are in a better position to handle the income and the property itself. For instance, if your beneficiaries are legally adults but they lack the emotional or intellectual training, experience, physical capacity, or willingness to handle large sums of money or assets that require constant, high-level decision-making ability, a revocable living trust may be a viable solution.

Through a trust, you don't have to make the all-or-nothing-at-all decision of an outright gift. You can specify that the income and capital that beneficiaries are to receive is to be spread out over a period of time. You can use your trust to create rewards for behavior you want to promote. For instance you could provide that extra payments of income or capital will be made on the achievement of certain financial goals (for example "when my daughter has held a job for more than 3 years," or "when my son has invested 10 percent of his salary for 5 consecutive years").

Some people are reluctant to make outright gifts to children or others because they want to maintain a degree of control over those individuals. They fear that once their children or other beneficiaries receive a significant amount of income or capital, they will be less dependent (financially or psychologically) on them. With a revocable living trust you can maintain some control over a beneficiary. If you wish to make gifts eventually but are worried about the possible results of an outright no-strings-attached transfer, a revocable living trust may be a solution.

Yet another control-related reason for setting up revocable living trusts is that in some states they minimize the possibility that details about assets you own and their disposition will become public knowledge. Unlike a will, which becomes a matter of public record once it is filed in the appropriate local court, in many states a revocable trust is not required to be filed anywhere that would open its provisions to public scrutiny. In most states an inventory of the assets that will pass under a will must be filed in court, and so the assets, too, become subject to inspection. Only a few states make the same information available if the assets are held in trust.

Still, because the typical will doesn't make exciting reading, as a practical matter, most of us shouldn't be overly concerned about the invasion of our privacy. But privacy does become important if you have (or anticipate) intrafamily conflicts. In that case, the relative privacy available through a revocable living trust may be an important factor. No one need know how much another beneficiary receives or upon what terms. This may be a major advantage if you want to disinherit a child or other relative, provide different levels of income or capital, or give a share of income or capital to a friend who is not a member of your family. Privacy is also important if you want to support a paramour, illegitimate child, or a child of a prior marriage, but you don't want anyone else to know.

Within reasonable limits, you can be assured that the amount you place into your trust, the terms and conditions you impose on transfers to recipients, the identity of the beneficiaries you have named, and the amount of their income and capital shares will be known only to you, your trustee, and each of your specified beneficiaries. (If a federal estate tax return must be filed, your executor will be required to attach a copy of your revocable trust. If there is any tax litigation, the terms of the trust may then become public. Successor trustees and beneficiaries will also become privy to what you've written. A few states also make an inventory of assets held in a revocable trust available to the public.)

- *Effective and efficient transfer.* There are a number of elements you must consider when you are trying to transfer wealth at the least possible cost or risk. For instance, assume you have four children and that you own property—a summer home in North Wildwood, New Jersey—that does not lend itself to fragmentation.

You want to spread the enjoyment (and any summer rental income) among all four of your children. When the summer home is eventually sold, you want the proceeds to be shared equally. And you want the home to be adequately maintained and insurance and real estate taxes paid until that time—without family squabbles as to who pays for what. By placing the home (or other asset) in a revocable living trust, you may accomplish these objectives.

Another common example is a life insurance policy that will provide income and capital for your children or grandchildren. It is much easier (and less expensive) in most cases for one trustee to hold the policy and collect the proceeds than for all four of your children each to purchase and pay their shares of the premium for a policy on your life. (Be sure to read chapter 16 to learn about the advantages of using an irrevocable life insurance trust as the *owner*—not beneficiary—of life insurance.)

A revocable living trust can serve as a unifying receptacle for a multitude of assets. Because a trust can be named as recipient of almost any type of asset and because you (or others) can transfer cash, stocks, bonds, or other property into a revocable living trust at any time, you can use the trust to unify not only the mix of assets you now own but also assets you may obtain in the future. That unification will be monitored and administered by one person (or party) or by co-trustees working together who can see the whole investment picture.

Another aspect of unification is that, if you are rendered mentally incompetent by a stroke or other disability, additional assets received on your behalf (perhaps through an inheritance or legal suit) can be added to your trust by others. (We suggest you specify in your power of attorney that the holder of that power is authorized to add property to your trust.) Even if you decide not to set up a revocable trust now, you may want to ask your legal counsel to consider a provision in your durable power of attorney that gives your attorney-in-fact the right to set up a revocable trust for your assets if you become disabled. You might require that the dispositive terms of the trust must be the same as those in your last will, or you could provide that upon your death, any assets remaining in the trust would pass to your estate.

Furthermore, you can "pour over" assets passing under your will at your death into the revocable trust you've established during your lifetime. This unification of assets will be particularly important if you own several different types of assets or you own property in a number of states. For instance, assume you live in Bryn Mawr, Pennsylvania, and you own a sailboat in Rock Hall, Maryland, and a condominium in Fort Lauderdale, Florida. By unifying all these geographically diverse assets in one legal "pot," you can save significant administrative costs at your death. For one thing, your executor will not have to incur what lawyers call "ancillary administration"—the multiple probate proceedings that are required when property is owned in more than one state. If you own real estate in one or more states outside of your domicile when you die, there will be an ancillary proceeding in every one of those states. These multiple legal procedures are necessary to give your executor the legal authority to act on your behalf and to pass good title to each of the properties. But if you convey the property to a revocable trust, only one estate administration will be required—in the state where you were domiciled. (Be sure to check with your lawyer to see if there are other ways to avoid ancillary administration, such as a family limited partnership or limited liability company, which may accomplish the same objectives more effectively and cost efficiently.)

Closely related to the unification advantage is a trust's ability to equalize both the beneficiaries' individual financial risk and their income and appreciation potential. In other words, you might consider a revocable living trust as a way to even out the value or income produced by a given asset among all the beneficiaries. For example, assume you own four different mutual funds of equal value from four different companies, and you have four children, all of whom you want to treat equally. At first glance, it seems that you could treat everyone fairly and equalize the potential for gain or loss by giving each child one of your four funds. But one (or two or three) of the funds could drop in value while another could increase dramatically. Alternatively, all four mutual funds could (and probably would) increase or decrease at different rates. Clearly, if you gave each child one fund, your children would not consider themselves treated equally. But if you put all four mutual funds into a revocable living trust, you could equalize the potential risks and rewards among your four children. The trustee could pay all four children equal shares of the total income of the trust and equal shares of any capital appreciation (or loss).

Forum shopping is a very special advantage of a revocable living trust that lawyers often utilize. Within reasonable limits, you can designate which state's law will govern the administration of your trust and the interpretation of its terms. This means that your trust does not necessarily have to be governed by the laws of your own state. You can pick a state where the laws are more favorable to accomplishing your objectives, and stipulate in your trust that it is your desire that the interpretation of trust terms to be governed by "State X."

The choice of forum can be a significant advantage if one of your objectives include to allow your trust to continue longer than might otherwise be permitted, reduce a surviving spouse's rights to a statutory share of your estate, or lessen the threat of a will contest, because laws in these areas vary greatly from state to state, and another state may have laws much more favorable to your situation. You should also consider forum shopping if another state has a more favorable law dealing with creditors' rights or charitable bequests, and your intentions may be thwarted under your own state's laws.

Your choice of state law will not be effective unless the trust has some relationship with the chosen state, but this can be accomplished by choosing a trustee located in that state. In fact, choosing a trustee in the desired state almost guarantees that the laws of that state will be applied, because anyone wishing to bring a legal action against the trust will have to sue the trustee, and the courts of the trustee's state will be naturally inclined to apply their own laws.

Generally speaking, by "wrapping" the trust around your assets, you make it harder for someone to disturb the plans you've made to distribute your property the way you want to when you die. A well-drawn trust is better able to withstand an attack than a will drawn shortly before your death—which is a very good reason to establish a trust now, rather than take a chance and create one in your will (that is, a "testamentary" trust).

Insulating your assets is particularly important if you intend to make provisions in your will that may be controversial or apt to stir up a family dispute. (You can often anticipate this type of problem if the provisions of your will are likely to disappoint certain would-be-heirs or if you are in a second or third marriage.) If there is any suggestion that your will might be challenged, you should consider a revocable living trust. In a few states, a revocable living trust can even help defeat a challenge by a surviving spouse who "elects against" your will (i.e., exercises a statutory right to take a share of the estate determined under state law regardless of the terms of the will).

A trustee can usually use trust assets to defend against an attack on the validity of the trust. Although your intended beneficiaries may still be bearing the costs of their own defense, it may help to discourage a claimant to realize that, even if the attack on the trust is successful, the claimant will have had to pay the legal fees of both sides to the dispute.

Q. How do I set up a revocable living trust?

A. Here is the typical process:

- Step 1: Find a lawyer who is knowledgeable about estate planning, trusts, and tax and financial planning, and who is willing to listen to your personal goals and objectives and take them into account in the trust planning process. (See chapter 6 for more information on choosing lawyers and negotiating legal fees.)

- Step 2: Explain to your lawyer your tax and personal planning objectives. He or she will ask you a number of questions about the extent, value, and legal title of your assets, life insurance policies, and employee benefit plans and their beneficiaries. Your lawyer should also ask you extensive questions about you, your beneficiaries, and your needs, circumstances, and objectives. You should ascertain the likely expense of retitling assets into the trust, decide what assets you'd like to continue to own in your own name (closely-held business interests, for example), and determine if there will be a surprise cost of transferring assets to the trust (for example, real estate transfer tax).

If a revocable living trust is appropriate, your lawyer will then draft a revocable living trust document (in addition to a *pour-over will*, a *durable power of attorney*, and perhaps also a *living will*). The trust document will name a trustee—the person (or persons) willing to accept the responsibilities of carrying out the terms of your trust. The trustee can be you alone, or you can serve together with one or more other individuals or even a trust company or bank. You should also name successor (backup) trustees or include a mechanism that will enable present trustees to name alternates in case you or another current trustee can't or won't serve for some reason. (No one you name as a present or future trustee can be forced to serve if they don't want to be a trustee.)

Your trust document (sometimes called a *trust indenture*) should spell out all the terms and conditions for distributions of income and principal. It should identify the beneficiaries (which can include yourself and your spouse), either by name or by class (for example, "my grandchildren"). The trust must also specify when distributions should be made during your lifetime and following your death, any conditions or restrictions on distributions (only after a certain age, or only for certain purposes), and the amounts or portion to be distributed to each beneficiary. Trustees are usually given investment and administrative powers by law, but it is a good idea to eliminate uncertainty by listing the powers of the trustees in the trust document. It may also be desirable to expand or restrict the normal powers of the trustee in order to carry out your particular planning objectives.

- Step 3: You must *fund* the trust initially and maintain the funding of the trust during its existence. This means you must legally change the ownership of assets from your name alone (or your name and your spouse's name jointly) to the name of the trustee (even if you are the sole trustee). It is very important that you segregate assets held in the trust's name from your own personal assets by retitling them. As trustee, you must keep separate records and hold cash in a bank account in the trust's name.

- Step 4: The trustee will then hold the legal title to the assets in the trust. It is the trustee's job to invest and safeguard trust assets, file tax returns (if needed) and pay the trust's income tax liabilities, pay out income and principal in accordance with the terms of the trust, and generally carry out the terms and conditions of the trust, subject always to the fiduciary duties described in chapter 4.

Remember that, as you acquire new assets, you must also change ownership to the trust, or better yet, acquire ownership originally in the name of the trustee. (At the end of this chapter, you'll find some forms that will assist you in the process of changing title.)

Before 1997, the IRS had taken the position that gifts from a trust fall within a special class of gifts that are still included in the gross estate for federal estate tax purposes if death occurs within three years after the gift, so it was usually recommended that gifts intended to qualify for the annual gift tax exclusion *not* be made from a revocable living trust. Fortunately, the Internal Revenue Code was amended by the Taxpayer Relief Act of 1997 to eliminate this problem.

Q. How does the living trust operate while I'm alive?

A. During your lifetime, the living trust serves as a kind of special savings account, separating the trust assets from your individual assets even though the trust assets are always available to you for withdrawal. Let's assume you've retitled whatever assets you want in the trust's name and have held back a modest checking account for day-to-day living expenses. The trust assets continue to produce the same income or capital growth that they produced before being transferred into the trust. The income earned by the trust is deposited into the trust's checking, savings, or money market accounts, or reinvested in the securities held in the trust's brokerage account. You can withdraw all or any part of the income and principal from the trust at any time, or the trustee can pay bills for you. You can also revoke the trust and withdraw all the assets whenever you want and at any time (or at least until you die, become incompetent, or voluntarily amend the trust to make it irrevocable).

Q. How does the living trust operate after I die?

A. If you should die, your trust becomes irrevocable, just like your will is irrevocable once you have died. After any debts, taxes, or other expenses have been paid, your trust assets will be distributed to the persons you have named, and under the terms and conditions you have specified in your trust document, just like a will directs the distribution of an estate. You can specify that part or all of the assets of the trust should continue to be held in the trust and that the trust continue for many years (even decades).

Your revocable trust may be given a "split personality" at your death—that is, you can direct your trustee to split your single trust into two more smaller trusts to accomplish various planning objectives. For instance, your revocable trust could be divided into one or more of the following types of trusts:

- a *qualified terminable interest property (QTIP) trust* to provide income for life to your surviving spouse. A QTIP trust qualifies for the federal estate tax marital deduction, so there is no federal estate tax (and usually no state death tax) on the transfer to the trust. At your spouse's death, all of the assets in the trust will be part of your spouse's taxable estate, but the assets will pass to the beneficiaries you have named, so that you can be sure your assets will pass to your children even if your spouse should remarry or have children from a prior marriage. See chapter 13 for more information on QTIP and marital deduction trusts.

- a *qualified domestic trust* (QDT), which is a special form of marital deduction trust for a surviving spouse who is not a U.S. citizen.

- a *"family" or "by-pass" trust* which can provide income and other benefits to your spouse and children, but will not be subject to federal estate tax at your spouse's death. This kind of trust is usually funded with an amount that is free of federal estate tax due to the federal estate tax unified credit, so the assets in the trust will escape federal estate tax at both your death and your spouse's death. For this reason, the family trust is often called a *credit equivalent by-pass trust* or *credit shelter trust*. No matter how much the assets in this trust increase in value after your death, the entire amount can by-pass any tax at your spouse's death, which can save hundreds of thousands of dollars in taxes. See chapter 13 for more information on "by-pass" or "credit shelter" trusts.

- *trusts for children* if your spouse does not survive you, or if you should decide to use your unified credit to skip your spouse entirely and benefit your children immediately.

- *charitable split-interest trusts,* such as a charitable remainder trust or charitable lead trust, if you want to benefit both your family and charity. See chapter 26 for more information on split-interest trusts.

Q. What is the difference between a living trust and revocable trust?

A. The terms living trust and revocable trust are sometimes used synonymously, but the terms "living" and "revocable" describe two different qualities. As we've noted earlier, almost all trusts are (1) either living or testamentary and (2) either revocable or irrevocable.

When you set up a trust during your lifetime, the trust is called a *living* trust. (It is also sometime called *inter vivos* trust, meaning that it is a trust between living people.) Alternatively, you can direct in your will that, after your death, some or all of the assets passing under your will should go into a trust. In that case, the trust is called a *testamentary trust.* ("Testamentary" means having to do with wills or testaments.) If you can terminate, alter, amend, or revoke a trust, it is a *revocable trust.* If you can't alter, amend, revoke, or terminate the trust, it is an *irrevocable trust.* (See chapter 16 for more about irrevocable trusts.) All testamentary trusts are irrevocable once they come into being, because the person who created them is dead and no longer able to make any changes. Therefore, all revocable trusts are living trusts, but a living trust can be either revocable or irrevocable.

Q. What rights do I have after I create a revocable living trust?

A. As the grantor of a trust, you have only the rights you specifically reserve in the trust document. That is why it is so very important to specify clearly at the beginning or end (or both) of the document that you intend the trust to be *revocable*.

Of course, if you name yourself trustee or co-trustee of your trust or you are the primary beneficiary (as is typically the case), you will have rights and powers of a trustee over the investment and management of trust assets, or the rights and powers of a beneficiary. So, if the trustee has the absolute discretion to distribute principal to the beneficiary, and you are the trustee and beneficiary, you can effectively terminate the trust by exercising your discretion as trustee to distribute all of the principal to yourself as beneficiary, regardless of whether the trust is expressly "revocable."

Q. What types of property can I put into my revocable trust?

A. Any property you can own in your own name can be placed into a revocable living trust. You can put cash, stocks, mutual funds, bonds, real estate, or any other asset you own into a trust. You can even put life insurance into a trust, or name the trust as beneficiary of your life insurance. (You can also name a trust as a beneficiary of your pension or profit-sharing plans, or an individual retirement account, but you can't transfer the actual assets of the retirement plan or IRA into the trust without realizing taxable income and perhaps incurring penalties for premature withdrawals. Because of the large tax liabilities that can result from retirement funds, and the complexities of tax planning for retirement fund distributions, we suggest you consult with both a tax lawyer and your accountant before naming a trust as a beneficiary of a retirement plan.)

We advise that at the time you sign the trust documents, you put at least a small amount of cash into the trust so there is no question that the trust has been funded. (Some lawyers will staple a $10 bill into the trust, so that it is clear that the trust has a valid "corpus.")

Assets can be transferred at the time you set up the trust, and you can add assets any time up until your death. You can even pour over assets into your trust from your will. (If your revocable trust is your primary estate planning document, you should have a "pour-over" will to make sure that any assets left in your name at death are added to your trust and distributed as you have directed in your trust.)

Q. How do I terminate a revocable trust?

A. Revoking the trust will enable you to resume possession and title to the assets in the trust, and you will have no obligation to its beneficiaries. The trustee should immediately turn over any assets in the trust to you.

If you have specifically reserved the right to revoke the trust, a written letter from you to the trustee (even if that trustee is yourself) is all that should be necessary to end the trust and recover your assets. The letter to the trustee should state that you wish to revoke the trust, and it should also specify that assets in the trust should be retitled in your name. The power to revoke typically also carries with it the power to amend the trust, since you could use your power to revoke to recover the assets and then create a new trust. (But it doesn't work the other way: A power to amend is not the same as a power to revoke. We suggest that you make sure your trust clearly gives you both powers.)

Some lawyers insert a *power of appointment* provision which essentially gives the holder of that power the right to demand trust assets be paid to the party specified. If the power of appointment is a "general power," you have the right to demand that the trustee pay the assets to you directly or to any other party you designate on your behalf (including your creditors). Holding a general power is like having a blank check that can be written against trust assets. It gives you the absolute right to recover all the assets you've placed into the trust at any time before your death.

It may also be possible to revoke a trust by your will. You can state in your trust that you have the right to revoke the trust in your will as well as during your lifetime, in which case the trust assets would be distributed to the executor of your estate.

Another way a trust can be terminated is through the trustee's discretionary power to make principal distributions to you. If the trustee invades the principal for you and pays out all the trust's assets, it will terminate. (A trust must have assets to exist.)

Q. If I am disabled, can someone exercise the right to revoke the revocable trust on my behalf?

A. If you are legally incapacitated because of mental illness (such as Alzheimer's disease), you will not be able to revoke your revocable trust. The power to revoke may still exist, but you will not be able to exercise the power if you are legally incompetent, just like you will not be able to sell property or sign contracts. However, if you have been wise enough to have given a *durable power of attorney* (see chapter 2) to a spouse, child, other relative, or friend, that person may be able to act on your behalf to revoke the trust or at least make withdrawals from the trust for your benefit, or to make gifts that will reduce the death taxes otherwise payable by your beneficiaries.

In most states, your attorney-in-fact (the person to whom you have given a durable power of attorney) will not be able to revoke your trust or withdraw from your trust unless very stringent requirements have been met. At a minimum, the durable power itself must specifically allow the attorney-in-fact to revoke or withdraw from the trust, and the trust itself must allow for that action. We suggest that the trust specifically authorize a conservator, committee, or guardian who represents you (or the person to whom you have given your power of attorney) the right to withdraw from the trust to the extent necessary to pay for your support and maintenance.

You may not want someone else revoking your trust—even though supposedly acting on your behalf—if you become disabled. If you don't want anyone other than yourself to revoke your trust—even someone acting with court approval—you should insert a provision in your trust specifically denying the right of revocation to anyone else, including any agent or guardian.

Q. Can I be the trustee of my own revocable trust?

A. Yes. You or your spouse (or both of you together) can serve as the trustee of your own trust, either alone or with any other person you might choose as a co-trustee. Instead of yourself (or yourselves), or as co-trustees, you can name a child or other relative, a friend, a legal or financial advisor, a corporate fiduciary such as a bank trust department, or any combination of them. In short, you can "have it your way."

There are obviously advantages in serving as the trustee of your own trust. You continue to have complete control over all investments, and you don't even need to ask for a distribution from the trust, because you can write yourself a check from your trust anytime you want.

Because a revocable trust is generally ignored for income tax purposes, there are no tax disadvantages in serving as the trustee of your own revocable living trust, or in your spouse serving. However, there may be tax complications if your spouse or other family members serve as trustees after your death. See chapter 3 for an explanation of these tax considerations.

There are some potential non-tax disadvantages in naming yourself as the sole trustee. If one of the purposes of the trust is to provide for continued management of your investments and other assets in the event of your disability, then serving as the sole trustee may result in complications or delays. Your mental or physical abilities may deteriorate gradually, through age or illness, and you may inadvertently neglect the management of the trust assets, or even mismanage or waste assets, because you were not aware of your own diminishing abilities. If you serve as sole trustee, your assets might suffer from the same mismanagement that the trust was intended to avoid, the only difference being that your disability occurred while you were the trustee of the trust instead of the owner of the assets. Even if your successor trustee recognizes your disability and steps in to take control of the trust, your disability might prevent you from resigning, in which case the successor trustee might have trouble getting the banks or brokers who are holding trust assets to accept the authority of the successor trustee, in which case a court proceeding may be needed to officially remove you as trustee and qualify your successor.

Even if you successfully serve as sole trustee until your death, your successor trustee may have difficulties in gaining control of all trust assets. In the past, most banks and brokers were satisfied with a copy of the trust document and a death certificate. However, more and more financial institutions are becoming concerned by the possibilities of undisclosed or unknown trust revocations or amendments, invalid trusts, or even fraud by those claiming to be the successor trustee. As a result, more and more financial institutions are requiring court approval of the successor trustee before turning over trust assets.

For these reasons, we would recommend that you consider having a trusted family member, such as a spouse or a child, serve as a co-trustee during your lifetime, even if you continue to perform all of the services of trustee. Having a co-trustee named on bank or brokerage accounts should eliminate or simplify the transfer of assets or control of the trust assets upon your death or disability. You can also consider a bank or other third party as a co-trustee, but you must remember that there are many responsibilities that a trustee must meet and liabilities a trustee must accept. Few people (other than yourself or a close relative) will perform these tasks for free, and certainly no banks will ever serve without compensation.

For additional information and guidance on selecting the best trustees, see chapter 3.

Q. Why do I need to have a trust document if I will be the trustee?

A. With only a few rare exceptions, the terms of any trust you create should be in writing. Why? Because you are not the only person affected by your trust. In fact, there are always at least four parties (other than the grantor) concerned with every trust:

- The trustee who is responsible for managing, safeguarding, investing, and paying out trust principal and income and who holds legal title to trust assets. While you might be the sole trustee while you are living, someone else will have to serve as trustee upon your death or disability, and that other trustee will need to know what you wanted done with the trust assets.

- The trust's beneficiaries, for whom the trustee serves and who are entitled to the benefits of trust assets and income. How are they to know whether they have gotten what they are supposed to get if the trust is not in writing. There can be disputes among trust beneficiaries when a written trust is vague or ambiguous. Imagine the possibilities for litigation when there is nothing in writing at all?

- The IRS and state tax authorities need to determine tax liabilities based on the terms of the trust. In the absence of written evidence of the terms of the trust, the trust may be ignored for tax purposes, and the tax liabilities might be considerably greater than what you intended or expected.

- Banks, brokers, mutual funds, creditors, and others who buy, sell, lend, or who have other dealings with the trust and its assets need to be sure that they are dealing with the right trustee and that the trustee has the proper power to sell or invest the assets.

All of these parties need an accurate recording of the terms of the trust and written documentation of the trustee's authority to act on behalf of the trust and its beneficiaries.

The trust document—sometimes called a *deed of trust, trust indenture,* or *trust agreement*—serves as evidence of the agreement between the grantor and trustee and lets the beneficiaries, federal and state taxing authorities, and others who deal with the trustee know:

- Who is to serve as trustee

- Who are the beneficiaries to be paid income or principal from the trust, and when and how much they are to be paid;

- What powers the trustee will have to sell, buy, or manage trust assets, and whether those powers are expanded or limited from what is otherwise allowed by law. Each state gives trustees certain powers (and responsibilities). You can expand the powers (and therefore the flexibility) of your trustee, or you can choose to restrict your trustee's ability to purchase or hold certain assets or take certain actions. For instance, if you are conservative and don't want your trustee to take certain risks or purchase certain types of assets, you can specify that in your trust document.

- How much compensation will be paid to the trustee.

- Whether there are any special limits on the liabilities or responsibilities of the trustee. You can exonerate your trustees (other than yourself) from certain liabilities or impose responsibilities beyond what your state's law normally provides. For certain types of trust investments or trustee decisions, it may be necessary to limit the liability of the trustees in order to get a trustee to accept the duties and responsibilities of trustee. For example, if you wanted a family business to continue to operate as long a least one of your children is active in the business, you could direct the trustees to continue the business and exonerate the trustees for any liability for business losses.

Q. Who can I name as the beneficiaries of my trust?

A. You have almost unlimited flexibility in naming beneficiaries. You can name yourself as the primary beneficiary during your lifetime. You can also specify that you'll receive all of the income from the trust annually, along with whatever principal you want or need, at whatever dates or in whatever installments, and under whatever terms, you specify in the trust document.

Any individual can be a beneficiary—even a minor or an adult who is legally incompetent—because the beneficiary does not need to manage any property, only receive the benefits from the trust. (Of course, if the beneficiary is a minor or legally incompetent, it may be necessary to have a guardian appointed to receive the income or principal if the trustee does not have the power to hold the income or principal for the beneficiary and apply it for his or her benefit. In order to avoid the need for guardians, most trusts have provisions for minor or disabled beneficiaries.)

You don't have to identify any of your beneficiaries by name. You can specify, for example, that "income is to be paid annually or more frequently to my children." In fact, beneficiaries don't even have to be alive when you create the trust. The law requires only that beneficiaries be an identifiable and definite class or group, such as spouse, children, grandchildren, nieces, or nephews. You could, therefore, include children or grandchildren not yet born as beneficiaries—even if you have no children at the time you set up and fund your trust.

Beneficiaries do not have to be related to you. For example, you can name a friend or employee as the beneficiary of your trust. (You could even name the authors of this book as beneficiaries!)

Charities and other organizations can also be named as beneficiaries, including corporations, other trusts, partnerships, federal, state, and local governments, and even foreign governments. However, complications can arise if the beneficiary is an unincorporated association or other organization unable to hold legal title to property. There are also strict rules regarding the types of organizations, and the types of interests, that will qualify for charitable deductions for gift or estate tax purposes. (See chapter 25 for details.)

You cannot name a dog, cat, or other pet as a beneficiary of your trust, because a pet cannot own property or sue in court, and so cannot receive money from the trust or sue in court to enforce the trust. (You can name an individual as a beneficiary with the request that the money from the trust used to take care of the pet. However, this is not legally binding and is sometimes called an "honorary" trust.)

See chapter 5 for additional information about who can be beneficiaries and types of beneficial interests.

Q. Do I have to tell my trustee that I've set up a trust?

A. Yes. Like other kinds of gifts, a trust is not valid until the trust property (or "corpus") has been delivered to the trustee. The trustee usually acknowledges receipt of the trust property by signing the trust document.

It is only the initial trustee who must acknowledge and accept the trust. If your trust document names successor trustees, they do not need to be told about the trust until it is time for them to serve, and they can decide whether or not to accept the trust at that time. (However, you should let a successor trustee know that the trust exists if you expect him or her to take over the administration of the trust at your death. Otherwise, it is possible that no one will know what to do following your death, or that finding and carrying out the trust will take more time.)

We recommend that you have the initial trustee acknowledge acceptance of that responsibility in writing and that you deliver the trust document to the trustee to create evidence that the trust is in effect. Ideally, the trustee should sign the deed of trust.

Q. Do I have to notify my beneficiaries that they have been named in the trust document?

A. No. You can create and fund a revocable living trust without ever notifying any of your trust's beneficiaries. No law requires that you tell your beneficiaries that there is a revocable trust or that they have an interest in it.

Q. Do beneficiaries have to accept their interests?

A. No. A beneficiary can refuse to accept an interest. If a beneficiary decides to renounce an interest, however, it is extremely important that the beneficiary do so in a way that minimizes gift and estate taxes. The technical term that tax lawyers use for the act of refusing a gift, inheritance, or trust is a *disclaimer*.

Why would anyone disclaim an interest in a trust? Suppose someone left you an interest in a trust worth $300,000, and you were wealthy and didn't need or want the money but did want your children to receive it, and they were the contingent beneficiaries named in the trust. If you were to accept the money and then give it to your children during your lifetime or by will, you might incur gift or death taxes. By disclaiming in a timely manner, the trust interest can go directly to your children without triggering any additional gift or estate taxes.

There's a catch: To be effective for tax purposes, a disclaimer must be "qualified." Some of the rules for a qualified disclaimer are that it must be

- an irrevocable and unqualified refusal to accept

- in writing

- delivered to the transferor of the interest (or the transferor's legal representative, the trustee, or the person possessing the property)

- given before acceptance of the property or any benefits from the property

Timing is important, and a disclaimer must also satisfy certain other rules and state laws. These requirements can be technical, and if you want to disclaim an interest, it is extremely important to contact tax counsel before signing any papers or accepting any benefits.

We'd like to use this discussion of disclaimers to point out the importance of flexibility and careful drafting of a revocable living trust. Revocable living trusts are complex and they require a skilled and experienced estate planning lawyer. As we've emphasized throughout this book, a revocable living trust is not a do-it-yourself project.

Q. Are revocable trusts a good choice for an unmarried individual or someone married more than one time?

A. Both situations are strong indicators that a revocable living trust might be appropriate and should definitely be considered. An unmarried individual who is living with another person will often wish to provide for his or her partner. Typically, that partner will have no state law survivorship rights. Worse yet, the property-owning individual may have relatives who will inherit that property if there is no will. This is a perfect recipe for a will contest, and it could easily lead to a bitter fight—almost certainly to a probate delay. The living trust can help avoid the entire problem because it will not be offered for probate; none of the disappointed relatives need know of the terms, or even the existence, of the trust and the assets it conveys.

A revocable trust may also be indicated for divorced clients in states that require an "affidavit of heirship" (essentially a family tree) and a copy of any divorce decree when an unmarried person dies. What if the marriage was terminated but there is no easily accessible evidence to prove it? (Perhaps the divorce occurred 40 years ago.) A revocable trust may avoid the delay, aggravation, and cost of searching for the evidence of a prior divorce.

Individuals who have married more than once would often like to make provisions for children of a former marriage, but they want to keep the terms and amounts private. A revocable trust is an excellent vehicle for accomplishing this objective.

Q. Is there a reason to use a revocable living trust to make a gift to charity?

A. In most cases you should make charitable gifts either outright or in an irrevocable trust that is designed specifically to qualify for the charitable deduction. There is one situation, however, when you should consider a revocable trust in lieu of leaving assets to charity in your will. Some states have what are called *Mortmain* statutes. These laws invalidate a gift made to charity by will within a specified period of death (typically 30 days). In some states you can circumvent such laws by making the gift through a revocable trust.

Q. Is there an FDIC problem with revocable trusts?

A. Yes. When spouses' separate accounts are lumped together in a single revocable trust, the insurance protection of the Federal Savings and Loan Insurance Corporation (FDIC) is limited. When the beneficiaries of a revocable living trust are solely husband and wife, your assets may not be fully insured since your trust account will be lumped together with your other joint accounts for testing insurance limits. Once that total exceeds

$100,000, the excess is not protected under FDIC insurance. (Trusts at the same institution that name beneficiaries other than the husband and wife are treated as separate accounts and should not be a problem.)

One solution is to set up your revocable living trust account at a financial institution separate from where your joint account is. This will help to guarantee that all your bank or thrift deposits are properly insured. We also recommend that you monitor your trust held bank accounts as carefully as you watch your stocks or bonds.

Q. Are the assets I place into my revocable living trust protected from the claims of creditors?

A. No. You can't protect yourself or your beneficiaries by placing assets into a revocable living trust. Avoidance of probate does not guarantee any creditor protection. In most states your creditors continue to have essentially the same access to assets that they had before you transferred those assets to a revocable trust. If you retain a beneficial interest in the trust, that interest is subject to your creditors' claims.

In some cases you may even place assets at a greater risk by transferring them to a revocable trust then you would if you left them by will. For instance, in many jurisdictions creditors of your probate estate have only 4 to 6 months to make their claims. Yet the creditors of a revocable trust have no such short deadline. In many states a creditor can file a claim for payment years after your death, assuming the claim is filed within the statute of limitations—as long as 6 or 7 years for a mortgage, credit card, or other contract claim in some states. Furthermore, some states (such as Florida) will not honor a *homestead exemption* (which allows a homeowner to designate a house and land as his or her homestead and then exempt that homestead from execution for the homeowner's general debts) from creditors if the deed is registered in the name of a revocable trust.

If your trustee distributes assets in your revocable trust before the IRS (the most senior creditor of all) is satisfied that the federal estate tax has been paid, your trustee can be held personally liable for any unpaid tax. Because the assets in the revocable trust are part of your taxable estate, any distribution to beneficiaries is at the trustee's peril until your executor receives a "closing letter" from the IRS for the federal estate tax. Tax liens for income taxes you have incurred during your lifetime can also be attached to revocable living trust assets. And a trustee in bankruptcy (a court-appointed party representing your creditors) can revoke your trust in order to obtain the cash to satisfy your personal creditors.

Q. What protection does a revocable trust provide from disgruntled heirs?

A. In most states a revocable trust will not provide a significant bar to the claims of potential heirs. Usually, you'll have no more protection than if you had made a will.

Generally speaking, a will can be contested on any the following grounds:

- Lack of testamentary capacity (i.e., competence).

- Fraud.

- Mistake.

- Undue influence.

- Failure to comply with formal requirements (witnesses and other formalities of execution).

Generally speaking, a revocable trust or other lifetime transfer can be contested on any of the following grounds:

- Lack of donative capacity (i.e., competence).

- Fraud.

- Mistake.

- Undue influence.

- Failure to comply with formal requirements (lack of valid corpus, trustee, or other element of a valid trust).

In other words, there is really no difference in the laws regarding the validity of wills and the laws regarding the validity of revocable trusts (aside from mechanical differences in the formalities of wills and the formalities of trusts). A successful will contest usually requires that the decedent, at the time of signing the will, didn't understand the extent of his or her property, didn't know who the natural objects of his or her bounty were, didn't understand the consequences of signing the will, or didn't comply with state law requirements to make a valid will. The degree of mental capacity needed to transfer assets to a trust will vary from state to state, and there might be a significant distinction in the degree of capacity needed between making a valid will and making a valid revocable trust in some states. If legal capacity is an issue, the difference may be quite important, and it should be researched by an expert in estate planning and administration. However, the difference between a will and trust is usually procedural. The trustee of a revocable trust is usually not required to give notice to heirs at law or other potential claimants, so it is possible that the trust could be distributed after death before any disgruntled heir is able to locate the trustee and begin any legal challenge to the trust. Also, the fact that a trust exists during the lifetime of the grantor, and the grantor lives with the trust for several years before his or her death, may help convince the court that the grantor knew what he or she was doing.

A revocable trust also provides little protection against the claims of surviving spouses. In most states, the surviving spouse can "elect against a will" and other transfers by a decedent. This right, called "dower," "curtesy," or an "elective right," typically allows a surviving spouse to take a specified share of your real and personal property (often one third) regardless of what your will provides—even in the absence of fraud, undue influence, or failure to meet statutory requirements for a valid will. In other words, a surviving spouse can claim a portion of your estate—including assets held in a revocable living trust—even if your will and revocable trust are completely valid for all other purposes. Of course, even in those relatively few states that do allow one spouse to block the other spouse's elective rights by transferring assets to a revocable living trust, if it can be shown that the transfer was specifically to do just that—to perpetrate a "fraud" on the other spouse—the courts may find this to be an unfair practice and invalid.

Q. Does my revocable living trust provide any protection for me if I should become divorced?

A. Probate laws in many states will automatically revoke any gift to a spouse by will if you have divorced before your death (unless you specifically provide otherwise). So if in your will you leave a spouse your entire estate, you then divorce, and you forget to change your will, your ex-spouse will receive nothing and your property will be distributed as if your ex-spouse had predeceased you. Likewise, if you have named your spouse as executor or executrix of your will and you die after you are divorced but before you've changed your will, that provision is automatically negated in many states.

This protection is usually not afforded to those with revocable trusts. In most states, there is no automatic change in your trust merely because you become divorced. You may therefore be stuck with an ex-spouse who is both a trustee and beneficiary of a revocable trust with assets you have placed into the trust. Of course, you could always revoke the trust and recover the assets—assuming you do so before your death or mental incapacity.

Some lawyers will include provisions in a trust that specifically state that your spouse must still be married to you at your death in order to be a beneficiary (and most married couples will accept those kinds of standardized provisions without offense or anxiety about the state of their marriage). However, no matter what estate planning tools or techniques you have used, we suggest that you review all of them immediately upon a divorce (or better yet, adjust them appropriately as you proceed in the divorcing process). The point is this: If you *do* forget to make changes, the odds are greater for your will to be corrected by law in the way you'd want it to be than your revocable living trust. Should you have a stroke or become mentally incompetent, trust provisions you've made for a spouse might not be correctable before your death. As a practical matter, your legally revocable trust then becomes irrevocable in favor of your ex-spouse.

Q. *How should my revocable trust be coordinated with my overall estate plan?*

A. Neither man nor woman can live (or die) by trust alone. The best resource books available to estate planners stress over and over that no tool or technique, no matter how useful, should be employed in a vacuum. We have also emphasized repeatedly that a revocable living trust should not, by itself, be viewed as the perfect (or sole) solution to estate planning problems. It is only one of many tools, and it must be coordinated with other tools and techniques by knowledgeable planners as part of an overall estate plan.

For one thing, you'll need a will. If you are an adult citizen or resident alien living anywhere in the United States, you should have an up-to-date valid will with or without a living trust. Why? As we've already mentioned, no matter how masterfully drafted your revocable living trust might be, it is operative only for property that has been placed into it. If, for any reason, you haven't retitled an asset and made the trustee the owner (even if you are the trustee), that asset will pass under the terms of your will (that is, through probate), rather than according to the provisions of the trust. None of the advantages of a revocable living trust are possible for these assets.

No matter how meticulous you are in retitling your property to a revocable trust, it is often the case that all of your assets will not be actually held in the name of the trust when you die. There can be some asset (a car, household items, or jewelry, for example) that you have overlooked. That asset will pass through intestacy if there is no valid will at your death. Suppose, for example, you die from a car accident that was clearly the fault of someone's negligence, and a large sum of money is paid as the result of the lawsuit you began on your deathbed. It may have been impossible for you to have assigned that money to your trust.

If your estate is large enough to require an estate tax return ($600,000 in 1996, but scheduled to increase to $1,000,000 by 2006), the IRS will prefer to deal with a formally appointed executor—someone qualified by state law to act on behalf of your estate. If you haven't appointed one, your trustee will be considered your "executor" by default, and able to make various tax elections available to your estate. (If there is no executor or administrator officially appointed by the court, then any person in actual or constructive possession of any of your property, including the trustees of your revocable living trust, may be considered your executor.) You may or may not want this result. Generally, it is better to specify an executor in your will and name at least two backups in case one of them cannot serve (or will not serve, or ceases to serve) for whatever reason, before completing the administration of the estate.

There is one more extremely important reason that you'll need a will. Some key non-tax objectives can be achieved only through a will. For example, a will may allow you to name a *guardian of the person* for each of your children (someone to care for your children, rather than your wealth). This is not possible in a trust. A will might also allow you to make anatomical gifts from your body after death, or exercise powers of appointment given to you under trusts established by others during your lifetime.

You'll also need a durable power of attorney. We believe that almost every adult should execute this relatively simple and inexpensive legal document and make sure it is constantly updated. A power of attorney is a document that gives your spouse, child, other relative, or trusted friend (the *attorney-in-fact*) the legal right to act on your behalf as you could have acted (or in more limited ways, if you decide to grant limited powers). A "durable" power ensures that the rights you give to the person or persons you name as your attorney-in-fact (or agent) are not nullified if you become physically, mentally, or emotionally disabled. Your durable power of attorney should specifically authorize your attorney-in-fact to add to your revocable trust, as well as withdraw from the trust to the extent needed for your support (or to make gifts for tax planning purposes). Your revocable trust should also specify that your attorney-in-fact can withdraw from the trust for those purposes. (See, "If I am disabled, can someone exercise the right to revoke the revocable trust on my behalf?", above in this chapter.)

Q. What legal capacity is needed to create a trust?

A. To create a valid trust under state law, you must have the same capacity needed to make a gift or other transfer of property. A trust can be set aside and disregarded if the grantor of the trust was a minor or was under a mental deficiency or derangement that would have invalidated a direct gift of property.

Q. If I set up and fund a revocable living trust, what must be done when I die?

A. Typically, the grantor of a revocable trust has retained rights to income and principal during his or her lifetime, and specified how the trust should be distributed (or for whom it should continue) following the grantor's death. After your death, your trustee will therefore have to:

- Collect all assets that may be payable to the trust at your death, such as the balance of your estate under will (after payment of debts and taxes), life insurance benefits, or retirement benefits.

- Pay any amounts owed to the executor of your estate, such as income earned during lifetime and undistributed at death, as well as any amounts needed by the executor to pay your debts and death taxes. Because of the likelihood that your trustee will be called upon to pay death taxes, or your estate will be reduced by death taxes (and therefore reduce the amount going into your trust), your trust (and your will) should include instructions regarding which beneficiary should pay those taxes, or which beneficiary's share of the trust should be reduced by those taxes. Lawyers call this an *apportionment clause* because it apportions taxes according to your wishes. An apportionment clause can mean a difference of thousands of dollars to your beneficiaries, and your will and your trust should contain apportionment clauses that are consistent with each other.

- Sell assets to the extent necessary to pay debts, taxes, or expenses, or make distributions. For example, if your home is in your revocable trust, your trustee may need to sell your home in order to divide your trust among your beneficiaries.

- Continue to manage investments and properties held in trust, making sure that all funds are properly invested, and any real property (such as a home) or tangible property (such as jewelry, cars, works of art, or other furnishings) are properly insured, stored, and maintained.

- File state and federal income tax returns for the years (or parts of years) following your death and until the trust has been completely distributed. Following your death, your trust will be considered an irrevocable trust and a separate taxpayer for income tax purposes. The trust will be entitled to a deduction for amounts distributed to beneficiaries, and the beneficiaries will be required to report distributions of income on their individual income tax returns, but the trust must still file tax returns so that the beneficiaries (and the government) know how much income they have received.

- Distribute the trust assets to the beneficiaries entitled to them. As part of the final distribution, the trustee will want to get releases from the beneficiaries, so that the distribution of the trust is final, and the beneficiaries cannot later sue the trustee, claiming that they received less than they should have. In order to get releases from the beneficiaries, the trustee may have to account to the beneficiaries for all of the receipts and disbursements during that trustee's administration of the trust, including receipts and disbursements during your lifetime if the trustee served during your lifetime (unless you released the trustee during your lifetime). (For more information on accounting by trustees, see chapter 5.)

If you have transferred all of your assets to your revocable trust, and there is a probate estate and no executor, your trustee will also have to take responsibility for the duties of an executor. Your trust may have to:

- Settle your lifetime debts, including the preparation of your final lifetime income tax return.

- Prepare and file your federal estate tax return (if required) and state death tax return (if any) and settle those taxes.

Finally, your trustee may become involved in disputes with your heirs at law or the beneficiaries of your trust, or disputes among the beneficiaries. For example:

- If there is a contest to the validity of the trust, your trustee must defend the trust against it.

- If your surviving spouse is not pleased with his or her share of your estate, he or she may elect to take a statutory share of your estate, which in many states may include up to one third of the value of assets in your revocable living trust. Your trustee would then have to segregate (and perhaps sell) trust assets in order to pay out the appropriate amount and settle with your surviving spouse as though a beneficiary of the trust.

- If your trustee claims compensation for his or her services, your beneficiaries may object to the amount of the compensation.

- In the administration and distribution of the trust, your trustee may be required to make a number of tax decisions and investment decisions, and your beneficiaries may not agree with all of those decisions.

Q. Mechanically, how do I transfer the title of bank accounts, mutual funds, and life insurance policies to my revocable living trust?

A. On the next few pages, we have provided some forms which may be useful to your advisers in transferring assets to your revocable trust.

Sample Form to Transfer Title

DATE: January 1, 1996

FROM: CHARLES PARKER
        1447 Market Street
        Philadelphia, PA 19111

TO: _____
         _____
         _____

RE: **Transferring Title to Revocable Living Trust**

To Whom It May Concern:

I have established a Revocable Living Trust solely for my benefit, and would like to transfer title of my account with you to the name of my Revocable Living Trust.

My account should be titled as follows:

"Charles Parker, Trustee
U/D/T dated January 1, 1998,
F/B/O Charles Parker"

Please change your records to reflect this change.

        Asset to be transferred: Refer to account no.:
        _____   _____
        _____   _____

There is no consideration for this change of title. If you have any further questions, please contract me at 215/555-4343.

Sincerely,

CHARLES PARKER

Sample Form to Change Beneficiary

DATE: January 1, 1998

FROM: CHARLES PARKER
         1447 Market Street
         Philadelphia, PA 19111

TO: NIGHT LIFE OF TEXAS INSURANCE COMPANY
         2054 Longhorn Boulevard
         Dallas, TX

         ATTENTION: Beneficiary Change Division

RE: **Policy No.: 123456**
         Named of Insured: Charles Parker

To Whom It May Concern:

Please send me the necessary forms to change the beneficiary of the above insurance policy under which I am the named insured and the owner. The beneficiary provision should read as follows:

"Revocable Living Trust of Charles Parker
dated January 1, 1998"

If you have any questions concerning the above, please contact me at 215/555-4343.

Sincerely yours,

CHARLES PARKER

Sample Form to Add Contingent Beneficiary

DATE: January 1, 1996

FROM: CHARLES PARKER
        1447 Market Street
        Philadelphia, PA 19111

TO: THE DISCOUNT PAJAMA COMPANY
        2020 Park Avenue
        New York City, NY

        ATTENTION: Beneficiary Change Division

RE: **Pension Plan of Charles Parker**
        with the Discount Pajama Company

To Whom It May Concern:

Please send me the necessary forms to change the beneficiary of my pension plan with The Discount Pajama Company as follows:

Primary Beneficiary: "Diane Parker, Wife"

Contingent Beneficiary: "Revocable Living Trust of Charles
                            Parker dated January 1, 1996"

If you have any questions concerning the above, contract me at 215/555-4343.

Sincerely yours,

CHARLES PARKER

HOW REVOCABLE LIVING TRUSTS ARE AFFECTED BY INCOME, GIFT, AND ESTATE TAXES

Chapter 10 explains:

- The federal and state death tax implications of a revocable living trust

- How to use a revocable living trust to provide estate liquidity

- How the federal gift tax law impacts on transfers to and from a revocable living trust

- How the federal income tax affects assets you've placed into the revocable living trust

- The special impact of the "alter ego" status of a revocable trust on certain assets

- What income tax reporting requirements must be met by the trustee

- How holding period and basis of capital assets are affected by a transfer into a trust

- The income tax implications of a revocable living trust after your death

---

Q. What are the federal (and state) estate tax implications of a revocable living trust?

A. Let's return to our analogy of a trust as a box. If you put assets into the box but keep a string on the box, you can pull the box back, reach into it, and regain all of the assets you have placed into it. Likewise, by using that string, you can change the terms of the trust and alter or amend it so that any time you want trust assets, you can have them. As a practical matter, therefore, because you hold the string, the assets in the box are still yours. You still have the right to use, possess, or enjoy the assets in that box or the income those assets produce (or at least the right to regain the use and possession of the assets at any time).

That string—representing your lifetime retention of the right to alter, amend, revoke, and terminate your living trust—causes all of the assets in the trust to be included in your gross estate for federal estate tax purposes even though the assets are not part of your "estate" under state probate law. The value of each asset in the trust, as of the date of your death, will be added to the value of the assets passing under your will and any other assets that were otherwise includible in your estate for federal estate tax purposes. This is a very important point: **Every asset in your revocable living trust will be included in your estate for federal and state death tax purposes just as if you never created the trust.**

In fact, the property in your revocable living trust will be in your estate for death tax purposes even if you are legally declared incompetent (some states call this "mentally disabled") before your death and are unable to exercise any power you retained in the trust. Even if you were trapped in a snow cave in Switzerland and physically couldn't revoke your trust, or even if you were standing in the trustee's office and it could be proven that you were legally insane at that time and could not revoke the trust, the assets in the trust would be part of your gross estate for federal estate purposes (and state death tax purposes).

Your trustee may be required to file federal and state death tax returns and pay the appropriate tax since the term *executor* is defined in the Internal Revenue Code as the party "in actual or constructive possession of property" if there is no executor appointed by a court. This means your trustee might have to order an independent professional appraisal to ascertain the value of trust assets on the appropriate valuation date, determine your taxable estate, compute the tax due, raise the cash (perhaps by selling trust assets if necessary), and pay the tax within nine months after your death.

Q. Is there a way to use a revocable living trust to provide estate liquidity?

A. Although we've stated several times that a revocable living trust is not, in itself, an income or estate tax savings device, it can serve as a very important planning tool. For instance, you can stipulate that assets in your trust at your death can (or even must) be used to pay your estate's expenses, administrative costs, and taxes. The trust could even specify that it must pay the same types of expenses and taxcs in your surviving spouse's estate if other funds are not available.

If you are married at the time of your death, your single revocable living trust can be split into one or more new trusts that can provide significant estate tax savings. Alternatively, some assets can be paid into other trusts you (or others) have established, or your revocable living trust (which at your death has become irrevocable) can be merged into a preexisting trust to accomplish various estate planning objectives and unify your planning efforts. These actions can assure that your unified credit will be fully and effectively utilized in coordination with your marital deduction. The trick in planning the estates of most married couples is to provide the surviving spouse with sufficient income and capital but pass as much as possible to the next generation with a minimum of overall federal and state death taxes.

It may be especially useful to have life insurance payable to your revocable trust. This will insure that (1) the life insurance is available to provide liquidity to pay debts, expenses, and taxes, (2) the life insurance proceeds are divided or disposed of along with your other assets, in accordance with the plan contained in your revocable trust, and (3) the life insurance proceeds do not become part of your estate, where they could be subject to the claims of creditors, beneficiaries you did not intend, or unnecessary administration expenses. (However, it may be even better to transfer your life insurance to an irrevocable trust. See chapters 17 and 18.)

Q. What are the federal gift tax implications of a revocable living trust?

A. Transferring assets to a revocable trust is not a gift for federal gift tax purposes (and should not be a gift for state gift tax purposes). So you will not need to file a gift tax return nor will you incur any federal or state gift tax cost when you set up a revocable living trust and put cash or other assets into the trust. Neither the creation nor the funding of a revocable living trust is a gift because you have not parted with "dominion and control" over the assets you transferred to the trust. Until a distribution is made from the trust to or for anyone other than yourself, or until you give up the right to alter, amend, revoke, or terminate your trust, you haven't made a gift subject to gift taxes because you can always get the property back.

At the moment you "cut the string" and give up or lose the right to get the property back, you will have made a completed gift subject to federal and state gift taxes. In other words, you will be treated as having made a gift at the instant your trust becomes irrevocable for any reason during your lifetime. For information on the gift tax consequences of transfers to irrevocable trusts, see chapter 16.

Of course, you are also making a gift subject to gift taxes if you withdraw money or other assets from your revocable living trust and then transfer it to someone else. In addition, you will also be considered to have made a gift subject to gift tax if the trustee, acting at your direction or in accordance with discretion given to the trustee, makes a distribution to someone other than you. For example, you might have retained the power to "appoint" assets to other people, as well as the power to withdraw assets for yourself.

If you direct the trustee of a revocable living trust to distribute assets to your son as a wedding gift, you will be considered to have made a gift. Or the trust document might give the trustee discretion to distribute money for the welfare of your children, as well as you and your spouse. If you become disabled, and your trustee decides to distribute money to your daughter for support while in graduate school, the distribution may be a gift for federal gift tax purposes. (Distributions to a spouse or minor child should not be considered gifts if they are within your obligation to support your spouse and children. However, graduate studies are not usually considered part of a parent's support obligation.)

The fact that a distribution from a trust is a gift is not necessarily bad, because the same gift tax exclusions and deductions will apply as would have applied to a direct gift. For example, a distribution to a child can qualify for the annual gift tax exclusion ($10,000, but may be adjusted for inflation after 1998), as well as the gift tax exclusions for educational and medical payments. (Tuition payments are not gifts if made directly to the educational institution, and payments of deductible medical expenses are not gifts if made directly to the health care provider.) A distribution to a spouse can qualify for the gift tax marital deduction and a distribution to a charity can qualify for the gift tax (and income tax) charitable deduction.

Before 1997, the IRS had taken the position that gifts from a trust fall within a special class of gifts that are still included in the gross estate for federal estate tax purposes if death occurs within three years after the gift, so it was usually recommended that gifts intended to qualify for the annual gift tax exclusion *not* be made from a revocable living trust. Fortunately, the Internal

Revenue Code was amended by the Taxpayer Relief Act of 1997 to eliminate this problem.

Q. What are the general federal income tax implications of a revocable living trust during my lifetime?

A. Generally, when you place cash, stocks, bonds, mutual funds, real estate, or other assets into a revocable living trust, there is no income tax effect, either favorable or unfavorable. You've merely put a "wrapper" around your assets, but you have not changed the essence of ownership. The revocable living trust is basically ignored for income tax purposes.

How are the assets you place into the trust—and the income those assets produce—treated during your lifetime? Generally speaking, you must report trust income, losses, deductions, and credits as if you personally received or incurred them. Stated another way, you are considered the real owner of the trust assets for income tax purposes. This means that:

- The IRS will ignore the trust as an entity and tax you directly on trust income whether or not it is distributed to you.

- Because you are treated as the owner of all trust assets, any allowable deduction is passed through to you, and you may take advantage of it on your own personal income tax return just as if you had paid the expense directly. If your home is held by your revocable trust, you are still considered the owner for income tax purposes and any real estate taxes or mortgage interest paid by the trustee are deductible on your personal income tax return.

- Any sales or other transactions between you and the trust are ignored for federal income tax purposes. You cannot realize any gain (or loss) in any transfer of assets or exchange of assets between you and your revocable trust.

- Any sales or transactions between your trust and any other person is considered to be a transaction between you and that other person. For example, if a loss on a transaction between you and a corporation controlled by your son would be disallowed for income tax purposes, the same loss will be disallowed on a transaction between your trust and your son's corporation.

Any trustee's commissions paid during your lifetime to a bank or other third-party trustee are deductible to the extent they are ordinary and necessary and paid for the collection of income or the maintenance of income-producing property. Therefore, commissions are not deductible to the extent paid for the management of tax-free investments, or for the management or maintenance of a home or other non-income-producing property. Also, the income tax deduction for those expenses are subject to the two percent "floor" for "miscellaneous itemized deductions."

The fee paid to a lawyer for tax advice and tax planning is also deductible for federal income tax purposes (subject to the two percent floor for miscellaneous itemized deductions). But fees paid for the preparation of wills, trusts, and other documents are usually not deductible. However, you may be able to deduct the legal fees and other expenses of establishing a revocable trust if the trustee is a bank or other third party and you can show that the creation of the trust was necessary for the management or conservation of income-producing property.

Q. What impact does the treatment of my revocable living trust as my income tax alter ego have on special tax treatment of certain assets?

A. Treating the trust as your income tax alter ego means that it is generally safe to transfer a U.S. savings bond, your principal residence, installment obligations, S corporation (Subchapter S) stock, or a partnership interest to a revocable living trust.

If you place a Series E, EE, or H savings bond into your revocable living trust, you don't have to worry that the transfer will trigger an acceleration of income. You don't have to report interest income until the trust cashes in the bonds or until they mature. At that time, you must report the total income interest not previously reported on your own tax return if the trust is still revocable when the trustee cashes in the bonds or when they mature. When you die, the accrued interest income that hasn't been reported may be included in your final income tax return. Therefore, U.S. savings bonds held in your revocable living trust are essentially treated as if you still owned them at death.

If you place your home in a revocable living trust, you don't have to worry that you are risking the ability to roll over gain on a tax-deferred basis. Since you and the revocable trust are considered the same for income tax purposes, you will not lose the right to roll over your principal residence income tax free.

Likewise, your right to the 1997 tax law's $500,000 gain exclusion for joint filers ($250,000 for others) is protected. (Warning: If for any reason, you are not considered the owner of the entire trust, the IRS may deny that exclusion). In some states the transfer of a home's title to a trust may trigger real estate transfer tax. These are just a few more examples of why the creation and operation of a revocable living trust is not a do-it-yourself project. You must use an estate planning lawyer and tax accountant who understand the complex interplay of both federal and state tax laws.)

Your trust can also own stock of an S corporation, even though ownership of stock of a Subchapter S corporation is generally held by individuals. (Ownership of S corporation stocks by most types of trusts can cause an involuntary loss of the S corporation status which in some cases amounts to a tax disaster).

Q. What are the income tax reporting requirements a trustee must meet?

A. Before 1996, the federal income tax reporting requirements for a revocable trust depended on whether or not the grantor (or the grantor's spouse) was also a trustee. Beginning in 1996, the reporting requirements of a revocable trust have been simplified, and the trustee of your revocable trust can use *either* of the following two methods to report the income, deductions, and credits of your revocable trust:

- The trustee can furnish *your* name and Social Security number to the banks, brokers, and other persons paying income to the trust, instead of an employer identification number (EIN) for the trust. In that case, the trustee does *not* file a Form 1041 or any other income tax return with the IRS. However, if you are not the trustee, the trustee must send you a statement with all of the information you will need to prepare your personal income tax return, including the amounts of income, deduction, and credits, and from whom the income was received.

- The trustee can furnish the *trust's* name, address, and employer identification number (EIN) to the banks, brokers, and other persons paying income to the trust, instead of your Social Security number. In that case, the trustee still files a Form 1041, but is required to file separate Forms 1099 for the total amounts of the interest, dividends, or other income received by the trust and taxable to you. If you are not the trustee, the trustee must also send you a statement with all of the information you will need to prepare your personal income tax return, including the amounts of income, deduction, and credits, and from whom the income was received.

If you create a joint revocable trust with your spouse and you file a joint income tax return, the same rules apply. However, if you file separate income tax returns, the trustee must follow the second reporting method described above, supplying the trust's EIN to payers of income and filing Forms 1099 to show the shares of income earned by you and your spouse during the year.

Notice that, under these rules, a revocable trust may never file a fiduciary income tax return (Form 1041). However, these rules do not apply if the grantor is not a citizen or resident of the United States, or if the grantor is a corporation or other entity with a taxable year that is not a calendar year.

Q. What happens to my holding period and basis for capital assets when I place property into a revocable living trust?

A. Basis, the starting point for determining an asset's gain or loss, is very important. If you purchase a piece of property for $60,000 and the property appreciates to $100,000, the $40,000 of gain that you realize when you sell the property is determined by subtracting your $60,000 basis from the amount you realize on the sale, $100,000. The higher your basis, the lower your reportable gain. Higher basis therefore means a lower tax. (To be eligible for the 28% rate for "mid-term" capital gains rates, you must hold a capital gain type asset for **more** than 12 months and to be eligible for the 20% rate for "long-term" capital gains, your holding period must be more than 18 months.)

What happens to your basis when you place that same asset into a revocable living trust that you have established? Nothing. Your basis will remain the same because there was no taxable event when you put the asset into the trust. Similarly, for purposes of the "more than 12 or more than 18 month" holding requirements, the trustee's holding period includes your holding period—that is, the trustee can "tack on" your holding period to the actual length of time the trust held the asset for purposes of determining capital gain and loss when the trustee sells the asset.

Upon your death, the assets in the trust will be included in your taxable estate and so they will receive a new basis equal to the federal estate tax value of the assets at your death (sometimes called a *step-up basis,* apparently in the belief that assets always increase in value, because the basis of a depreciated asset will step *down*). This means that your beneficiaries will have a tax basis in your trust assets equal to the fair market value of the assets at your death (or six months after death, if your estate elects so called "alternate valuation"), and not the basis you acquired during your lifetime.

A step-up in basis at death is highly advantageous because it eliminates all the income tax on the capital gain that had accumulated up until that point. Your beneficiaries will pay capital gains tax only on the gain (if any) that arises after your death. For instance, if you paid $60,000 for an asset that is worth $100,000 at your death, your heirs will receive a $100,000 basis. The $40,000 of appreciation is never subjected to income tax. If your heirs later sell the asset for $110,000, their reportable gain is only $10,000 (the $110,000 amount realized minus the $100,000 stepped-up basis). Warning: As of the date this book was published, an heir's holding period is automatically deemed to be "more than 12 months" (unless Congress amends this oversight). This is not sufficient time to qualify for the new 20 percent long term capital gains rate since more than 18 months is required.

Q. What are the income tax implications of a revocable trust after I die?

A. At your death, the revocable trust becomes irrevocable. New income tax rules apply. These rules are complex and, compared to the taxation you experienced during your lifetime, may be exceptionally harsh.

Essentially, the trust itself is considered a new taxpayer, separate from any of its beneficiaries. However, the trust can also act as a "pass through" entity. Income of the trust that is distributed to the beneficiaries during the year is taxed to the beneficiaries, not the trust. Only income that is retained by the trust and not distributed before the end of the year is taxed to the trust.

What would be taxable income for an individual (e.g., interest, dividends, rents, capital gains, etc.) is also taxable income for an estate or trust. The important tax differences are in the area of deductions, especially legal fees, trustee commissions, and other administrative expenses. For an individual, expenses of administering income-producing property are deductible, but are subject to the 2% floor for "miscellaneous itemized deductions." For an estate or trust, the expenses of administration are not subject to the 2% floor as long as the expenses are of a type that would not have been incurred if the property were not in trust. For example, investment fees will remain subject to the two percent floor because those expenses would have been the same inside or outside of the trust. However, all of the trustee's commissions and all of the legal fees relating to the administration of the trust should be fully deductible.

Even expenses that are otherwise fully deductible are still not deductible to the extent they are incurred to administer stocks or bonds generating tax-exempt income. For example, trustee commissions usually must be allocated proportionately between taxable income (deductible commissions) and tax exempt income (nondeductible commissions).

Another limitation is that administration expenses cannot be deducted for income tax purposes if they have already been deducted for estate tax purposes. If no estate tax return is required, then the expenses should obviously be claimed as income tax deductions. But if an estate tax return is required, then the trustee must sit down and figure out which will be best for the beneficiaries, to claim legal fees, trustee commissions, and other administration expenses as estate tax deductions or as income tax deductions. (These decisions sometimes affect different beneficiaries in different ways, and those differences can cause conflicts among the beneficiaries or between the beneficiaries and the trustee. For example, if your trust continues after your death for your spouse or other income beneficiary, and the expenses payable after your death are payable from principal but claimed as an income tax deduction, the income beneficiary gets a benefit, in the form of tax-free income, paid for by the remaindermen out of the principal of the trust. To eliminate these unintended shifts in benefits, courts will sometimes order "equitable adjustments" between income and principal.)

If the beneficiaries of your trust are in the top income tax brackets, it might seem that your trustee could reduce their income tax liabilities by delaying distributions for a year or two, allowing the income to be taxed at the lower income tax rates available through the trust's separate income tax brackets.

However, this won't really work, because trusts (and estates) have their own tax tables with incredibly small (that doesn't mean low) tax brackets. For example, in 1997 an unmarried individual was subject to an income tax rate of 15% on the first $24,650 of income. (Income tax brackets are adjusted annually for inflation and therefore change each year.) For a trust during the same year, only its first $1,650 of income was subject to tax at 15%. Income above $1,650 was subject to tax at higher rates. Income of a trust therefore is pushed into higher income tax brackets much sooner than single or married taxpayers. In fact, in 1997, a trust's income would be subjected to 39.6%, the top federal income tax bracket, with only $8,100 of income. Comparatively, married taxpayers filing jointly could earn as much as $271,050 before income is subjected to the same rate. Because of these narrow tax brackets, accumulating income in a trust can result in an annual tax reduction of no more than $920. (Still, that's almost $1,000 a year and in 20 or 30 years the savings can be considerable).

A second problem in the past was that accumulating income in a trust could result in an additional income tax imposed when the accumulated income was finally distributed to the beneficiaries of the trust. However, these complex "throw-back" rules were repealed by the Taxpayer Relief Act of 1997.

In chapter 16, you will find a more complete explanation of some of the complexities regarding the calculation of "distributable net income" and how that income is taxed to the beneficiaries receiving distributions from your trust. If your trust terminates following your death, and the assets in the trust are distributed to your beneficiaries, you should be aware of the following:

- Gifts and inheritances are not taxable income, so the distributions from your revocable trust to your beneficiaries are taxable income only to the extent that the trust has taxable income (interest, dividends, or rents received during the year).

- If your trust has taxable income, then distributions to your beneficiaries will carry that taxable income out to your beneficiaries regardless of whether the distribution is "income" or "principal" under state law. The exceptions to this rule are that gifts of specific dollar amounts (such as a gift of $25,000 to a friend or other named individual) and gifts of specific assets (such as a gift of your home, or 100 shares of stock) do not carry out taxable income.

- Distributions of property usually do not result in taxable gain or loss, unless the distribution is used to satisfy a gift of a specific dollar amount. For example, if a particular beneficiary is supposed to receive $20,000, a distribution of $20,000 worth of stock may result in taxable gain or loss to the trustee if the trustee's basis is not exactly equal to $20,000, just as if the trustee had sold the stock for $20,000. (Gain or loss is not likely for a revocable trust, because all of the assets of the trust received a new basis equal to fair market value at death, but it is still possible if there are changes in fair market value between the date of death and date of distribution.) However, if your trust is to be divided between your two children in equal shares, then distributing half of the stock to each child will not result in any taxable gain or loss unless the trustee specifically elects to treat the distribution as a taxable exchange. (Theoretically, gain or loss can also result if your trustee distributes different assets to different beneficiaries, instead of dividing them proportionately, unless the trust document specifically authorizes the trustee to make disproportionate distributions of assets.)

- Generally speaking the beneficiary will have the same cost basis in property received from the trust as the trustee had just before the distribution (and the same holding period, for purposes of determining whether the sale of an asset results in short-term or long-term gain or loss). The only exception is when the distribution results in gain or loss for the trustee (see above), in which case the beneficiary's basis will be the fair market value of the asset on the date of distribution (or the dollar amount of the gift satisfied by the distribution).

- If the deductions of the trust (such as legal fees, trustee commissions, or other expenses of administration) exceed the income of the trust for the year in which the trust makes its final distribution, then the beneficiaries of the trust are entitled to income tax deductions for the excess deductions of the trust. (However, the deductions may be subject to the 2% floor for miscellaneous itemized deductions.)

The above rules are the same for both trusts and estates. However, there are many income tax rules that apply only to trusts, and those rules are less favorable than the rules for estates. Fortunately, a revocable trust can now elect to be treated as part of the estate for federal income tax purposes (with the consent of the executor, if there is an executor). The election can last until six months after the federal estate tax liability of the estate has been settled, or for two years after death if no estate tax return is required. If this election is not made, there will be some significant tax differences between your revocable trust and your probate estate after your death:

- After your death, your revocable trust is entitled to a special deduction of $100 (kind of like a personal exemption for a trust). So only $100 can accumulate in the trust free of income tax. An estate is entitled to an annual deduction of $600.

- A trust must file tax returns for a calendar year. An estate can file income tax returns on the basis of a fiscal year ending during any month of the year. This gives an estate a significant advantage, because beneficiaries must report income from an estate or trust in the year in which the tax year of the trust or estate ends, not the year in which the income is earned or distributed.

  For example, suppose a decedent died in February of 1997. In the absence of election to be treated as part of his estate, his revocable trust will file an income tax return for 1997. All of the income earned by the trust and distributed to the beneficiaries during the year will be reported by the beneficiaries on their 1997 income tax returns. If the revocable trust makes the election to be treated as part of his probate estate, the trust (as part of the probate estate) could file its first income tax return for a tax year beginning in February of 1997 and ending on January 31, 1998. All of the income earned by the trust (and probate estate, if any) and distributed to the beneficiaries in 1997 must be reported by the beneficiaries on their 1998 income tax returns, not their 1997 returns, because the estate's tax year ended in 1998, not 1997. The beneficiaries have therefore deferred their income taxes for one year. The advantage? They receive the equivalent of an interest-free loan from the government for the money they would otherwise have had to pay in taxes for 1997. This one-year deferral of income can continue year after year until the election ends (six months after the federal estate tax is settled, or two years after death if no federal estate tax return is required).

An estate is not required to make any estimated tax payments for its first two tax years. This is the equivalent of an interest-free loan from the government for the amounts which otherwise would have been paid in estimated taxes. A similar rule applies to revocable trusts (even if the trust is not considered to be part of the estate) if the trust is the beneficiary of a "pour-over" will from the decedent's estate, or the trust is primarily responsible for the payment of the decedent's debts and taxes.

WHAT ASSETS SHOULD NOT BE PLACED IN A REVOCABLE LIVING TRUST?

Chapter 11 explains:

- Types of property that should not be placed into trust and the problems that may result

- The potential problem if S Corporation stock is transferred to a revocable living trust

- Why professional corporation stock is not appropriate as a revocable trust asset

- Why closely-held (Section 1244) stock should not be transferred to a revocable living trust

- Why a transfer of a partnership interest to a revocable living trust may not be wise

- What an ISO is and why it may be a poor asset to place into a revocable trust

- Why funding a revocable living trust with an IRA or pension or profit-sharing plan may result in problems

- Problems associated with funding a trust with stock, bonds, or other securities

- Problems real estate poses when transferred to a revocable trust

- How household items can be transferred to a revocable living trust

- How a revocable living trust can own a safe deposit box

- Issues associated with a transfer of life insurance to a revocable living trust

- Possible problems if oil or gas rights are transferred to a revocable living trust

- How ownership of livestock and farm equipment can be shifted to a revocable living trust

- What cannot or should not be placed into a revocable living trust other than those discussed above

Q. Are there types of property that may trigger tax or other problems if placed into a revocable living trust?

A. Yes. There are a number of assets that, if transferred to or from a revocable living trust, may result in adverse tax consequences. These assets include S corporation stock, professional corporation stock, Section 1244 stock, flower bonds, incentive stock options (ISOs) individual retirement account, (IRAs), retirement plans (pension and profit-sharing), and assets generating passive activity losses. Real estate in general presents a number of problems for trusts, and few corporate trustees are comfortable with a closely held business or unimproved real estate. Let's take a look at the most critical of these problems.

Q. What is the potential problem in funding a revocable living trust with S corporation stock?

A. An "S corporation" is a closely-held corporation that has elected under Subchapter S of the Internal Revenue Code to have the income, losses, and credits of the corporation passed through to the shareholders of the corporation, and reported on their individual income tax returns, so that the S corporation itself pays no federal income tax. The taxation of an S corporation flows through to its owners and in that sense is very much like a partnership. (State tax treatment of S corporations varies from state to state.)

Generally speaking, only individuals can be shareholders of an S corporation, subject to certain exceptions. One exception is that a trust can be a shareholder if the grantor of the trust is treated as the owner of all of the assets of the trust for federal income tax purposes (i.e., it is a "grantor trust.") A revocable trust is a grantor trust during your lifetime, but unfortunately becomes an irrevocable trust upon your death. (See chapter 10.)

There are only two ways an irrevocable trust can continue as a shareholder of an S corporation:

- If the trust has only one beneficiary and distributes all of its income, the trust (and its beneficiary) can elect to be a "qualified Subchapter S trust" (or QSST), in which case the beneficiary will effectively be considered to be the owner of the S corporation stock, and not the trust.

- A trust with more than one beneficiary may elect to be an "electing small business trust" (or ESBT), but there is a heavy tax cost for the election. All of the income of the trust must be taxed at the highest possible income tax rate *even if the income is distributed* and the trust is denied many deductions and credits ordinarily allowed to trusts.

The bottom line is that a trust that is to continue for some period of time with more than one beneficiary cannot safely and economically continue to hold S corporation stock after your death. Specifically, the permissible holding period for your trust after your death is two years. At that point, your trust must divest itself of the stock, distribute it outright to a qualified beneficiary, or transfer it to a qualified Subchapter S trust (QSST) that is eligible to hold S corporation stock. Otherwise, the benefits of the S election will be lost to all of its shareholders.

For this reason, if a significant portion of your wealth is invested in S corporation stock, a revocable living trust may not be the most appropriate long-term receptacle. The inadvertent risk of losing the S corporation election after your death is often not worth taking. If you nevertheless want to hold your S corporation stock in trust during your lifetime and following your death, make sure that your lawyer is familiar with the types of trusts that can hold S corporation stock, and that your revocable trust is written to take those rules into account.

Q. Why is professional corporation stock inappropriate as a revocable trust asset?

A. If you hold stock in a professional corporation such as a medical or dental practice, law practice, or engineering practice, you cannot place that stock in a revocable living trust. Under state law, only licensed professionals may hold the stock of a professional corporation engaged in a licensed profession. Even though a revocable living trust is considered your alter ego for income tax purposes, most states will not allow any type of trust to hold professional corporation stock either during your life or after your death. (As is the case with all the different types of assets discussed in this chapter, it is important to check with a lawyer in your state, because at least one state does allow the stock of a licensed lawyer to be held in a revocable trust.)

The best course of action for most closely held stock, including S corporation stock, is a fully funded buy-sell agreement. That way, your estate will receive cash at your death, the surviving shareholders can continue the practice, and there are no disputes or uncertainties about how to dispose of your stock (which state law will require your estate or trust to dispose of immediately following your death).

Q. Is there a disadvantage to transferring certain closely held stock to a revocable trust?

A. When a closely held or family-owned corporation is set up, most tax lawyers and accountants classify the stock of the business as "Section 1244 stock." Section 1244 of the Internal Revenue Code gives extremely favorable treatment to stock that meets certain requirements. An "Ordinary" rather than "capital" loss deduction is allowed when stock in a "small business corporation" (essentially one in which the aggregate amount of money and other property received by the corporation for its stock is $1,000,000 or less) is sold at less than its basis. Up to $50,000 per tax year ($100,000 on a joint return) is deductible.

Unfortunately, under current law, this favorable Section 1244 stock treatment is allowed only if the seller is an individual. Ordinary loss treatment is not permitted if the seller is either an estate or trust. If you placed stock in your closely held or family-owned business into your revocable living trust and the trust later sold that stock at a loss, the loss would be a capital loss rather than an ordinary loss for income tax purposes, thus severely limiting the tax effectiveness of the deduction.

There may be an easy solution. We suggest you ask tax counsel about TOD (transfer on death) registration of your closely held stock. This is a simple means of conveying the stock to the party you desire, and it avoids probate. (Unfortunately, not all states allow the TOD procedure.)

Q. Can I transfer my partnership interest into a revocable living trust?

A. Yes. A trust may hold an interest in a partnership. In most cases, however, a buy-sell agreement with the partnership is a better idea. An alternative in states that have adopted the Uniform Probate Code is to provide in the partnership agreement itself that each partner may designate a beneficiary of his or her partnership interest at the partner's death. That way, you could hold your partnership interest personally as long as you lived, and at your death your interest would pass directly to the named beneficiary without going through probate.

Q. Is an incentive stock option (ISO) a poor asset to place into a revocable trust?

A. If I you are a senior-level executive, your employer may issue you an incentive stock option. An ISO is a "grant"—a legal right to purchase stock in the employer's business—with certain tax advantages. You are not taxed on the gain either when you receive the grant or when you exercise your option under the grant to purchase stock from your employer. You report gain only if and when you sell, exchange, or dispose of the stock.

Nevertheless, there are problems when an ISO is transferred to a revocable trust. Neither the ISO nor the stock acquired through its exercise are good assets to place in a revocable living trust for the following reasons:

- An ISO has to be issued to a specific employee and can only be exercised by that employee, his or her estate, or an heir who inherits the ISO. It must be expressly nontransferable as long as the employee lives. It can't be exercised by a revocable living trust.

- If you transfer your ISO to a revocable living trust—even as a gift—the IRS may consider that transaction similar to a sale and tax you on gain realized in the disposition.

- Worse yet, there is a 2-year "danger zone," starting at the time the ISO option is granted, during which disposal of the stock will trigger gain. If the stock acquired by exercising an ISO is disposed of within one year of the date you receive it, you'll also have to report the gain.

Q. What are the problems I might face funding a revocable trust with my IRA or pension/profit-sharing plan proceeds?

A. First of all, you can't transfer assets from your IRA or pension or profit-sharing plan without immediately realizing taxable income on the transfer. You can withdraw the money from your retirement plan, pay the income taxes on the withdrawal, and then transfer the money to your revocable trust. But withdrawing money from a retirement plan before you need the money or are required to withdraw the money makes absolutely no sense, because you will be paying taxes before you need to pay the taxes and will be losing the advantage of tax deferral on the future earnings of the retirement plan. Therefore, the most you can do is name your revocable trust as the *beneficiary* of your IRA or qualified retirement benefits, to receive the balance of the proceeds upon your death. However, you probably don't want to do that, either. Why not?

The problem with IRAs and pension and profit sharing plans (which we will group together with the general term "retirement plan") is that the distributions that are (or would have been) taxable income to you during your lifetime are also taxable income to your beneficiaries after your death, even though the benefits are also subject to federal (and in many cases state) estate tax. (Any non-deductible contributions you made with after-tax income during your lifetime can be received income tax free either during your lifetime or after your death) So there are at least two and in many cases at least three levels of tax on IRAs and pension/profit-sharing distributions. Unfortunately, there is no "step-up" in basis which eliminates the income tax on retirement benefits. All your beneficiaries will get is an income tax deduction for whatever estate tax might be paid on the benefits. Tax planning for retirement benefits therefore means that you have to take into account both the potential estate tax liabilities and the potential income tax liabilities.

If you are married, current law allows your spouse to receive retirement benefits payable by reason of your death and roll the benefits over to her (or his) own IRA. That means that your spouse would be able to continue to defer any income tax on the retirement benefits, and the future income from the retirement benefits, until he or she begins to withdraw from the IRA after age 59-1/2 (or is required to make withdrawals after age 70-1/2). (And the retirement benefits payable to your spouse would also qualify for the federal estate marital deduction, so there would be no estate tax payable on the retirement benefits at your death.) Therefore, naming your spouse as the beneficiary of your retirement benefits will probably allow for the greatest deferral of income, and will not necessarily result in any unnecessary death taxes.

(Some experts have suggested that it *might* be possible to name your spouse's revocable trust as the beneficiary of your retirement benefits instead of your spouse, because your spouse and the trust are usually considered to be the same entity for income tax purposes. However, there is no tax benefit to this arrangement and many authorities believe it is most likely that your spouse will *not* be able to roll over benefits from an IRA or qualified pension or profit-sharing plan to a revocable living trust tax free.)

If you want to minimize income taxes on retirement plan distributions by delaying those distributions as long as possible or spreading them over as long a period as possible, then naming your revocable trust as the beneficiary of your retirement benefits, instead of your spouse (or instead of your children, if your spouse has predeceased you), creates a number of difficult tax problems:

- Retirement benefits can be paid out over the lifetime of a "designated beneficiary." A trust can qualify as a "designated beneficiary," but only if a number of technical requirements have been met. One technical requirement is that, if you have already reached retirement age and started receiving distributions from the retirement plan, the trust you name as beneficiary must be *irrevocable,* not revocable.

- If the beneficiary designation of your revocable trust does not comply with the technical requirements for a "designated beneficiary," all of the retirement benefits must be paid out within 5 years after your death. Distribution within this relatively short time means that the benefits of tax deferral have been greatly reduced, if not lost entirely. (In the past, there have been advantages to distributions in a lump sum from pension or profit-sharing plans, but those benefits have been reduced to five-year averaging, and even that benefit will end in the year 2000.)

- If you want your retirement benefits to be distributed to your trust over your spouse's lifetime *and* qualify the trust for the federal estate marital deduction, the trust must guarantee that your spouse receive that portion of each retirement plan distribution representing the current income of the retirement plan. (The failure of the trust to qualify for the marital deduction could be a tax disaster, because it could mean that the retirement benefits are taxed at your death and, after they have been received by your spouse, are taxed again at your spouse's death.)

- If you want your revocable trust to divide into separate trusts after your death, such as the creation of a *by-pass trust* to use your federal estate tax unified credit (see chapter 13) or separate trusts for each of your children, there is a danger that the division of the retirement benefits will cause them to become taxable income immediately, even if you or your trust have elected to receive the retirement plan distributions in installments.

Of course, there may be non-tax reasons that lead you to name your revocable trust as the beneficiary of your retirement benefits, such as the fact that your children are minors. In that case, you and your legal counsel should consider naming your spouse as *primary beneficiary* and naming your revocable trust as *contingent beneficiary,* so it will receive the benefits only if your spouse predeceases you.

Naming your spouse as the primary beneficiary does not foreclose all estate tax planning, because if your combined estates are more than the unified credit applicable exclusion amount ($600,000 in 1997 and increasing by steps to $1,000,000 in 2006) and your own estate is not sufficient to fund a *by-pass trust* (see chapter 13) with the amount that would pass tax free using the federal estate tax unified credit, your spouse can *disclaim* (refuse to accept) part or all of the retirement benefits, in which case the disclaimed portion of the benefits will go into your revocable trust. This plan can give your spouse a great deal of flexibility in planning for both estate taxes and income taxes following your death.

The law in this area is unfortunately arcane, hair-pulling complex, and terribly important to understand and plan for in advance. You should therefore not name your revocable trust as beneficiary of your IRA or pension or profit-sharing benefits unless you obtain the advice of a knowledgeable tax advisor.

Q. What problems may occur in funding a revocable living trust with stocks, bonds, or other securities?

A. There is no question that you can transfer both listed and closely held stock to a trustee. A specific law adopted by many states, called the Uniform Act for Simplification of Fiduciary Security Transfers (UASFST), specifically permits such transfers. Often, the stock transfer company will request that you title the stock in the name of the trustee as follows:

"Charles Parker, Trustee, Charles Parker Revocable Trust, U/A 1/1/95"

For administrative convenience, most authorities suggest opening an account with a broker so that the broker can register the securities in "street name." This allows the brokerage firm to execute buy or sell orders for the trustee without the need to give each stock transfer agent a copy of the trust. The monthly statements of income and stock values from the brokerage firm will also facilitate the trustee's record keeping. (Call and ask your stockbroker if there will be any additional charge for this service. Usually, there is not.)

Bearer bonds are securities that are not registered in the name of the owner and can be negotiated by whoever possesses them. They are generally transferred to the trustee by a general assignment or bill of sale adequately describing them. For security purposes, we suggest that the trustee open a special safe deposit box in which to keep bearer bonds safely and to avoid the problems that could occur if the trustee commingled bearer bonds with his or her personal assets.

Q. What problems does real estate pose as a revocable trust asset?

A. There are a number of advantages to transferring real estate (particularly real estate outside of the state in which you live) to a revocable trust. The single biggest advantage is that once the title to real estate is transferred to your trust, the need for "ancillary" (multiple) probate proceedings outside of your home state is eliminated. That in turn can result in significant savings.

However, there can be disadvantages to transferring real estate to a trust. So before you transfer real estate to a trust, be sure to check with your tax counsel. If you own real estate which is located outside of your home state, check with tax counsel in the state in which the real estate is located. State or local law may impose a real estate transfer tax when title is changed to the trust even though it is your revocable trust. Even though no consideration changes hands in the transfer of title and even though you essentially own and control the same property in the same degree as before, the conveyance could trigger a state transfer tax.

You may also lose the creditor protection afforded by your state's statutory homestead exemption. (Homestead exemption laws allow a homeowner or head of family to designate a house as his or her homestead and to exempt that homestead from execution for his or her general debts.) For example, if you record a homestead deed in Florida to a revocable trust, you may lose your homestead exemption for property tax purposes.

You must also consider the impact of contributing real property that has potential environmental problems to a revocable trust. As explained in chapter 4, recent legislation has limited the liability of trustees and other fiduciaries for personal liability relating to contamination that occurred before the property was placed in trust, or before the trustee became trustee. That means, if you do not put the property in trust, your executor will not be responsible for any environmental contamination that occurred during your lifetime. However, if during your lifetime you transfer to your revocable trust a commercial property or other property on which there are activities that could cause environmental liability, your trustees could become personally liable for any contamination that occurs during your lifetime and while they are serving as trustees.

The trustee of a revocable (or irrevocable) trust should know that he or she may be personally liable, for fines, cleanup costs, and damage to the environment caused by hazardous waste deposited in real estate. Most professional trustees therefore require a "Phase I environmental report" before they will accept trustee responsibilities if nonresidential real estate is involved. (Obviously, the potential liabilities are even clearer if underground petroleum storage is involved.)

There are difficult issues even when the real estate will generate no transfer tax and has no environmental cleanup problems associated with it. For example, what type of deed should be used to convey title to the property to the trust? Many authorities believe that a "quit claim" deed is most suitable because it conveys only such title as the grantor has at the time of conveyance. However, many recording clerks are not accustomed to dealing with quit claim deeds or real estate titles owned by a trust. Often, they will require a copy of the trust instrument before they will allow the trustee to transfer title to the property, or when the trust ends or if the trust's real estate is sold.

Real estate title companies will require an affidavit (typically one or two pages) certifying that the trustee has authority to make a given conveyance. What if the deed was originally recorded in the name of "Martha Feinstein, Trustee of the Samuel Feinstein Trust" and Martha has died? The successor trustee would have to prove (presumably by presenting a death certificate of Martha's demise) why Martha couldn't convey the real estate. The successor will also have to document his or her authority to act as the new trustee. Some authorities have suggested that the answer is simply to take title as "John Doe, Trustee." Supposedly, title can then be transferred without the need to disclose the terms of the trust itself or names and shares of the various beneficiaries.

Banks and trust companies operating as trustees may find that state law creates another impediment: Your state may not allow a bank or trust company to hold title to real estate that is located outside of the state where the bank is incorporated or authorized to conduct business. If the bank is authorized to operate in a number of states, this may minimize or eliminate the problem. But bankers often worry that holding title to real estate in another state may mean that they are "doing business" in that other state, perhaps becoming subject to taxes or regulations in that other state, or subject to the jurisdiction of the courts of that other state for lawsuits having nothing to do with your trust. One solution to this potential problem is to stipulate in your trust that for real estate located outside your state, the bank may appoint a substitute trustee from that state just for that particular piece of property.

Yet another problem might arise if you are transferring title of real estate to a revocable living trust but the property in question is mortgaged and the mortgage includes a "due-on-sale" clause that accelerates the entire debt if the property is sold or transferred. Federally insured lenders are prohibited from exercising a due-on-sale clause for a transfer of residential real estate to a revocable trust (and for certain other transfers among family members).

But a mortgage from a state chartered bank or private mortgage company, or a mortgage on non-residential property, might allow the lender to demand payment of the mortgage. Although many lenders are willing to waive that right, the lender might be tempted to demand repayment (or refinancing at a higher rate) if interest rates have increased significantly. (The federal prohibition on exercising due-on-sale clauses is also subject to certain conditions: There must be no transfer of the right to occupy the property, the request for waiver of the lender's right must be in writing, and there must be no change in the borrower's obligations.)

One way to avoid the potential acceleration of the loan when property is transferred to a trust is to make the legal transfer to the trustee but hold back on the actual recording of the deed (another cost to consider) until you (the grantor) die. The unrecorded deed can be reclaimed and destroyed if you revoke the trust, reclaim the property, and later decide to sell it. Because the rules regarding delivery of a deed and its importance in conveying title vary from state to state, the exact implications of an unrecorded deed depend on the laws of the state in which the property is located. Typically, however, even an unrecorded deed is sufficient to raise a presumption that you meant to complete delivery. Ordinarily, therefore, it will be valid and binding on everyone but an unsecured creditor.

Some practitioners have also reported that the transfer of a residence to a revocable trust can cause problems with homeowners insurance. You may therefore wish to consult with your insurance company or insurance agent before transferring title to your home to a revocable trust.

Q. How do I transfer my household items to my revocable living trust?

A. At first glance, it seems to be impossible. How could you possibly transfer ownership of something that doesn't have a formal title or form of registration? This same problem seems to apply to your jewelry, clothing, and even valuable art and other collectibles.

There is a solution. Your lawyer can prepare a *deed of gift* (or in some cases a *bill of sale*) from you to your trustee (which may be from you to yourself as trustee). The document by which you transfer ownership should specify that the trustee is the legal owner and your physical possession of the item is consistent with the terms of the trust and with the express permission of the trust, rather than a personal retention of ownership. In other words, you must meticulously document the fact that you have transferred legal title to the trustee, even though you appear to continue to use, possess, and enjoy the furniture or other item. Perhaps the best way to evidence the trustee's title is to write to your insurance agent, requesting that the ownership of household property be changed and that the insurer pay proceeds in the event of a fire, theft, and so on to the trustee. All correspondence from that date forward should be between the insurer and you as trustee. Whenever the owner's signature is required, you should sign as trustee.

When transferring valuable items such as furniture, art, or jewelry to a revocable trust, always check with your insurance company or insurance agent to make certain that your homeowners insurance (or the trust's homeowners insurance, if your home as been transferred to the trust) will continue to cover the theft or loss of those items after title has been transferred to your trust.

Q. Can my revocable living trust own a safe deposit box?

A. Yes. It is possible for a revocable living trust to open a safe deposit box at a bank. The bank will require a copy (probably certified) of the trust document. The procedures for what happens if one or more trustees should die vary widely from state to state. Typically, the box will be sealed if the sole trustee dies (especially if the trustee is also the grantor). Once the box is inventoried by a state death tax official and a successor trustee is appointed, the contents of the box will be released.

Q. Can I transfer life insurance on my life to a revocable living trust?

A. Yes, although there is no tax or administrative advantage in transferring *ownership* of the policy to the trust. We advise merely naming your revocable living trust as the beneficiary of your life insurance. A change of beneficiary form created by the American Bar Association and the Trust Division of the American Bankers Association will be accepted by almost all trusts and insurance companies. Your insurance agent or lawyer should be able to obtain this form for you at no charge. (More on the taxation of life insurance in trusts is available from *Tax Planning With Life Insurance: Financial Professional's Edition*, which can be obtained by calling 800 950 1210, or *Tools and Techniques of Life Insurance Planning*, which can be obtained by calling 800 543 0874).

In most cases when a life insurance policy and revocable trust are to be used in tandem, estate tax savings are not a major objective. This is because (1) the estate is likely to be well under the unified credit applicable exclusion amount ($600,000 in 1997 and increasing by steps to $1,000,000 in 2006), (2) the combined estates of the husband and wife are less than (or not significantly above) the amount sheltered by their combined unified credits and the life insurance proceeds can be used to fund a *by-pass trust* (see chapter 13) that will use up the insured spouse's unified credit and minimize (or eliminate) any estate tax in either estate, or (3) the marital deduction will eliminate the estate tax and the surviving spouse is young and healthy enough to consume (or give away) all or most of the insurance proceeds during his or her lifetime. In those cases, the trust's main charge will be the division, conservation, investment, and management of the insurance proceeds. If saving estate taxes are a major objective, we suggest you read chapter 17 for an explanation of the advantages of irrevocable life insurance trusts.

Before you set up a revocable living trust as the receptacle for life insurance proceeds, you should check with your insurance agent about the advantages of different life insurance settlement options. For instance, without any of the costs of setting up a trust, you can have the insurance company pay out proceeds to your beneficiaries in a series of periodic payments lasting for a fixed number of years, in a series of payments of fixed monthly amounts, or even for the lifetime of the beneficiary (or beneficiaries). If you want to guarantee your beneficiaries a come-hell-or-high-water payment in each month, life insurance settlement options are a viable alternative to a revocable trust. In fact, life insurance settlement options have been called the "poor man's trust" but should be considered even by wealthy people in certain situations.

Your trust should specifically allow (but not require) your trustee to use life insurance proceeds to purchase assets from your estate or to make fully secured interest-bearing loans to your estate. This will give your estate cash to pay federal and state death taxes and other estate administration expenses. It will also ensure that your beneficiaries keep the property you now own.

Occasionally, someone will try to get the life insurance out of their taxable estate by transferring ownership of the policy to their spouse, yet have a revocable trust named as the beneficiary of the policy. We strongly recommend against this course of action. Here's why: When a policy is owned by someone other than the insured, the payment of the proceeds to anyone other than the owner is considered to be a taxable gift by the owner. If your spouse is the owner of your insurance and your revocable trust is the beneficiary, your spouse will be considered to have made a taxable gift to the beneficiaries of your trust upon your death, which could result in gift tax. Even worse, your spouse's interests as a beneficiary of your trust may cause the trust to be included in your spouse's taxable estate even after paying gift tax on the gift to the trust. This arrangement is therefore a potential tax nightmare and should be avoided.

Q. What are the problems, if any, in transferring my oil and gas rights to my revocable living trust?

A. The answer to this question depends largely on two factors: First, what rights do you own? Second, what form of conveyance is required by the state in which the mineral interests lie?

The problems are relatively minor mechanical ones, which can be solved with patience and good legal advice. If you have mineral rights, you may need a mineral deed and an assignment of your oil and gas lease. If your property is already producing oil or gas, once you've transferred your rights to your trust, the trustee must give the operator a copy of the conveyance of your rights to the trust. Future royalty payments will then be made to the trust under a "division order" prepared by the oil or gas operator.

Q. I'm a rancher. Can I place my ownership of livestock and farm equipment into a revocable living trust?

A. Yes. Your livestock brand can be registered in the name of your revocable living trust. Once you've placed the livestock brand in the name of the trust, all future livestock with that brand on it will automatically become part of the trust's assets.

To transfer crops and farm equipment to a revocable living trust, you'll have to have your lawyer draft a bill of sale (or deed of gift) for both growing and stored crops and change the registration of tractors, trucks, vans, and other titled equipment,

Q. Is there property that I can't or shouldn't place into a revocable living trust?

A. There are several types of property interests which can't be assigned.

You can't assign your future earnings to your revocable trust. (Or, even if you can, the assignment would be a meaningless exercise with no tax or legal consequences.)

Typically, personal service contracts are nontransferable. You can't assign the right to another individual's personal services to a revocable trust unless your contract with that person specifically permits such an assignment.

There are many types of litigation claims, such as personal injury claims or claims for libel or slander, which can't be assigned until after a judgment has been entered.

You can't assign your interests in other trusts or estates if the trust document or will has a "spendthrift" clause, and you usually can't assign any interest in the estate of a living person.

You can't transfer the obligation to pay your own debts to a revocable trust (at least not without the consent of your creditor, who has absolutely no reason to agree to such an assignment and many reasons not to agree).

SHORT-FORM SECURITIES TRUSTS

Chapter 12 explains:

- What a totten trust is

- How a "short-form" securities trust can serve as a totten trust for stocks and bonds

- What a P.O.D. or T.O.D. account is and how it works

- The disadvantages of the P.O.D. or T.O.D. account and how the short-form securities trust avoids those problems

- How to create a short-form securities trust (and provides a sample form)

Q. *What is a totten trust?*

A. Assume you want to control a bank savings account while you are alive but would like whatever cash is in the account at your death to pass automatically and without probate to a specified person. One of the most common and convenient ways of titling bank savings accounts to accomplish those objectives is called a *totten trust*. (The term *totten trust* comes from the name of an early case on this point of law.)

In a totten trust, the depositor places money into a savings account in the name of the depositor "in trust for" a child, niece, or nephew, or other person. The account is still considered to be the property of the depositor who retains total control of the account. However, after the depositor's death, the account and all proceeds of the account pass to the named beneficiary immediately and without probate.

Similar to a totten trust is a bank account which is "payable on death" to a named beneficiary, sometimes called a "P.O.D." account, as described below.

The totten trust is a way for you to be sure that a particular account will pass to a named beneficiary upon your death and it will avoid probate. But it will not avoid income, estate, or inheritance taxes.

Q. Is there a totten trust for stocks and bonds?

A. Historically, most states have not allowed securities (stocks and bonds) to pass "in trust for" a beneficiary unless the investor has created a formal written trust (usually with the aid of a lawyer). The cost of preparing a trust for a relatively small account usually discourages the depositor, and he or she usually opts for putting the assets in joint names (which can be a taxable gift) or just ignoring the whole thing and letting the securities pass as part of the probate estate (which may be a more costly result).

Fortunately, some states (such as Pennsylvania) have enacted statutes allowing securities (and brokerage accounts) to be registered "payable on death" (POD) or "transfer on death" (TOD) to a named beneficiary, as explained below.

Q. What is a POD. or TOD account?

A. A few states have enacted legislation permitting *payable on death* (POD) accounts or *transfer on death* (TOD) accounts or security registrations. With this type account or security registration, which is essentially the same as a totten trust, a beneficiary may be named in the same fashion as with savings accounts in banks. POD. and TOD designations are a big step forward, and are becoming increasingly popular. This enables you to register a stock or bond or security account in a way that states who your beneficiary will be if you die while owning that security. In some states you can name a trustee as beneficiary.

In most cases you include the words, "transfer on death" (TOD) or "payable on death" (POD) after the name of the owner and before the name of the beneficiary (or beneficiaries since you can name more than one). If your beneficiary dies before you do, the security will pass as part of your probate estate. Some states allow you to avoid this result by indicating an intent to substitute other beneficiaries. Pennsylvania, for example, allows you to name the children and other descendants of the deceased beneficiary by adding the letters "LDPS" (lineal descendants per stirpes) after the primary beneficiary's name.

Q. Is there a better way to hold securities than a P.O.D. or T.O.D.?

A. The *short-form securities trust* may be an even a better way to hold securities. Merely naming a beneficiary on an investment account is just one of several steps that you should take for sensible estate planning. Using the short-form securities trust gives you the following choices, which are not possible with P.O.D. or T.O.D. accounts:

- You can select a successor trustee to manage your account if you are physically or mentally disabled. You can also specify an alternate successor trustee to take over if the first successor trustee fails or chooses not to serve.

- You can name alternate beneficiaries so that if the primary beneficiary predeceases you, the security will pass directly and immediately to the secondary beneficiary without passing through probate.

- You can impose limitations on the authority of the trustee(s) to invest. This gives you, the investor, indirect control of broad-based decisions concerning rollovers, renewals, or alternative investments.

- You can specify the percentages of the proceeds for each of your named beneficiaries. For instance, an investor with five children does not have to leave each child an equal share.

- A successor trustee can be directed to distribute funds when minors are involved. This will allow assets to be held until the minors are not only of legal majority but are also ready emotionally and intellectually to handle the investment.

- The trust can specify how the various beneficiaries will bear the burden of federal and state death taxes on their share.

- It is possible to amend or revoke the account without interrupting the compounding of interest and accruals. This makes it easy to retitle an account and change beneficiaries. (Most banks require that beneficiaries can be changed only at a renewal date and not during the term of a certificate of deposit.)

Although the short-form securities trust is relatively simple and inexpensive, it is not a panacea. Check with your lawyer and accountant to be sure the form is appropriate and is compatible with your will and other estate planning documents. Your lawyer may need to make certain modifications so that the form complies with your state's law. Remember that the short-form securities trust, just as any other trust, should be viewed as just one part of an overall plan to reduce your estate costs and accomplish your personal and tax objectives.

Q. How do I create a short-form securities trust?

A. You must sign a form created by your lawyer (see the sample form that follows), and have it notarized before presenting a photocopy to your securities broker for the broker's records. The broker then makes all future purchases in the name of the trust. You must specify the name of the trust-for example, "The John Doe Family Trust."

Trusts/Leimberg Associates Books: 610-527-5216

Sample Short-Form Securities Trust

DEED OF TRUST

DATE _____, 19__

1. NAME OF THIS TRUST:

2. GRANTOR/TRUSTOR: _____
   ADDRESS: _____
   _____

3. TRUSTEE: _____
   ADDRESS: _____
   _____

4. CO-TRUSTEE: _____
   ADDRESS: _____
   _____

5. SUCCESSOR TRUSTEE: _____
   ADDRESS: _____
   _____

   ALTERNATE SUCCESSOR TRUSTEE: _____
   ADDRESS: _____
   _____

7. BENEFICIARIES OF TRUST (Name, address, relationship, and share):
   _____
   _____
   _____
   _____

8. ASSET   INVESTMENT   LIMITATIONS:
   _____
   _____
   _____
   _____
   _____

I (we), the undersigned and above named, hereby create a trust wherein I designate myself as Trustee, and shall hold and invest the assets of this trust (item 8) in a depository of my choice or that of my successor trustee, for the purposes intended and upon the following terms:

I.   LIFETIME TRUST: During my lifetime, I or my successor trustee shall keep principal invested and distribute as follows:

A.   As much of the principal and income as I desire to consume, or direct to be paid, or as my successor trustee may from time to time think desirable to be used for my support, health, maintenance and comfort shall be distributed to me or used by the trustee for my benefit, and

B.   Any remaining income not so used shall from time to time be accumulated and added to principal.

II.   DISPOSITION AT DEATH: Upon my death, all undistributed principal and income shall be paid to my Beneficiaries in the manner and shares as listed above in item 7.

III.   MINORITY/DISABILITY CLAUSE: In the event that any share becomes distributable to a person under twenty-one (21) years of age, such distributable share shall be held in trust by my successor trustee until that person becomes twenty-one (21) years of age, or if in the opinion of my successor trustee, a beneficiary is disabled and unable to manage his or her own business or financial affairs, then in the discretion of my trustee, the income and principal of such share shall be applied toward the support, health, education and welfare of such person, directly without the intervention of a guardian. The receipt of such funds by any person or institution, as my successor trustee shall select to receive disbursements of income and principal, shall be a complete release of my successor trustee.

IV.   SUCCESSOR TRUSTEE: If any trustee ceases to act or is incapable of acting, the successor trustee shall then assume all the trustee's authority, powers, and obligations and shall prepare and submit an affidavit as to the former trustee's failure or inability to act, and such affidavit together with a certification from a physician shall be accepted and relied upon by any person, financial institution, depository, firm, or corporation. Should my successor trustee or co-trustee predecease me, or be incapable of acting for any reason, I then appoint my alternate successor trustee, or such of them living if more than one, to serve as sole trustee, upon the preparation and supervision of an affidavit and physician's certificate as set forth above.

V.   DEATH TAXES: Unless my will provides otherwise, my successor trustee shall pay all inheritance, estate, or death taxes (including interest and penalties) attributable to each beneficiary's share or amount of trust principal, and deduct same prior to distribution of this trust.

VI.   PROTECTIVE PROVISION: To the greatest extent permitted by law, no interest in income or principal shall be assignable by any beneficiary or available to anyone having a claim against a beneficiary before actual payment to the beneficiary.

Trusts/Leimberg Associates Books: 610-527-5216

VII.   POWERS RESERVED BY ME: I shall have the following powers, exercisable whenever and as often as I may wish:

A.   To withdraw any or all of the principal;

B.   To add to this trust;

C.   To amend, alter, or revoke this trust in whole or in part by a writing, other than a Will at any time before my death.

VIII.   MANAGEMENT PROVISIONS: I and my successors are authorized to exercise the following powers:

A.   To retain and to invest in all forms of real and personal property (including proprietary stock and bond mutual funds operated by my corporate trustee), regardless of any limitations imposed by law on investments by trustees, or any principal of law concerning investment diversification, subject, however, to any limitations as defined under "Asset Investment Limitations" (item 8).

B.   To sell any investments held by this trust or terminate any accounts when the account is of little or no value;

C.   To join in any merger, reorganization, voting-trust plan or other concerted actions of security holders, and to delegate discretionary duties with respect thereto;

D.   To allocate any property received or charge incurred to principal or income or partly to each, without regard to any law defining principal and income;

E.   To distribute in kind and to allocate specific assets among the beneficiaries (including any trust hereunder) in such proportions in accordance with Article II, providing that the market value of any beneficiary's share is not affected by such allocation.

These management authorities shall extend to all accounts in this trust, and at any time held by any trustee in this trust, and shall continue in full force until the actual distribution of all such property, except as specifically stated by amendments to this trust, if any. All powers, authorities and discretion granted by this trust shall be in addition to those granted by law and shall be exercisable without leave of court, and shall terminate when all distributions have been made to the named beneficiaries, or their heirs.

IX.   MANAGEMENT RESTRICTIONS: I direct that the reinvestment of principal payments and income resulting from this trust and made by successor trustees be restricted to the types and kinds of investments as specified in item 8 of this trust.

X.   RIGHTS OF INCOME: All income shall be distributed proportionately and any undistributed income does not vest in a beneficiary until it has been distributed.

XI.   MISCELLANEOUS: I direct that:

A.   The use of the masculine shall be deemed to include the feminine or neuter and the use of the singular to included the plural, and vice versa.

B.   The term "minor" shall be deemed to refer to any individual who has not attained the age of twenty-one (21) years.

C.   Any trustee may resign at any time without court approval;

D.   Should any corporate trustee be appointed by my successor trustees, the said corporate trustee shall be compensated in accordance with its fee schedule that is in effect at the time the services are performed.

XII. SPECIAL   PROVISIONS:

IN WITNESS WHEREOF, I have hereunto set my hand and seal.

WITNESSETH:

_____   _____(GRANTOR)

_____   _____(TRUSTEE)

COMMONWEALTH OF PENNSYLVANIA   :
                                                   :

COUNTY OF   :

On this _____ day of_____, 19_____, before me, a Notary Public, personally appeared _____known to me (satisfactorily proven) to be the person_ whose name_ is/are subscribed to the within instrument, and acknowledged that _he_ executed the same for the purposed therein contained.

IN WITNESS WHEREOF, I have hereunto set my hand and official seal.

                                       _____

                                              NOTARY PUBLIC

Classic Marital/Family Trusts

MARITAL TRUST

Amounts passing to this trust are estate tax free because of the marital deduction

When you die:

FAMILY TRUST

Amounts passing to this Trust are estate tax free because of the unified credit

There will be no Federal Estate Tax at your death

Classic Family/Marital Trusts

Your Spouse Receives:

FAMILY TRUST

- All Income for life
- Principal at Trustee's Discretion
- Right to demand principal for health, education, maintenance, and support

  Power to annually withdraw up to greater of $5,000/5%

Amounts remaining at spouse's death escape untaxed

MARITAL TRUST

- All income for life
- Any and all trust assets on demand
- Spouse can consume, use or leave to anyone

Amounts remaining at spouse's death taxed in spouse's estate

QTIP Trust

**Your spouse
for life**

**When you die
trust created**

*Trust pays
all income to*

**No estate tax at your
death due to marital
deduction**

**At spouse's death, assets
paid in time/manner to
parties you choose**
*Assets included in
spouse's estate*

TRUST

· Trusts/Leimberg Associates Books

MARITAL AND BY-PASS TRUSTS

Chapter 13 explains:

- What the marital deduction is and why it is so important

- What's wrong with the marital deduction: the downsides

- What the unified credit is

- The tax trap of over-using (or "over-funding") the marital deduction

- A marital trust is not necessary to obtain the marital deduction

- What a marital trust provides and how it works

- What a by-pass (nonmarital) or family trust is and why this trust is usually drafted together with a marital trust

- Typical by-pass trust provisions

- How additional flexibility can be built into your by-pass trust

- What a QTIP trust is and how it works

- Wording often found in QTIP trusts

- The estate tax cost of the QTIP trust at the surviving spouse's death

- Other disadvantages of a QTIP trust

- What an estate trust is

- What an estate trust provides

- Disadvantages of an estate trust

- What a QDT is

- What's wrong with a QDT

- A solution to the QDT dilemma

- Special factors to consider in ultra-large estates

Q. What is the marital deduction?

A. To understand the importance of the marital deduction trust and its very special companion, the credit equivalent by-pass trust (CEBT), you must first understand and appreciate the incredible opportunity that the federal estate tax marital deduction presents.

For most married couples, no estate tax deduction is more important—nor is any estate planning tool more powerful—than the federal estate and gift tax marital deduction. This is a deduction allowed to a married couple that makes it possible (in most cases) to leave your entire estate to your surviving spouse—yet pay not one penny in federal estate taxes. (Actually, you can leave all or any portion of your estate to your surviving spouse but only the net amount actually passing qualifies for this marital deduction.) Many states have similar marital deductions.

The federal estate and gift marital deduction is based on the net value (gross value of assets less any debts, expenses, or taxes payable on or from the assets) of the property left from one spouse to another at death or given to one spouse by the other during lifetime.

For example, Ted could leave his wife Alex his entire $3,000,000, estate. Because of the federal estate tax marital deduction, no federal estate tax would be due from his estate. In fact, because the marital deduction is unlimited, his estate could be $10,000,000 or even $100,000,000 (or more), and in most cases there would be no tax at Ted's death. The difference, as you can see in the accompanying table, is significant:

Trusts/Leimberg Associates Books: 610-527-5216

Taxable Estate	Federal Estate Tax if Marital Deduction Is Allowed	Federal Estate Tax with No Marital Deduction (1997)	Additional Money Surviving Spouse Can Invest, Spend, or Give Away
$1,000,000	0	$119,800	$153,000
2,000,000	0	488,400	588,000
5,000,000	0	1,806,400	2,198,000
10,000,000	0	3,880,400	4,948,000
20,000,000	0	8,281,200	10,948,000

Note that these figures significantly understate the true advantage to the marital deduction because they show only the federal estate tax and do not illustrate state death taxes.

Q. What's wrong with the marital deduction?

A. Nothing. The federal estate tax marital deduction is real. It does permit a person to leave all (or any portion of) his or her entire estate to a surviving spouse and pay no federal estate tax.

But there is no free lunch in the tax law. When the surviving spouse dies, the IRS will be there to impose estate taxes not only on what the surviving spouse owned before he or she received your property but also what you've left your spouse as well. In other words, the federal estate tax marital deduction delays—but doesn't eliminate—the federal estate tax—*unless* your surviving spouse can use up or give away what he or she receives under your marital deduction.

So the marital deduction is like an interest-free loan from the IRS in the amount of the deferred tax (to the extent that it's still there when your surviving spouse dies). At that point, all of your assets (and all appreciation from the date the surviving spouse receives your assets) plus all of the survivor's own assets are taxed at cumulatively higher and higher rates.

Fortunately, the longer your spouse lives, the longer he or she will have to give the property away or use it up during his or her lifetime. Since each person can give away up to $10,000 each year per donee (including children, grandchildren, siblings, and even people or organizations who are not related to you), your surviving spouse can give away (as well as consume) an incredible amount that will never be subject to federal estate tax. (The $10,000 figure may be adjusted for inflation after 1998.)

The following table illustrates life expectancy according to the IRS annuity tables. Consider how much a spouse can give away gift and estate tax free if the spouse has two children and three grandchildren (five donees) and gives each one the maximum $10,000 a year. That's as much as $100,000 a year that escapes gift and estate tax altogether. The following chart, courtesy of the *NumberCruncher* program (610-527-5216) illustrates the life expectancy a person has at given ages. Multiply this number by the maximum amount your surviving spouse can give away gift tax free each year (number of donees x $10,000) and you'll see that it's substantial.

Current Age	Life Expectancy (Years)	Life Expectancy (Age)
50	33.1	83
55	28.6	84
60	24.2	84
65	20.0	85
70	16.0	86
75	12.5	88

Q. What is the federal estate tax unified credit?

A. The federal gift and estate tax unified credit is a credit against the federal gift tax or federal estate tax that would otherwise have to be paid on gifts you make during your lifetime or your estate at death. Under the Taxpayer Relief Act of 1997, the unified credit is scheduled to increase in steps from 1997 to 2006. If you have not yet made any taxable gifts, the unified credit will be equivalent to one of the following exclusions from your estate:

Year of Death	Applicable Exclusion Amount
1997	$600,000
1998	$625,000
1999	$650,000
2000 & 2001	$675,000
2002 & 2003	$700,000
2004	$850,000
2005	$950,000
2006 and later	$1,000,000

If you are not married and have not made any gifts using your unified credit, only that part of your estate in excess of the applicable exclusion amount is subject to federal estate tax. If you are married, the unified credit can avoid estate tax on any part of your estate that does not pass to your spouse and does not qualify for the marital deduction.

Q. Is it possible to over-use (or "over-fund") the marital deduction?

A. The tax trap! Most (but not all) people reading this book should take full advantage of the marital deduction. However, if your assets are appreciating very rapidly and the total is greater than your surviving spouse could possibly consume or give away, leaving everything to your spouse will set up the survivor's estate for what planners call the "second death wallop!" That's another way of saying that a large part of what you leave your spouse—and all the growth on it—will be involuntarily left by her to the IRS.

Suppose, for example, Ted had a $600,000 estate and Alex, his wife, had a $1,000,000 estate. Ted could leave everything to his spouse. At his death, because of the marital deduction, there would be no federal estate tax. So far, so good. If Alex dies in 2006 or thereafter, the first $1,000,000—the assets she owned on her own—would be estate tax free because of the federal estate tax unified credit (for which the applicable exclusion amount is $600,000 in 1997 but increases to $1,000,000 in 2006, as explained above). But the $600,000 Ted left her—assuming she hadn't spent or given it away—plus any growth that occurred between Ted's death and Alex's death—would be subjected to federal estate taxes when she died. The tax on that additional $600,000 would be $184,200. (Federal estate tax rates start at 37 percent above the $600,000 exclusion amount, or 41% above the $1,000,000 exclusion amount, and they can range as high as a confiscatory 55 percent on every dollar, with a 5 percent surtax on ultra large estates, i.e., estates in excess of about $10,000,000.)

The point is, leaving everything to a surviving spouse may needlessly expose your assets to unnecessary estate tax and make the IRS (and your state) an unintended beneficiary of a large portion of the present worth and future growth in your estate. One solution is the CEBT, the credit equivalent by-pass trust used in combination with one or more of the marital deduction trusts described in this chapter.

Q. Do I need to use a marital trust to obtain the marital deduction?

A. No. The federal estate tax marital deduction is allowed for transfers that are outright—or tantamount to outright—as well as transfers made in trusts specifically designed to qualify for the marital deduction. So you could leave your cash, stocks, bonds, home, or other assets directly to your surviving spouse in your will, and there would be no federal estate tax at your death. Property you own jointly with your spouse as tenants by survivorship or tenants by the entirely passes directly to your surviving spouse at your death. That property would also qualify for the estate tax marital deduction. Likewise, life insurance payable outright to your spouse will be estate tax free.

Why, then, doesn't everyone just leave property outright? Why use a trust at all? Take a look at the following reasons you may want to consider a marital trust:

- Your spouse is unwilling or unable to invest, manage, or handle the responsibility of an outright transfer of a large amount of money, sizable investment portfolio, or a family business.

- You want to avoid probate, both in your estate and your spouse's estate.

- You want to keep all the details of your wealth as private as legally possible.

- You want to be sure that if your spouse becomes physically, mentally, or emotionally disabled in the future, or for any reason cannot handle the assets you have left, the trustee will continue to invest and manage the property and pay your spouse's bills.

- You want the assets you leave your spouse to qualify for the marital deduction, but you would like them eventually to pass to your children or some other person or persons you specify. (You may be concerned that an outright bequest to your spouse at your death may end up in the hands of your spouse's next spouse—or his or her children. This problem can be solved by using the QTIP marital deduction trust discussed later in this chapter.)

- You do not want to "over-qualify" and leave too much in assets to your surviving spouse, because you want to avoid the "second death wallop" that occurs when the surviving spouse dies and all the assets he or she owns—plus all the assets you have left to him or her (and all the appreciation on those assets from the moment of your death)—are subjected to federal estate taxes. A formula in the master trust divides assets between the marital and the credit equivalent by-pass trusts to minimize taxes in both your estate and your spouse's estate.

Q. What does a marital trust say?

A. Typically, a marital deduction trust (sometimes called the "A" trust because it is established in the first clause of the master trust document) states that at your death all the trust's income will be paid to your spouse for as long as he or she lives. Usually, the trust also gives your surviving spouse the power to consume, use, give, or leave trust property to anyone. This is called an *inter-vivos general power of appointment*. In a nutshell, this means your spouse has a blank check for the assets in the trust. He or she can "appoint" trust assets (i.e., channel the trust property) to practically anyone, including himself or herself. What's left at your spouse's death goes to the party specified in your spouse's will (or to the party you specify in your trust should your surviving spouse not make a specific designation).

If you give your spouse the right to name the ultimate recipient of the assets in your marital trust at his or her death, that right is called a *testamentary general power of appointment*. Again, your spouse's blank check enables him or her to specify—by will—any recipient (related or unrelated to you or your spouse), including your spouse's estate or creditors. This type of marital deduction trust is appropriately called by estate planners a *general power of appointment marital deduction trust*, since your surviving spouse can take all the trust assets whenever he or she desires during lifetime or alternatively leave all the assets to anyone he or she names by will. (You can specify that your surviving spouse has either a lifetime or at-death power—but not both—if you so desire.) Additional flexibility can be built into the marital trust to protect and care for your spouse. The catch is that because of these sweeping powers, everything that's in the marital trust when your spouse dies will be taxed in your spouse's estate.

Marital Deduction General Power of Appointment Trust

- Income to spouse for life
- Spouse has unlimited and unfettered power to consume, give away, or leave property to anyone
- What remains at spouse's death goes to party he or she specifies (but if he or she makes no specific provision, to the party you have specified)
- Additional flexibility and protection can be built in for spouse
- Assets in trust will be subject to federal estate tax when spouse dies

---

Q. What is a credit equivalent by-pass trust, and why do most estate planning lawyers draft both a marital and a by-pass trust?

A. As you've probably realized by now, it's no great trick to obtain the federal estate tax marital deduction and eliminate estate taxes when the first spouse dies. You merely leave everything outright (or in a manner that's tantamount to outright, such as the general power of appointment trust described above) to your surviving spouse. The mark of good estate planning in most family situations is to eliminate—or significantly reduce—the federal estate tax at the survivor's death. In other words, to the extent possible, you want to by-pass estate taxes at both spouse's deaths.

The *by-pass trust* (also called the "credit-equivalent by-pass" or "nonmarital" or "family" or "B" trust—because it's established in the "B" clause of the master trust) is where the big tax dollars are saved. Rather than leaving your spouse everything you own (outright or in a marital deduction trust) and having it all later taxed in your spouse's estate at confiscatory estate tax rates, you "hold back" an amount roughly equivalent to the unified credit exclusion amount (which is $600,000 in 1997 and increases by steps to $1,000,000 in 2006) and have it paid (by a formula clause in the master trust agreement) to the by-pass trust rather than the marital trust. Why? To by-pass the federal (and state) death tax when your spouse dies.

Remember, none of the assets going to the marital deduction trust will be taxed at your death (because of the marital deduction) and none of the assets going into the by-pass trust will be taxed (because of the unified credit). So there will be no federal estate tax when you die, no matter how large your estate. This is exactly the same result as if you had left all your assets to your spouse either outright or in a marital deduction trust. The real savings through the marital/by-pass trust combination comes at the second spouse's death.

As you've already noted, the by-pass trust is, by definition, designed to avoid the federal estate tax when your surviving spouse dies. None of the assets in the by-pass trust, therefore, will be subject to estate tax at your spouse's death. For a $2,000,000 estate in 2006 (when the unified credit exclusion amount will be $1,000,000), the by-pass trust can translate into an estate tax saving of $435,000! In a large estate, at the 55% tax rate, the tax saving could be as much as $550,000!

Actually, the real advantage of the by-pass trust just begins at that point. For example, suppose the by-pass trust is fully funded with $1,000,000 of assets at your death in 2006. Assume your spouse lives for 20 years after your death, and the trustee of the by-pass trust can invest the $1,000,000 of cash or other assets at a 6 percent after-tax rate of return. That $1,000,000 will grow to $3,207,135. By using the combination of a marital trust and the by-pass trust, not one penny of that money will be taxed in either your estate or your spouse's estate. If your spouse is in a 55 percent estate tax bracket at death, the amount saved will be more than $1,700,000!

Q. What does a by-pass trust say?

A. A by-pass trust typically states that the surviving spouse will receive all the income from the trust annually or more frequently for life. But the spouse has no right to take trust assets or dispose of trust principal. When the surviving spouse dies, what's left in the trust passes, not according to the surviving spouse's wishes, but under the terms of the trust you have provided. (You can give the trustee discretion to make additional distributions to the surviving spouse without endangering the tax advantages, and the surviving spouse can be safely empowered to withdraw money for health, education, maintenance, or support.)

By-pass (Family) Trust

- Income to spouse for life
- Spouse has no power to use or dispose of principal
- Remainder goes to party specified by first to die
- Additional flexibility and protection for spouse possible
- Assets in trust (including appreciation) not subject to federal estate tax at surviving spouse's death

---

The larger the estate, the more dramatic the tax savings can be. But even in more modest estates, this combination of trusts can save a surprising amount of money for your ultimate beneficiaries. For example, assume a husband has an estate that totals $800,000 (net of expenses and debts) and his wife has assets of her own of $50,000. If the husband leaves his entire estate to his spouse, the unlimited marital deduction will wipe out the tax when he dies. His wife lives on the after-tax income from the trust, income from her $50,000, and social security. But when she dies, her $50,000 is added to the $800,000 she received from her spouse. So her total taxable estate is $850,000, $250,000 more than the $600,000 unified credit exclusion amount. The tax on that $250,000 is $70,800! Because the husband never used any of his own $600,000, he completely wasted that credit, and it didn't shelter anything from tax in the surviving spouse's estate when she died.

Now let's change the example. Assume, instead of leaving all his assets to his spouse, the husband's will directed that his assets were to go into a master trust—which, by formula, created two trusts, a marital trust and a by-pass trust. Assume the first $600,000 of the husband's $800,000 went into that by-pass trust and the balance—the remaining $200,000—was channeled into the marital trust for his spouse. Although the $600,000 going into the by-pass trust is technically taxable in the husband's estate, it is shielded from any actual tax by the unified credit, and the husband's estate pays no tax on this amount at his death. The remaining $200,000 passes to the marital deduction trust, and no tax is paid on that amount either.

The bottom line: In this example, when using the marital/by-pass trust combination, almost $71,000 more can pass to the couple's children.

The following table compares the two trusts:

	If All Left to Spouse	Marital/ By-pass Formula
Tax at first spouse's death:	$0	$0
Tax at second spouse's death:	$70,800	$0
Total tax:	$70,800	$0

Q. Can I build any additional flexibility into the by-pass trust?

A. The price for the incredible estate tax savings potential of the credit equivalent by-pass trust is that the surviving spouse cannot be given carte blanche over the assets the trust holds. There are ways, however, to give your spouse a great deal of flexibility— without making trust assets includible in his or her estate. For instance:

- The surviving spouse can be given all of the trust's income.

- The spouse can be given an absolute right to demand trust principal to the extent necessary to pay for the costs of health, education, maintenance, and support (we call this the "HEMS" power). Trust assets will not be included in your survivor's estate as long as his or her rights to principal are limited by an "ascertainable standard."

- An independent trustee can be given unlimited power to make additional payments of principal to your spouse at the trustee's discretion.

- Your surviving spouse can be given a tax-free power to use trust assets essentially to make gifts to children, grandchildren, or others under what is called a "limited power of appointment."

- Your surviving spouse can be given a noncumulative right to withdraw—each year—the greater of $5,000 or 5 percent of the value of the trust's assets in that year. (The most that will be included in your surviving spouse's estate under this clause is the amount that he or she could have taken in the year of death.)

Q. What is a QTIP trust?

A. In addition to qualifying the assets transferred to it for the marital deduction a QTIP trust accomplishes an objective that other marital deduction trusts can't. The letters QTIP stand for *qualified terminable interest property* trust. Typically, you can qualify for the marital deduction only when you leave your spouse property either (1) outright (by will, joint ownership, or as the direct beneficiary of your life insurance, pension plan, IRA, or tax-deferred annuity) or (2) in the traditional marital deduction trust, which gives the surviving spouse the power either (or both) to take the trust's assets during lifetime or to determine who receives those assets when he or she dies.

If the surviving spouse's interest is *terminable*—that is, if the spouse could possibly lose the right to use, possess, enjoy, or dispose of it as he or she wishes upon the occurrence of some event (for example, remarriage) or the nonoccurrence of some event (for example, having to survive probate to receive it)—the marital deduction will usually not be allowed.

This means that you would be faced with a most difficult decision: Choice 1: You could leave your property outright or in trust in a manner that essentially gives your surviving spouse absolute power to dispose of your property in a way or to a person that might not be your choice (for instance, a wife could leave the property to a friend, her second husband, or even to his children) in order to qualify for the marital deduction.

Choice 2: You could leave your property in a manner that restricts your surviving spouse's interest and thereby ensures that it would ultimately pass to the party you select. But this restriction will mean your assets will not qualify for the marital deduction, and the up-front tax payable at your death could cause a serious lack of liquidity (not enough cash to pay tax), resulting in both a forced sale (a loss of your most valuable assets and perhaps control of a family business) and a fire sale (a sale at sacrifice prices to raise the necessary cash to pay the tax).

Fortunately, Congress passed a provision that allows terminable interest property that would otherwise not be eligible to qualify for the marital deduction. This *qualified terminable interest property trust* is particularly useful in second marriages or even in first marriages where, after the death of the first spouse, the second spouse might remarry or decide to leave the property owner's assets to someone other than that owner would have chosen. A QTIP trust might be the right choice for anyone worried that his or her assets may end up in the hands of a surviving spouse's future spouse, children of a future marriage, the spouse's favorite charity, or squandered or totally consumed by the surviving spouse.

Keep in mind that even if your spouse doesn't deliberately leave your assets to his or her next spouse, that spouse may be entitled to a portion of those assets in one of two ways: First, if your spouse dies without a valid will, state *intestacy* laws may name your spouse's next spouse as the beneficiary of all or a large portion of his or her estate. Second, even if your spouse dies with a valid will leaving everything to your children, many state right-of-election laws give surviving spouses certain inalienable rights, regardless of what your will says. In most states, for example, a second spouse could end up with at least the amount he or she would receive if your spouse died without a valid will.

So the peace of mind you receive when you know your estate will eventually go to the party of your choice is one major advantage of the QTIP trust. There are other significant advantages to a QTIP trust. Not only can you specify who will receive your assets when your spouse dies, but your executor can also determine how much of your assets will qualify for the marital deduction. This is an important tax-planning device that can save hundreds of thousands of dollars for your children and grandchildren. Moreover, you can authorize your spouse to make gifts of the assets in your QTIP trust to people you've selected. This adds to your trust's overall flexibility.

Sophisticated lawyers and other advisers may even suggest that you create more than one QTIP trust to increase your executor's planning flexibility. The combination of two QTIP

trusts and a by-pass trust is often used in larger estates—
sometimes with yet a fourth (irrevocable life insurance) trust.

Q. What does a QTIP trust say?

A. A QTIP trust states that all the income of the trust must be paid annually or more frequently to the surviving spouse. That income must be paid for as long as the surviving spouse lives. But at the surviving spouse's death, what remains in the trust (the *remainder*) will pass to the children (or other party or parties) that you, the property-owner spouse, specify. The surviving spouse has no power to either take the trust's principal during lifetime or at death.

At your death, your executor must make a special election on your estate tax return to have the assets passing to the QTIP trust qualify for the federal estate tax marital deduction. Technically, there are four conditions that must be met for QTIP treatment to be allowed:

- The decedent-spouse (or donor in the case of a lifetime gift) must make a transfer of property. The transfer can be in trust, through insurance proceeds, or in other ways, such as the death proceeds of a nonqualified deferred-compensation plan.

- The surviving spouse (or donee in the case of a lifetime transfer) must be given the right to all the income. It must be payable at least annually, and the surviving spouse must be entitled to that income for life.

- No one can be given the right to direct that the property will go to anyone other than the spouse as long as that spouse is alive. (It is permissible to give someone other than the surviving spouse the power to appoint QTIP property if that power can be exercised only after the surviving spouse dies.)

- The executor of the first decedent-spouse must make an irrevocable election on that decedent's federal estate tax return. The election stipulates that to the extent the QTIP property has not been consumed or given away during the lifetime of the surviving spouse, its date-of-death value (at the surviving spouse's death) will be included in his or her estate. In the case of a lifetime gift of QTIP property, the donor-spouse must file a similar election on the gift tax return so that the QTIP property will be in the estate of the donee-spouse unless that spouse disposes of it during his or her lifetime.

Qualified Terminable Interest Property (QTIP) Trust
• Income to surviving spouse for life annually or more frequently
• Remainder to children or other party designated by grantor
• Surviving spouse has no power to take principal during life
• Surviving spouse has no power to take principal at death

Q. What is the "cost" of a QTIP trust?

A. Many times throughout this book we've pointed out that *every* estate planning tool has both its advantages *and* disadvantages. QTIP trusts are no different. To qualify assets in a trust that otherwise would not qualify for the marital deduction, your executor has to agree to have the QTIP trust property taxed in your surviving spouse's estate when he or she dies even though your spouse will not be able to take that property or decide who receives it when he or she dies. Of course, it is typically well worth that cost because your spouse may live and enjoy trust income for many years, you will have succeeded in accomplishing your dispositive objectives, and at the same time you will have delayed massive federal estate taxes on the money or other assets in the trust.

Q. What's wrong with a QTIP trust?

A. At first glance, it appears that the QTIP concept satisfies all needs for all people. Unfortunately, however, this is not the case. The QTIP trust may not work if all or the bulk of your estate consists of unproductive real estate or stock in a closely held corporation that has not paid, and probably never will pay, any significant dividends. Why not? Because the IRS might claim your surviving spouse may not receive the statutorily required "all income at least annually."

What's wrong with that? According to most experts, your surviving spouse must be given an interest that is realistically expected to produce income consistent with its value. Most closely held stock will never do that. For example, stock worth $300,000 that generates either no dividends or dividends significantly below the lowest reasonable rate of return on an investment of $300,000 cannot be said to produce an income "consistent with its value." Therefore, without planning, you could lose the marital deduction.

What can you do to save the marital deduction? Without a state law giving your surviving spouse the power to require that trust assets be sold and that trust property be made productive in a reasonable period of time, the lawyer drafting the marital formula must insert a provision in the will or trust that clearly gives the survivor that power, that is, the power to demand that "unproductive" (non-income-producing) property be made productive. If your surviving spouse can demand that the trustee sell the stock (or other unproductive assets) and use the proceeds to purchase income-producing property, the marital deduction can be saved (even if the power is never actually exercised).

Unfortunately, even if your surviving spouse is given the power to demand that the trustee sell the stock, there are practical problems. Assume, for instance, that your objective was to pass the stock of your family business to your adult daughter—the one working in your business—at your wife's death. If your wife can force a sale, what assurance does your daughter have that she, the daughter, will be the purchaser? Who will purchase the stock if it is a minority interest? If it is a majority interest, what happens to your daughter's job if the stock is sold to a third party?

Even if your wife is not given the power to require that the trustee sell the stock, can she obtain the corpus of the trust by electing against your will? (Under the laws of many states, a surviving spouse has a statutory right to elect against the will of a spouse who leaves her with merely a life estate.) If your spouse doesn't force a sale of trust assets, where will she (or he) obtain income sufficient to maintain her (his) current standard of living? Most corporations don't pay any significant dividends and in many cases surviving spouses can't justify the type of salary they'd need to live as they do now.

A good lawyer will find solutions. One solution to the example above is to create an irrevocable trust funded by life insurance on your life. At your death the trust would provide income to your surviving spouse for life, and the principal would pass to your children. That would relieve pressure on your spouse to force the trustee to sell the stock in the QTIP trust. In fact, the irrevocable trust might condition your surviving spouse's right to that income on her making no demand for a sale of QTIP assets. If she demands that the trustee sell the QTIP assets, she'll lose her right to income from the irrevocable trust. Another alternative solution is a funded buy-sell agreement between you (the father) and your child. If your daughter, for instance, has the insurance proceeds at your death, she can purchase the stock from your estate so that cash, rather than stock, goes into the QTIP trust.

Q. *What's an estate trust?*

A. An estate trust is yet another way of placing assets in trust but still qualifying for a marital deduction. The major advantage of an estate trust is that, unlike both the general power of appointment marital deduction trust and the QTIP marital deduction trust, an estate trust is not required to pay out all income annually or more frequently to the surviving spouse. In fact, the estate trust is the only type of marital deduction trust that allows the trustee, at the trustee's discretion, to accumulate rather than pay out income. Because of currently high tax rates on trust income, this does not seem to be advantageous. But when your assets consist mainly of non-income-producing property (such as closely held stock or undeveloped real estate or a large family home), this may be the best choice among the three types of marital deduction trusts. In fact, it may be the only choice.

Both general power of appointment trust and QTIP trust rules require both that income be payable and that the amount of that income be commensurate with the value of the assets in the trust. For instance, the general power of appointment trust will not qualify for a marital deduction if its only asset is stock in your $3,000,000 business and that stock pays a $300-a-year—or even a $3,000-a-year—dividend. The marital deduction may be disallowed—a tax disaster—if the trust's beneficiary can't demand that a non-income-producing asset, such as that stock, be sold and replaced by an asset that generates income at a rate closer to current market rates. Unfortunately, giving the surviving spouse the ability to force a sale may not be what you wanted or intended.

An estate trust may be the answer if your estate meets the following three criteria:

- Non-income-producing property comprises all or a sizable portion of your estate.

- Your surviving spouse is independently wealthy and will not need either trust assets or trust income.

- The property you transfer to the trust at your death is not likely to significantly appreciate in value after your death.

Q. What does an estate trust say?

A. Essentially, an estate trust gives your surviving spouse a *life estate* (the right to receive income or use of trust property for life) coupled with a *remainder* (what's left when your spouse dies) to his or her estate. In other words, an estate trust stipulates that a surviving spouse is to be paid income from the trust for life whether annually or more frequently. But, at the trustee's sole discretion, that income can be accumulated in the trust. The remainder of the trust (both income that has been accumulated and not paid out and the trust's principal) will be paid to the surviving spouse's estate at his or her death and will pass under the terms of the surviving spouse's will.

Because no interest can pass to anyone other than the surviving spouse, the trust qualifies for the estate tax marital deduction. Income that is needed for the surviving spouse's support or medical care, education, or other needs can be paid to him or her.

The objective of an estate trust is to achieve a balance between attaining the estate tax marital deduction and restricting the surviving spouse's ability to access trust property during his or her lifetime. The cost is that the first-to-die spouse gives up the right to control who receives the property when the surviving spouse dies. That determination is made under the surviving spouse's will.

Marital Deduction Estate Trust
• Income paid out—or accumulated—for surviving spouse • Remainder payable at surviving spouse's death under terms of that spouse's will • Assets in trust taxed at surviving spouse's death • Assets in trust subject to probate in surviving spouse's estate

Q. What are the disadvantages of an estate trust?

A. One drawback of an estate trust is that your surviving spouse has no right to trust income. You can partially overcome this obstacle by giving your spouse a noncumulative right (perhaps one month each year to limit estate tax exposure in the year of death) to withdraw a minimum amount each year (for example, $5,000 or 5 percent of trust corpus, whichever is greater).

A second drawback is the key to the estate trust: To qualify assets for the estate tax marital deduction, property in the trust must be paid to your surviving spouse's estate at his or her death. The problem this creates is that trust assets become subject to all the potential and actual problems of probate—that is, assets are subjected to administrative costs, claims of the surviving spouse's creditors, and a subsequent spouse's right of election. Obviously, if these disadvantages greatly concern you, you should use a general power of appointment trust or QTIP trust rather than an estate trust.

An estate trust is a good alternative to the general-power-of-appointment trust or QTIP trust when (1) non-income-producing property is involved and the parties want to make sure it is not sold during the surviving spouse's lifetime or (2) when the surviving spouse has substantial income and/or wealth from other sources. The estate trust is also a tool to use in conjunction with a power-of-appointment trust or a QTIP trust whenever the marital deduction amount is large enough to justify two trusts and there are income-tax-saving opportunities by doing so.

Q. Compare the advantages of outright distribution to a power-of-appointment trust, QTIP, and estate trust.

A. The following table will help you understand some of the key pros and cons of each method of qualifying for the estate tax marital deduction.

WAYS TO QUALIFY FOR MARITAL DEDUCTION				
	Outright Transfer	General Power of Appointment Trust	QTIP	Estate Trust
Simplest method	Yes	No	No	No
Surviving spouse has great lifetime control over assets	Yes	Yes	No	No
Most effective for personal assets such as jewelry	Yes	No	No	No
Spouse can be protected against financial immaturity, inexperience, and undue influence	No	Yes	Yes	Yes
Marital assets can be managed on behalf of disabled surviving spouse	No	Yes	Yes	Yes
Spouse relieved of investment and property management burden	No	Yes	Yes	Yes
Estate administration expenses lowered on surviving spouse's death	No	Yes	Yes	Yes
Estate owner's dispositive wishes can be ignored	Yes	Yes	No	Yes
Non-income-producing (unproductive) assets can fund marital trust	N/A	No	No	No
Maximum post-date tax planning available	No	No	Yes	

Q. What is a QDT?

A. No estate tax marital deduction is allowed when the surviving spouse is not a U.S. citizen. If your spouse is Canadian, Mexican, English, German, Swiss, Israeli, or the citizen of any other foreign country, your estate will not receive a marital deduction and will have to pay the federal estate tax 9 months from the date you die.

Denying a marital deduction in the first estate when the surviving spouse is not a U.S. citizen is revenue motivated;

Trusts/Leimberg Associates Books: 610-527-5216

Congress was concerned that the alien-spouse, having received the estate, would literally "take the money and run" (back to a foreign country and beyond the reach of the IRS).

Fortunately, there are exceptions to the general rule that no marital deduction is allowed if the surviving spouse is a non-U.S. citizen. The two major exceptions occur when

- the surviving spouse becomes a U.S. citizen before the decedent-spouse's estate tax return is filed and has been a U.S. resident at all times after the death of the decedent-spouse and before becoming a U.S. citizen, or

- the property passing to the surviving spouse goes into a qualified domestic trust (QDT)

A QDT is a trust that benefits the surviving resident-alien-spouse and meets the following requirements:

- It must be created and maintained under U.S. federal or state law.

- It must require that at least one trustee must be either an individual who is a U.S. citizen or a domestic corporation.

- The trust must provide that no distribution can be made from the QDT unless the U.S. trustee "has the right to withhold the QDT tax from that distribution" without the approval of any other trustee.

- The executor of the decedent-spouse who is transferring property to a resident-alien surviving spouse must make an irrevocable election for QDT treatment.

- Certain other requirements must be met to ensure the collection of any tax imposed on the trust.

- The QDT must otherwise qualify as a transfer eligible for the marital deduction under the normal rules applicable to marital transfers.

QDTs are divided into two types: (1) "big" (assets of more than $2,000,000 at the citizen spouse's death) QDTs and (2) "small" ($2,000,000 or less of assets at the citizen spouse's death) QDTs. Big QDTs must require that at least one U.S. trustee be a bank or that the U.S. trustee furnish a bond or other security at least equal to 65 percent of the fair market value of the trust's assets. Small QDTs can meet similar bank-requirement tests or must require that no more than 35 percent of the trust's assets consist of real property located outside of the U.S.

An estate tax payable at the death of the first spouse to die will result if a transfer to a resident alien surviving spouse is made in a way that does not qualify under QDT rules. The transfer will be subject to federal estate tax in the estate of a citizen spouse who predeceases the resident-alien-spouse.

Q. What's wrong with a QDT?

A. There are some very significant distinctions between a QDT and the other marital deduction trusts we've described. The most important is this: Your surviving spouse can't take the principal out of the QDT without paying an estate tax. And that tax is based, not on the size of the surviving spouse's estate, but on the size of *your* estate.

The estate tax payable at your surviving spouse's death is computed by adding the assets in the QDT to the assets you owned at your death. In fact, some planners call this a "Dracula" tax because every time any principal is paid out of the QDT, it's as if you had died again. A new tax must be recalculated. Unless there is a financial hardship, your spouse can safely receive only trust income without incurring an additional round of federal estate tax. Payment of principal to her triggers the "Dracula" tax.

Even in the case of transfers that do qualify for QDT treatment, the estate tax is not forgiven; it is merely delayed. This follows the basic theory (but not actual practice) of the estate and gift tax marital deductions allowed to U.S. citizens: The marital deduction defers the estate tax on the assumption that the deductible property will eventually be included in the surviving spouse's estate. Keep in mind, however, that with a general-power-of-appointment marital deduction trust, surviving spouses who are U.S. citizens can freely take trust assets, consume them or give them away before death without triggering any tax. This can't be done with a QDT without generating an immediate estate tax.

Four events can trigger an estate tax on QDT assets:

- Any distribution other than

    (1) income to the surviving spouse or

    (2) a distribution to the surviving spouse on account of hardship made prior to the surviving spouse's death will result in an immediate tax. Under proposed regulations, a hardship distribution is "one made in

response to an immediate and substantial financial need relating to the noncitizen spouse's health, maintenance, or support."

- At the time of the surviving spouse's death, the entire value of the property in the QDT will be subject to federal estate tax. So the QDT is a tax bomb waiting to explode. There's no way to get asset appreciation out of the trust without setting off a series of tax explosions.

- As soon as the QDT fails to meet any QDT requirement, the estate tax will be imposed as if the surviving spouse had died on the date the trust failed the requirement.

- If the QDT pays the tax imposed on any of the triggering events above, that payment is considered a taxable distribution that sets off yet another tax. In other words, the QDT's payment of the estate tax on a distribution is itself a distribution (equal to the amount of the tax) subject to a further estate tax.

There is yet another trigger to the time bomb: a QDT is disqualified if the trust uses any device or arrangement, the principal purpose of which is to avoid liability for the deferred estate tax. In our opinion the QDT transfer is probably a transfer that you should avoid. The tax imposed on the occurrence of a taxable event proves the QDT to be a cleverly devised trap for the unwary planner for the following reasons:

- The QDT tax is imposed at the citizen spouse's highest marginal rate (if the citizen dies first). This is an unusual penalty on the resident-alien, particularly if the survivor has insignificant individual wealth.

- The surviving resident-alien-spouse cannot avoid the QDT tax by consuming the trust corpus (absent permissible hardship distributions).

- The unified credit is not available to the surviving spouse for QDT taxable events. Therefore, the resident-alien-surviving spouse's unified credit is wasted unless he or she has sufficient individually owned property to qualify for the credit.

- When combined with the regulations, QDT law is complex, confusing, and potentially draconian in harshness.

Q. Is there a solution to the QDT problem?

A. One solution is to avoid exposure to the QDT tax by making provisions for the resident-alien-spouse through lifetime transfers. Gift tax rules permit intra-spousal transfers in amounts up to $100,000 a year. This opportunity is significant for planning purposes, since lifetime gifts to a resident-alien-spouse do not otherwise qualify for the unlimited marital deduction.

To obtain this "super annual exclusion," the gift to the resident-alien-spouse has to qualify under the normal rules for an annual exclusion gift and has to meet the requirements for a marital deduction as if the donee is a citizen. Through effective use of this gift exclusion, the citizen-spouse can transfer substantial assets to the resident-alien-spouse over time. The surviving spouse can use these assets for his or her support after the citizen-spouse dies and thereby reduce the need to fund a QDT.

Moreover, the assets received through the lifetime gifts can avoid all transfer tax to the extent that the resident-alien-spouse consumes them, and they will qualify for the unified credit if the resident-alien-spouse holds them until his or her death. In addition, the resident-alien-spouse is free to take the gifted property outside the U.S. and avoid U.S. transfer tax entirely if he or she is not a resident at the time of his or her death.

Your non-U.S.-citizen spouse may even want to leverage the power of the super exclusion by using each year's gift to purchase life insurance on your life. None of that life insurance will be in your estate nor will any of it be subject to the claims of your creditors. When you couple the super annual exclusion with an irrevocable life insurance trust, you can secure incredible amounts of wealth for your spouse and children through this planning technique.

Q. My estate is large. Are there any special factors I should consider in trust planning?

A. If the size of your estate exceeds twice the exemption equivalent, you must give careful thought whether to (1) pay no first-death tax or (2) split the estate and pay a tax at the first spouse's death. If you choose the first course of action, all the property passing

Trusts/Leimberg Associates Books: 610-527-5216

to your surviving spouse will be added to his or her taxable estate (to the extent your spouse does not consume it or give it away).

Why would anyone ever chose to pay tax before it is required? If you choose to have your estate pay an "up-front tax", the portion taxed at the first death (and all growth from the time of your death until the date of your surviving spouse's death) escapes taxation at the second death. In many cases, a family can save tens, hundreds of thousands, or even millions of dollars by paying a relatively small estate tax at the first death to save large taxes when the second spouse dies.

For example, suppose your estate is worth $3,000,000 and your spouse has a $50,000 estate. If you, the spouse with a net estate of $3 million, leave an amount equal to the $1,000,000 unified credit exclusion amount (in 2006) to your children and the $2,000,000 difference to your spouse, there will be no federal tax. At your survivor's death the estate tax on $2,050,000 ($2,000,000 plus your spouse's $50,000 estate, assuming no consumption or gifts of the property) will be $356,300 (after considering the federal credit for state death taxes). If, on the other hand, you split the estate into two equal portions and leave $1.5 million to your spouse and an equal amount to your children, the tax at the first death will be about $145,600. The tax at the second death (based on a $1,550,000 tentative tax base) will be about $164,900—a total of $310,500. The difference—the tax saved—is $45,800.

The factors that you and your advisers must consider, therefore, are the following:

- If the no-tax-at-the-first-death option is chosen, how much after-tax interest will assets earn each year, and how long will they continue to earn interest? (What is the life expectancy of the surviving spouse?)

- Will each spouse's estate be taxed at more or less than the maximum 55 percent federal estate tax rate?

- How much growth will occur in the portion of the estate not passed to the surviving spouse?

- How important is it to provide for children during the surviving spouse's lifetime?

- How beneficial would it be to shift income to your children's tax brackets? (What is the impact, if any, of the "kiddie tax" rules, under which investment income of minor children can be taxed at the parents' income tax rates?)

- What are the basis implications of each action? (Passing property at death from you to your spouse and from your spouse to your children achieves two basis step-ups at the cost of only one estate tax.)

Here are some other factors to weigh:

- Does your spouse intend to leave the property to charity?

- What is your surviving spouse's standard of living?

- How many dependents does your surviving spouse have?

- How likely is it that your surviving spouse will remarry?

In summary, then, there are four major arguments for paying no up-front tax:

- The liquidity need for estate tax dollars is removed as a problem at the first death (but will probably be greater at the survivor's death because the first decedent's assets are taxed at higher rates as a result of being placed on top of his or her assets).

- The surviving spouse has more actual (and psychological) security and may have more usable dollars.

- The possibility of a second step-up in basis exists.

- The surviving spouse may consume or be able to give away much of what would otherwise be taxable.

The major arguments for paying an up-front tax, on the other hand—and against deferral of the tax—are the following:

- The tax might be paid at lower tax rates.

- To the extent that a QTIP trust is not used, if your surviving spouse receives assets outright, they may end up in the hands of a second spouse or that spouse's children.

- Your children may have to wait until your surviving spouse dies to enjoy the property.

- Spreading wealth at the first death may facilitate a spreading of income and therefore an overall reduction in income taxes.

- If there is significant growth in the value of the property left to the by-pass trust or directly to your children, avoiding a second tax on the now-appreciated property can result in sizable overall death tax savings.

It is important to recognize that, believe it or not, there is no-time-value-of-money advantage to deferral of federal estate tax. Any income not consumed by your surviving spouse will be subject to federal estate tax rates as high as 55 percent (plus a potential 5 percent surtax on ultra-large estates) at your surviving spouse's death.

Deferral of federal estate tax at your death is merely investing the deferred tax for the benefit of the IRS. So paying taxes at the first death may make sense—unless your family will need to invade trust principal for living expenses so much that they will consume the assets subject to tax. In that case, the estate of the second to die will be smaller, and it would be poor planning to pay taxes voluntarily on the death of the first spouse.

Obviously, the choice is complex and should be made only in consultation with skilled and experienced tax advisers. Keep in mind that a small outlay of cash currently in the form of life insurance premiums can provide the cash to pay an up-front tax that in turn could save hundreds of thousands or even millions of dollars for future generations of family members.

JOINT TRUSTS

Chapter 14 explains:

- What a joint trust is

- The mechanics of a joint trust

- The advantages of a joint trust

- The federal gift tax implications of a joint trust

- The possible gift tax complications for a surviving spouse upon the death of the first spouse to die

- The federal estate tax complications of a joint trust

- The income tax implications of a joint trust

- The possible tax basis advantage of a joint trust

- State tax considerations when a joint trust is used

- Why a joint trust may be suitable for community property

Q. What is a joint trust?

A. A joint trust is a single-document form of revocable living trust created by a married couple. It provides lifetime asset management for both spouses and contains essentially all of the dispositive provisions of the couple's estate plan. The key features are that both spouses have joint control of—and access to—the assets placed into the trust and that both spouses receive equal shares of trust income and principal for life or it is paid to the person or persons they direct.

Q. Mechanically, how does a joint trust operate?

A. It might work like this: You and your spouse can create a joint revocable trust naming yourselves as co-grantors. You can amend or revoke the trust at any time while both of you are alive and even after one of you dies. The trust can stipulate that, upon notice of revocation, trust assets will be paid to you (the couple) or to the survivor or to the party you name.

Either or both of you can be trustee(s), and you can name one or more successor trustees. You might choose to name a third-party individual, bank or other professional trustee to give investment advice and professional management, to provide continuity, and to see that things go smoothly if either of you is unable to act as trustee for any reason. (In larger estates an independent trustee might minimize some of the potential tax problems that can arise in a joint trust).

You can transfer both jointly held assets (such as mutual funds or real estate) and assets either of you own in your own name. When you transfer jointly-owned property to a joint trust, that asset continues to have many of the same characteristics it had before it was retitled into the trust's name.

You and your spouse will continue to share the income. Trust income will automatically continue to the survivor (in trust) when either of you dies. Technically, the joint property is no longer joint property; that form of ownership ends when you named the trustee (or trustees) as the new legal owner and the trustee took legal title to the assets in the trust. But as a practical matter, your interests are similar to joint ownership.

You and your spouse can jointly retain the right to any principal you need or want. You can provide in your trust document that all trust income must be paid to you (the couple) as long as you both are alive and when either of you dies, to the survivor. You can also give your trustee the discretion to pay income and principal in his, her, or its discretion if you are disabled and need money for your health or support. The same power can protect the surviving spouse after the first death.

In smaller estates, you can stipulate that the joint trust will remain intact and continue to operate the same way it had before the first spouse's death. In other words, the trust will become the revocable trust of the surviving spouse, and part of the survivor's taxable estate. Alternatively, you can provide that at the first death, the trust will be split into several portions. An amount could be carved out of the trust equal to the decedent's unified credit exclusion amount ($600,000 in 1997 and increasing by steps to $1,000,000 in 2006). If the unified credit has not been used by lifetime gifts, this exclusion amount that is placed in a new *family trust*, as its name implies, will pay income to the surviving spouse and children.

This new family trust is sometimes also called a *by-pass* or *credit-shelter* trust because it will by-pass estate taxes on an amount equal to the unified credit exclusion amount when the surviving spouse dies. This family/by-pass/credit shelter trust is irrevocable, so that the assets in it are protected from being taxed in the surviving spouse's estate. Any remaining property in the original joint trust will stay there and be used for or on behalf of the surviving spouse. You can specify that this trust will remain revocable, or you can make it an irrevocable marital deduction *QTIP* trust upon the first death. (See chapter 13 for a thorough discussion of both the family/by-pass/credit shelter trust and the marital deduction trust.)

Finally, your joint trust can provide that upon the death of the surviving spouse, everything in the trust will remain in trust for the children or other remaindermen, or be paid out directly to them.

Q. What are the advantages of a joint trust?

A. The concept of a joint trust appeals to many people because it is purported to be simple, short, and relatively understandable. It is also appealing because it maintains the "joint property ownership" sharing of rights. Many people feel that the joint trust helps to maintain the mutuality of interest they had in jointly held property with rights of survivorship. It eliminates "mine-versus-yours" feeling in separate trusts; instead, there is a complete sharing of burdens and benefits of property. Such a trust also gives a married couple the same immediate access to property they had before placing the asset into the joint trust.

As is the case with all revocable trusts, to the extent that you and your spouse transfer your assets to it, the joint trust will avoid probate at the first death. At that time, the joint trust will become a regular revocable living trust. Your surviving spouse will have unrestricted access to the assets in the trust because of his or her retained right to require distributions and to revoke the trust. When the surviving spouse dies, the trust can pass any of its assets to your designated beneficiaries and thus avoid probate a second time.

If the combined value of the assets of you and your spouse is below the value where federal estate taxes are a consideration ($600,000 in 1997 and increasing in steps to $1,000,000 in 2006), a joint trust can be advantageous and accomplish most— if not all—of the objectives described above. Although there are disadvantages to a joint trust (see below), if you don't have to worry about the federal estate gift or estate tax consequences, you can ignore many of them.

Q. What are the possible disadvantages of a joint trust?

A. Some authorities feel that a joint trust is indicated only if the assets in your estate are relatively modest and your dispositive scheme is relatively simple. If your combined wealth (you and your spouse) is significantly more than the unified credit exclusion amount, however, you may trigger a number of these complex tax traps:

- The entire trust may be included in the estate of the first spouse to die—even if that spouse didn't contribute all the assets to the trust (or any assets to the trust).

- Even worse, the entire trust may be included in the estate of the second spouse to die, even if part of the trust was intended to qualify as a *unified credit* or *by-pass trust* that was *not* supposed to be included in the estate of the second spouse. It is because of this danger that most lawyers recommend a joint trust *only* when the combined estates are less than the unified credit exclusion amount, because then the entire trust can be sheltered by the surviving spouse's unified credit regardless of how the trust is treated on the death of the first spouse. If your combined estates are more than the available exclusion amount, the joint trust could "waste" the unified credit of the first spouse to die and more than $200,000 in needless estate taxes might be payable upon the death of the surviving spouse because the surviving spouse's estate was "loaded up" with more property than necessary.

- You may be making taxable lifetime gifts subject to gift tax when you transfer assets in your own name to a joint trust.

- In many states, property owned by a husband and wife jointly, as "tenants by the entireties," is not subject to the claims of a creditor of one spouse. Assets transferred to a joint trust will probably lose that protection. For instance, if one spouse signs as guarantor for a business loan, you expose all your property to those claims if all your assets are in a joint revocable trust. It may therefore be preferable to keep assets separate, or in joint names, whenever one spouse has potential debt or litigation.

- If your joint trust becomes irrevocable when either you or your spouse dies, the survivor may be treated as having made a taxable gift to your children or other beneficiaries.

Because the joint trust is a relatively new concept, neither federal nor state law has fully developed. Since even the brightest and best lawyers and accountants have little guidance from cases and rulings, this means that they can't predict with certainty the consequence of various actions. The person drafting your document, therefore, will have to spend considerable time researching the problems and creating new solutions. That time will cost you money. (A lack of research can cost even more.) You may be the test case that proves the accuracy (or fallacy) of your lawyer's efforts. If your estate is above the unified credit exclusion amount, the savings of one document over two are outweighed by the potential litigation it may take to make you famous and prove you right.

Q. What are the federal gift tax implications of a joint trust?

A. When you and your spouse place assets into a joint trust, your rights are similar, but not identical, to joint ownership. It is this subtle but important difference that may cause a number of sophisticated estate planning problems.

Starting with joint ownership with rights of survivorship or tenancy by the entireties and then changing to something else (that is, a beneficial interest in a trust) can trigger unintended adverse tax implications. Remember that the legal relationship you have to the property in the trust is as a beneficiary, rather than a joint tenant. Even if you transfer only jointly held property to your joint trust, your property rights change. Whenever there is a shift in ownership rights, federal (and possibly state) transfer taxes may be imposed.

In order to try to figure out the gift tax implications of a joint trust, you have to start by determining the nature and value of the property each party puts into the trust. Then you have to determine the nature and value of the interests of each party in the trust after the transfers to the trust. When you place assets into a joint trust, each of you has contributed property to the trust and each of you has retained—as a beneficiary—an interest in that property. You each have a present interest in the trust, and you each also have what lawyers call a *contingent remainder interest*. This means each of you has the potential to receive (should you be the surviving spouse) the other person's share of the assets in the trust (what remains upon the other's death if you survive).

Whether the right to revoke or amend the trust can be exercised by each spouse separately, or only jointly, can have gift tax consequences. For example, if one party contributes less than the other, or if one party has a greater actuarial interest in the trust's assets than the other, but both parties must agree in order to demand a trust distribution or revocation, a taxable gift may occur. If you anticipate these potential technical problems, it may be possible to minimize them by drafting the trust document appropriately. But if you ignore or overlook these issues, you or your estate may incur significant gift or estate taxes.

The value of your interests in the trust must also be considered. For instance, if you put $30,000 of your own money into a joint trust with your wife, she has an interest in that money she didn't have before. This is easy to see if your wife puts none of her own money in the trust, but it is also true even if she puts her own $30,000 into the trust. Why? It would appear the two amounts balance each other out and that there could be a gift only to the extent that one spouse puts in more than the other. Unfortunately, even if you and your spouse put identical amounts into the trust, the IRS might claim that your wife's greater life expectancy makes it more likely that she'll receive everything in the trust than you will. Therefore, in creating the trust, you are making a gift to your wife of the potential to receive the entire principal upon your prior death. You are also making a gift to her of the lifetime right to the income from the property you placed into the trust.

Even if you wind up making a gift to your spouse, won't it qualify for the gift tax marital deduction? Probably not, because of the technical requirements the law imposes. A gift in trust usually qualifies for the marital deduction only if the spouse is entitled to *all* of the income of the trust. In the classic joint trust you *both* receive the right to the income. This could cause a forfeiture of the inter-spousal marital deduction.

The apparent solution to these problems is to be sure each spouse has the unilateral and unconditional right to withdraw his or her separate contributions to the trust. This will render the gift incomplete, so there is no gift and no gift tax problem. (If you live in a community property state such as California or Texas, your interests inside the trust continue to be considered community property, so the result may differ. See the discussion of community property at the end of this chapter.)

The drawback to this solution is that this requires very carefully tracing and documenting of the source of all income as well as gains and losses from each and every income-producing property in the trust, for as long as both spouses are alive. This obviously complicates the joint trust and increases its expense and aggravation. And it defeats the "share and share alike" simplicity and community of interest that was the original reason for the joint trust.

Some lawyers believe that the separation and tracing of the contributions of the spouses is not necessary, and that a carefully worded joint trust can be created in which each spouse will be considered to be the owner of one half (and only one half) of all of the trust assets. Any gift that might occur when the trust is funded during lifetime should qualify for the marital deduction if each spouse always has the right to withdraw his or her half of the trust assets, just like the purchase of jointly owned assets qualifies for the marital deduction.

Unfortunately, there have been no rulings by the IRS on the gift tax and estate tax consequences of joint trusts, and lawyers are divided in their opinions. If your combined estates are not likely to exceed the unified credit exclusion amount, the federal transfer (gift and estate) taxes can largely be ignored. But if your combined assets will eventually exceed this amount, a joint trust can cause severe transfer tax problems. Proceed with great caution.

Q. Can the death of a spouse result in a taxable gift of a part of a joint trust?

A. Yes, it is possible for the death of one spouse to result in a taxable gift by the *surviving* spouse.

The problem is that the surviving spouse will probably be considered the owner of part (or all) of the trust at the death of the first spouse to die, either due to that spouse's contributions to the trust or the rights of revocation held by that spouse before the death of the first to die. For example, if the husband transfers all of his assets to a joint trust and the wife contributes nothing, but the wife has the right to withdraw from the trust during the husband's lifetime, the wife has an interest in the trust which can result in a taxable gift upon the death of the husband.

A couple will often want make a joint trust irrevocable after one spouse dies. This is sometimes done to control the ultimate disposition of the money in the trust. For instance, if you and your spouse each place $700,000 in assets into the trust, and you both want to be sure that at the survivor's death the assets in the trust will go to your children, you might not only name them as beneficiaries but also provide that the surviving spouse cannot withdraw the principal or change the terms of the trust when either spouse dies. (Many couples worry about the spouse or children of a second marriage and the diversion of family funds to someone other than their intended beneficiaries.) Another reason couples sometimes chose to make a trust irrevocable at the first death is to protect the surviving spouse from unwise withdrawals and lifetime use of trust assets.

In either case, making the trust irrevocable at the first death can trigger federal gift tax problems for the surviving spouse, because the surviving spouse has lost (in reality given up) the right to take the trust property and do with it what he or she wants. At that instant, value shifts from that spouse to the remaindermen (those who will receive what remains in the trust when the second spouse dies). For instance, if the trust gives you and your spouse income for life and the power to revoke the trust while you are both alive, but the trust becomes irrevocable when one of you dies, the survivor may still be entitled to income but will not be able to require a distribution of the principal. That signals a shift of wealth, a gift from the surviving spouse to the remaindermen you've named. Your surviving spouse has lost dominion and control over what happens to the principal, and he or she is making a taxable gift to the remainder beneficiaries based on the actuarial value of the 'their rights. If the taxable gift exceeds the surviving spouse's unified credit, there will be gift tax payable.

Unless it is contrary to your objectives, a simple solution to this problem is to be sure that the trust remains revocable by the surviving spouse.

If you are not worried about who gets the trust property when your spouse dies but want to protect your spouse against foolish uses of principal during lifetime, there is another solution. Speak to your lawyer about a *testamentary power of appointment* over the trust property. This gives the surviving spouse no lifetime power of revocation but allows him or her to appoint (name) the recipient of the joint trust principal in a last will and testament. This makes the gift incomplete, eliminates the gift tax problem, and assures you that the property will remain in the trustee's hands for as long as your surviving spouse lives.

One drawback to this approach is that you lose the ability to control who will be the eventual owner of the trust assets. If your spouse remarries, it could result in property passing to someone other than your intended beneficiary, which would defeat the purpose and function of the irrevocability clause.

These two solutions can also assure that the trust qualifies for the marital deduction and results in no estate tax for the deceased spouse. However, it also means that the entire value of the trust will be taxed upon the death of the surviving spouse. This means that the unified credit of the deceased spouse will not be used, and unnecessary federal estate tax may be payable upon the death of the surviving spouse. (See chapter 13 for an explanation of *by-pass trusts* and unified credit planning.)

Q. What are the federal estate tax implications of a joint trust?

A. If a couple's combined estates exceed the unified credit exclusion amount ($600,000 in 1997 and increasing in steps to $1,000,000 in 2006), there are a number of complex and potentially expensive tax problems that the use of a joint trust creates. Although there are solutions to these problems, in many cases the solutions will themselves either create new problems or thwart your planning objectives. Even some of the brightest minds who have studied these problems admit that the solutions are neither elegant nor simple. Complexity leads to additional cost and hidden tax traps. In most cases (particularly involving larger estates), tax planning professionals will take the more conservative route and draft separate revocable trusts for each spouse.

There are two different types of problems that could arise. One type of problem arises if the entire trust is included in the taxable estate of the first spouse to die. The other type of problem arises if the *surviving* spouse was still considered the owner of the trust upon the death of the first spouse to die.

If each spouse is considered to have powers over the property in the entire joint trust, it is possible the IRS will argue that those retained interests will cause all of the assets in the trust to be included in the estate of the first spouse to die. If the trust exceeds the deceased spouse's unified credit exclusion amount ($600,000 in 1997 and increasing in steps to $1,000,000 in 2006, but reduced by taxable gifts made during lifetime) and the interests of the surviving spouse do not qualify for the federal estate tax marital deduction, there may be an estate tax payable.

The simple solution to this problem is to draft the trust with the assumption that the trust could be entirely included in the taxable estate of the first spouse to die. The trust should therefore provide a marital deduction trust for the surviving spouse if the value of the deceased spouse's estate exceeds the amount sheltered by the unified credit. (See chapter 13 for an explanation of marital trusts and unified credit planning.)

The second type of problem is that the surviving spouse might still be considered the owner of part (or all) of the trust at the death of the first spouse to die. As explained above, a couple will often want make a joint trust irrevocable after one spouse dies. However, making the trust irrevocable at the first death can trigger federal estate and gift tax problems, because the surviving spouse has lost (in reality given up) the right to take the trust property and do with it what he or she wants. The loss of the right to revoke the trust is equivalent to a gift by the surviving spouse which may result in gift tax payable. Even worse is that the surviving spouse may still have beneficial interests in the trust, such as the right to income from the trust, and the retained interests may cause the *entire* value of the trust to be included in the surviving spouse's estate at his or her later death. (The fact that the surviving spouse can make a taxable gift and that the subject of the gift can remain part of the taxable estate does not mean that there is a double tax, because there is essentially a credit for the gift tax when the gift is still included in the taxable estate. However, it shows the complexity of the estate and gift tax problems that can arise.)

These two different types of problems show that the gift tax and estate tax uncertainties create a real tax planning dilemma for large (i.e., above the unified credit exclusion amount) joint trusts. If the surviving spouse is given the right to revoke the trust (or other broad powers) after the first death, there may be unnecessary federal estate tax payable at the first death. If the rights of the surviving spouse are restricted, in order to use the unified credit in the first estate, the surviving spouse may be found to have made a taxable gift at the first death and still owe federal estate tax at his or her own death.

The solution to this dilemma that is recommended by most lawyers is the same as the solution suggested for the gift tax problems, and that is to be sure each spouse has the unilateral and unconditional right to withdraw his or her separate contributions to the trust but has no rights over the contributions by the other spouse. Only in that way can you be sure of the estate and gift tax consequences at death.

The drawback to this solution is that this requires very careful tracing and documenting of the source of all income as well as gains and losses from each and every income-producing property in the trust, for as long as both spouses are alive. This obviously complicates the joint trust and increases its expense and aggravation. And it defeats the "share and share alike" simplicity and community of interest that was the original reason for the joint trust.

There are some lawyers who believe that a joint trust can be drafted so that half, and only half, of the trust is included in the estate of the first spouse to die, and that the trust can then be safely divided in half, with half of the assets included in the deceased spouse's estate (with whatever unified credit or marital deduction provisions might be appropriate for that half of the trust), and the other half remaining the property of the surviving spouse. If these tax results can be obtained, it would be an ideal estate plan for many married couples, because they could enjoy the convenience of a joint trust during their lifetimes and be assured of minimizing estate taxes through both unified credits regardless of which of them might die first.

As noted before, there have been no rulings by the IRS on the gift tax and estate tax consequences of joint trusts, and lawyers are divided in their opinions. If your combined estates are not likely to exceed the unified credit exclusion amount, the federal transfer (gift and estate) taxes can largely be ignored. But if your combined assets will eventually exceed this amount, a joint trust can cause severe transfer tax problems.

Q. Are there any income tax problems with a joint trust?

A. In most cases there will be few—if any—income tax problems with a joint trust. As is the case with most revocable living trusts, all income, deductions, and credits are reportable by you and your spouse on your own joint return just as if there were no trust. Since you are both considered the owners of the property actually owned by your joint trust for income tax purposes, if you put a jointly held home in the trust, you can still deduct real estate taxes and mortgage interest.

See chapter 10 for other information on the income tax treatment of revocable trusts.

Q. Is there a tax-basis advantage to a joint trust?

A. According to some authorities, it should be possible to create a joint trust in which *all* the assets in the joint trust receive a step-up in basis to fair market value at the death of the first spouse, without any adverse estate tax consequences. This could be extremely advantageous because a later sale of those assets by the survivor would result in relatively little, if any, gain.

The reasoning that leads to this result is complicated, and requires you to tip-toe through the minefield that is the Internal Revenue Code. What is especially troubling is that the lawyers who claim to be able to achieve this result also claim to have solved all of the gift and estate tax problems described above. In other words, these lawyers say that you can have an estate plan with all of the administrative advantages of a single joint trust, the optimum estate tax result regardless of which spouse dies first, *and* get an additional income tax break through a step-up in basis for all trust assets.

Most lawyers would be delighted to be able to create a joint trust in which each spouse was considered the owner of one half of the trust, with a step-in basis for one half of the assets and no estate tax complications at the second death. But the additional trust provisions that are needed to try to achieve the additional step-up in basis would also jeopardize the favorable estate tax results.

Q. Are there state tax considerations I must consider with a joint trust?

A. All estate planning must take the state death tax implications into consideration. For those relatively few states with estate taxes or inheritance taxes that are independent of the federal estate tax system, the state death consequences could vary greatly from state to state. Does your state consider a joint trust as the equivalent to jointly held property owned by husband and wife? The answer may be very important.

The death tax results may also differ if the trust becomes irrevocable after the first death. Some states may allow a marital deduction or joint trust exemption if the trust is revocable after the first death, but they may deny the exemption if the joint trust becomes irrevocable at the first death.

You should also check to see if placing real estate into a joint trust could trigger real property transfer taxes.

Q. Is a joint trust suitable for community property?

A. Although joint trusts can raise difficult issues in most states, as discussed above, there are a few states with special property laws for married couples, called "community property" laws, which eliminate or minimize the problems of joint trusts.

In most states which have adopted the English "common law" legal system (i.e., every state except Louisiana, which adopted the French "civil law" system), all property belongs to either the husband, or to the wife, or to both jointly. Money earned by the husband belongs to the husband and money earned by the wife belongs to the wife and property is jointly owned only if the husband and wife choose to take title in joint names.

In the 1800s, seven western states (Arizona, California, Idaho, New Mexico, Nevada, Texas, and Washington) joined Louisiana in adopting a marital property system based on Spanish civil law. The Wisconsin Marital Property Reform Act of 1984 does not use the term "community property," but the IRS has ruled that the Wisconsin system is a community property system for federal tax purposes, so Wisconsin should also be considered a community property state for estate tax planning purposes.

What is "community property"? In those nine states, all property acquired during a marriage is "community property" of the husband and wife, belonging to both of them regardless of who took title to the property. Even the earnings from the labor of a spouse are considered to be community property, not the separate property of the working spouse. Gifts by a married couple of community property are considered gifts by both spouses (and may require the consent of both spouses). So the surviving spouse may be entitled to a one half share of the community property at the death of a spouse, regardless of what the will of the first spouse might provide with respect to the community property. In short, both spouses have rights in the community property of the marriage regardless of how the property is titled.

In a community property state, community property may retain its character as community property even after it has been transferred to a joint trust. As a result, there is no gift by either spouse when the joint trust is created, and only one half of the property is included in the estate of the first spouse to die. Therefore, many of the estate and gift tax problems discussed above no longer apply, while the convenience and other advantages of a joint trust remain. For this reason, joint trusts are popular estate planning tools in several community property states.

Even in community property states, it is typical for a joint trust to keep separate schedules of community property and separate property contributed to the trust, to trace and document the source of all income as well as gains and losses from each income-producing property in the trust for as long as both spouses are alive, and to provide separate directions for the distribution or other disposition of the community property that are different than the directions for the distribution and disposition of the separate property. This obviously complicates the administration of the joint trust and greatly reduces the desired simplicity and convenience that were among the original reasons for the joint trust.

TRUSTS FOR MINORS

Chapter 15 explains:

- Why you (and almost everyone who has children) may want to set up a trust for a minor—or even an adult child

- What a UGMA or UTMA account is and why it may be a viable alternative in some cases to a trust

- The advantages of a UGMA/UTMA

- The disadvantages of a UGMA/UTMA

- What a Section 2503(c) trust is

- Requirements of a Section 2503(c) trust

- Tax savings possible under 2503(c) trusts

- How a trust that distributes all of its income can qualify for the annual gift tax exclusion

- What a Crummey trust is and how it can accomplish the same objectives as a 2503(c) trust

- How a trust for a minor grandchild can avoid the federal generation-skipping transfer tax

Q. Why set up a trust for a minor?

A. It is dangerous, inefficient, and expensive to leave large amounts of money or other assets to minor children, either outright or in installments, or to children of any age who do not have the emotional or intellectual maturity to handle those assets properly. An outright gift (during your lifetime, by will, or by intestacy) of a large amount of cash or any other asset is a classic example of what estate planners consider an improper disposition of assets: the wrong thing going to the wrong person at the wrong time and in the wrong manner. For instance, take a look at the following situations:

- Joint accounts in your name and your minor child's name (or a U.S. savings bond or note in joint names or a minor's sole name) can result in giving that child direct access to money—sometimes even before that child reaches majority. (Minors who are competent enough to sign their name to the request for payment can cash U.S. bonds).

- To a great extent, property titled in the name of a minor is legally "frozen." The minor's signature on a transfer document gives little assurance of good title to the buyer, so it is difficult to engage in transactions pertaining to that asset. This is why property passing outright to minors almost invariably requires the court appointment of a legal guardian, a costly and often frustrating process under which every dollar spent on the minor's behalf must be accounted for and approved by the court (which often will not approve certain expenditures).

  Because very rigid procedures and operating standards are mandated for guardians, investments are highly restricted and very inflexible. Some states require that the guardian of a child's money be someone other than the child's parent. Many states require that a guardian of a minor's property post a bond, a form of insurance that must be paid for by the minor out of the minor's assets.

- Property left directly to a minor is controlled by the minor without restriction when he or she attains legal majority, which is 18 in almost all states. But does (or will) your 18-year-old child have the intellectual capacity, maturity, and willingness to handle the investment properly over a long period of time? If you leave life insurance, pension money, a family business, stocks, bonds, real estate, or almost any other asset outright, you have no way to be sure that an immature child will not squander money intended for the child's college education or for the child's lifelong financial security.

- Stock and real estate brokers don't want to deal with minors. Why not? Because when minors reach legal majority, they can accept the benefits of a transaction that works in their favor yet legally disaffirm one that has fallen in value.

Q. What are the UGMA and the UTMA?

A. There is a way gifts can be made for a minor without a trust or a guardian. This trust alternative is known as the Uniform Transfers to Minors Act (UTMA), which is the successor to the to Uniform Gifts to Minors Act (UGMA) which is still in force in many states. The UTMA allows you to make a gift of property such as securities, cash, life insurance, annuities, or even real estate to a minor. (The UGMA is more limited than the UTMA, but still permits gifts of stocks and bank accounts.) Usually, the transfer is made easily and quickly. In fact, the custodial account is much more simple to create and much less expensive to administer than a trust. Typically, the custodial account is the most appropriate vehicle for small, one-time-only, or sporadic modest gifts.

In the case of securities, for example, you merely have your broker register the stock or bond in the name of the custodian "as custodian for (name of minor) under the (name of state) Uniform Transfers to Minors Act." Typically, the custodian is an adult family member (preferably not the person making the gift or a parent of the minor, because of estate tax complications discussed below).

Technically, although the adult custodian holds physical possession of the property or the instrument representing the property and acts on the minor's behalf, it is the minor who is considered the owner of the property for tax purposes. For that reason, all income earned by the custodial property is taxable income to the minor, not the custodian or the donor.

Generally, you can name any adult, a trust company, or a bank with trust powers as a custodian, although some states limit custodians to an adult member of the minor's family. (It is essential that you check your state's laws to see if the person you have selected is eligible.) If you are concerned about keeping the property in question out of your estate for tax purposes, name someone other than yourself as custodian. (Estate tax law would treat a parent's custodial power to use account income or principal to satisfy his or her obligations to support the minor child as an incomplete gift and thus require the account to be included in the parent's estate).

The types of property that can be given to a minor under the UGMA or the UTMA may be limited under your state's law. Under the UTMA (the newer and broader of the two laws), you can give all the types of property that can be transferred under the UGMA, as well as real estate and personal property (such as artwork and even oil or gas leases). Intangible property (such as the right to payment on a mortgage or the right to repayment of a debt) can also be given to a custodian for a minor under the UTMA. In addition, the UTMA allows transfers from estates, trusts, and guardianships. Most states have either expanded their UGMA laws or replaced them with the more liberal and flexible UTMA rules.

The person you have selected as custodian may use the property to provide either a luxury or a necessity for the minor. Custodial property, therefore, can be used to support, maintain, educate, or provide other benefits for the minor donee. Note that the custodian has total and absolute discretion to determine whether to pay out or accumulate income and to decide how much principal—and for what purposes—to expend for the minor's use and benefit.

Only one custodian can be named for each account and only one minor can be the beneficiary of each custodial account. But there is no limit as to how many different custodial accounts you may set up. In many states, if the custodian dies while serving, the minor's legal guardian will take over unless the custodian had specified a successor. Some states allow a minor age 14 or older to select a successor custodian. In other cases, a state court will select a successor.

Q. What are the advantages of an UGMA/UTMA account?

A. There are many advantages to the UGMA/UTMA. Consider the following:

- Typically, there are no out-of-pocket costs in using either an UGMA or UTMA. If you would like to make a gift of relatively small amounts of cash each year for a child's or grandchild's (or other minor's) benefit but do not want to make an outright gift and for whatever reason do not want or cannot afford to set up a trust, the UGMA or UTMA is a good device.

- You can give gifts to minors of relatively modest amounts of land, stocks, bonds, and especially mutual funds quickly, easily, inexpensively through an UGMA or UTMA custodial account.

- The UGMA/UTMA device will shift income taxation on any investment earnings from you to your child. So technically, your child is liable for reporting income earned by custodial account assets.

Up until age 14, income earned is taxed to the child—but at your tax bracket. Once your child reaches age 14, income earned by the asset(s) in the custodial account will be taxed to the child at his or her bracket rather than yours. This could shift income from as high as a 39.6 percent bracket to as low as a 15 percent rate. This incredible tax bracket shift is essentially equivalent to increasing the return on the investment by about 25 percent! The more children, grandchildren, nieces, nephews, or other donees you have, the more effective this income-splitting technique is. Income is taxed to the child whether or not the investment income is actually distributed to him or her (unless it is used by the custodian to discharge a parent's legal obligation, such as support; in that case, it is taxed to the parent at the parent's income tax bracket).

- Gifts under the UGMA or UTMA qualify for the federal gift tax annual exclusion, so you can give each minor donee (related or not) up to $10,000 a year ($20,000 if you are married) each year (and every year), without paying a gift tax and without using a nickel of your unified credit (which shelters $600,000 to $1,000,000 from estate or gift tax, depending on the year of the death or gift). (And the $10,000 annual exclusion may be adjusted for inflation after 1998.)

- If you no longer own an asset, it can no longer be taxed in your estate. The UGMA/UTMA gift, therefore, will save estate taxes on the asset you give away and on any appreciation from the date of the gift. For example, if you are 40 years old, married, and have three children, you can give up to $60,000 ($20,000 per account) gift tax free each year. If you continue gifts for, say 10 years, you'll save the federal estate tax on over $600,000—resulting in a tax saving of about $300,000 if you are in a 50 percent estate tax bracket!

- Custodial income can be accumulated so that when the child begins college, some or all of the income can be paid out each year to that child, who can then pay his or her own tuition, room, and board and use any additional funds for other expenses and luxuries. (Some state divorce courts will impose a legal duty on a financially "wealthy" parent to pay for the children's college education. Whether or not the UGMA/UTMA gifts will reduce that legal obligation will depend on the specific laws of that state.)

- Transfers you make to a UGMA or UTMA are no longer subject to probate in your estate and, absent fraud, are no longer subject to the claims of your creditors.

Q. What's wrong with the UGMA/UTMA?

A. The UGMA/UTMA is a kind of simplified trust defined by statute. Because it is defined by statute, you can't change it. You are stuck with the provisions of the statute. This can cause a number of problems, including the following:

- The minor may get control of the custodial property earlier than you would like. In the majority of states, the custodial account ends (and is distributed to the beneficiary) at age 21, which you might consider to be too young. In a sizable minority of states, the custodial account ends as 18 (or 19), which may *really* be too young. So your child, upon the date specified by the UGMA/UTMA statute in your state, must then take over the investment and management of the property. At that point, there are no restrictions on how he or she may invest—or spend—the money or other asset. Therefore, there is no guarantee that he or she will not make an unwise investment or spend money foolishly. Creditors or predators can pounce.

In a few states, the account ends at 18 unless you specify that it ends at age 21. So you need to specify the age you want when you make the gift. Even if you live in a state in which custodial accounts end at eighteen, you might be able to choose the laws of a different state, in which the account will not end until 21, by naming a custodian who lives in that state and naming that state in the custodial registration. (For example, if you live in South Carolina, where accounts end at 18, and you want to appoint a custodian who lives in Georgia, where accounts end at 21, you would register the account in the name of the custodian "as custodian for (name of minor) under the Georgia Uniform Transfers to Minors Act.")

You may also be able to restrict the rights of your beneficiary after the custodial account ends by getting the custodian to transfer the custodial account to a family limited partnership in exchange for a limited partnership interest. That way you shift both income and wealth to your children but they receive no cash to spend or squander—unless you—as the general partner chose to make a partnership income distribution.

- If you have two or more children to whom you'd like to make a gift, you must set up a separate custodial account for each one. You can't establish one custodial account for all three of your children.

- Assets in one account can't be used for the other child or children no matter how deserving or needy they may be. There is no flexibility, therefore, to combine custodial accounts or make transfers from one UGMA/UTMA account to another.

- Gifts to either a UGMA or UTMA are irrevocable. So you can't take them back.

- At the minor's death, assets in his or her custodial account will pass to his or her executor (if there is a valid will) or the administrator of his or her estate. This means that assets will pass through probate in the minor's estate, will typically be administered under state intestacy laws—which may means delays and costs—and will often ultimately pass back to the parent who made the gift.

- The custodial account may also be subject to inheritance tax under state law. If the parents disclaim (renounce) their interests in the child's estate, so that the custodial property passes to the deceased child's siblings and is not added back to the parents' taxable estates, there may have to be guardians appointed for minor siblings, which results in the same problems and expenses of guardianship proceedings that the UGMA/UTMA gifts were intended to avoid.

- All of the property you have given under the UGMA/UTMA will be included in your taxable estate at your death if you are the custodian for the minor beneficiary and you die prior to the date the assets are payable to the child under your state's laws. This is because, as custodian, your powers over the custodial property are extensive enough to be considered a retained right to control the disposition of the property.

If federal estate tax planning is a concern (i.e., your estate or the combined estates of you and your spouse are likely to exceed the unified credit exclusion amount), you should not name yourself as custodian of any gifts you make. One solution is to name your spouse as custodian. But if you live in a community property state, you should not name your spouse to serve as custodian because your spouse will be considered to have given one half of the value of the transferred property. Consider naming another responsible adult family member as custodian.

- Some authorities also believe that custodial property could be included in the taxable estate of the custodian if the minor beneficiary is the child of the custodian, even though the custodian is not the donor, because the custodian could use the custodial property to discharge the custodian's duty to support his or her minor child. For that reason, it may be better for grandparents who want to make gifts for grandchildren to name as custodian a child who is *not* a parent of the grandchild (i.e., an aunt or uncle of the grandchild) rather than a parent of the grandchild. (Some state laws provide that the custodian cannot use the custodial property to discharge a legal obligation of support, in part to try to avoid estate taxes on the death of the custodian.)

Q. What is a Section 2503(c) trust?

A. Generally speaking, gifts in trust do *not* qualify for the federal gift tax annual exclusion. That's because the law requires that the recipient of a gift have the immediate, unfettered, and ascertainable right to use, posses, or enjoy the gifted property— which is exactly what most trusts are designed to prevent.

However, Section 2503(c) of the Internal Revenue Code Section allows you to make a gift to a child, grandchild, or other minor that does qualify for the federal gift tax annual exclusion, so that up to $10,000 (or $20,000 if you are married and you and your spouse elect to split the gifts) can be given to the trust each year without any gift tax consequences.

A Section 2503(c) trust is similar to a UTMA gift, because the trustee *must* have the power to apply the income and principal of the trust for the benefit of the minor, and the minor *must* have the right to withdraw all of the income and principal of the trust at age 21.

However, a Section 2503(c) trust can be more flexible than a UTMA gift for the following reasons:

- In addition to naming a trustee, you can select one or more co-trustees and one or more "back-up" trustees in case the ones you've named, for whatever reason, resign or no longer perform their duties. Don't name yourself as trustee--or your spouse if you live in a community property state--because your powers as trustee will cause the trust assets to be included in your taxable estate if you should die while the beneficiary is under 21. Another reason not to name yourself as trustee is that income of the trust could be taxable income to you, and taxable at your income tax bracket, if trust income is used for the support of your child for whom you have a legal obligation of support.

- Although the beneficiary must have the right to withdraw the income and principal of the trust at age 21, you can provide in the trust that the beneficiary's withdrawal right can expire if it is not exercised within a limited time. The IRS has approved a trust in which the right to withdraw from the trust ended after 60 days from the day the beneficiary reached age 21. This is significantly different from a custodial arrangement under the UTMA, because the beneficiary automatically has the right to the custodial property without doing anything, and there is no time limit within which the beneficiary can exercise his or her rights to the custodial property.

- If the beneficiary should die, the trust must allow the beneficiary to direct ("appoint") the property in the trust to whomever the beneficiary wants, including his or her creditors and the creditors of his estate. This "general power of appointment" means that the property in the trust is included in the beneficiary's taxable estate for federal estate tax purposes and for state death tax purposes in most states). However, the beneficiary cannot validly exercise the power of appointment under the laws of most states if the beneficiary is under 18 years of age.

Your trust can therefore direct that, if your child dies while under 18 (or over 18 but without exercising the power before death), the property will stay in trust for the benefit of your other children and not return to you or become part of your child's probate estate. (Under the UGMA/UTMA, the custodial property always becomes part of the deceased beneficiary's probate estate.)

The usual reason for a Section 2503(c) trust is to take advantage of the federal gift tax annual exclusion. Each $10,000 gift that qualifies for the annual exclusion is free of both gift tax and estate tax. If your estate is more than the unified credit exclusion amount, your estate may eventually have to pay estate tax on the value of your estate above the exclusion amount at rates of 37% or more. Each $10,000 gift therefore saves at least $3,700 of federal estate tax. With enough children (or grandchildren) to whom to make gifts each year, the annual exclusion can save a significant amount of estate tax within just a few years of starting a gift program.

Another reason your estate planner might advise using a Section 2503(c) trust is to save income taxes if your income tax bracket is high and your child is in a relatively lower bracket. Shifting property to a child in a 15 percent bracket could save a great deal of income tax on investment income. For instance, if you are in a 40 percent state and federal bracket and your child is 14 years old or over and in a 15% bracket, there will be an immediate net increase of 24%. (Until a child is 14, his or her unearned income is taxed to the child—but at the parent's bracket.)

Q. What are the requirements for gifts to a 2503(c) trust to be gift tax free?

A. The tax law device that makes transfers to a 2503(c) trust gift tax free up to $10,000 a year ($20,000 if you are married) is called the *annual gift tax exclusion*. The usual rule is that a gift must be a gift of a "present interest" to qualify for the exclusion. That means that the *donee* (recipient) of your gift must have the immediate, unfettered, and ascertainable legal right to use, possess, and enjoy the gift. Gifts are typically made in trust to do just the opposite, restrict the donee's use, possession, and enjoyment of the gift. That is why, as noted above, gifts in trust usually do not qualify for the annual exclusion.

Section 2503(c) provides an exception to the general rules regarding present interests. If your lawyer drafts the trust properly, you'll obtain the favorable gift and estate tax treatment the 2503(c) trust is designed to bring. Here's what the trust must specify:

- Trust income and principal may be used by or on behalf of the beneficiary of the trust at any time before he or she reaches age 21. You can *not* limit the discretion of the trustee and direct that the income and principal only be used for certain purposes, such as the education of the minor.

- To the extent income or principal have not been used by or for the trust's beneficiary by the time he or she reaches age 21, it must pass to the beneficiary at age 21. (The references to age 21 is a matter of federal tax law, and is not affected by states laws regarding majority or the ages specified in the UGMA or UTMA in a state.)

- If the beneficiary dies before age 21, the assets in the trust (including any accumulated income) must be paid either to the beneficiary's estate *or* as the beneficiary may direct ("appoint") during his or her lifetime or by his or her will. (The fact that the beneficiary might be legally incompetent to execute a will or otherwise exercise the power of appointment is not relevant.)

Although these provisions seem to be very strict, there is actually a certain amount of flexibility:

- You may include an "extension feature"--that is, you may specify that the trust will continue for your selected beneficiary even beyond his or her 21st birthday--as long as he or she has the right to withdraw the trust's assets at age 21. For example, you can stipulate that the trust will continue until your beneficiary's 30th birthday unless she files a written notice within 2 months of her 21st birthday demanding that she be paid all trust principal and accumulated income. This type of provision obtains a gift tax exclusion yet prevents assets being "forced out," as they are in a UGMA/UTMA account. It is one reason the 2503(c) trust is favored when gifts are large or are expected to grow substantially in value.

- You can also provide for contingent gifts or contingent trusts if your beneficiary should die before withdrawing all of the trust assets. At the death of the beneficiary, the trust assets do not have to be paid to the beneficiary's estate. You can give the beneficiary a "general power of appointment" (the right to name who gets the assets in the trust if he or she dies) but provide that the power is exercisable only in his or her will, and only if the beneficiary specifically refers to your trust.

If the beneficiary fails to exercise the power, the trust can (for example) direct that the trust assets be distributed to your other children or held in trust for your benefit. Under state law, a beneficiary under the age of 18 cannot exercise a valid will, so as a practical matter you can exert almost complete control over the disposition of the trust funds upon the death of the beneficiary.

A Section 2503(c) trust—into which you've placed $20,000 of cash, stocks, bonds, mutual funds, or other assets—could provide as follows:

"The OverFlowing Bank and Trust Company is named trustee of this trust for my son, Farnsworth. The trustee shall pay to my son, or apply for his benefit, as much of the income and principal of this trust as the trustee may from time to time consider appropriate for my son, in the trustee's sole discretion. As soon as my son is 21 years of age, he shall have the right to withdraw all or any part of the principal and undistributed income of this trust. If my son should die before he is 21 years of age, the principal and undistributed income then remaining shall be distributed to whatever persons and in whatever amounts or proportions, and subject to whatever trusts or other conditions, my son may appoint by will or codicil specifically referring to this power. To the extent my son should fail to exercise that power of appointment, the balance of principal and undistributed income then remaining shall be distributed to his descendants then living or, if there is no such descendant, to my descendants then living."

Q. What tax savings are possible under 2503(c) trusts?

A. It is possible to save at least four types of taxes using a 2503(c) trust:

- If the income of the trust is distributed to the beneficiary, it is taxable to that person instead of you. Assuming your beneficiary is aged 14 or older, tax will be imposed at his or her income tax bracket rather than to you at yours. (If the child is younger than 14, distributed income in excess of $1,300—indexed each year for inflation—will be taxed to the child but at your top bracket.)

Although income accumulated by the trust is taxed at the trust's bracket, some tax savings may be possible by splitting income between the trust and its beneficiary. Thus income tax savings are possible every year in which your income tax bracket is higher than each of your children or grandchildren or the other minor beneficiaries you have named. (This assumes that the trust is not a "grantor trust" (one in which the grantor is treated as if he or she—and not the trust—owned trust assets) for federal income tax purposes, and that income of the trust is not used to support a child whom you are legally obligated to support. See chapter 16 for an explanation of the grantor trust rules.)

- To the extent that they don't exceed $10,000 a year, gifts you make to a Section 2503(c) trust are gift tax free. In fact, you can make taxable gifts up to a total of $1,000,000 (in 2006) without payment of any gift tax if you are willing to utilize your federal estate and gift tax unified credit.

- Property you place into the 2503(c) trust can avoid federal estate tax because is no longer yours. As long as you don't name yourself as trustee (or name your spouse as trustee if you live in a community property state), you can remove an asset from federal estate taxation in your estate, and your children will benefit from the estate tax savings. All of the property plus all of the appreciation realized on the property is removed from your estate from the date you put it into the trust. (Note that to remove life insurance from your estate, you must give up all rights and survive the gift by more than three years.)

- Many states with inheritance taxes have no gift taxes, so that gifts to a Section 2503(c) trust can avoid state death taxes as well as the federal estate tax.

Q. Can a trust that distributes income qualify for the annual gift tax exclusion? (What is a 2503(b) trust?)

A. As we have previously explained, a gift does not qualify for the federal gift tax annual exclusion unless the gift is a "present interest," and gifts in trust are usually not considered to be present interests. One exception is the Section 2503(c) trust, described above. Another exception is a trust which is required to distribute all of its income each year, sometimes called a "simple trust" for federal income tax purposes. The present right to receive a stream of income is considered to be a present interest, even though the income itself will be received in the future. However, the annual gift tax exclusion only applies to the present value of the income stream. This value is determined from the government's present value tables using a federal interest (discount) rate called the "Section 7520 rate" and the term of the trust or the life expectancy of the beneficiary (if the trust is for the life of the beneficiary). (These calculations can be quickly done using the *NumberCruncher* program, which can be purchased by calling 610-527-5216).

The advantage of a "simple trust" is incredible flexibility and control over trust assets: Here, the trustee does not have to pay out trust principal when the child reaches 18 or 21 or any other age required by federal tax law or state law. As long as you are willing to have the child receive all the income of the trust, you can spread out payments of trust principal over as many years or at whatever ages you'd like. For instance, you can specify that your son is to receive no principal until he reaches age 35, then receive a portion of trust principal every 5 years until it is used up. In fact, the simple income trust can last for your son's lifetime (or for any shorter period, such as a specific term, for instance 10, 15, or 20 years).

You can even provide that the trust beneficiary will never receive the principal in the trust and you can specify who will receive the principal instead. Or you can allow your income beneficiary to pick the ultimate beneficiary of the principal.

The fact that all of the income must be distributed each year does not mean that you have no control over the income. You can control the application of income generated by the trust by directing that the trust income be distributed to a custodian under the UGMA or UTMA instead of being distributed to the minor beneficiary. You can also arrange for the trust to invest in high-growth, relatively low-yield securities or an interest in a family limited partnership or limited liability company, enabling you to control income distributions if you are the general partner of the family partnership or the manager of the limited liability company. However, the trust document cannot direct (or specifically allow) the trustee to invest in non-income-producing assets. If it did, the present income interest you provided in the trust will not be meaningful and the IRS would disallow your annual gift tax exclusion.

If you decide to use a simple income trust, the income from the trust will be taxed to your beneficiary as it is earned. However, you should be careful that you have not retained any powers over the trust that would cause the trust to be considered a grantor trust for federal income tax purposes, as explained in chapter 16. Regardless of the terms of the trust, you can still be taxed on income that is applied to pay for the support of a minor child which you have an obligation to support under state law.

When you put assets into a simple income trust, the entire amount you transfer to the trust is a gift. But only a portion of it, an amount equal to the present value of the income stream, will qualify for the annual exclusion from the gift tax. Your lawyer or accountant will compute the value of the present interest by actuarially determining which portion of the gift is the beneficiary's annual right to income—the *term certain* or *life estate*—and which is the principal that will remain when the term expires or the life income beneficiary dies and the trust ends—the *remainder interest*.

You'll be allowed an annual gift tax exclusion for the present value of the guaranteed term or life interest. No exclusion will be available for the value of the remainder interest. For example, if you establish a trust for the lifetime of your 5-year-old son, the present value of his income interest could be about 98% of the value of the gift (depending on Section 7520 federal discount (interest) rate in effect at the time of the gift). If you make a gift of $10,000 to his trust, $9,800 could qualify for the gift tax annual exclusion, while only $200 remains a taxable gift, using part of your unified credit (if not already used by other gifts).

A simple income trust allows you greater control over the disposition of trust principal at the cost of some relatively small gift tax liability. Even that small gift tax exposure should not cause any out-of-pocket gift tax payments until you have used up your unified credit or unless your total transfers to the trust are quite large.

Q. What is a Crummey trust, and can it be used to accomplish the same objectives as a 2503(c) trust?

A. The obvious disadvantage of the 2503(c) trust is that the beneficiary must have the right to take all of the trust's assets and accumulated income at age 21. This legal right must be specified in the 2503(c) trust in order for you to obtain the annual gift tax exclusion that allows gift-tax-free gifts year after year.

The disadvantage of the simple income trust is that a portion of every transfer you make to the trust is not eligible for the gift tax annual exclusion. Once you've used your unified credit (an exclusion of $600,000 in 1997 and increasing by steps to $1,000,000 in 2006), you'll have to pay gift taxes. (Of course, your total gifts to the simple income trust must be very large to reach this point).

A possible solution to the disadvantages of the Section 2503(c) trust and simple income trust is yet a third type of irrevocable trust—one that gives its beneficiary a "Crummey power." A Crummey power is a good thing. According to a case named after a taxpayer named Crummey, you can obtain the annual exclusion for a gift in trust if you give the beneficiary an immediate right to withdraw the gift from the trust. It's like providing a window that the beneficiary can open, reach in, and take the cash or other asset you put in the trust. That satisfies the gift tax annual exclusion requirement that the beneficiary have the immediate, unfettered, and ascertainable right to use, possess, or enjoy the property.

The fact that the right of withdrawal cannot be exercised by a minor beneficiary does not prevent the right of withdrawal from being a present interest as long as their is no reason why a guardian could not be appointed to exercise the power. Typically, the beneficiary's right of withdrawal ends (or "lapses") after a relatively short period of time (usually no less than thirty days), and the trust is completely irrevocable after the right of withdrawal lapses. So the window can be set to open for only a certain period of time each time you make a gift—and then it locks shut.

You can require written notice by your beneficiary that he or she is electing to take that year's contribution and, if he or she fails to make a withdrawal during the specified time and in the specified manner, the assets and income cannot be withdrawn at a later date. After the window of withdrawal opportunity closes, the trust can continue for many years, and a great deal of money and other assets can be placed into it for a child's benefit without risking that the child will be tempted to withdraw from the trust when he or she is 21.

A "Crummey trust" can therefore qualify for the federal gift tax annual exclusion even though the beneficiary has no right to income and no right to any principal at age 21. You can postpone payments of both income and principal and keep them from a child or grandchild until an age (e.g. 25, 20, or 35) or event (marriage or birth of a child or start of a business) at which you feel more confident that he or she will have the emotional and intellectual maturity to safely handle trust assets.

The preparation of a trust with Crummey powers raises a number of technical tax issues, and the wording of the trust can be very important:

- The power to withdraw is intended only to qualify the gifts to the trust for the annual gift tax exclusion. So the rights of withdrawal you give each beneficiary should be limited to the $10,000 annual exclusion. In order to provide for possible future increases in the annual exclusion, most lawyers limit the right of withdrawal to either (a) the value of the property given to the trust or (b) the maximum annual gift tax exclusion allowed under the Internal Revenue Code, whichever is less.

- In order for the right of withdrawal to qualify as a present interest, the IRS has ruled that the beneficiary must be given written notice of the right of withdrawal within a reasonable amount of time after each gift is made.

- The trust must specify how long the right of withdrawal may remain unexercised before it lapses. We recommend that you give a beneficiary at least 30 days from the date of notice within which to exercise the right before it can lapse. This can be a problem if the rights of withdrawal lapse on December 31 and you want to make gifts to the trust in December (which people often want to do to take advantage of their annual exclusions before the end of the year).

- The failure of the beneficiary to exercise the right of withdrawal, resulting in a lapse of the right, can itself be a taxable gift by the beneficiary to the ultimate beneficiaries of the trust. In other words by choosing not to take money which the beneficiary could choose to withdraw and by leaving it in the trust, the beneficiary is making a gift of that asset to the person or persons who take it when the trust ends. (Obviously, if there is only one beneficiary, i.e., if the same person gets both all income and all principal, no gift is made when the beneficiary allows the right to take a contribution earlier to lapse since he or she will eventually get it).

Different lawyers have different strategies to avoid this gift by the trust beneficiary to the remainder interests. Some lawyers will limit the beneficiary's right of withdrawal to $5,000, instead of the $10,000 annual exclusion, because of a provision in the Code that allows lapses with a value of $5,000 or less each year to be ignored for gift tax purposes.

Other lawyers will draft the trust so that the beneficiary has the right to withdraw $10,000, but only $5,000 lapses each year. (This is sometimes called a "hanging power," because the power to withdraw continues to "hang" over the trust from year to year until enough years has passed for the power to lapse.)

A third approach is to give the beneficiary powers over the trust (such as a power to direct by will who gets the principal of the trust after the death of the beneficiary) which will prevent the lapse from being a completed gift for federal gift tax purposes, so no taxable gift occurs even though the lapse of the $10,000 right of withdrawal exceeds the $5,000 exception.

- The trust document should recognize that a guardian may be appointed for the minor beneficiary to exercise the rights of withdrawal for the beneficiary. But the trust document should not in any way obstruct the appointment of a guardian. In some states, it may be possible within the trust document to name a guardian for the minor for the purposes of the trust, which may be helpful in establishing that the rights of the minor really could have been exercised by someone for the minor.

  Parents of the minor (other than the grantor of the trust) may also have the power to act for the minor as "natural guardians" under state law, and the trust should not prevent the parents from exercising the rights of the minor. We would also recommend that the guardian named in the trust (if any) and the natural guardians of the minor receive written notices of any gifts.

- There should also be some way to increase the right of withdrawal from $10,000 to $20,000 if the you are married and want to "split" the gifts with your spouse in order to use both annual exclusions.

Unlike a UGMA/UTMA gift or a 2503(c) trust, a Crummey trust can have more than one beneficiary. Instead of having three trusts for your three children, you could have just one trust for all three children. This increases the trust's flexibility because the trustee can provide income or principal to the beneficiary who needs it most.

Gifts to a Crummey trust can have the same income tax, gift tax, and estate tax advantages as gifts to other types of trusts described in this chapter. And as is the case with the other devices discussed in this chapter, it is important that you name a party other than yourself (or your spouse if you live in a community property state) as trustee. Otherwise, because of the broad discretionary powers given to the trustee over trust principal and income, the assets in the trust may be included in your taxable estate and subject to estate tax if you die before the trust ends.

If your estate is large ($1,000,000 or more) and you intend to make a gift to a grandchild, you may need to consider how your trust might be affected by the federal generation-skipping transfer tax (GSTT). If you create a trust for a minor child and the child dies during the term of the trust, survived by his or her own children to whom the trust then passes, the trust may be subject to GSTT at the almost confiscatory rate of 55% unless either (a) the child has been given interests in the trust which cause the trust to be included in the child's taxable estate (in which case there will be no estate tax to pay unless the child's own estate is more than the unified credit exclusion amount) or (b) you have applied your $1,000,000 GSTT exemption to the trust.

Most trusts for minor children are expected to end during the child's lifetime, hopefully at the point the child has matured sufficiently to manage the trust assets wisely and not spend them foolishly. Most donors do not want to waste the $1,000,000 GSTT exemption on a trust which is not intended to be a generation-skipping trust. For that reason, it is often best to give the child taxable interests in the trust and avoid any possible GSTT that accidentally arise if the child dies during the term of the trust. (See chapter 27 for more information about the generation-skipping tax.)

Q. Are trusts for minor grandchildren subject to the generation-skipping transfer tax (GSTT)?

A. Yes, as noted above, a gift to a trust for a minor grandchild can result in generation-skipping transfer tax (GSTT) at the almost-confiscatory rate of 55% (in addition to any gift tax payable), unless one of the following exceptions apply:

- The transfers to the trust are nontaxable gifts for GSTT purposes.

- You elect to apply part of your $1,000,000 GST exemption to the trust. (Note: The $1,000,000 exemption may be adjusted for inflation after 1998.)

- Your child (the grandchild's parent) is dead. (This is usually known as the "predeceased child" exception.)

A gift to a trust for a grandchild will be a nontaxable gift for GSTT purposes only if all the following conditions are met:

- The gift to the trust qualifies for the federal gift tax annual exclusion. A trust that qualifies for the annual exclusion under Section 2503(c), or a Crummey trust, could both qualify as nontaxable gifts for GSTT purposes.

- The trust is for the benefit of only one individual and, during the lifetime of the individual, no distributions may be made from the trust to anyone but that individual.

- The value of all of the assets of the trust will be included in the taxable estate of the beneficiary if the beneficiary dies before the end of the trust. (This does not mean that the trust must be distributed to the probate estate of the beneficiary, only that the assets of the trust will be subject to federal estate tax if the beneficiary's taxable estate, including the trust, is more than the unified credit exclusion amount. What happens to the assets of the trust after the death of the beneficiary depends on the terms of the trust.)

Both a Section 2503(c) and a Crummey trust for the benefit of a grandchild can satisfy all of these conditions as long as (1) the grandchild is the only beneficiary of the trust during the grandchild's lifetime and (2) the grandchild continues to have a power over the trust which will cause the entire trust to be included in the grandchild's taxable estate at death (such as a *general power of appointment,* which is a power to direct the distribution of the trust property to anyone the grandchild wishes after his or her death, including his or her own estate or creditors).

A gift to a grandchild under the UTMA or UGMA will be considered to be a gift directly to the grandchild, and not in trust. For this reason, it will not be subject to federal GSTT as long as the gift is within the federal gift tax annual exclusion. Only to the extent the gift is in excess of the annual exclusion will it be necessary to apply part of your $1,000,000 GSTT exemption (or pay the GST tax).

The draconian generation-skipping tax and the $1,000,000 exemption from that tax—as well as the predeceased child exception—are all described in more detail in chapter 27.

Irrevocable Trust

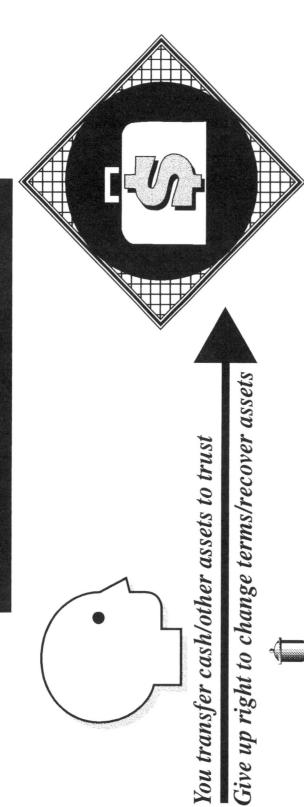

You transfer cash/other assets to trust

Give up right to change terms/recover assets

Irrevocable Trust

Trust pays income and principal to parties you specified in time/manner you specified when you create trust

At your death:

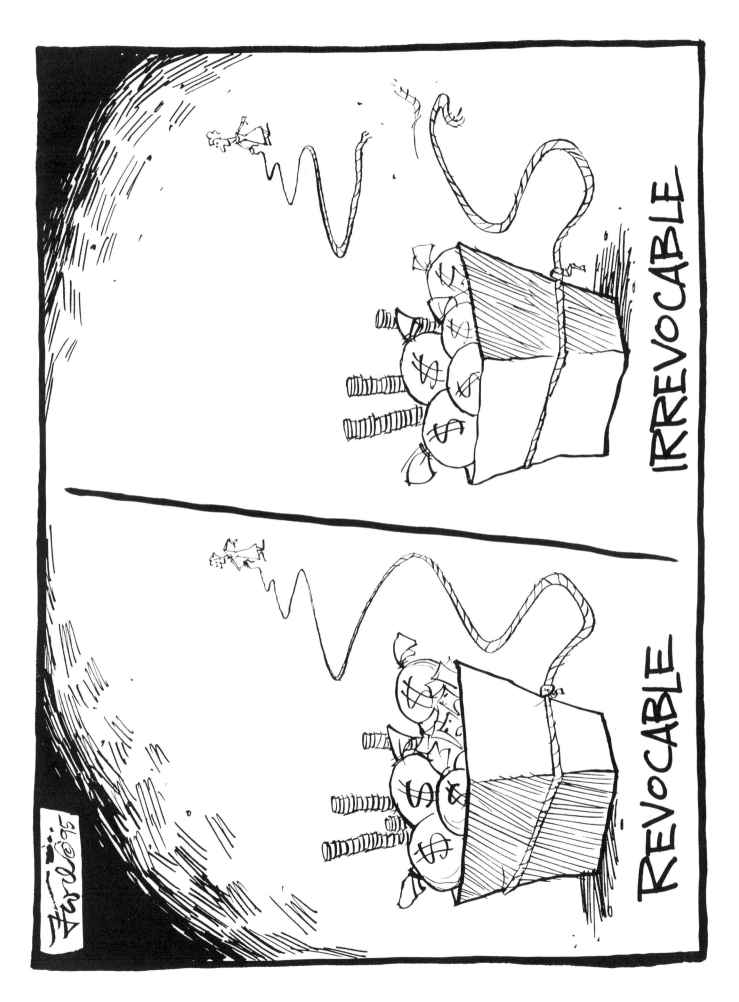

IRREVOCABLE

REVOCABLE

IRREVOCABLE TRUSTS

Chapter 16 explains:

- What is an irrevocable trust

- How an irrevocable trust works

- Why make gifts in trust rather than outright

- Why you may want to create a trust you can't revoke or terminate

- How an irrevocable trust can be the center of an estate plan

- How an irrevocable trust can be used to pay your estate taxes

- What the downsides and costs of an irrevocable trust are

- What types of assets are best to place in an irrevocable trust

- Implications of retaining the right to income from assets you have transferred

- Problems when the assets contributed are subject to debt

- Situations in which you rather than the trust will be taxed on trust income

- How an irrevocable trust (and its beneficiaries) are taxed on trust income

- How a trust calculates taxable gain or loss on a sales of an asset contributed to the trust

- Advantages of creating multiple trusts

Q. *What is an irrevocable trust?*

A. Let's return to our analogy of a trust as a box into which you can put all types of assets. You'll remember that we described a revocable trust as a box with a string on it. By pulling the string, you can recover the property you placed into the box or change the terms of the agreement you made when you set up the box.

If you set up the box without a string or if you cut the string you had kept when you set up the box, your trust becomes irrevocable. You can no longer reach in and get back cash or other assets you put into the trust. Nor can you unilaterally change the terms of the trust.

The term "irrevocable trust" is usually used to describe a "living" or "inter vivos" trust created during the lifetime of the *grantor* (that's you, the person who creates and funds the trust) that cannot be revoked, altered, amended, or terminated by the grantor. The grantor transfers legal title to property (called *corpus* or *principal*) to the *trustee* (the person or parties) who holds legal title to the property placed into the trust. The trustee is responsible for administering that property for the benefit of the trust's *beneficiary* (the person or party for whose benefit the trust was created).

Even when you create a trust that is irrevocable, you can still retain broad powers over the trust. For example, you can keep the power to direct ("appoint") distributions of income and principal from the trust to the beneficiaries of your choice. You can retain extensive interests in the trust, such as the right to income and the right to principal in the discretion of the trustee. (However, retention of these powers or strings may cause the income to be taxed to you and the assets in the trust at the time of your death to be includable in your estate for tax purposes).

The term "irrevocable trust" really describes a broad spectrum of possible trusts, from a trust in which the grantor has absolutely no interest and absolutely no power to a trust which is almost (but not quite) revocable and almost indistinguishable from a revocable trust. As we've just noted, which strings you keep—and how many—will have a direct impact on whether or not you will be taxed on trust income and whether or not trust assets will be included in your estate. But if taxes are not a major consideration, you may want to consider holding on to one or more of these powers.

Q. Give me an example of how an irrevocable trust works.

A. Assume you are a widower. You transfer property worth $300,000 into a trust. You are the grantor of the trust, and you irrevocably give up the right to revoke the trust, amend it, or end it. So the trust is irrevocable.

You might provide in the trust that income from the trust will be paid to your primary beneficiary—your daughter, age 30—for her lifetime and, at her death, everything that remains in the trust at that time will be paid to her children, the *remaindermen*. You could name the XYZ Trust Company as your trustee and give the trustee certain discretionary powers to pay principal to your daughter (or her children) in addition to the required distributions of income.

Q. Why would I want to create a trust that I couldn't revoke or amend?

A. No one would give up the right to recover cash and other property or change the terms of a trust unless the stakes were very high. They are. Not everyone needs to set up an irrevocable trust. No estate planning tool should be used just because it is popular—or even because it may save huge amounts of estate taxes. Don't use an irrevocable trust unless it will accomplish a number of objectives that are very important to you.

The decision to use an irrevocable trust is really two separate decisions. The first decision is whether to make a gift. The second decision is whether to make the gift outright or in trust. (We'll discuss that decision in just a moment). A gift to a revocable trust is not really a gift, because you still have your string and can still pull the gift back. So if you want to make a gift in trust that is a real, final, irrevocable gift, you need an irrevocable trust, not a revocable trust. But why make a gift at all? Many (perhaps most) gifts are made from generosity or love, but if you are looking for a less altruistic reason for gifts to irrevocable trusts, the answer is usually, "to save taxes".

Lifetime gifts can save death taxes (and income taxes) in a number of different ways:

- The federal gift tax annual exclusion allows you to give $10,000 each year to as many different people as you like (or $20,000 if you are married and your spouse agrees to "split" the gifts for gift tax purposes). Once you give it away, it can't be taxed. When your estate exceeds the unified credit exclusion amount ($600,000 in 1997 and increasing by steps to $1,000,000 in 2006), the excess is subject to tax rates beginning at 37% and climbing to 55%. For someone with an estate potentially subject to federal estate tax, each $10,000 gift saves at least $3,700 in estate tax. (The $10,000 annual exclusion may be adjusted for inflation after 1998.)

- The federal estate and gift tax unified credit allows you to give up to a total of the applicable exclusion amount ($600,000 in 1997 and increasing by steps to $1,000,000 in 2006) during your lifetime without paying any gift tax. A gift of the exclusion amount does not itself save any tax, but it removes the future income and growth of the gift from your taxable estate. It is common to use the unified credit to create "family" or "credit equivalent by-pass" trusts at death (see chapter 13), but there are even greater tax benefits from creating similar irrevocable trusts during your lifetime.

- Many times, the benefit of one spouse's unified credit can be wasted if that spouse does not have the exclusion amount in his or her separate estate and that spouse dies before the richer spouse. In order to avoid this tax loss (which can cost $200,000 or more in additional estate tax), it is common to transfer a measured amount of assets from the wealthier spouse to the poorer spouse. The transfer can be made in an irrevocable trust in order to provide better management or to guard against the problems of disability, second marriages, creditors problems, or other diversions of assets from the family.

- Each person is entitled to a $1,000,000 exemption from the generation-skipping transfer tax (GSTT), a tax of 55 percent that is imposed on gifts to grandchildren and others in generations below your children. (This $1,000,000 exemption may also be adjusted for inflation after 1998.) Because the exemption is so high, the GSTT is an affliction suffered only by the highly financially successful. But when the tax strikes, it strikes with a vengeance. Because of the "money value of time", it is usually better to use the exemption sooner rather than later, and by lifetime transfers rather than at death. When used, this exemption is almost always applied to fund a generation-skipping trust (with or without life insurance to "leverage" the exemption) that will benefit several generations. (See chapter 27.)

- Shifting income-producing assets from high income taxpayers to low-income taxpayers can result in the income being tax at lower rates, reducing the total tax burden of the family. (Although accumulating income in a trust doesn't save income taxes, or at least doesn't save very much, because of the "compressed" tax brackets that push trusts into the top income tax rates very quickly.)

- Avoid state death taxes. State death taxes can be surprisingly high. Many states with death taxes have no gift tax. So lifetime gifts can completely avoid the death tax. In Pennsylvania, for example, if you left $1,000,000 to your sister, the state tax alone would be $150,000! However, if you give her that same amount during your lifetime (and more than one year before your death), there is no state transfer tax at all.

- Life insurance can be transferred during lifetime with very little "cost" in terms of taxes or loss of financial security, and yet save tremendous amounts in federal estate tax and some death taxes. The proceeds of a life insurance policy are subject to federal estate tax if the policy is owned by the insured or the insured has any "incidents of ownership" in the policy (such as the power to change life insurance beneficiary designations). However, if life insurance is owned by an irrevocable trust, with no incidents of ownership in the insured, the proceeds can be applied for the benefit of the insured's family after death, free of any death taxes. A life insurance policy often has relatively little value during the insured's lifetime. So giving away the policy costs the insured very little and yet provides a tremendous benefit to the insured's family. (See chapters 17 and 18.)

- In order to get a current income tax deduction for a charitable gift to a private foundation (see chapter 25) or a charitable lead trust or charitable remainder trust (see chapter 26), the trust must be irrevocable.

There are also some non-tax reasons for gifts:

- Protect your assets from the claims of creditors. Suppose your profession makes you a potential subject of a lawsuit for professional errors, or your business operations expose you to financial risks in the event of unexpected market or business changes. You may want to transfer some of the assets you have accumulated to your spouse or children to make sure that they will be able to enjoy them and benefit from them even if you might not. A revocable trust offers no significant creditor protection in any state. As a general rule, if you can reach an asset or the income it produces, so can your creditors. But by placing an asset and its income in an irrevocable trust beyond your reach, assuming there is no fraud, you are also placing that asset beyond the reach of your creditors. (See chapter 28.)

- Protect your assets from a surviving spouse's rights of "dower," "courtesy," or "election" under state law. Every state gives a surviving spouse certain statutory rights to the assets you own at your death, no matter how little you leave that spouse in your will. In other words, without proving anything except that he or she is your surviving spouse, that person will be legally entitled to a share of your estate. In most states, this includes assets you've put into a living revocable trust. However, if the trust is irrevocable and you have no rights to the trust's assets, neither does your spouse (unless you've purposely made the transfer to the trust close to death to "defraud" your spouse).

Q. Why should I make gifts in trust rather than outright?

A. There are many reasons, both tax and non-tax, for making gifts in trust rather than outright. We call these people-oriented goals. If you examine the list below, you'll find that most of the reasons for making gifts in trust fall into one of these three categories:

- You want to guarantee proper management for the assets.

- You want to conserve principal for as long as possible.

- You want income and principal paid out in the time and manner and to the persons of your choice.

See if any of the following situations apply to you or your beneficiaries:

- You are afraid that your beneficiary is unable to handle the asset. If you feel that your spouse, friend, children, grandchildren, niece, nephew, parent, or other beneficiary is unwilling or unable to invest, manage, or handle the responsibility of an outright gift, you should consider making a gift in trust. Minors and legal incompetents are obvious members of this class. So are adults who lack the emotional or intellectual maturity or who do not have the physical capacity or technical training to handle large sums of money or assets that require constant, high-level decision-making capacity such as a family business.

Legally, a minor cannot buy or sell assets or enter into binding contracts. This means that if property is given to a minor, the property cannot be purchased, sold, exchanged, or mortgaged without the appointment of a guardian by a court and the accounting to the court for every dollar spent on behalf of the minor. Using an irrevocable trust could minimize or avoid that often expensive, troublesome, and inflexible process.

- You fear that your beneficiary will not feel dependent on you. You may want the income and estate tax advantages (which we'll describe shortly), but you don't want to put all of the ownership rights in your child or other beneficiary's hands. Suppose you want to start a gift program but you are afraid that if you make no-strings-attached-gifts, your child will no longer feel dependent on you. Unlike an outright gift, an irrevocable trust will *not* allow a beneficiary to "take the money and run" because he or she will not receive it all at one time.

- The property is not fragmentable. Perhaps the property doesn't lend itself to fragmentation, but you still want to spread the benefits among a number of people. (For example, a large life insurance policy and its eventual proceeds may be best held by a single trustee, rather than jointly by a half a dozen individuals.)

  Say you have 10 children and grandchildren. You also have 10 acres of real estate, which may be more valuable to them if it is not subdivided into 10 one-acre plots. If you placed the real estate into an irrevocable trust, all 10 of your children and grandchildren could enjoy the property's growth and income without the need to subdivide it. Upon the occurrence of a specified event (for instance, when the youngest of them reaches age 25 or when the property can be sold for an amount in excess of $100,000 an acre), your trustee could sell the property and divide the proceeds or hold the money for the trust's beneficiaries.

- You want to limit ownership. Consider an irrevocable trust in place of an outright gift if you want to limit the class of beneficiaries. For instance, suppose you want to be sure that stock in your family business, the family vacation home, or Grandpop's pocket watch does not end up outside the family. With an irrevocable trust you can make sure that doesn't happen. You can set up a trust that will retain family control and provide protection against the fallout from a beneficiary's unsuccessful marriage, for example, and thus prevent his or her spouse from acquiring that asset. Such ownership restriction is not possible if you make an outright gift.

• You don't want the property to return to you once you have given it away. If a parent makes a direct gift to a child and the child predeceases the parent, absent a valid will (which a minor child probably can't create), the property may return to the parent rather than pass directly to another child under state intestacy laws. To then remove the asset from the parent's estate, he or she would have to make yet another taxable gift. This second gift may be even more expensive than the first because the asset may have appreciated in the hands of the deceased child. Placing the gift in an irrevocable trust, however, can ensure that it doesn't end up back in your estate.

• You'd like to familiarize your trustee with managing your trust. Initially, your irrevocable trust may have only a life insurance policy and a relatively small amount of investment assets in it. You may plan to "pour over" other assets from your probate estate (assets you own in your own name when you die), from a revocable trust you've established during your lifetime, or from a group life insurance plan into the trust. In other words, your trust may be relatively small now but at your death contain a sizable sum of money and other assets. You may want to know now how well your trustee will perform and so you need to familiarize the trustee with your assets, your family, your plans, and the relationship of each to the other. Even though the trust is irrevocable, you can give the trustee suggestions as to property investment and management.

• You desire to "hide assets" from creditors or predators. You may want to ensure your beneficiary's financial security, yet not make him or her the target of a fortune hunter. You can do this—create significant economic security for someone else, but protect the beneficiary from himself and others—by using a trust that provides only income, with additional amounts of principal—at the trustee's sole discretion—for the beneficiary's health, education, maintenance, and support. Alternatively, you could give the beneficiary the right to demand certain amounts for specific needs but stipulate that amounts above those levels or beyond those categories of need would be paid out only if the trustee deemed it desirable.

- Increase the control you have over your assets beyond your death. An irrevocable trust offers both control and flexibility. In the trust agreement, you can dictate who receives both income and capital, when they receive it, and upon what terms. You can also add flexibility to the "iron rules" you set up in your document by selecting a trustee (or co-trustees) not only whom you trust but also whose investment and personal finance philosophy is similar to yours. You can thereby extend your control and your investment and management philosophy well beyond your death.

Giving your trustees what lawyers call *sprinkle and spray powers* allows them the discretion to "sprinkle" income and "spray" capital among your beneficiaries in the way that best matches your way of thinking, accomplishes your objectives, and meets the beneficiaries' needs. Through these powers, more could be paid to needy than to financially successful beneficiaries or to industrious and deserving individuals than to those who are not.

The trustee's discretion could be both "carrot and stick." For example, your lawyer could draft an "incentive trust" that rewards children—perhaps by increasing this year's payout to them—who invest a certain portion of last year's trust income wisely or who perform certain other conditions or refrain from specified actions. You could also stipulate that if—in the independent trustee's sole discretion—trust money was not invested wisely last year, less would be paid out this year.

Such flexibility can also be used to reduce intrafamily income-taxes by shifting income to lower bracket family members on a year-to-year basis. For example, if one beneficiary has deductible losses in a given year, more can be paid to him or her that year, while less might be paid to a beneficiary with significant income in a high tax bracket.

Still another control-flexibility element in an irrevocable trust is objectivity. You can direct your trustee to deny payments when the trustee deems it appropriate. This "just say no" ability places the hard decisions on an independent, objective third party (someone other than a family member), and it reduces the likelihood of family conflict. Think how hard it would be, for example, for a mother to deny her son the large sum of money he'd like when she knows he is not emotionally mature enough to handle it properly. In the trust document, however, you can specify that a child using drugs, will for instance, be rewarded with additional income or principal if the child can prove sustained abstinence, but that income or principal will be reduced or stopped temporarily if the child tests positive in a drug test. Likewise, you can encourage a child who has dropped out of school to return by giving him or her additional payments from the trust (perhaps in the form of trust-to-school payments for tuition, room and board, or spending money).

- Provide for those you love or feel a responsibility toward—in complete privacy—even if they are not family members. For instance, you may feel responsible for the welfare of a friend, or employee, or you may want to be the benefactor of someone needy, but you would like to keep your identity secret and avoid publicity. Except for financial accounting to the court, only the trustee and beneficiaries need know the amounts involved and the terms and conditions of the trust. It is even possible to make the gifts without disclosing your identity to the recipients.

Q. Can I use my irrevocable trust as the center of my estate plan?

A. Because you can use it to unify all of your assets, your irrevocable trust can be the pivotal device for your overall estate plan. Here's how:

- Your will can direct that any asset or property right you own at your death can pass (pour over) by will through a "funnel" to your previously established irrevocable trust. This is what lawyers call a *pour-over*.

- Assets you've placed in a revocable living trust can also be poured over into your irrevocable living trust, thus

Trusts/Leimberg Associates Books: 610-527-5216

combining the lifetime flexibility you've gained by placing assets into your living revocable trust with the estate tax savings you've realized by placing other assets into your irrevocable trust before your death.

- Alternatively, two or more trusts can co-exist even after your death. For example, you might create an irrevocable trust as the owner of your life insurance (see chapter 17) and have your revocable trust add to the irrevocable trust after your death so that your irrevocable trust would also use up your federal estate tax unified credit and thereby serve as a *family trust* or *by-pass trust* (see chapter 13) for the benefit of your spouse and children. If properly written and properly funded, this credit equivalent by-pass trust (CEBT) will not cause any estate tax at your death, due to the removal of the life insurance from your taxable estate and the application of the federal estate tax unified credit. Nor will assets in the CEBT be taxable at your spouse's death because your spouse will have no taxable interest in the trust. (It is possible to provide significant financial security for your spouse through the CEBT without having it taxable in his or her estate).

The balance of the assets in your revocable trust could continue to be held for the benefit of your surviving spouse, in the form of a *marital deduction QTIP trust* (see chapter 13), qualifying for the marital deduction and yet assuring you that the principal will pass to your children or grandchildren at the death of your spouse. This marital trust will not cause any estate tax at your death, due to the marital deduction, but will be taxable at the death of your spouse. These two trusts, working together, may be sufficient to minimize or eliminate any estate tax for your children.

Q. Can I require my trustee to use trust cash to pay my estate taxes?

A. You could. But this would defeat any estate tax saving objective. If your trust document *requires* your trustee to use trust assets to pay the debts, expenses, and taxes incurred at your death, the IRS will include the trust assets in your taxable estate. It's as if all the money and other assets you've so carefully kept out of your estate while you were alive were dumped back into your estate a moment before your death. Such a requirement would defeat the major goal of the irrevocable trust—keeping wealth *out* of your taxable estate.

But you can still accomplish your goal with little trouble. Simply insert a provision into your trust authorizing—but *not* directing—your trustee to purchase assets at their fair market value from your estate. You can give the same authorization for purchases of assets from your spouse's estate. Those funds can be used to pay estate taxes and other at-death expenses.

Alternatively, you can authorize your trustee to lend money to your estate and your spouse's estate. All loans should be fully secured and made at an interest rate equal to (or reasonably in excess of the current bank-lending rate in your geographic area).

Q. What are the disadvantages of an irrevocable trust?

A. Every tool or technique of estate planning has its downsides and costs. Irrevocable trusts—even with their tremendous tax-savings potential, creditor protection, and other advantages—are no exception. Some of the costs of an irrevocable trust (including those with life insurance) include the following:

- You lose control over your assets. In return for the tax and creditor advantages, you must be willing to give up all significant ongoing control over the right to recover trust assets and to select (or deselect) trust beneficiaries.

  "Irrevocable" means just that. You cannot revoke or terminate an irrevocable trust at your whim. Within the narrow exceptions described below, every transfer you make to the trust must be both complete and permanent. Despite the significant control and flexibility a creative and experienced lawyer can build into the trust document, you must be willing to give up a substantial amount of control.

  Once assets are put into an irrevocable trust, they are no longer yours. You must retitle or absolutely assign ownership of every asset placed into the trust. Not one of those assets can come back to you—without a possible adverse tax implication. It's no longer your property. If you place life insurance on your life into the trust, you can no longer name or change the policy beneficiary, veto a change, or borrow against the cash values of the policy. The same applies to any other asset you put into an irrevocable trust. You can't even safely retain the right to accelerate one beneficiary's interest or the ability to withhold another beneficiary's income or principal—even for a month.

- There is a loss of flexibility. Closely related to the loss of control over assets is the loss of the right to change the terms of an irrevocable trust. You must give up the flexibility associated with outright ownership. You cannot alter or amend the trust in any way once you have put it into effect.

Why is this loss of flexibility so important? Events that were totally unpredictable at the time you placed assets into an irrevocable trust could change your financial circumstances or your beneficiary's situation drastically. You may divorce, remarry, or lose your job or much of the wealth you didn't put into the trust. Your health or your spouse's (or beneficiary's) could deteriorate. Business opportunities could blossom—if only you could get to the money you can no longer unilaterally reach. You may not like your beneficiaries any longer, or they may not need or want your money.

We rarely make predictions, especially those about the future. But one thing we can predict with certainty, and that is that Congress will change (again) the tax laws. There is no guarantee that if a tax law change occurs between the time you sign and fund your trust and the date you die that Congress will be thoughtful enough to "grandfather" the law in existence at that time. Whether that change is fair or not, your beneficiaries may be stuck with an estate or gift tax law that neither you nor any of your advisers could possibly have anticipated. That law may be very detrimental to your financial health.

For instance, if the annual gift tax exclusion (discussed below) is eliminated or severely restricted, the irrevocable trust's cost efficiency could drop precipitously. (At this date, we have no notice that Congress is planning such a drastic step, but in an age of revenue starvation, nothing—except truly lower taxes—is impossible from a hungry Congress).

There are countless other things that can also change, but the terms of your irrevocable trust are not one of them. Once you place assets into the trust (aside from the "escape valve" devices we'll describe below), you can't change the terms of your gift. Do not underestimate the psychological effect of losing this control and flexibility. The younger you are, the more likely you and your beneficiaries will experience significant changes in your personal and financial circumstances.

You should not create an irrevocable trust—in spite of the tremendous potential death tax savings and other advantages—if the lifetime loss of flexibility will upset you. At the very least, never put all your financial eggs in one basket. (One solution often suggested is to place term life insurance on your life into the trust as its sole or major asset. If you no longer were satisfied with the trust or wanted to change its terms, you could effectively end the trust merely by not paying any more premiums.)

If, after all these warnings and a thorough examination of other costs and disadvantages with each of your financial services professionals, you still feel that an irrevocable trust is appropriate, be sure your lawyer builds into the trust document as much flexibility and as many escape valves as possible in case your objectives, your circumstances, or the tax laws change. (See our discussion on "escape valves" below.)

• An irrevocable trust can be complex. It has to be, since it must anticipate the changing needs of its beneficiaries for decades—in some cases, for generations. It must also achieve its tax savings objectives through carefully worded phrases and clauses that don't interfere (more than necessary) with your desires. For instance, you may want to limit a beneficiary's access to funds completely until he or she reaches a certain age. Yet if you give that beneficiary no right at all to money you place into the trust, every one of your transfers to the trust will result in immediate gift tax implications. (See our discussion of Crummey powers below.)

An irrevocable trust's complexity and the meticulous drafting it takes to achieve your intended objectives is expensive. Expect a well thought out irrevocable trust to cost more—in some cases much more—than a revocable trust, if for no other reason than the fact that you don't get a second chance to get it right. The process may require several meetings with your lawyer before you sign the document. Insist he or she go through every single clause so that you both understand what it says and does and why it's there. Never feel any question you have is "dumb"; you are paying the freight so you should drive the train. Your life's efforts are at stake!

- You may have to pay federal gift taxes. Each transfer you make to an irrevocable trust—every time you part permanently with cash or any other asset—is a completed gift. However, through creative drafting and qualifying your gifts—up to $10,000 a year ($20,000 if you are married) per donee (recipient)—for the gift tax annual exclusion, your lawyer may make it possible for you to give gifts to the trust each year that don't attract any gift tax at all. Over a period of years, this could enable you to shift huge amounts of wealth gift tax free.

  In some cases, the gift tax impact of those gifts can be reduced even further by the federal estate and gift tax unified credit which shelters a total of up to $1,000,000 from tax (depending on the year of death or gift) during lifetime or at death. But at a certain point, if the amount you want to shift to your beneficiaries is large or you have made significant gifts in the past, you may have to incur gift taxes or, as a tradeoff, accept the risk of shifting control over assets to a beneficiary before you'd like.

- You may incur state gift taxes. A few states, such as New York, impose a state gift tax in addition to the federal tax (although the New York gift tax will end in the year 2000). If your state has a gift tax, there may or may not be a credit or exemption that you can apply to reduce the gift tax cost of a gratuitous transfer. (New York, for instance, currently allows a $2,750 credit against its gift tax. That translates into a total shelter from state gift taxes for up to $108,500.)

- There can be a loss of income. When you place any income-producing assets into the trust, you lose the right (assuming you are not an income beneficiary) to the income it produces.

- A trust generates ongoing administrative, accounting, and legal costs. Records must be kept, income tax returns must be filed, and communication with beneficiaries must be maintained. From time to time, a trustee may face a question that cannot be answered easily and legal interpretation—perhaps even court adjudication—may be required. None of these time-consuming and potentially costly responsibilities can be ignored. All add to the continuing expense of maintaining an irrevocable trust.

Even with the disadvantages we've just described, for many individuals, an irrevocable trust may be a good estate planning tool. But it may not be a great tool. There may be another more appropriate vehicle for shifting your wealth and accomplishing your other planning objectives. Be sure to talk to your lawyer, CPA, and other financial advisers about the pros and cons of FLPs (family limited partnerships) and LLCs (limited liability companies), as well as other devices such as GRATs (grantor-retained annuity trusts), GRUTs (grantor-retained unitrusts), GRITs (grantor-retained income trusts), SCINs (self-canceling installment notes), and private annuities. (See *The Cutting Edge*, which can be purchased by calling 610-527-5216, for a very thorough explanation of these sophisticated tools).

Often, the best solution to your estate planning problems involves a combination of several tools and techniques. As we caution you repeatedly throughout this book, never look at any solution, no matter how appealing, in a vacuum or as the total panacea. You have invested a whole lifetime building your wealth. Transferring it to those you love cannot (and should not) be a one-hour instant process.

Q. What types of assets are best to place in an irrevocable trust?

A. Generally, the best assets to transfer are those you do not need personally or in your business and that you would like to hold within your family. Select assets likely to appreciate in value. The more rapidly an asset is appreciating, the more appropriate it is to transfer quickly to your irrevocable trust. The reason is that you will remove a great deal of value from your estate at relatively little current gift tax cost. If you wait, the cost of transferring the asset after it has already appreciated will be much higher.

For example, suppose you are 55 years old, married with five adult children, and among your possessions is an asset worth $100,000 that is growing at a 6 percent after-tax rate. Your life expectancy is about 29 years. In that time, your asset will have grown to a value of over $542,000! If you do nothing and are in a 50 percent federal estate tax bracket at your death, your heirs will lose more than a quarter of a million dollars! If you and your spouse put the asset in irrevocable trusts for your five children, however, the gifts can be made currently while the asset is worth only $100,000—at no gift tax cost. Because you and your spouse can each give up to $10,000 (adjusted for inflation after 1998) each year for each child gift tax free, you can give the entire $100,000 away in one year, pay no gift tax, and still have your entire unified credit exclusion amount remaining. None of the $542,000 will be taxable at your death. Your gift giving program will enrich your children by hundreds of thousands of dollars. But if you wait until the property is worth, say $400,000 before giving it away, you'll use up a great deal of your unified credit (which exposes more of the estate you leave to tax). Our advice: Use your annual exclusions and your unified credit as quickly as possible with property that is likely to appreciate significantly.

Another general rule is to transfer assets that have a tax basis (cost) that is fairly close to fair market value, or assets that you do not expect your trustee to sell for many years. This is because assets that you give away during your lifetime do not receive a new, stepped-up tax basis at death, but continue to have the same tax basis you had. That means that your trust will eventually have to pay tax on the capital gain that has occurred, while your estate (and its beneficiaries) would not have to pay any tax on that gain if you held the asset until your death. This income tax cost may not be important if the asset is a family business or farm that you do not expect your trust to sell for many years after your death.

Q. Can I safely maintain the right to receive the income produced by the assets I place into my irrevocable trust?

A. Not if the purpose of the trust is to avoid estate taxes at your death. The retained right to receive the income of the trust, the power to change the income beneficiaries, or even the power to change the timing of income distributions, will cause the entire value of the trust to be included in your taxable estate at your death. In fact, almost any meaningful "string" you hold on trust income or principal may cause all of the principal in the trust—no matter how large it's grown and no matter how long ago you put the property into the trust—to be pulled back into your estate. To meet your estate tax planning and wealth-shifting objectives, you must give up both control over and the benefits of the property you place into the trust.

Q. What are the problems, if any, of contributing encumbered property to my irrevocable trust?

A. Beware of using assets subject to debt as the subject of a gift to a trust. There may be income, estate and gift tax, and practical problems if you contribute encumbered property to your irrevocable trust. For instance, if you transfer property subject to a mortgage, consider these questions:

- Who will pay the interest and principal each month, and where will that person get the money?

- Will your creditor allow you to shift the liability to another person?

- If the trust's payments satisfy your personal obligation, will you be considered to have received taxable income from the trust each time the trust makes a payment?

Also consider these issues:

- The IRS will take the position that the transfer of encumbered property should be treated the same as if you sold the property, in which case you would be taxable on any gain. For instance, say you borrow $100,000 on property for which you paid $40,000 that is worth $120,000 at the time you place it in the trust. If the trust takes over the $100,000 debt, the IRS will claim that you have gain equal to the $60,000 difference between the $100,000 you now have and the $40,000 you paid.

- The IRS might also take the position that by paying your mortgage, the trust is satisfying your personal legal obligation. In that case, the trust assets in your estate would be included in your taxable estate on the grounds that you retained an income interest in the trust.

The bottom line is that you must check with competent tax counsel before transferring any property subject to debt to your irrevocable trust. This even applies to life insurance subject to a policy loan. Although it is tempting to take a loan out on your policy shortly before transferring it to your life insurance trust, doing so may trigger ordinary income.

Q. What might cause me, the grantor of an irrevocable trust, to be taxed on its income rather than the trust itself or its beneficiaries?

A. Rules known as the *grantor trust rules*—which apply to income tax but not to estate tax—treat the grantor of the trust, rather than the trust itself, as owner of the trust assets and therefore taxable on trust income (and eligible to take deductions directly that are otherwise usable by the trust or its beneficiaries). These rules are among the most technical and difficult to understand rules in the Internal Revenue Code, and we will try to describe them in only a general way.

Under these rules, you, the grantor of the trust, will be treated as the income tax owner of trust assets if the trust meets any one of the following conditions:

- You (or your spouse) *could* receive income of the trust, or it could be used to pay your debts. For example, suppose your trustee has discretion to distribute income to your spouse or to your children. You will be taxable on all of the income of the trust even if the income is actually distributed to your children.

- You (or your spouse) keep a *reversionary interest* (the right to receive it back or determine its disposition) in the income or the principal of any portion of a trust—but only if the actuarial value of the retained reversionary interest is greater than 5 percent of the value of the income or principal that may revert. Similarly, the trust will be a grantor trust if *anyone* could terminate the trust and return the principal to you, unless the power is held by someone with a substantial interest in the trust (and who would therefore be adversely affected by the termination of the trust).

- The power to control distributions from the trust, even if you don't hold the power. For example, the power to distribute income to one or more of your children will cause the trust to be a grantor trust unless the trustee is independent (i.e., is not you or your spouse, children, parents, or siblings, or an employee of a business you own or control). However, a power to distribute principal does not cause an income tax problem (although it may cause an estate tax problem), even if you are trustee, if the power is limited to an "ascertainable standard" such as health, education, support, or maintenance.

- You (or your spouse) keep certain administrative powers such as (1) the power to purchase, deal with, or dispose of the income or principal of a trust for less than adequate and full consideration and (2) the power to borrow from income or principal without adequate interest or security.

- Someone other than your trustee can vote corporate stock held by the trust, can control the investment of stock or securities held by the trust, or can reacquire the principal of the trust by substituting property of equal value.

- The income of the trust is used to pay premiums on insurance on your life or the life of your spouse.

- The income of the trust is used to pay for the support of someone whom you are obligated to support (such as a minor child).

A person other than the grantor can be considered the owner of a trust, and taxable on all of the income of the trust, if the person has the power to withdraw from the trust, even if the power is not exercised. For example, it is common to give a spouse an unlimited power to withdraw the principal of a trust intended to qualify for the federal estate tax marital deduction, or to limit the power to not more than five percent of the principal of the trust each year. The unlimited right of withdrawal would mean that the spouse is taxable on all of the income and capital gains of the trust, while the limited right would mean that the spouse is taxable on five percent of the income and gains.

There are exceptions to all of these rules, and exceptions to the exceptions, which is why the creation and operation of an irrevocable trust requires the services of a knowledgeable lawyer and CPA.

Q. How is an irrevocable trust (and its beneficiaries) taxed on trust income?

A. If the trust is not a grantor trust (as described above), then the trust is a separate taxpayer and is required to file an income tax return separate from the grantor and all of the beneficiaries. (The return is known as Form 1041.) However, the trust is entitled to a deduction for income distributed to beneficiaries, and the beneficiaries are required to include those distributions in their income. The income of the trust that is distributed to the beneficiaries during the year is therefore taxed to the beneficiaries, not the trust. Only income that is retained by the trust and not distributed before the end of the year is taxed to the trust (unless the trust is a charitable remainder trust described in chapter 26, which is subject to special rules).

A trust is a kind of "pass-through" funnel-like entity, because not only are the beneficiaries taxed on the income of the trust that is distributed to them, but the *character* of the income remains the same in their hands. Dividends received by the trust and distributed to the beneficiaries are still considered dividends, interest income is still interest, and tax-exempt income is still tax-exempt. What would be taxable income for an individual (e.g., interest, dividends, rents, capital gains, etc.) is also taxable income for a trust.

Most of the important tax differences are in the area of deductions, including the following:

- For an individual, expenses of administering income-producing property are deductible, but are subject to the 2% floor for "miscellaneous itemized deductions." For a trust, the expenses of administration are not subject to the 2% floor as long as the expenses are of a type that would not have been incurred if the property were not in trust. For example, investment fees will remain subject to the two percent floor because those expenses would have been the same inside or outside of the trust. However, all of the trustee's commissions and all of the legal fees relating to the administration of the trust should be fully deductible.

- Even expenses that are otherwise fully deductible are still not deductible to the extent they are incurred to administer stocks or bonds generating tax-exempt income. For example, trustee commissions usually must be allocated proportionately between taxable income (deductible commissions) and tax exempt income (nondeductible commissions).

- As noted above, a trust is entitled to a deduction for income distributed to beneficiaries. The first complexity in determining the taxable income of a trust and its beneficiaries is calculating "distributable net income" (or "DNI"). DNI is the taxable income of the trust (excluding capital gains) after the deductions for the administration expenses, interest paid by the trust, state income taxes paid, and other usual deductions, and before the distribution deduction.

- Because capital gains are excluded from DNI, the trust (and not the beneficiaries) will usually pay the taxes on the capital gains realized by the trust (unless the trust includes specific provisions that capital gains are part of income for the purpose of trust distributions).

- There are two types of irrevocable trusts for income tax purposes: The first type is the "simple trust. "Simple" trusts are required to distribute all of their income and do not distribute any principal. The beneficiaries of a simple trust are taxable on all of the DNI of the trust regardless of whether or not it is actually distributed. A simple trust (or a complex trust required to distribute all of its income each year) is entitled to a deduction of $300 against the capital gains taxable to the trust.

The second type of irrevocable trust is the "complex" trust.

"Complex" trusts can either accumulate income or distribute principal. The beneficiaries of a complex trust are taxed on DNI actually distributed. A complex trust is entitled to a deduction of $100 against its income (kind of like a personal exemption for trusts).

- Amounts that the trust is required to pay currently to a charity are deductible, but amounts accumulated by the trust for future distribution to charity are not deductible.

Many people believe that income that is accumulated in a trust will be taxed at lower tax rates, because of the separate tax rates applicable to trusts. For example, if your beneficiaries are in the top income tax brackets, it might seem that you could reduce your family's total tax liabilities by accumulating income in the trust and distributing it only when needed, allowing most of the income to be taxed at the lower income tax rates available to the trust.

However, this won't really work, because the tax tables for trusts have incredibly shallow tax brackets. Very little income results in a very high tax rate. For example, an unmarried individual is subject to an income tax rate of 15% on the first $24,650 of income in 1997. (Income tax brackets are adjusted annually for inflation.) For a trust, only $1,650 of income is subject to tax at 15%, and income above that is subject to tax at higher rates. A trust therefore moves into the top income tax brackets much sooner than single or married taxpayers. In fact, a trust is now in the top income tax bracket with only $8,100 of income, compared to $271,050 for married taxpayers filing jointly or single taxpayers. Because of these narrow tax brackets, accumulating income in a trust can result in an annual tax reduction of no more than $920. (Still, a savings of $920 a year for 10 or 20 years adds up).

In the past, the accumulated income of a trust has also been subject to a complex additional tax when the income was finally distributed to a beneficiary. These "throwback" rules were repealed by the Taxpayer Relief Act of 1997.

Like individuals and corporations, trusts are subject to the AMT, the alternative minimum tax. The alternative minimum tax was originally enacted by Congress to make sure that *some* tax was paid by taxpayers with accelerated depreciation, oil depletion allowances, and other "tax shelters." However, like most things created by Congress, it has grown steadily more complex, and "alternative minimum taxable income" can now include things as mundane as the deduction for state income taxes.

A trust is entitled to a distribution deduction for alternative minimum taxable income, just like the trust is entitled to a distribution deduction for regular income. This means that the trustee must calculate (are you ready for this?) the *distributable net alternative minimum taxable income* (or DNAMTI, usually pronounced "dammit!") for the trust and each beneficiary's share of DNAMTI. The beneficiaries are required to include their share of the trust's DNAMTI in the calculation of their own alternative minimum tax on their personal tax returns.

There are a few other mechanical rules for the taxation of irrevocable trusts that should be mentioned:

- Trusts are required to file their tax returns on the basis of a calendar year, and are not allowed to select a fiscal year.

- The trustee must make estimated tax payments, just like individuals. If the trust makes larger distributions to beneficiaries than originally expected, so the trust has paid more estimated tax than was needed and the beneficiaries have paid less estimated tax than was needed, the trust can elect to let the beneficiaries claim credit for the estimated tax payments made by the trust.

- Before the due date for the income tax return (usually April 15), the trustee is required to give each beneficiary a Schedule K-1 that shows the beneficiary's share of the taxable income of the trust, the tax-exempt income, and any alternative minimum taxable income, as well as other information about the tax character of the distributions from the trust.

Q. If I own appreciated investments and contribute them to my irrevocable trust, who pays the tax if the trustee later sells the assets?

A. The trustee will pay the tax on any gain realized on the sale of the assets, including the gain on the pre-gift appreciation.

The gift tax consequences of a gift of an asset to a trust are based on the fair market value of the asset at the time of the gift. However, to calculate taxable gain for income tax purposes, the trustee is required to use the donor's cost basis (increased only by any gift tax paid on the contribution to the trust). So if your trust sold an asset right after you gave it to the trust, the taxable gain would be the same as if you had sold the asset. If the trust is a separate taxpayer and not a "grantor trust" as described earlier in this chapter, then the trust will add the gain to its income and calculate the tax based on its other income and deductions and its separate income tax brackets (which may result in a higher tax than if you had sold the asset, because of the trust's compressed income tax brackets, as described above).

An older rule required that gain on assets sold within two years be taxed at the grantor's income tax rates, even though the trust paid the tax. When the tax brackets for trusts were compressed, this often resulted in a *reduction* in tax, not an increase, which was not what Congress intended, and this two-year rule was repealed in the 1997 Tax Law.

The tax basis of a contributed asset is calculated differently if the asset is sold at a loss. For losses, the trustee must use either the donor's cost basis for the asset or the fair market value of the asset at the time of the contribution to the trust, whichever is less. So a capital loss cannot be transferred to a trust. (If depreciated property is contributed to a trust and is sold at a price that is less than the original cost basis but more than the fair market value at the time of the contribution, there will be neither gain nor loss on the sale.)

These rules regarding the basis of contributed assets are the same rules that apply to gifts between individuals, so trusts are not being treated harshly and there is no capital gains tax "penalty" for a gift in trust.

In determining whether a gain or loss is long-term, mid-term, or short-term, the trustee can add the length of time the asset was held by the trust to the length of time the asset was held by the trustee.

These rules for calculating gain and loss also apply to charitable remainder trusts, but charitable remainder trusts are exempt from federal income tax, and so the gain or loss is not taxed unless it is distributed to the non-charitable beneficiaries of the trust. (See chapter 26 for additional information on charitable remainder trusts and how they can be used to avoid or defer taxes on capital gains.)

Q. Are there any advantages to creating multiple trusts rather than one big trust?

A. There are a variety of reasons your lawyer may suggest multiple trusts, including the following:

- You have a number of beneficiaries with diverse needs and circumstances, and you would like to include significantly different provisions for each.

- You don't want one beneficiary (or group of beneficiaries) to know what you have provided for other beneficiaries.

- Your beneficiaries are in vastly different geographic locations, and you'd like to set up trusts with trustees close to each of them.

- You own assets (such as rental property and businesses) that require close, day-to-day supervision. These properties and your beneficiaries are widely scattered, and you'd like to have a trustee close enough to interact more frequently with both the property and your beneficiaries.

When trust income tax rates were lower than individual rates, many people tried to lower overall taxes by creating multiple trusts so that each trust's income was taxed at the lowest possible bracket. That divide-and-conquer technique will no longer work for two reasons: First, as mentioned above, trust tax brackets have been compressed and so trusts reach the top tax brackets with very little income. Second, no matter how many trusts you set up, they will all be consolidated and taxed as one trust for income tax purposes—unless the trusts have different primary beneficiaries and you can show that the principal purpose of the multiplicity of trusts is to accomplish an objective other than income tax avoidance.

For example, if you set up five trusts for five different sets of beneficiaries and have different provisions in each trust reflecting differing bona fide non-tax objectives, each trust will be considered separately for income tax purposes. On the other hand, if all the beneficiaries are the same and all five trusts have essentially the same terms, the IRS will tax all the income retained in each trust as if only one trust earned it. The result will probably be that the highest tax rates will apply to your trusts.

Irrevocable Life InsuranceTrust

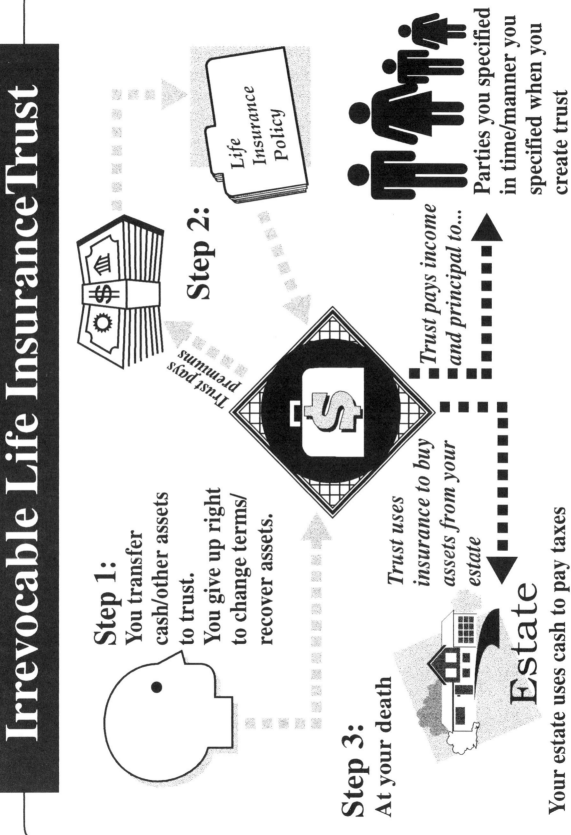

Step 1:
You transfer cash/other assets to trust.
You give up right to change terms/ recover assets.

Step 2:

Life Insurance Policy

Trust pays premiums

Trust pays income and principal to...

Parties you specified in time/manner you specified when you create trust

Step 3:
At your death

Trust uses insurance to buy assets from your estate

Estate

Your estate uses cash to pay taxes

17

IRREVOCABLE LIFE INSURANCE TRUSTS

Chapter 17 explains:

- What an irrevocable life insurance trust is

- The advantages of an irrevocable life insurance trust

- Why life insurance should be added to an irrevocable trust rather than giving the insurance directly to your beneficiaries

- The type of life insurance that should be in your irrevocable trust

- What is meant by the terms "funding" and "unfunded"

- The disadvantages of trust owned life insurance

- Traps to avoid when setting up an irrevocable trust

- How to get life insurance coverage in force as quickly as possible

- "Escape valves" you can build into your irrevocable life insurance trust

- How to select the trustee of an irrevocable life insurance trust

- How to change trustees of an irrevocable life insurance trust

- Why it is not possible to retain the right to policy cash values yet keep insurance out of your estate

- Gift tax implications of a transfer of life insurance to an irrevocable trust

- Valuation of life insurance for gift or estate tax purposes

- How to minimize or eliminate the gift tax cost of transferring life insurance to an irrevocable trust

- How to minimize the gift tax cost of annual contributions to the trust through "Crummey" powers

- How to make a Crummey power more flexible

- What a "5 or 5" power is and why you may want to use it

- How to go beyond "5 or 5" limits

- Why you may want to set up an irrevocable life insurance trust without giving anyone a withdrawal power

- How to increase the size of the annual exclusion if you are purchasing ultra large amounts of insurance

- Income tax implications of an irrevocable life insurance trust

- Why survivorship (second to die) life insurance may be advantageous in your irrevocable trust

- Downsides of survivorship life insurance

- Potential taxes to avoid when using survivorship life

- Why group term life insurance may be a good asset to transfer to your irrevocable trust

- How group term insurance can be transferred to a trust, and the premiums paid by the employer can qualify for the gift tax annual exclusions

- Possible problems associated with group term life as the sole asset of an irrevocable trust

- What split dollar is and why you may want to use this concept in conjunction with your irrevocable life insurance trust

- Community property issues

- How an irrevocable life insurance trust can be a generation-skipping trust

Q. What is an irrevocable life insurance trust (ILIT)?

A. An irrevocable life insurance trust is created either by transferring one or more life insurance policies to an irrevocable trust or creating an irrevocable trust and permitting the trustee of the irrevocable trust to purchase one or more life insurance policies. Although these policies are generally on the life of the grantor and the grantor's spouse, they can also be policies donated by others or purchased on the lives of others. (The trust should specifically provide for such contributions or purchases.)

Q. Why would I want to add life insurance to an irrevocable trust?

A. Adding life insurance to an irrevocable trust makes attaining your financial goals much more likely. The reason is simple: Almost certainly, there will be much more money in the trust with life insurance than without it. So if your goal is to give the maximum amount of after-tax income and capital to your beneficiaries, you should strongly consider an irrevocable life insurance trust.

If you are in the wealth-building stage, an irrevocable life insurance trust is the most efficient way to create an "instant estate." At the stroke of a pen, the payment of a relatively small premium can assure your beneficiaries of hundreds of thousands—even millions—of dollars of financial security.

If you are already financially successful, there is no better way under current law—nor is there a more certain or dramatic way—to transfer large amounts of wealth and provide financial security. Through the life insurance/irrevocable trust combination, you can transfer massive amounts of wealth—free of the federal estate tax system.

Aside from the instant estate that life insurance creates and the assurance of meaningful financial security to those you love, placing life insurance in an irrevocable trust adds a unique element: leverage. Usually, you can shift wealth to others with little or no gift tax through life insurance rather than other assets. The gift tax cost is relatively low because the IRS measures the gift tax value of life insurance at its lifetime rather than its at-death value. You cannot obtain this degree of "tax judo" in any other currently existing estate transfer tool or technique. For instance, think of the gift taxes you'd pay if you transferred $1,000,000 of mutual funds, stocks, bonds, or real estate to an irrevocable trust. Now consider how little gift tax there would be if the trustee purchased a $1,000,000 policy on your life and you made annual gifts to the trustee sufficient to pay the premiums on the policy.

You may want to place life insurance in an irrevocable trust for the most obvious reason of all: You may not have excess non-insurance assets. You may feel that you need the principal of all (or most) of the assets you have and don't want to (and wouldn't feel comfortable if you had to) part with them irrevocably. Or you may just not want to pay the gift taxes that it would take to transfer those assets to the trust.

The best part about accomplishing all your objectives through life insurance is the relative lack of pain. Psychologically, life insurance is an easier asset to part with than most other property. Why? When you give up life insurance, you are not transferring an income-producing asset, so you are not giving up income. Compare how you would feel about giving $1,000,000 of life insurance to an irrevocable trust to making a gift of $1,000,000 of dividend-paying mutual funds.

Few of us want (or can afford) to part with large amounts of wealth while we are young and healthy. Yet that is the very time when it makes the most sense—and dollars—from a tax-savings, wealth-shifting standpoint. Using life insurance in an irrevocable trust, we can assure our beneficiaries of significant financial security by committing a relatively small, budgetable amount of income or capital each year.

Q. Why would I want to put life insurance in a trust rather than giving the life insurance directly to my beneficiaries?

A. There are several reasons why you might want to put life insurance in a trust rather than have an adult beneficiary own the coverage:

- You can limit and restrict how policy proceeds are to be invested or used.

- There is a lot of flexibility in how the money is paid out. For example, through "sprinkling" powers, your trustee can make additional payments to beneficiaries who need extra money because of a medical emergency, a divorce, or educational expenses.

- You can coordinate and consolidate multiple policies into one trust.

- Your family will avoid the often expensive and aggravating burdens of court-appointed guardianships for minor beneficiaries.

- You can ensure that the premiums will be maintained and the proceeds used for the purpose for which the policy is intended—regardless of what that intention is or whether or not the beneficiaries agree. This assurance is especially important if the child has creditors or if you are worried about the soundness of a child's marriage and the possibility that the child's spouse could reach the policy cash values in the event of a divorce. This is especially important if that child is in business. For instance, if the life insurance is crucial to pay taxes so that a family business will not have to be sold to raise tax money or if you want to prevent a forced sale of real estate that your family has owned for generations, you may not want to risk that the money will not be available. If you make an outright gift of the insurance, instead of placing it in an irrevocable trust, an adult child might cash in the policy or borrow against the cash values.

Furthermore, if you have four children and give each one a policy on your life, your executor may have a difficult time getting all four to purchase assets from your estate to provide estate liquidity. This problem is compounded if all four children receive different-size policies or some are mature enough not to make loans against the contract while others are not. On the other hand, if an irrevocable trust buys one large policy on your life, you can be almost certain that there will not be similar problems. (It's also more cost efficient to have a trustee purchase one big policy, rather than having four adult children each purchase a separate policy—even if the total coverage is exactly the same.)

There is still one more major advantage to placing life insurance in an irrevocable trust. If you can be sure that your beneficiaries are well provided for—because of the life insurance in the irrevocable trust—you may feel free to use other assets to attain a higher standard of living now. Spending more of your assets now also has the collateral benefit of reducing the size of your taxable estate. So creating an irrevocable life insurance trust can help you save estate taxes and pay estate taxes, and can also give you more freedom to enjoy the assets you presently own.

Q. What type of life insurance should be in my irrevocable life insurance trust?

A. The best advice with life insurance is to match the product to the problem and to the objectives and circumstances of the parties. For this reason, we generally advise that the trustee of an irrevocable trust purchase some form of permanent protection such as whole life, variable life, universal life, or variable universal life insurance.

Why do we suggest permanent coverage? If the main purpose of your irrevocable trust is to provide estate liquidity (large amounts of cash to pay federal and state estate taxes and other death-related expenses) at an indeterminate date (your death or your spouse's death), a term contract may not suit your objective, because it may expire before you and your spouse.

Term insurance, as its name implies, is the appropriate coverage where you can accurately predict how long the need will last and you are sure that coverage will not run out before the need for cash occurs. It typically is indicated when the highest amount of coverage is required for a relatively short period of time. For example, if you were concerned about paying for a child's college education, you could buy insurance that ended at the same time you expect the child to finish college. The flaw of term insurance is that it is, as its name implies, insurance for only a term. At the end of the term, coverage terminates.

Furthermore, term rates are very favorable only while you are young. Premiums increase astronomically as you grow older and the probability of death grows greater. There is no way to be sure, therefore, that you can afford the ever-increasing costs of term insurance at older ages—the very time when you are most likely to die.

An irrevocable life insurance trust can hold permanent insurance for your entire life, even though you may not have to pay premiums that long. Most permanent products have features allowing you to pay up the policy at a given point through accumulated cash values or the judicious use of policy dividends.

Q. How do I set up an irrevocable life insurance trust?

A. The best way to establish an irrevocable life insurance trust is by following these four steps:

- Step 1: Your lawyer drafts an irrevocable trust document specifying the terms and conditions of payouts. The trust document should be carefully written so that you do not have interest or power over the trust that would be an "incident of ownership" in any policy that may be owned by the trust. If the trust may own insurance on the life of your spouse, then your spouse must also have no interest or power in the trust.

- Step 2: You then transfer cash or income-producing property to the trust either annually or in a large lump sum (or a combination).

- Step 3: Your trustee uses that cash (or income from investments you've placed into the trust) to purchase insurance on your life, your spouse's life, or both. To ensure that you keep the insurance out of your estate, the trustee should arrange with the insurance agent to purchase and own the policy in the name of the trust. Then you merely sign the insurance application as the "proposed insured," not as the policy owner. There should be a specific provision in the trust document authorizing (but not requiring) your trustee to purchase life insurance not only on your life and the life of your spouse but also on the life or lives of anyone in whom the beneficiaries have what life insurance companies call an *insurable interest*—someone whose death would cause a financial loss to the beneficiary, usually a close relative or business associate. For instance, you may want the trust to be able to purchase insurance on the life of your business partner.

- Step 4: The trust will then be the premium payer, owner, and beneficiary of the insurance. Any premiums to be paid must be paid by the trustee, not by you as insured. At your death (or the death of the insured, if you are not the insured), the trust will receive the policy proceeds estate tax free and income tax free.

Of course, it may not always be possible or expedient to create the irrevocable life insurance trust in the classic way. There are alternatives. One alternative—which assumes the trust is established solely for children, grandchildren, and other relatives on these generational levels and is designed to avoid estate tax in both husband and wife's estate works like this:

- Step 1: Your spouse applies for a policy on your life as policy owner and initially names himself or herself as beneficiary.

- Step 2: After the irrevocable trust is created, your spouse immediately transfers ownership of the policy to the trust through what is called an *absolute assignment* (a way to transfer *all* policy rights). Using this approach, the policy should not be included in your estate since you never owned it—even if you die within 3 years after the policy is issued. Moreover, if your spouse makes the gift to the trust almost immediately after the trust is created, there should be relatively little (or no) gift tax implications. (Note: This approach assumes that your spouse has no beneficial interest in the trust. The IRS might include the insurance proceeds in your spouse's estate if you've given him or her a lifetime interest in the trust.)

There is still another approach:

- Step 1: You purchase term insurance on your life to ensure that if you die before the creation of the irrevocable trust, your heirs will have the coverage you desire. Initially, you are the owner and you name your children as beneficiary. (You may want to purchase enough extra coverage to pay the potential estate tax you would incur if you die before you can accomplish Step 2. Alternatively, you could name your spouse as beneficiary so that if you do die before Step 2 can be implemented, the proceeds will pass to your spouse in a manner that will qualify for the federal estate tax marital deduction and thereby wipe out the estate tax.)

- Step 2: When your lawyer has completed the trust document (assuming you are still insurable), the trustee purchases permanent coverage on your life. As soon as the permanent coverage is issued and fully effective, you allow the term policy to expire (or "lapse").

There are many variations on these themes. We suggest you discuss the strategy with your lawyer, accountant, and CLU, ChFC, or CFP.

Q. What is the procedure if I want to create an irrevocable life insurance trust with existing policies?

A. At this point, you must realize that any insurance you own on your own life will be taxed in your estate when you die. Furthermore, even if you don't own the insurance at your death, it will still be part of your taxable estate unless you transferred it out more than three years before you died.

You can transfer existing policies on your life to an irrevocable trust by gift. Your insurance agent will give you an *absolute assignment of ownership* form. This will transfer all your rights in the policy to the trust. The trust will then become the owner and should immediately name itself beneficiary of the insurance. (There should be no charge for this transaction from either the insurance company or the agent.)

As we just mentioned, you must survive for three years after the insurance is transferred, beginning on the date of the transfer. Otherwise, the policy proceeds will be included in your estate and taxed at your highest federal estate tax bracket. This places a certain amount of urgency in the creation of the trust because, until it is drafted and executed, the policy can't be transferred to it. Although a trust document must be tailored to meet your individual needs, and the needs of your family, and cannot just be spat out by a computer, most competent estate planning lawyers are familiar with the issues and alternatives and can create these documents relatively quickly.

Could you—or your advisers—backdate the trust to beat the three-year clock? Not without committing tax fraud. The IRS would quickly find that your records didn't match those of the insurance company. You therefore need to get the process started now, and not wait any longer. Because time is of the essence, you may want to use some of the techniques we discussed earlier in this chapter to ensure sufficient amounts of cash for your beneficiaries. However, if you must make a choice between waiting for the drafting of the trust document and obtaining insurance which might be estate tax includible, the later course of action is preferable. Even after taxes, your heirs will always be better off with the life insurance. They can spend the dollars but they can't spend the trust documents.

If you are married and must transfer an existing policy to an irrevocable trust (because you are no longer insurable or otherwise cannot replace the insurance at a comparable cost), make sure that your trust document includes a *contingent* marital deduction trust or gift to your spouse if your death occurs within the three year period following the transfer of the policy to the trust. The trust or gift is "contingent" because the insurance proceeds are only payable to the trust or to your wife if your death occurs within three years and the proceeds are included in your taxable estate. In the absence of this kind of contingent gift, the insurance proceeds might exceed your unified credit exclusion amount and result in the payment of estate taxes even though your spouse survived you. Under these circumstances, we believe it is usually better to take advantage of the marital deduction (see chapter 13) and defer any federal estate tax until you and your spouse have both died.

Q. What does the term "funded irrevocable life insurance trust" mean?

A. An irrevocable life insurance trust may be either unfunded or funded. Funding implies that you have placed income-producing assets into the trust. Most irrevocable life insurance trusts are unfunded. In other words, you don't put anything in the trust except for one or more life insurance policies.

If the trust doesn't have any income-producing assets, how does it pay premiums? The trustee pays premiums on policies in your unfunded life insurance trust from cash gifts you make to the trustee from time to time in amounts large enough for the trustee to pay the premiums and have enough cash left over to cover any incidental trust expenses. Your trustee has no obligation to keep the life insurance coverage in force if you do not make cash gifts to the trust, and probably does not even have any obligation to remind you when policies are due.

As noted above, "funding" implies that you have put income-producing assets into the trust in addition to life insurance to generate enough income to pay premiums on that insurance. If you do fund your trust with income-producing property, be sure the trust specifies what should be done if the income isn't enough to pay the entire premium or if there is an excess of income.

As a backup, your trust document should specifically authorize the trustee to borrow policy cash values to keep the policy in force. The trustee should also check with the insurance agent and make sure that if premiums are not paid for whatever reason, some coverage remains in force. There are two ways to accomplish this: First, the policy's cash values can be used to purchase term insurance (an option insurance agents call *extended term*) that will provide full coverage for a period of time stated in the policy. Second, cash values can be used to purchase a reduced amount of insurance that will be paid up for the rest of the insured's life (an option insurance agents call *reduced paid-up* coverage). With some older policies, dividends can be quite considerable and they can often be used to reduce your outlay; in some cases, the dividends are enough to pay most—or even all—of the premium.

Note that to the extent trust income is used to pay premiums on your life or your spouse's life, that income will be taxed to you as if you had earned it personally. However, this is not necessarily bad, for two reasons: First, income taxed to a trust may be subjected to much higher rates than if it is taxed to you or any of the trust's beneficiaries. Second, many lawyers believe that the income tax paid by the grantor on the income earned by an irrevocable trust is not a taxable gift, even though it effectively increases the value of the trust. Every dollar you use to help your beneficiaries is a dollar that will not be taxed in your estate. Taxes you pay on their behalf are a kind of transfer to them—on which you pay no gift tax.

Q. What are the disadvantages of transferring life insurance into an irrevocable trust?

A. There are a relatively few (but perfectly sound) reasons why you may not want to transfer existing life insurance into an irrevocable trust or to have the trustee purchase new insurance on your life. These disadvantages include the following:

- The arrangement is more complicated and requires more attention to detail than if you or your beneficiaries owned the insurance outright on your life.

- You lose the ability to reach the policy cash values of contracts that the trust holds.

- You cannot use trust-owned life insurance policy cash values as collateral for personal or business loans.

- You can no longer name new policy beneficiaries or remove those presently named.

- You cannot change the size or terms of a life insurance policy beneficiary's interest.

- There are up-front and continuing costs involved with an irrevocable life insurance trust, even if the trustee "isn't doing anything." First, there are legal fees for preparing the trust agreement. Expect lawyer's costs to range from a low of $1,500 to more than $10,000, depending on the nature and extent of your assets and the part the irrevocable trust plays in the overall planning process in your estate. (Always demand a written estimate of overall costs and hourly fees—*before* any work is done.)

  Second, there are accounting and investment costs. Of course, if the trust has no income, no tax returns will be required. Until you put income-producing property in the trust or until your death, tax return preparation costs should be nil. Likewise, until there are assets in the trust other than life insurance policies, no investment expertise is required. Nevertheless a trustee has set-up costs and annual record-keeping expenses. In addition, documents and correspondence must be exchanged between you and the trustee, the trustee and the trust's counsel, the trust and its beneficiaries, and the trustee and the IRS—even if it's just to say, "We had no income and that's why no income tax return was filed."

For these reasons, expect to pay an "acceptance fee" and charges for management and investment services. You rightly can anticipate that these fees will be nominal as long as you are alive, your trust has little or no assets, and your trustee has few responsibilities other than the payment of insurance premiums and safeguarding the trust document. But that will change if you fund the trust with income-producing assets during your lifetime (or when you die) and policy death benefits and other assets are paid by your will into the trust.

Therefore, we suggest that you shop around for professional trustees. Don't automatically accept the first one you are introduced to, even if you already do business with the same bank's commercial department. We highly recommend you obtain—in writing—the schedule of fees the bank intends to charge, not only after your death but also while you are alive and before the trustee holds anything but life insurance policies. Some banks don't feel it is profitable enough to be trustees of irrevocable life insurance trusts and charge fees designed to discourage trusts without significant amounts of income-producing property. (For this reason, you may want to use an individual as trustee during your lifetime and add a professional trustee such as a bank at your death.)

- You may be charged a *termination fee* by a corporate trustee if the trust is terminated for any reason before your death and prior to the time the trustee has had the opportunity to recover set-up costs. Find out if there will be such charges before you sign any documents. Get either written confirmation that such charges will not be imposed or a statement of exactly what those fees will be. Again, note that different banks have different policies regarding these fees.

- To minimize gift tax costs on transfers to an irrevocable trust, planners build into the trust what is called a *Crummey power*. In a nutshell, this power gives the beneficiaries of your trust (usually, your spouse and children) the right to make current withdrawals of the money you put into the trust each year. This is the price the tax law demands in return for an annual gift tax exclusion that shields from gift tax up to $10,000 a year for each beneficiary. (The $10,000 exclusion may be adjusted for inflation after 1998; Crummey powers will be discussed in detail below.) You must consider the possibility that, rather than letting your annual contribution of cash stay inside the trust and be used when appropriate to pay insurance premiums, one or more of your beneficiaries might chose to take the cash. Because the tax law requires that beneficiaries must be notified of their right to make a withdrawal, the potential for back-door drainage of cash you put into the trust to pay life insurance premiums is real. Nonetheless, it is a relatively small risk you must be willing to take in return for the significant rewards an irrevocable trust may offer. (Note that the IRS will disallow the annual gift tax exclusion where it feels the Crummey power you provide is a "sham" and could not really be exercised.)

- The rules regarding the estate tax treatment of life insurance are very strict and unforgiving, and you may go to all the trouble and expense of setting up an irrevocable life insurance trust but never realize the intended estate tax benefits. If the lawyer who drafts the document relics on legal research that is incomplete or makes even a slight mechanical error, an inadvertent misstatement, or omission from the trust instrument, that error may eviscerate an otherwise brilliant estate plan. A faulty irrevocable trust may not only fail to achieve your goals, but it may also cause the loss of the desired tax savings. This is just one more reason to use only a lawyer who specializes in estate planning, preferably one who belongs to an estate planning council. The risk is too great to use anyone less than a highly competent and experienced practitioner. Estate planning is not the place to cut corners; your entire family's financial safety and hundreds of thousands (or perhaps millions) of dollars are at stake!

- To the extent that your transfer to an irrevocable trust does not qualify for an annual gift tax exclusion, or to the extent that you've already used your exclusion for a given beneficiary because of another gift, you will have to utilize your unified credit (shielding up to $1,000,000 of lifetime gifts from each spouse by 2006) and then pay gift taxes on any transfer in excess of that amount. Of course, if you think about it, the ability to transfer up to $1,000,000 during your lifetime—in addition to $10,000 ($20,000 if you are married) annual exclusion gifts—is an enormous opportunity. Combine that amount with life insurance purchased by the trustee, and you can shift vast amounts of wealth with little or no out-of pocket costs.

  For example, suppose you are 50 years old, have five donees (i.e., children or other beneficiaries), and give each $10,000 a year in trust. By the end of your life expectancy, you will have given away (and protected from estate tax) a total of $1,655,000. Assuming you are in a 50 percent estate tax bracket, your children (or other beneficiaries) will have received $827,500 more than they would have if you had done nothing. Furthermore, if the trustee invests the $50,000 each year at only 4 percent net after taxes, your gifts will grow in the trustee's hands to about $3,328,398. Then the potential estate tax savings increases to $1,664,199! This estate tax savings is the result of *only* the annual exclusion.

  If you are wealthy and use some or all of the unified credit to shelter lifetime gifts to your children's trust, you can further increase the benefits of giving gifts in trust. For instance, your unified credit allows you to give $600,000 (in 1997, but increasing by steps to $1,000,000 in 2006)—over and above any annual exclusion gifts—to anyone you want without any out-of-pocket federal gift tax cost. At a 4 percent after-tax return, that $600,000 will grow to well over $2,000,000 in 33 years. Since none of that will be in your estate, the savings will be considerable if you are in a 50 percent estate tax bracket.

- There are simpler alternatives. You want to give cash directly to your (mature) adult children and obtain an annual exclusion for your gifts of cash. Your children can then use that cash to pay the life insurance premiums and you won't have to worry about a Crummey power or the complex wording and consequent expense of a trust. Life can be simpler—if you are willing to take more risks.

- Life can also be simpler if estate tax savings and creditor-proofing assets are not your major objectives. In that case, consider naming a revocable trust as beneficiary of life insurance on your life.

Q. What are the estate tax and other traps to avoid when setting up an irrevocable trust?

A. If your objective is to shift the maximum amount of wealth possible and by-pass federal estate taxation in your estate (and your spouse's estate if you are married), you must be willing to give up certain rights, accept certain limitations, and meet certain guidelines. These include the following:

- You cannot serve as trustee, or have any right to direct how the trust is distributed, or how it is invested. You cannot have any right to withdraw from the trust in any way, any right to exchange assets with the trust, or any right to revoke or modify the trust. However, many lawyers believe that it may be possible to retain the right to appoint additional successor trustees.

- Your spouse must not have the power to withdraw from the trust, or amend or revoke the trust, or else the trust will be considered part of your spouse's estate and subject to estate tax at his or her death. However, you can accomplish your goal of keeping the trust out of her or his estate and still give your spouse considerable benefits, control, and flexibility. For instance, you can safely give your spouse all of these rights without fear of estate tax inclusion:

  - the absolute right to all of the income from the trust

  - the right to any principal necessary to provide for his or her health

  - the right to any principal needed for your spouse's education (including tuition, books, and related expenses)

  - the right to any principal needed for his or her support and maintenance (food, clothing, and shelter at the standard in which he or she has been living at the time the trust is created)

–   an absolute right to withdraw the greater of $5,000 or 5 percent of the trust's principal each year

–   a power to appoint (that is, to specify who receives) assets in the trust. This power can give your spouse the right to direct how the trust should be divided among your children at your deaths, or it can be a broader power, including charities and almost anyone else *except* your spouse, his or her estate, his or her creditors, and the creditors of his or her estate (and you, of course).

•   If you are relatively young, you may be worried about what will happen if your spouse divorces you after you have created and funded your irrevocable trust. It is perfectly appropriate to provide in the trust document that all powers and interests of your spouse will end upon divorce, and most married couples today will accept that kind of "boilerplate" provision without offense, understanding the ever-present danger of divorce. Some lawyers will go still further and define the primary beneficiary of the trust as "the person to whom I am married on the date of my death." This definition of the beneficiary by description—-without specifying a name—is legally valid and the IRS has ruled that it does not create any estate tax problems for the grantor of the trust.

•   The biggest tax trap is the possibility that your life insurance will be included in your taxable estate if your death occurs within three years after you create the trust. You can't avoid that result if you transfer an existing policy to the trust, but you should be able to avoid that result if you contribute nothing but cash to your trust and your trustee is the original applicant and owner of the policy. If you were never the owner of the policy, and never had any "incident of ownership," the policy should not be included in your taxable estate even if your death occurs within the three year "danger zone." To be sure the policy is not included in your estate, your trustee should contact the insurance agent and apply for the policy listing you as the "proposed insured" (but *not* as applicant or owner). The trustee should pay both initial premium and all later premiums, whenever possible, with a check drawn on the bank account of the trust.

- Another tax trap is the unnecessary estate tax that might result if the life insurance is included in your taxable estate (which would occur, for example, if your transferred an existing policy to your trust and then died within three years of the transfer) and your trust does not qualify for the federal estate tax marital deduction (which it typically would not). Speak to your lawyer about a *contingent* gift to or for your spouse, so that if for any reason a policy on your life owned by the trust is estate tax includible, it will pass to your surviving spouse in a way that qualifies for the estate tax marital deduction, instead of being distributed or held in trust as originally planned. In other words, build a "fail-safe" provision into the trust so that if the policy is included in your estate, the estate tax will be offset by an equal deduction.

  This fail-safe is not without its costs. If the purposes of the trust included not only saving taxes but also controlling the disposition of the life insurance proceeds, the fail-safe marital deduction will avoid (or at least defer) the estate tax, but may result in a disposition of the life insurance proceeds that is different than what you intended. Because your spouse may be receiving additional income or principal, or may even be able to withdraw and control the life insurance proceeds, your spouse may be able to give that additional money to someone (including a future spouse) or use it in a way that is contrary to what you intended. As a result, the trust may wind up fulfilling *neither* of the original purposes of the trust.

Q. Suppose I want to get life insurance coverage in force as quickly as possible. Is there a way to do it even before my irrevocable trust is fully prepared?

A. We suggest, whenever possible, that you create the trust first. Although this may take some time because of the complicated issues involved, a careful, well-drafted document is worth the wait. Since every document is as different as the people it is designed to protect and the objectives it is created to meet, a good estate planning lawyer can—and should—not rush to draft your trust. Contrary to some people's impression, computers cannot merely crank out a well thought out trust document. Furthermore, you should not rush to sign any document until you have read it and considered the consequences and alternatives.

Your insurance agent will (rightfully, in our opinion) want to be sure coverage is effective as quickly as possible. Given a choice between effective insurance coverage that is not estate tax free and a perfect irrevocable trust that has no life insurance or any other assets, the decision should be obvious. (Many problems can be corrected with cash, but few can be solved with a trust that has no assets. If you need the cash that life insurance creates, we strongly advise that it be placed into effect as quickly as possible.)

But must you chose? As we've just stated, the best procedure is to create the trust quickly and the trustee apply for the insurance. But the next best alternative is as follows:

- Your spouse could apply for the insurance on your life as quickly as might be necessary to protect your family.

- Ask your lawyer to begin drafting the irrevocable trust document simultaneously with your application for insurance. Let your lawyer know that life insurance will be the main vehicle for providing cash in the trust, and tell him or her that you'd like the trust to go into effect as quickly as possible.

- Your spouse can sign as the applicant for the life insurance on your life in what agents call a "preliminary application." You would sign as the "proposed insured."

- Take whatever physical examination will be necessary. Ideally, by the time word comes back that you have passed the exam, you and your lawyer will have completed the trust document.

- After the trust document has been executed, your trustee can sign a new application for insurance on your life and your spouse can withdraw the old application or let it lapse. Because the insurance company was willing to accept the risk of insuring you under the first application, the company should be willing to accept the new application by your trustee—assuming no changes in your health or other factors affecting insurability. At not time did you own the insurance or any rights in it. Because the "transfers within three years of death" rule applies only to insurance you owned on your own life and then transferred, there should be no federal estate tax inclusion in this scenario even if you die within three years of either application.

There are still other alternatives. First, your spouse can purchase term insurance on your life while you are waiting for the trust to be set up. Assuming your health has not deteriorated by the time the trust is drafted, your trustee can apply for permanent coverage; once it becomes effective, you can drop the term insurance your spouse owns. If your health does deteriorate (or if for any other reason the trustee is unable to purchase the new policy), your spouse can make a gift of the original policy to the trust. There will be relatively little, if any, gift tax payable on that transfer. The trustee can then convert the term insurance to a permanent form of coverage on your life. (If your spouse is a beneficiary of the trust, that transfer makes your spouse a grantor of the trust. At least part of the trust will be included in your spouse's estate if your spouse is a beneficiary of the trust, or has any power over it. Therefore, this procedure works best only if your spouse is not a beneficiary or trustee of the trust.)

Second, some companies will issue policies with a *rider* (attachment) that provides (for a small additional premium) that if you die within three years from the date the policy is purchased, the death benefit will be doubled, or increased by an amount sufficient to pay any additional estate tax, whether or not the IRS actually includes the policy in your estate. If you are really concerned about the impact of the death-within-three-year rule, you can purchase a regular term rider yourself for a relatively small additional premium. You can then drop this additional coverage when the policy has been in the trustee's hands for more than three years.

Do not take any of these steps—or any other suggestion in this book, for that matter—without the concurrence of your lawyer working with your insurance agent. You must insist these two professionals work together for you. Without a team effort, you risk making some potentially expensive mistakes.

Q. What are some of the "escape valves" I should build into my irrevocable life insurance trust?

A. When you set up an irrevocable life insurance trust, there is always the possibility that, at some point, for whatever reason, the terms of your trust will no longer meet your objectives or your beneficiary's needs or circumstances. Building escape valves into your trust is important if for no other reason than to anticipate changes in the tax law or the circumstances of the parties. Discuss the pros and cons of the following ways to add flexibility to your irrevocable life insurance trust with your lawyer and other advisers (keep in mind that none of these solutions is a "free lunch" and each has its own costs):

- You can build flexibility into the terms of the trust. For example:

  - You can give your independent trustee (someone other than you, a beneficiary, or someone subservient to either of you) discretionary power to "sprinkle" income or "spray" principal among a class of persons. This can add significant additional flexibility to the dispositive terms of your trust without adverse tax consequences.

  - Your lawyer can include a provision in the trust allowing the lifetime use of policy cash values by trust beneficiaries. Although this isn't as appealing as making it possible for you to reach the money directly, it serves its purpose by freeing up your personal assets without risking the federal estate tax exclusion of the life insurance in the trust. For example, if a married child asks you for cash to buy a house, he or she can get money from the trust, rather than from you personally.

- If the terms of the trust become completely unacceptable, and you are still insurable, you can choose to discontinue premium payments. Term insurance, which generally builds up no cash values, will quickly lapse with no benefit. If permanent coverage inside the trust has cash values, you can stop paying premiums and allow policy cash values to purchase extended term insurance for a limited time or a lower amount of paid-up insurance for your life. In either event, you can create a new trust with new terms and new insurance—assuming you are still insurable at affordable rates. It may also be possible to create a new trust and have that trust purchase assets—including life insurance—from the old trust. (There are serious potential tax problems to this technique unless it is handled very carefully. This technique is discussed in detail below.)

- You can petition the court for a change or termination. In spite of all we have said about the unchangability of an irrevocable trust, under certain circumstances it may be revoked or modified by a successful court petition.

Generally, the court allows revocation only if significant and unforeseen events (such as a major tax change) occurs after the trust was created. The catch is that a change in trust terms or the revocation of an irrevocable trust entails:

– the written consent of all (including guardians for minor) beneficiaries

– the expense of legal representation and court action

– the cost of drafting a new trust with the appropriate terms

– the strong likelihood that otherwise excludable assets will now be included in your estate at their current value (unless the old trust contained a clause that paid them over to specified beneficiaries in the event of a premature termination of the trust).

- You can buy the trust-owned life insurance for full fair market value from the trust. This gives the trust a relatively small amount of cash but returns the insurance to you. The trustee can terminate the old trust under a built-in provision to "pull the plug" if the value of trust assets drops below what the trustee feels is economically feasible. You can then create a new trust with new provisions and contribute the old policies to that new trust.

Where will the money come from to buy the policy from the trust? You can borrow it from a bank for a long enough time to buy the policy and once you become the new owner, borrow from the policy cash values to pay off the bank loan at your own pace.

An alternative mentioned briefly above is to create a new trust that reflects your changed objectives or the beneficiary's changed circumstances and have the new trust purchase the policy for fair market value from the old trust. However, this could trigger an arcane income tax trap called the *transfer-for-value rule*. In a nutshell, if a policy or an interest in a policy is purchased or "transferred for value" it loses its income tax-free status at death. Ironically, the arcane rule that creates the trap has arcane exceptions. Under one such exception, if you are a partner of the party that buys the life insurance, a transfer to that partner (even if it is a trust) falls within a "safe harbor" and eliminates the problem. One possible solution is for you to enter into a bona fide partnership with the new trust (perhaps involving an investment venture) before it purchases the policy from the old trust.

Note that you can't safely put a provision in the trust requiring the trustee to sell you the policy or lend you policy cash values. That right is quite likely to cause the policy to be included in your estate.

Keep in mind, too, that the fair market value of the policy may be considerably more than its cash value, especially if you are in worse health than you were when you purchased the policy. If you are terminally ill, the policy's fair market value may be closer to its death benefit than its cash value.

Also remember that once you've purchased the policy, it's a "hot potato." Hold it and it will be included in your estate and taxed accordingly. Give it away within three years of your death and it will still be taxed in your estate. If the trust paid less in premiums than you pay the trust for the policy, the old trust will have a taxable gain at the time you buy it.

- You can have your lawyer insert a clause giving someone else the power to remove the policy from the trust. Such a provision is called a *special power of appointment*. This special power can give your independent trustee (or some independent third party) the right to require the trustee to transfer trust-owned life insurance to a specific person or a class of beneficiary consisting of anyone other than you (the grantor of the trust), your spouse, your estate, your creditors, or your estate's creditors.

We advise that you specify in the trust that the policy may not be appointed to you, your creditors, your estate, the creditors of your estate, or the creditors of your spouse's estate. If the policy can be shifted back to you or be used for your benefit under the terms of the trust, the IRS will include it in your estate. Even if that power is held by an independent trustee or an individual who is totally unrelated and non-subservient to you, if the policy can be appointed back to you, and your creditors under state law could compel that distribution, the IRS will certainly include the policy proceeds in your estate.

- Can the limited power of appointment to shift policy ownership be given safely to your spouse? Our opinion is that you should act conservatively in this area. The stakes are too high. There are two reasons for this suggestion: First, if neither you nor your spouse has a right to remove life insurance on either of your lives from the trust, the IRS can't claim that a policy owned by the trust should be included in either of your estates. Second, if you do give that power of appointment to your spouse, if there is a divorce or your spouse predeceases you, there will no longer be a way to remove the life insurance and have it transferred in a direction consistent with your objectives. Obviously, if there is marital discord at the time of planning, the decision is clear.

- You can name an adult child as the initial holder of a limited power to appoint trust-owned life insurance to another irrevocable trust you create or to a child or other relative. However, be sure to stipulate that he or she cannot appoint the insurance either to you or your spouse in any event and has no power at all over a trust-owned policy on his or her own life. Specify that the power ceases if he or she predeceases you. Provide further that the power will pass to a contingent holder (such as an another adult child) if the initial powerholder becomes legally incompetent, bankrupt, or divorced.

• You may condition a gift on the existence of a relationship.

- It is very common for a trust to benefit your "children" without naming them, so that any children who might be born in the future will automatically become beneficiaries of the trust without any need to try to change the trust or create a new trust. Similarly, trusts routinely provide for possible future grandchildren, and the possibility that one of your children may predecease you, or not survive to the end of the trust.

- As previously explained, you can also make any benefits or interests of your spouse conditioned on your continuing marriage, specifying that any rights in the trust end upon divorce. You can even designate your spouse as a beneficiary by description, not name, so that if you should divorce and remarry, your new spouse would become beneficiary.

— Any benefits that you might provide for daughters-in-law, sons-in-law, or other relatives by marriage can also be conditioned upon the continuing existence of the relationship (although many people have great affection for former in-laws, particularly former in-laws who are the parents of their grandchildren).

• You can empower your independent trustee (neither a beneficiary, grantor, nor someone subservient to either) with the right to terminate the trust if it no longer meets stated objectives due to unforeseen circumstances. In the trustee's (or co-trustee's) sole discretion the trust can be ended and the life insurance and other trust assets distributed to predetermined beneficiaries specified in the trust.

There are two possible problems with this approach. First, your trustee may be understandably reluctant to exercise this power unless all beneficiaries will sign an agreement that the action is proper and in conformance with the trustee's fiduciary responsibilities to all beneficiaries. Second, the beneficiaries may end up receiving substantial assets before they are mature enough to handle them.

• You might give your independent trustee the right to amend the trust as necessary to preserve your stated tax objectives, although that kind of "savings clause" is not always effective.

None of these techniques will work in every case, and all have their flaws or costs. A gain in flexibility might entail an unacceptable risk that a beneficiary will have more control than you wanted or receive an asset sooner than you desired. Increasing flexibility may also result in a retention of power that is broad enough to warrant estate tax inclusion. For these reasons, you must carefully weigh the advantages of an irrevocable trust against the costs, and you must be sure you have a lawyer who understands the intricacies of a very complex tax law.

Q. What criteria should I use to select a trustee for my irrevocable trust?

A. The selection of a trustee is covered in detail in chapter 3. The same basic selection factors apply to both an irrevocable trust and a revocable trust. However, the word "irrevocable" should point to the need for even greater caution because, once an irrevocable trust is created and funded, it is difficult—sometimes impossible—to make changes without severe adverse tax and non-tax consequences. Moreover, because the death benefits from the life insurance policies placed into most irrevocable trusts are generally larger than many entire estates, the trustee's investment expertise is particularly important. At your death (or your spouse's death), there may be more than a million dollars that must be invested wisely for a long period of time.

Here are some of the tasks. The trustee of your irrevocable trust has to:

- check to be sure that the trust document is not defective and will accomplish your dispositive and tax objectives
- create a trust bank account
- purchase and continue the appropriate type and amount of life insurance on your life
- receive cash and property transferred to the trust
- notify beneficiaries holding demand powers (i.e., "Crummey powers") of their rights to make withdrawals
- pay premiums to the insurance company

Do not allow yourself to be named as trustee, or your spouse if he or she is an insured under any life insurance held by the trust, or has made any gifts to the trust. Either choice might result in estate tax inclusion of the life insurance proceeds in your estate(s). At the very least, you will likely end up in a dispute with the IRS. (If you insist on naming your spouse as trustee, we strongly recommend naming a bank or other individual as a co-trustee and forbidding your spouse from voting on any issue or making any decision that may affect him or her.)

You may want to consider a two-tiered approach to naming a trustee. Ask yourself these questions: (1) Who should be the trustee of my trust while I'm alive? and (2) who should be the trustee of my trust after I die?

While you are alive, there isn't a great deal of work or responsibility for your trustee (compared to what must be done after your death). Generally, the time commitment (and therefore your trustee's compensation) is minimal. Your trustee, therefore, should be someone who knows you, your family, your business, and your assets and is willing to handle the few necessary details for relatively little payment. You may want to consider a friend, adult child, or financial adviser for this first stage of the trust's existence.

When you die, there is a dramatic change in the duties of the trustee of an irrevocable trust if its major asset is life insurance. Now, your trustee will have a significant amount of cash that must be invested, safeguarded, and managed. These proceeds, in addition to any other assets you placed into the trust while you were alive, assets that "poured over" into the trust under your will, or proceeds from employee benefit plans or life insurance you didn't transfer to the trust during your lifetime, will now have to be invested and managed for as long as the trust lasts.

For this second stage of the trust's existence, you might want to consider a corporate trustee (with or without individual co-trustees). We strongly advise you to consider naming a bank or other professional trustee as a backup trustee in case persons you've named as trustee die, become disabled, move, or for any other reason are unable or unwilling to perform the duties of trustee.

A good reason for the use of a corporate trustee is to avoid any tax traps. Having your spouse or other beneficiary as a trustee can cause unforeseen estate tax and income tax problems if the trustee has the power to distribute money to himself (or herself) or a beneficiary that the trustee is obligated to support. A corporate trustee can also offer your beneficiaries a professional level of investment, management, and record keeping services. Your beneficiaries will be relieved of the countless bothersome and time-consuming details that trust management requires. With a corporate trustee, all of these services will be performed seamlessly year after year, even if one or more family member dies or becomes incompetent. This continuity takes on more meaning when you remember that your irrevocable trust may continue for several generations.

One last reason to enlist the services of a corporate (or other professional) trustee in the second stage of your trust's existence is that such trust companies employ legal counsel either full-time or on a permanent retainer basis. Your individual trustee may often need to rely on this counsel's expertise on the tax or state law impact on an action the trustee is about to take. (The authors highly recommend the book, **TAX PLANNING WITH LIFE INSURANCE** (800-950-1210) for detailed and in-depth authoritative information about the income, estate, gift, and generation skipping transfer taxation of life insurance in and out of trusts).

Q. Can I safely reserve the right to change trustees of my irrevocable trust?

A. As explained in chapter 3, the choice of trustee is often more important than any other decision you make in creating a trust. The ability to change trustees is extremely important for these reasons:

- Personnel of trust departments change over time; individuals named as trustees may move out of the state or even out of the country.

- Your beneficiaries may move out of the state or out of the country as well.

- Beneficiaries may not like or get along with the trustees you have selected.

- The original trustee may no longer have the time or inclination to perform trust functions properly.

For these and many more reasons, it is important to be able to change trustees. As you might expect, if you reserve the right to change trustees and appoint yourself as trustee, you will be considered to have the powers of the trustee and (in the case of an irrevocable life insurance trust) the entire value of the trust will be included in your taxable estate. However, the IRS has ruled that the power to change trustees and appoint a third party as the trustee will not ordinarily cause an estate tax problem. Nevertheless, the IRS ruling did not involve a life insurance trust, and life insurance is an especially sensitive asset, so we would recommend that you and your legal counsel consider this issue very carefully and be very cautious in giving you a power that could cause adverse estate tax consequences and defeat the primary purpose of the trust.

Here are two overall guidelines and tips for adding flexibility without triggering taxation:

- You should *never* have the power to name yourself as trustee. Even if you never use the power, its mere existence could cause trust assets to be included in your estate.

- For you to have the power to name a trustee if a vacancy should arise (due to death or resignation) should be permissible, and not cause any estate tax problems, as long as you do not have the power to name yourself as trustee.

- If a bank or trust company is appointed as a trustee, we would strongly recommend that there be a way to remove and replace the corporate trustee with another corporate trustee. This will insure that the needs of the beneficiaries are met, and that trustee fees remain competitive. Ideally, that power should be held by an independent individual trustee (not a beneficiary) so that there are no possible tax consequences to the beneficiaries, and no possible conflicts among the beneficiaries. However, you might also consider giving your beneficiaries the right (by majority vote) to remove and replace a corporate trustee, if you and your legal counsel consider the risks acceptable and worth the flexibility given to the beneficiaries.

Q. How can I retain access to policy cash values but keep the life insurance I place into an irrevocable trust out of my taxable estate?

A. In our opinion, you can't. To the extent that you retain access to policy cash values personally, you risk a very high likelihood that the IRS will include all of the trust-owned life insurance in your estate. If it is extremely important to you to have instant and unrestricted access to policy cash values, an irrevocable life insurance trust is not an appropriate receptacle for a life insurance policy. You can't have both access to policy cash values and estate tax exclusion.

Q. Am I making a taxable gift when I transfer a life insurance policy on my life to an irrevocable trust?

A. Yes. Any asset you contribute to an irrevocable trust will be considered a taxable gift to the beneficiaries of that trust. This includes a gift of a life insurance policy on your life or on the lives of anyone else.

Fortunately, in most cases you will not have to pay any out-of-pocket tax even if the gift itself is subject to gift taxes. Here's why:

- Your gross gift for tax purposes is the value of the policy, essentially its *replacement cost* on the day you make the trust the new owner. The insurance company will give you this value at no charge. (Request Form 712, Life Insurance Statement, from the insurer.)

- Regardless of the value of the gift, you may be able to reduce the taxable portion of that gift by what is called the *gift tax annual exclusion.* This exclusion allows you to give—each year, every year, to an unlimited number of individuals, even if they are not related to you—up to $10,000 gift tax free. (The $10,000 may be adjusted for inflation after 1998.) The catch is that to be eligible for this exclusion your gift must transfer to the recipient the "immediate, unfettered, and ascertainable right to use, possess, and enjoy" the property. That's where the *Crummey power*, discussed below, comes in.

- To the extent that the annual exclusion has already been used or for whatever reason is not allowed, you still don't have to pay any out-of-pocket tax—until you've used up your *unified credit.* It's called "unified" because you can apply it during lifetime to shelter gifts you make now, or your executor can use what's left of it when you die to shelter assets remaining in your estate. Currently (1997), the unified credit exclusion amount is $600,000, but it is scheduled to increase by steps to $1,000,000 in 2006. If you are married, your spouse has the same credit. For this reason, you'd have to have a very large policy in your trust or have made sizable other lifetime gifts to trigger an out-of-pocket gift tax cost.

Q. How does the IRS value a life insurance policy I transfer to an irrevocable trust?

A. Valuation of a life insurance policy depends on a number of factors. If your policy was just purchased and you transfer it to your irrevocable trust immediately after you receive it from the insurance company, the gift tax value will be based on the amount of net premiums you have paid. So your cost determines the gift tax value.

If you have a *paid up* or *single premium* policy (a policy with no further premiums necessary to keep it in force for the rest of your life), the value is what insurance agents call *replacement cost*—the price the insurer would charge for an actuarially equivalent policy on your life at your age at the date of the transfer to the trust. (The insurance company will generally compute this figure for you or your tax advisers at no charge.)

Suppose the policy you are transferring to the trust is still in what is called the *premium-paying* stage. In other words, to keep it going you have to continue to pay premiums. In very loose terms, the policy's cash value determines the gift tax value. More technically correct, the gift tax value is the sum of (1) the policy's *interpolated terminal reserve* (the amount the insurer has set aside to meet its obligations under the policy as of the date of the transfer) plus (2) any *unearned premiums* (premiums that were paid and that will carry the insurance beyond the day you transfer it to your trust). Subtracted from these two amounts is the total of any loans outstanding against the policy. (The insurance company will give this figure to you or your advisers at no charge.)

You can also transfer group term life insurance to an irrevocable trust. The gift tax on your gift will be the lower of the actual cost of coverage on a year-by-year basis or the cost of term insurance in the amount you are transferring. The IRS calls this the *Table I cost* since it provides a table with rates that increase in 5-year increments for measuring the economic benefit (essentially what the IRS feels the group term premiums should be worth) you are receiving from your employer each year. Your tax counsel can easily calculate this amount.

Does a policy have the same gift tax value, regardless of the condition of the insured at the time of the gift? For instance, what if you had a $10,000,000 policy and you were on your deathbed at the time you assigned it to your irrevocable trust? Would it be worth the same amount as if you were in perfect health on that date? Obviously not. In such cases the IRS may attempt to value the policy at or near the amount it would pay as a death benefit. Even so, there may be advantages to transferring it to your irrevocable trust.

Q. How can I minimize the gift tax cost when I contribute a life insurance policy on my life to an irrevocable trust?

A. There are a number of techniques your advisers may consider to help you keep gift tax costs as low as possible. One technique is to borrow a portion of the cash values out of the policy before you transfer the policy to the trust. Creating a loan against the policy will lower the gift tax value of the policy. (But be sure you don't borrow out more than your net cost—the total of premiums you've paid less any tax-free dividends you've received. If you do, the difference may be taxed to you as ordinary income.)

Another technique is to split one large policy into several smaller ones and contribute them to the trust over a period of time, rather than all in one year. This will help you use your annual exclusions more efficiently.

Q. How can I minimize the gift tax cost each year when I contribute money to an irrevocable trust so the trustee can pay life insurance premiums?

A. As you know by now, every time you place cash or any other type of property into an irrevocable trust, you are making a gift, regardless of what the trustee does with that money. You also make a gift if you transfer property *indirectly,* such as by paying debts of the trust or spending money to increase the value of property owned by the trust. For that reason, the IRS will treat you as if you are making a gift to the trust's beneficiaries whether you place the cash in the trustee's hands or pay the premium directly to the insurer.

The best way to minimize the gift tax cost of contributions to your irrevocable trust is to maximize the use of the annual gift tax exclusion. But as we've already noted, the IRS will deny an exclusion unless you give each donee what lawyers call a *present interest.* A gift in trust is ordinarily not a present interest unless either (a) the beneficiary has an immediate and unrestricted right to the present and future income of the trust or (b) the beneficiary has an immediate and unrestricted legal right to take what you put into the trust. If your beneficiary's right to take what you contribute to the trust can possibly be obstructed or delayed for even one minute, the IRS will not allow your annual exclusion. For example, if a beneficiary has to wait, even one day, before he or she receives the legal right to property you place into the trust, you've lost the annual exclusion for the entire gift.

Obviously, if you give a child an outright gift of a life insurance policy, that transfer will qualify for the gift tax annual exclusion ($10,000, but adjusted for inflation after 1998). But remember the reason you set up the trust in the first place: You don't want your beneficiaries to have an immediate, absolute, and uncontrolled right to the property. You want to withhold those rights until your beneficiaries are older and, hopefully, more mature.

Think about it. The tax law demands that you give your beneficiaries immediate, absolute legal control while the trust itself is designed to do just the opposite. The problem is how to have your cake and eat it too.

The solution of choice is to create a "window" through which the beneficiary can reach to take all or a portion of each annual contribution you make to the trust. Professionals call this window a *Crummey power*, named after a person who convinced a court to rule in his favor, and against the IRS, on whether he should be allowed an annual gift tax exclusion because of the rights he gave his beneficiaries to make a demand of the trustee.

Crummey powers are a compromise. Essentially, they create a legal right for the beneficiary to demand an amount equal to the portion of your contribution that qualified for the annual gift tax exclusion—but no more than that. The Crummey power is simply a limited withdrawal right designed to satisfy the requirements of the annual gift tax exclusion.

Q. How flexible can a Crummey power be?

A. Crummey powers can work even if

- the selected beneficiaries are still minors

- there is no guardian for a minor beneficiary (In this case, notice of the right to make a withdrawal should be sent to a parent or the closest other relative and your trustee should be specifically authorized to deliver the notice to that person.)

- the power to demand a distribution was never actually exercised by either the children or by a guardian on their behalf

- none of the beneficiaries given Crummey powers receive any payment from the trust fund

- the power has a limited duration (For example, the window of opportunity for the beneficiary to take money you contribute to the trust each year could be restricted to one month per year.)

You can retain a great deal of control in your trust and still qualify your gifts for the annual gift tax exclusion as long as your Crummey power gives beneficiaries a reasonable and realistic legal right to enjoy what you've placed in the trust.

Your trust document must keep the window (the period during which a beneficiary can make a withdrawal) open long enough to give the beneficiary a realistic opportunity to withdraw the interest in the property given to the trust. Moreover, your trustee should keep sufficient funds in the trust during the open-window period so that a demand can be realistically and immediately satisfied. (If you put money into a trust but the trustee pays the premiums for trust-owned life insurance the very same day, the IRS could argue that your annual exclusion should be denied. Why? Because, again, your Crummey power beneficiaries were never given a realistic chance to make a withdrawal and the power to withdraw was a sham.)

The trust should notify the beneficiary (or guardian in case of a minor) by registered mail (request return receipt) of his or her right to make a withdrawal. We suggest that the trustee ask the beneficiary to initial a copy of the letter and return it in a stamped Self-Addressed envelope so that if you are ever audited you can prove the beneficiary had sufficient notice. The IRS has issued rulings indicating that beneficiaries cannot waive future notices, so we recommend that you send notices for *every* gift for which you wish to use the annual gift tax exclusion. There is no formal statutory language that you must use as long as you can show that the beneficiary had actual notice of his or her right to make a withdrawal of the proportionate share of what you've placed in trust that year.

Consider creating a Crummey (demand) power that continues each year unless you send a letter stating that no demand power applies in a given year. Alternatively, you could state in your letter that the demand power applies in a given future year but for a lesser amount.

Can you enlarge the amount you can put into the trust gift tax free each year by creating artificial Crummey powerholders?

In other words, can you select names at random, place them in the trust, give them Crummey powers, but never notify them of their right to make a withdrawal? We strongly advise you not to. The IRS has expressed its intention to attack those powers as shams. We suggest that you give withdrawal powers only to those individuals you genuinely want to receive income or principal from your trust—or who you want to be "contingent" beneficiaries who may receive income or principal upon the prior death or disclaimer of the income and principal beneficiaries you've named.

Q. What is a "5 or 5 power"?

A. In many irrevocable trusts you'll see a limit on a beneficiary's right to take money from the irrevocable trust. This limit is quite often stated as a noncumulative (use it now or lose it) right of withdrawal to the lower of (1) the beneficiary's share of the annual contribution to the trust (the total value of the contribution, divided by the number of beneficiaries who have been given a Crummey power) or (2) the greater of $5,000 or 5 percent of the value of the trust's assets at the time of the withdrawal. (We'll explain the reason for the second limit in a moment.)

You may be wondering why a lawyer might draft a trust with a limit potentially lower than $10,000 per year. After all, that's the size of the annual exclusion, so why should the beneficiary be given a withdrawal right less than that amount? Why limit the size of the window at all? There are several issues:

- You are creating the window through which a beneficiary can reach to make a withdrawal in order to qualify each year's transfer to the trust for the annual gift tax exclusion, but you do not want to make the opening so large and keep the window open so long that the beneficiary will actually reach in and take the contribution. If the beneficiary does exercise the right to withdraw, the money will not be available to pay premiums on the life insurance that is meant to provide estate liquidity and financial security for the trust's beneficiaries.

- Even if the beneficiary does not take the money he or she could have taken, the unlimited ability to do so could cause estate tax inclusion of the entire principal in your beneficiary's estate. Likewise, each year, the money the beneficiary could have taken but didn't could be considered a gift that beneficiary is making to remaindermen (beneficiaries who will receive the principal when the trust terminates). That would result in a need to file annual gift tax returns and in some cases pay a gift tax.

- If a powerholder actually takes money one year, you can decide not to make a contribution subject to that beneficiary's withdrawal right the next year by providing in your trust each powerholder has a right to withdraw funds from the trust only if notified in that year that a right to withdraw exists.

- You can specify in the trust that if a beneficiary is subject to a bankruptcy proceeding, the right to make a withdrawal lapses. This will prevent the bankruptcy trustee from exercising a withdrawal right.

- If the window stays open too long, there may be adverse tax implications to your Crummey powerholder. For example, if your beneficiary dies during a time when he or she has an absolute right to a specified amount, the assets subject to that power to withdraw will be included in his or her estate.

  That is why we suggest limiting the duration of the opening. Assume, for example, that the withdrawal right lasts only one month each year, starting at the moment you add money to the trust. If the beneficiary dies in any other month of the year (during which he or she had no power to make a withdrawal), none of the trust's assets should be included in his or her estate since the beneficiary had no rights to take the money once the allotted time expired.

- If the window is opened too high—that is, if you don't insert a 5 or 5 limitation in the withdrawal limitations— all or a significant portion of the value of the trust could be included in the Crummey beneficiary's estate. On the other hand, if the powerholder doesn't take the money, he or she may be making a taxable gift to the other beneficiaries. In other words, if there is no limit on how much a beneficiary can reach in and take, there may be serious estate and gift tax implications, as well as practical problems.

What's the solution to these problems? Under a special exception in the tax laws, there are no gift or estate tax problems for the powerholder who doesn't exercise the Crummey power to the extent that the lapse of the power each year does not exceed the greater of $5,000 or 5 percent of the value of the trust's assets at the time of the lapse. This "5 or 5 rule" is the reason for the familiar "5 or 5" limitation in many irrevocable life insurance trusts.

Q. Is there a way to expand the "5 or 5" limit?

A. You may want to set up a separate trust for each person who will be given a Crummey power, provide that assets not paid out to that person during lifetime will be paid to his or her estate at death or as that person directs under a power of appointment, and end the trust at the beneficiary's death.

This type of trust will allow you to avoid the 5 or 5 limitation altogether and may also have generation-skipping advantages. You may therefore be able to contribute more cash each year on a gift-tax-free basis, and the trust can purchase more insurance on your life without using your unified credit.

Q. Can I set up an irrevocable life insurance trust without giving anyone a withdrawal right?

A. Yes. There are some very good reasons why you may not want to build a Crummey power into your trust or why you may not want to give every beneficiary such a power. The most obvious reason is that some beneficiaries, upon being informed they have such a power, will use it. It is, of course, their legal right to do so. But this would defeat the whole purpose of your annual contributions—to provide future wealth in significant amounts by leveraging relatively small gifts with trust-owned life insurance on your life.

A second reason you may not want to put a Crummey power in a trust is that you may already be making gifts of other property to the beneficiary. You have only one annual exclusion per year per donee (two exclusions if you are married and split the gift) and, if the exclusion is already used up because you've made another gift, you will not receive an extra annual exclusion by adding a Crummey power in a trust.

Q. How can I lower gift tax costs if I intend to have my trustee purchase a very large life insurance policy on my life?

A. Most irrevocable life insurance trusts limit the demand power of beneficiaries to the 5 or 5 power we've just described. This may restrict your annual exclusion to only $5,000 ($10,000 if you are married and your spouse agrees to split the gift). Your Crummey power window may not be sufficient to shelter the large annual gifts you may be making to the trust to support a multimillion dollar life insurance policy held by the trust.

You can increase the size of your exclusion and fully utilize the $10,000 annual exclusion ($20,000 if you are married) by giving each beneficiary a pro rata share of the assets you contribute to the trust each year (based on the number of beneficiaries, but limited to the maximum annual exclusion in that year). The beneficiary's withdrawal right could be satisfied by taking any asset of the trust equal to that value.

Speak to your lawyer about the income and estate tax trade-offs of this approach. It may cause some income tax liability, gift tax, or estate tax inclusion in your beneficiaries' estates if they die before you do. However, in many cases, such problems are more academic than actual. (Most irrevocable life insurance trusts don't have much taxable income, and most beneficiaries don't have estates large enough to trigger any estate tax.) In a few cases where an irrevocable trust is funded with income-producing property, this technique could result in an advantageous shift of income from the trust's high brackets to the lower brackets of one or more beneficiaries.

Q. What are the income tax implications during my lifetime of an irrevocable life insurance trust?

A. Typically, an irrevocable life insurance trust will not be funded. Because it holds no income-producing assets, it generally creates no income tax problems.

If you fund an irrevocable trust—place income-producing assets into it—the income tax implications depend mainly on whether the trust retains income or pays it out to the trust's beneficiaries. Although the tax rules are extremely complex, in general terms they provide as follows:

- Income used to pay premiums on a policy insuring the grantor's life or his or her spouse's life will be considered taxable income of the grantor and taxed to the grantor, not the trust or the beneficiaries. As noted above, this may be a tax advantage because individuals are subject to a much lower set of rates than trusts.

- If the income of the trust exceeds the insurance premiums paid by the trust, the excess income might still be taxable to the grantor, not the trust or the beneficiaries. The Internal Revenue Code refers to income which "may be" applied to insurance premiums, but a few courts have ruled that the income is not taxed to the grantor unless *actually used* to pay insurance premiums. Whether the courts will continue to rule in that way is not certain.

- There may be other reasons why the grantor might be considered to be the owner of the income of the trust. For example, if your spouse is a beneficiary of your trust and the trustee has discretion to distribute income and principal to your spouse, you will be considered the owner of the trust for federal income tax purposes (even though you are not the owner for federal estate tax purposes). If the trust is a grantor trust, the income from the trust will be taxed to the grantor and any deductions, gains, losses, or credits the trust realized can be used by the grantor.

- Any income that is earned by the trust, is not considered to be owned by the grantor, and is paid to or for the trust's beneficiaries is taxed to them rather than to the trust. (This is similar to a partnership in the sense that income earned is taxed directly to the partners in proportion to their ownership interests.)

- Any income that is earned by the trust, is not considered to be owned by the grantor, and is not paid to or for the trust's beneficiaries is taxed to the trust as a separate taxable entity. (This is similar to a corporation that earns income. That income is taxed to the corporation at its separate tax rates.)

In the past, trustees always had to obtain an employer identification number (EIN) for a trust, because it was required to have a taxpayer identification number. However, beginning in 1996, a trust which is a grantor trust for federal income tax purposes can decide whether or not to apply for a separate taxpayer number or use the grantor's Social Security number.

We would recommend that any irrevocable life insurance trust you create should apply for an EIN, and not use your Social Security number, for the following reasons:

- The trust's own EIN will help to demonstrate that the trust was considered a separate entity, and not part of your estate. Using your Social Security number for the trust could confuse the insurance company and even the IRS, and the price of confusion could be thousands of dollars of unnecessary taxes for your family.

- The trust might have income during your lifetime, and will not necessarily be a grantor trust.

- The trust will certainly need its own EIN following your death, and your trustee might as well obtain it now.

To obtain an EIN, you must file Form SS-4, Application for Employer Identification Number. However, it is now possible to file the form by fax machine, or even get an EIN over the telephone. See the instructions to Form SS-4 for details.

Q. What is survivorship life insurance, and why should I consider it as a type of life insurance policy for my irrevocable trust?

A. Survivorship life insurance—also called second-to-die insurance—is a life insurance contract that pays only when the second of two insureds dies. Quite often, this type of contract is used to insure a husband and wife. But survivorship life insurance contracts can be used to insure any two (or more in some cases) individuals, whether or not they are related.

The single most common use of the survivorship life contract is to create estate liquidity at the second death of a financially successful married couple who used the federal estate tax marital deduction to defer tax at the first death. Survivorship life provides a large amount of cash to the trustee who can then use that money to purchase assets from the surviving spouse's estate, preserving those assets for the family.

Why are survivorship policies so appealing? The answer is "lower premiums." Because proceeds are payable under a survivorship contract when they are needed the most—at the death of the surviving spouse—the insurance company has a longer period of time to build up policy reserves to meet the death benefit obligation. (Compared to the amount of time an insurer has to accumulate reserves to meet claims under a single life contract, the period is much longer.) For this reason, premiums charged under a survivorship policy can be significantly lower than a single life policy with the same death benefit. This lower premium rate under survivorship life makes it possible to purchase a higher death benefit with the same amount of premium dollars or to pay fewer premium dollars for the same amount of coverage.

Q. What are the costs or downsides of survivorship life?

A. The disadvantage of survivorship life insurance is that, by definition, it doesn't make any payment until the survivor dies—no matter how many years that takes after the first death or how much money is needed at the first death. In many cases, there will be significant state death taxes that are not deferred, debts, and estate administrative expenses which must be paid at the first death. Furthermore, the surviving spouse may not have enough income to meet food, clothing, shelter, and educational needs at the same standards as before his or her spouse dies.

One further problem: If the first spouse to die was the breadwinner, where is the surviving spouse going to get the money to pay the premium on the survivorship policy? A solution to both of these problems is to have a separate policy that will pay at the first death or to attach a *first-death rider* (additional coverage for an additional premium) to the survivorship policy that will pay at the first death.

Q. Are there special tax traps to avoid when using a survivorship policy inside an irrevocable trust?

A. The primary problem with survivorship life insurance is remembering that both spouses are insureds under the policy, and so both are subject to the estate tax rules regarding "incidents of ownership" in life insurance policies. When only one spouse is insured, it is possible to give the other spouse some beneficial interests in the trust or some powers as trustee. However, if both spouses are insureds, then neither can have any interest in the trust or any power over the trust, or else the policy will wind up back in one (or both) of their taxable estates.

For example, it is particularly important that neither you nor your spouse serve as a trustee of a trust holding survivorship life insurance. The trustee of a trust holds legal title to the assets of the trust, and holding title to a life insurance policy is a clear "incident of ownership." If either of you served as a trustee, the policy would be included in that trustee's taxable estate.

Because the costs of ignorance of these estate tax rules will be very high, we urge you to work only with a lawyer and insurance agent, preferably a CLU (Chartered Life Underwriter) ChFC (Chartered Financial Consultant), or CFP (Certified Financial Planner), who specializes in estate planning and tax planning with life insurance.

Q. Can I put my group term life insurance in an irrevocable trust and keep it out of my estate?

A. Yes. Group insurance is a very good asset to transfer to your irrevocable trust. You can save a substantial amount of federal estate tax with little or no gift tax cost. For instance, if your employer provides you with $500,000 of group term life and you do nothing, at a 50 percent bracket, your heirs would lose $250,000! By assigning ownership of that insurance to your irrevocable trust, however, you can enrich your heirs by a quarter of a million dollars! (Assuming you live more than three years after the date of the transfer.)

The best part is that you haven't reduced your income by a penny; nor have you lost the use of policy cash values (because there aren't any). Again, we caution you that group term life, just as any individual term coverage, will expire—perhaps before you do. Also, when you retire, your group coverage will probably be reduced considerably. So don't count on this coverage for the bulk of your long-term needs.

If you own, control, or significantly influence your employer's employee benefit decisions, you can indirectly maintain a lot of control without attracting estate tax inclusion. How? Through the ability to cancel the master group insurance contract and replace the group term coverage with coverage from a different insurance company.

Q. Are there any problems using group term life as an asset to fund an irrevocable trust?

A. We've already mentioned the single biggest problem with group term insurance: It may run out at perhaps the very time it is needed most. Furthermore, if you have to pay some or all of the premiums after retirement (or if you leave your present employer), you will be paying ever-increasing premiums. At some point, your annual outlay may become prohibitive.

An irrevocable trust with group term insurance will have all of the problems previously discussed for irrevocable trusts generally. For example, you will lose the flexibility to change trust provisions in the future due to changes in your family's circumstances. There are other special technical problems with group term life insurance that your lawyer and CLU or ChFC should be prepared to discuss with you and help you solve. These include the following:

- Group term insurance is normally one policy covering all employees, but you don't want to transfer the employer's entire policy, just your rights to your insurance coverage. The employer's policy must recognize your insurance coverage as a separate, assignable part of the policy (sometimes represented by a certificate or individual coverage number) and your right to transfer your own insurance coverage must be recognized under state law.

- If your employer changes insurance companies, it may be necessary to make an immediate assignment of the new coverage to your trust. Your transfer of ownership of the old insurance company's coverage typically will not protect your new coverage. You must start your three year period all over again by making a new assignment.

  Believe it or not, the IRS has ruled that employees can assign to an irrevocable trust both the present group term coverage *and any replacement insurance that might be issued in the future,* and if the employee makes that kind of "future assignment," the replacement policies will *not* be included in the employee's taxable estate once the original three year period has run. You should therefore talk to your tax and insurance advisors about making an assignment of future replacement policies to your trust, to try to keep the three year "danger zone" from reappearing if your employer changes insurance companies or policies.

- Even though you have assigned your interests in the policy, you must still pay income tax on the economic benefit of the group term insurance coverage you are receiving as an employee. The employer will continue to report that you have taxable income for the costs of insurance in excess of the $50,000 in benefits that is allowed tax-free.

- The IRS has ruled that each premium payment by your employer is in fact a gift to the trust by you, the employee, but that the gift can qualify for the annual exclusion if the trust has *Crummey powers* described above. However, the trust will have no cash, because the employer paid the premium directly to the insurance company, not to the trustee. How can a beneficiary withdraw from the trust when the trust has no cash? According to the IRS, the right of withdrawal will be meaningful, and the gifts to the trust will qualify for the gift tax annual exclusion, if the trustee can satisfy the withdrawal rights in cash *or any other asset held by the trust, including the life insurance policy itself.* A life insurance policy for which a premium has just been paid has value, and so the IRS is willing to recognize the withdrawal right even if the only asset in the trust is the policy itself, as long as the trustee has the power to use the policy itself to satisfy the right of withdrawal.

  (It is because of this ruling that some lawyers believe that it is not necessary for the trustee to retain cash in the trust to satisfy the rights of withdrawal, but that the trustee can immediately use the cash to pay life insurance premiums, as long as the trust document authorizes the trustee to apply the policy itself to "pay" any beneficiary who might actually exercise a right to withdraw from the trust.)

Q. What is split dollar-life insurance, and does it make sense to use this concept with my irrevocable trust?

A. Split-dollar insurance is not a type of life insurance policy or contract but a way to divide the costs of life insurance and make it easier to pay life insurance premiums. There are an almost infinite number of ways to accomplish this objective, but the classic arrangement is the corporation that pays money into an insurance contract owned by a key employee or employee-shareholder to reduce the cash outlay for that employee. The corporation's outlay is protected by a contract that spells out each party's rights and duties and assures the return of corporate money whether the insured employee lives to retirement, quits prior to that date, or dies. If death occurs, the employer's dollars are first repaid to the corporation, and any balance passes to the beneficiary selected by the employee.

Many split-dollar plans are structured so that the employer pays the bulk (or all) of each year's premium while the employee pays relatively little (or none). This is commonly referred to as an "employer-pay-all" split-dollar plan.

If the employee owns the policy on his or her life, it will be subject to estate tax at his or her death. To keep the proceeds out of the insured employee's estate, the employee can transfer the insurance policy to an irrevocable trust, just like any other policy, the only difference being that the policy is still subject to the rights of the employer to recover its investment in the policy upon the maturity of the policy (or if the employee quits or retires). To avoid the three year estate tax inclusion after transferring a policy to a trust, it is also possible for the trust to purchase a policy and then enter into a three-way split dollar agreement with the employer and the employee-insured. In that way, the trust will be the owner from the policy's inception, the employee will never own the insurance, and it will not be included in his or her estate.

This technique will work both for regular corporations and for those that have elected S corporation (similar to partnership) tax treatment. (The IRS has confirmed that a split-dollar arrangement will be treated as a fringe benefit and can be safely used in an S corporation without violating the single-class-of-stock rule that forbids such a business from possessing more than one class of stock.)

Suppose you control (own 51 percent or more) of a closely held corporation and find it attractive to have your corporation lay out all (or most) of the money to pay for your personal life insurance. If your irrevocable trust owns the life insurance from the very beginning and splits the premium dollars with your corporation, can the life insurance proceeds be kept out of your estate? Tax lawyers will tell you that almost any meaningful power over the policy—no matter how indirectly held—can be considered a string that the IRS will use to pull the policy back into your estate. In fact, the IRS will claim that if you control the corporation and the corporation has an "incident of ownership" over a life insurance policy on your life (such as a power to borrow against the cash surrender value of the policy), you will be considered to have an "indirect" incident of ownership (or "string") that will cause the policy to be included in your gross estate. In order to avoid this result, it is important that the corporation's *only* right is to recover its outlay when you die and that the corporation has no other rights in the insurance.

The law in this area is based on a number of different rulings by the Internal Revenue Service, and no one knows whether new rulings might be issued in the future that modify or even contradict the old rulings. Therefore, no one can completely assure you of estate tax success if there is a split dollar agreement with a business entity you control. If avoiding estate tax is important, we suggest that you explore the alternatives with your legal, tax, and insurance advisors.

Q. *Are there special problems if I set up an irrevocable life insurance trust in a community property state?*

A. Yes. If you are married and living in any one of the community property states (Arizona, California, Idaho, Louisiana, Nevada, New Mexico, Texas, and Washington are community property states, and Wisconsin is "quasi-community"), one half of the compensation (and therefore the assets purchased with or because of that portion of your compensation) is considered half yours and half your spouse's from the moment it is earned. In essence, if you are living in one of these states, the law says that both spouses have a *community interest* in anything earned by either spouse during the marriage.

How can you successfully remove the insurance from both of your estates? Consider having your spouse transfer ownership of his or her one half of the future premium payments to you before you make the transfer of life insurance to the trust. Or you can reimburse your spouse for his or her share of the insurance from your separate property. Be sure to check with your tax counsel on this issue if you live in a community property state.

Your lawyer may draft a document classifying the life insurance as the separate property of the insured spouse so that spouse can then transfer it to the irrevocable trust. Technically, your lawyer will draft what is called a *waiver of rights* that the noninsured spouse will sign.

Alternatively, the noninsured spouse's rights can be "sold" to the insured spouse (in return for a payment from non-community funds) or transferred by gift. The insured can then (or some time later) transfer the insurance to the trust. We suggest that if you use this route, don't make the noninsured spouse a beneficiary of the trust. This will prevent an IRS argument that he or she was a grantor of the trust but retained a string on the trust for life and therefore the life insurance should be included in his or her estate.

Q. Can an irrevocable life insurance trust can be a generation-skipping trust?

A. Yes. In fact, an irrevocable trust is almost an ideal candidate for a generation-skipping trust. By creating an irrevocable life insurance trust, you have (we hope) created a trust that is not subject to estate tax at your death or your spouse's death, so that the life insurance proceeds can ultimately pass to your children free of federal estate tax. It takes only a little bit of extra planning to create a trust that will benefit your children and yet not be included in their taxable estates either, ultimately passing to your grandchildren (or even great-grandchildren) free of federal estate tax.

The problems with the federal generation-skipping tax, and the advantages of generation-skipping trusts, are discussed in more detail in the following chapter 18, and will not be repeated here. However, there is one technical problem that should be mentioned here, and that is the generation-skipping transfer tax problem with Crummey powers.

As previously explained, a trust can qualify for the federal gift tax annual exclusion if each beneficiary has a limited right to withdraw a share of each gift to the trust, limited to the annual exclusion. The gifts to the trust then qualify as "present interests" and there is no gift tax. The federal generation-skipping transfer tax (GSTT) applies to gifts and estates that skip generations, going directly to grandchildren or into trusts that benefit children but are not part of their taxable estates. Generally speaking, the definition of what is a taxable gift for GSTT purposes is the same as the definition of a taxable gift for federal gift tax purposes, with one important exception: *A Crummey power will usually not qualify for the annual exclusion for GSTT purposes.* This is explained in more detail in chapter 18, but the important thing to remember is that gifts to an irrevocable life insurance trust that is a generation-skipping trust may require annual gift tax returns, even though no tax is due, so that the generation-skipping tax exemption can be applied to the gifts to the trust.

Generation-Skipping Transfer Trust

Grandchild

Trust avoids estate tax at child's level

Grandparent

Leverages $1,000,000 exemption!
Avoids or minimizes 55% tax

GENERATION-SKIPPING AND "DYNASTY" TRUSTS

Chapter 18 will explain:

- What a "generation-skipping" trust is

- What the generation-skipping tax is

- How best to apply the $1,000,000 generation-skipping tax exemption

- The advantages of life insurance in generation-skipping trusts

- What a "dynasty" trust is and how it can be used to transfer great wealth to many future generations

- How to create a dynasty trust

- What the "rule against perpetuities" is and how it limits dynasty trusts

- How laws of some states might be better for dynasty trusts, and how to establish trusts in those states

- What a perpetual trust is

Q. What is a generation-skipping trust?

A. Typically, a generation-skipping trust is a trust that distributes only income to a child of the grantor. Then, upon the death of the child, the trust ends by distributing the principal in the trust to the child's children (the grandchildren of the grantor). This is why planners say that that the ownership of the principal of the trust has "skipped" the child's generation.

There are many variations on this estate plan. Instead of a trust for one child, the trust might be a common fund for all of the grantor's children and terminate only when all of the children have died. Or a trust might exclude the children entirely, so that only the grandchildren are beneficiaries and the children receive neither income nor principal. Or a trust might last for two (or more) generations, the principal of the trust skipping both the children and the grandchildren and ultimately being distributed to the great-grandchildren (or great-great-grandchildren).

A generation-skipping trust might be set up because a child is disabled or financially irresponsible. But most generation-skipping trusts are set up to avoid federal and state death taxes. The federal estate tax (and the various state inheritance taxes) are imposed at death on the property owned by (or controlled by) the decedent.

If a beneficiary of a trust does not own or control the principal of the trust, that principal is usually not subject to any tax at the death of the beneficiary (unless the beneficiary contributed to the trust or has a taxable power over the principal of the trust). A grantor may be required pay gift tax or estate tax when a generation-skipping trust is created, but there will be no estate tax or inheritance tax to pay upon the death of the grantor's child, or upon the death of any other beneficiary of the trust, until after the trust ends and the grantor's grandchildren (or great-grandchildren) become the owners of the trust assets.

Q. What is the generation-skipping tax?

A. In 1976, Congress decided that the federal estate tax should be imposed at each generation. There was a feeling that the generation-skipping transfers described above were a "loophole" in the federal estate tax system. Congress therefore enacted a "generation-skipping transfer tax" (GSTT) upon property that passed in trust to a younger generation upon the death of a beneficiary. The GSTT enacted in 1976 was ultimately found to be too complicated to administer, and so the tax was repealed in 1986 and a new (and equally complicated) and perhaps even more draconian GSTT was enacted in its place.

The present GSTT is a flat tax of 55 percent (the maximum federal estate tax rate) imposed on every taxable dollar of three types of transfers:

- Gifts during lifetime or at death to grandchildren (or other "skip persons") or to trusts for the benefit of skip persons. (A "skip person" is anyone two or more generations below the grantor.) This type of generation-skipping transfer is called a "direct skip."

- Any distribution from a generation-skipping trust to a grandchild or other "skip person." This is called a "taxable distribution." So, if a generation-skipping trust which can make distributions to both children and grandchildren makes a discretionary distribution to a grandchild, the distribution is taxable and the GSTT applies. And the GSTT applies regardless of whether the distribution is considered to be income or principal.

- If the beneficial interests of a child in a generation-skipping trust come to an end (which would happen upon the death of the child) and, as a result, all of the remaining beneficiaries of the trust are grandchildren (or other skip persons), there is a "taxable termination". Here, the GSTT is immediately imposed on the value of the trust, regardless of whether the trust ends or continues for the benefit of the grandchildren.

The federal GSTT can therefore apply to a generation-skipping trust in one of two different ways:

- If the grantor has decided to make an immediate (or "direct") skip over the grantor's children to a generation-skipping trust for the benefit of grandchildren or great-grandchildren, there is an immediate tax on the direct skip.

- If the grantor sets up a trust for both children and grandchildren, there will be no GSTT payable when the trust is created. But the trust will have to pay GSTT when taxable distributions are made to grandchildren, or when the children die and a taxable termination occurs.

The GSTT on direct skips and taxable terminations and taxable distributions is calculated in two different ways:

- The GSTT on a taxable distribution or taxable termination is based on the amount of the distribution or termination before taxes. The calculation is therefore *tax inclusive*, because the tax is based on an amount which may include an amount which must be paid in taxes. For example, if a $1,000,000 generation-skipping trust terminates and is subject to the 55 percent GSTT, the tax will be $550,000 and the grandchildren will get only $450,000.

- The GSTT on a direct skip is based on the amount actually received by the grandchildren (or other skip persons) after the tax has been paid. The calculation is therefore *tax exclusive*. For example, if an estate of $1,000,000 (after federal estate tax) is left to (or in trust for) the grandchildren, and is subject to the 55 percent GSTT, the tax will be $354,839, leaving $645,161 for the grandchildren. Why? Because 55 percent of $645,161 is $354,839, so if you start with $1,000,000 and give $645,161 to the grandchildren, you will have $354,389 left to pay the GSTT on that $645,161. Therefore, the effective rate of tax for direct skips is really 35.484 percent, not 55 percent.

Because the effective tax rate for direct skips is only 35.484 percent, not 55 percent, it is often better to make direct skips to grandchildren (and great-grandchildren) than it is to create taxable generation-skipping trusts that must pay GSTT at 55 percent upon the deaths of children. (These and other generation-skipping computations can be performed by the *NumberCruncher* program. For additional information, call 610-527-5216).

There are a number of exceptions and exemptions to the GSTT:

- The most important exemption is the $1,000,000 exemption which each taxpayer can apply against generation-skipping gifts or generation-skipping trusts. This $1,000,000 exemption can be applied to direct skips to (or in trust for) grandchildren, or to establish generation-skipping trusts that are exempt from the generation-skipping transfer tax. (Beginning in 1999, the $1,000,000 exemption may be adjusted for inflation.)

    Together, a husband and wife can exempt $2,000,000 from the GSTT. So if you do not expect that your estate at death will exceed these amounts, you need read no further since the confiscatory GSTT will not ravage your grandchildren's inheritance. The application of this exemption is discussed in more detail below.

- The $10,000 annual gift tax exclusion (which may also be adjusted for inflation after 1998) also applies to direct skips. So gifts to a grandchild (or great-grandchild) of not more than $10,000 each year are not subject to GSTT. Gifts in trust for the benefit of grandchildren (or great-grandchildren) may also qualify for this exception, but only if the trust is for only one grandchild or great-grandchild and the assets of the trust will be included in the beneficiary's federal taxable estate at his or her death. Most trusts for minors (see chapter 15) that qualify for the federal gift tax annual exclusion should also qualify for this GSTT exclusion.

- There is also an exemption for payments made directly to an educational institution for tuition, or made directly to a doctor or hospital for medical expenses. This means that a payment from a generation-skipping trust for a grandchild's college tuition is not a taxable distribution for GSTT purposes if the payment is made directly to the college.

- A gift to a grandchild is not a direct skip if the grantor's child (the grandchild's parent) is already dead. This is sometimes known as the "predeceased child" exception.

Q. How can I make the best use of the $1,000,000 generation-skipping tax exemption?

A. If you want to minimize death taxes not only for your children but also for your grandchildren and future generations, then you want to get the maximum benefit from your $1,000,000 GST exemption.

- You obviously want to use up all of the GST exemption, which means making gifts during your lifetime or at death of at least $1,000,000 to grandchildren, to trusts for grandchildren, or to generation-skipping trusts for the benefit of both children and grandchildren. (The $1,000,000 exemption may also be adjusted for inflation after 1998. If the exemption increases because of inflation, you would obviously want to make additional gifts to use up any additional exemption.)

- It is usually considered to be best not to create a generation-skipping trust in excess of the $1,000,000 exemption. Why not? Because every dollar of the excess will be subject to the extremely high tax rate of 55 percent, the highest possible estate tax rate.

  Technically, the generation skipping tax rate is multiplied by an "inclusion ratio" to reflect the percentage of assets covered by the $1,000,000 exemption, but the net effect is the same. If you create a $1,500,000 generation-skipping trust and have only a $1,000,000 exemption, the tax code may say that the tax rate on taxable distributions is only 18.33 percent, or one third of 55 percent, but the additional $500,000 is still going to result in $275,000 of tax, and it doesn't make any difference whether you call that 55 percent of $500,000 or 18.33 percent of $1,500,000. You therefore want to create a generation-skipping trust (or trusts) of at least the exemption, but not more than the exemption.

- If you are married, you want to be sure that you get the benefit of both GST exemptions. This can be tricky, because, without proper planning, the GST exemption can be "lost" at the first death, just like the unified credit can be "lost" at the first death by qualifying the entire estate for the federal estate tax marital deduction. (See chapter 13.)

This can happen if one spouse dies before 2006, while the unified credit exclusion amount (which is only $600,000 in 1997 but which will increase to $1,000,000 in 2006) is less than the $1,000,000 GST exemption (assuming no adjustments for inflation). For example, if one spouse dies in 1997 and creates a $600,000 "by-pass" or "nonmarital" trust to use up his or her federal estate and gift tax unified credit, that $600,000 trust can become a generation-skipping trust and use up $600,000 of the decedent's $1,000,000 GST exemption. However, if the rest of the estate qualifies for the marital deduction (in order to minimize federal estate tax at the first death), then the other $400,000 of the GST exemption will be lost.

Fortunately, the tax code allows what is usually called a "reverse QTIP election." Instead of giving everything in excess of the $600,000 by-pass trust to the surviving spouse, or in a regular qualified terminable interest property (QTIP) trust from which the surviving spouse will receive the income for life, the first spouse to die can put the balance of the GST exemption ($400,000 in the example above) in a separate QTIP trust which will become a generation-skipping trust upon the death of the surviving spouse. The decedent's executor can elect to qualify that trust for the marital deduction for federal estate tax purposes but also elect *not* to qualify the trust for the marital deduction for GST purposes. In that way, the first spouse to die will still be considered to be the grantor of the trust for GST purposes, and use up the $400,000 balance of the $1,000,000 GST exemption, even though the trust will be included in the surviving spouse's taxable estate for federal estate tax purposes.

We know it's confusing—why do you think Congress called it the Internal Revenue *Code*? It is not important whether you understand all the details of this special tax election. But you should understand the extreme importance of good tax planning and getting competent tax advice if you have a multimillion dollar estate and you want a significant portion of it to pass to one or more grandchildren.

- In order to make sure that your already wealthy children's estates are not unnecessarily enlarged by distributions from your generation-skipping trust, you may want to limit the interests of your children in the trust. For example, if you provide that all of the income from your generation-skipping trust must be distributed to your children and your children don't need or want that income, they will have to find ways to give the income away in order to prevent it from accumulating and being taxed as part of their estates at their deaths.

  One solution would be to give your trustee the power to "spray" or "sprinkle" income among your children and grandchildren, or accumulate the income in the trust, so that income is distributed only as needed and only to the beneficiary that actually needs it.

- Once you have created a generation-skipping trust, you may want to make it last as long as possible, in order to skip as many generations of death taxes as possible. (See the discussion of "dynasty trusts" below.)

- It may be possible to "leverage" the GST exemption through charitable split-interest trusts described in chapter 26. For example, if you set up a charitable remainder trust for the benefit of grandchildren, the charitable deduction allowable for the remainder interest in the trust will allow the trust to be more than $1,000,000, which may result in benefits in excess of $1,000,000 for your grandchildren, depending on their ages and how long they actually live.

- Another (and perhaps more certain and simple) way to maximize the $1,000,000 GST exemption is to "leverage" the exemption with life insurance, as explained below.

Q. What are the advantages of life insurance in a generation-skipping trust?

A. If used properly, the protection provided by the $1,000,000 GST exemption can be leveraged. You can allocate all or any part of your $1,000,000 exemption in such a way that it forms an "invisible shield" (remember the Colgate Guardall toothpaste commercials?) around what you put in the trust and protects whatever that amount grows to. For instance, you can allocate your $1,000,000 exemption to $1,000,000 you put into a trust during your lifetime. Even if it grows to $10,000,000 by the date it is distributed to your grandchildren, the entire $10,000,000 is free of the GSTT. At 55 cents on the dollar, the savings can be amazing.

You can significantly leverage the GST exemption if the trustee of your generation-skipping trust purchases life insurance on your life, your spouse's life, or on both of your lives under a survivorship type policy. With a $1,000,000 fund to pay premiums, think of how much death benefit you can generate—all exempt from the 55 percent GSTT.

A generation-skipping trust of this type will use up the $1,000,000 GST exemption even though the gifts to the trust qualify for the federal gift tax annual exclusion. Because of technical provisions in the laws relating to the GSTT, the "crummey" powers that are used to qualify the gifts to the trust for the federal gift tax annual exclusion will not qualify for any generation-skipping tax exclusion. That means a gift tax return must be filed each year so that the GST exemption can be allocated to the gifts to the trust—even though the gifts to the trust qualify for the annual gift tax exclusion and are not taxable for gift tax purposes. However, the time and expense of filing annual gift tax returns may be a very small price to pay for what is potentially astounding savings in death taxes for your grandchildren (and later generations).

If your estate is large (substantially in excess of $1,000,000) and your lawyer has recommended generation-skipping, you should consider sheltering relatively small life insurance premiums now to protect significantly larger policy proceeds later.

Q. What is a dynasty trust?

A. A dynasty trust (also called a "megatrust") is simply an irrevocable life insurance trust (see chapter 17) or generation-skipping trust taken to its logical conclusion. Rather than distributing property outright to ongoing generations, the dynasty trust or megatrust continues for as long as legally permissible and makes trust capital or assets *available* to beneficiaries without giving them actual outright ownership.

The objective of a dynasty trust is to keep huge amounts of wealth in a family for as long as state law limits allow and at the same time to avoid federal estate and generation-skipping taxes as the use of the property moves from generation to generation.

In our opinion, you should consider a dynasty trust only if

- your wealth is in excess of $10,000,000;

- your wealth is growing too fast for your personal living expenses, personal gifts, and charitable gifts to keep pace;

- you are willing to embark on a major gift-giving program;

- you are seeking asset protection from malpractice suits or creditors.

The tax objective of the dynasty trust is to avoid the imposition of transfer taxes on a continually growing "bank" of wealth, while affording your beneficiaries the enjoyment of these assets that approaches outright ownership.

Q. How do I create a dynasty trust?

A. Creating a dynasty trust entails placing a very large amount of assets (typically a minimum of $600,000 to $1,000,000) into a specially designed irrevocable trust. You will probably use up all or most of your unified credit exclusion amount and $1,000,000 generation-skipping transfer tax exemption, and in most cases you will still pay some gift tax.

What you are doing, in essence, is creating what some planners call a "money pump." Your trustee then harnesses that "engine" you have created with the large initial infusion of capital by investing that capital in ways calculated to produce the largest possible return over time. That can be investments in long-term growth stocks, but is typically an investment in life insurance on your life, your spouse's life, and in some cases, your children's lives. The insurance can be whole life, variable life, universal life, variable universal life, or some other form or combination of permanent coverage. Quite often, this insurance is at least partially of the second-to-die (survivorship) type we described earlier in this chapter.

Under the terms of your dynasty trust, the trust will continue to exist for the longest period of time permissible under the law of the state where the trust is to be formed. In almost all states, the trust will be limited by the "rule against perpetuities," discussed below. This rule limits how long property may be held before someone must be given absolute ownership rights.

Because the purpose of the dynasty trust is to withhold such ownership as long as is legally possible, it may be advisable to set up the trust in a state which has modified or abolished the rule against perpetuities, as suggested below. Your trust document will also specify that your dynasty trust should be managed for its beneficiaries in such a way that federal estate and generation-skipping taxes are avoided or minimized for as long as possible, while achieving your beneficiaries' objectives and satisfying their needs for as many generations as possible.

To achieve these twin objectives, your trustee will make trust assets available without making actual distributions of principal. For example, the trust might purchase a family compound on the lovely shores of the Chesapeake Bay for your children and grandchildren's *use*. But the property itself would remain a trust asset, rather than become the property of any one or more specific beneficiaries.

We want to specifically note that some of the most brilliant estate planning lawyers in the United States are setting these trusts up for their ultra-wealthy clients—and also to state that there are no specific Code sections, regulations, rulings, or court cases that sanction or bless the concept of a dynasty trust. According to its advocates, a dynasty trust can give beneficiaries the use and enjoyment of trust property without the transfer tax problems, protect trust assets from the claims of a spouse who divorces a beneficiary, and insulate property from creditor's claims. This is all accomplished in much the same way you might allow your children to use your cabin in the mountains for a month at no charge.

Here is an example. If a beneficiary wants a $1,000,000 home, rather than paying out $1,000,000 to a child or grandchild who will use that money to purchase a home that the child or grandchild and his or her spouse will own (and eventually have taxed in their estates), your trustee will purchase that home for the trust. The dynasty trust considers the purchase an investment and makes it available for the use and enjoyment of trust beneficiaries.

Although distributions from the trust are permissible, they will not be made unless they are necessary or appropriate in the trustee's opinion. In other words, the trustee has the sole discretion to pay out more than income to beneficiaries, if the tax law or planning strategies change or if the beneficiary cannot maintain a suitable standard of living. You can also authorize the trustee to make loans to enable a trust beneficiary to purchase a home, start a business, or obtain estate liquidity. Finally, many dynasty trusts contain a provision that allows distributions of principal in order for trust beneficiaries to purchase sufficient life insurance to begin yet another round of dynasty trusts.

As noted above, the tax implications of allowing trust beneficiaries to use but not possess trust assets has not yet been thoroughly tested by the IRS and the courts. So it is possible that there could be adverse tax consequences of that part of the dynasty trust concept. The IRS already imposes taxes on certain large intra-family loans, and it might find a way to impose income or gift taxes on the rent-free use of trust property.

The IRS has also expressed concern about the creation of generation-skipping trusts which extend past the period allowed by the traditional rule against perpetuities. As explained below, several states have modified or even abolished the common law rule against perpetuities, and most of these changes have occurred since the enactment of the GSTT. It is apparently the view of the IRS that Congress did not expect that states laws would change or that trusts would last more than the 90 to 100 years commonly allowed. It is therefore possible that Congress or the IRS may act to limit the generation-skipping tax benefits of dynasty trusts.

Since this concept should only be considered for the transfer of millions of dollars of wealth, we urge you to seek the advice of only the best and the brightest tax professionals if you feel a dynasty trust is appropriate for your family to consider.

Q. What is the "rule against perpetuities"?

A. The "rule against perpetuities" is a rule of law that limits the duration of trusts. In its original form, as created by the courts of England, the rule was that all interests in a trust must *vest* (be owned or controlled by a beneficiary) within twenty-one years after the deaths of the lives in being when the trust was created. The purpose of this rule was to limit the "dead hand rule" of trusts, i.e., to make sure that property could be sold and managed in accordance with the wishes of the living, and not according to the dictates of those long dead.

The net effect of the rule was to allow a person to create trusts which could last for the lifetimes of children ("lives in being at the trust creator's death") and until the creator's grandchildren were adults (which would occur no later than twenty-one years after the deaths of all of the grantor's children).

At least four states have modified or abolished this traditional rule against perpetuities. In Delaware, for example, a trust may last for 110 years, regardless of the lives in being at the time the trust was created or the ages of the beneficiaries. South Dakota has modified the rule against perpetuities to permit some longer trusts. Idaho and Alaska have apparently abolished the rule entirely, and permit trusts that could legally last forever.

Q. Are the laws of some states more favorable to dynasty trusts?

A. Yes. A number of states have enacted laws which make those states considerable more hospitable to dynasty trusts and generation-skipping trusts. These new laws allow trusts to last longer, reduce the taxes on the trusts, or make it easier to administer the trusts.

- As explained above, the "rule against perpetuities" in most states limits generation-skipping trusts to children and grandchildren, which works about to about 90 years in most cases. However, at least four states (Alaska, Delaware, Idaho, and South Dakota) have limited or abolished the rule against perpetuities, so that trusts created in those states can last longer than trusts in other states, or perhaps last forever. (See the discussion of "perpetual" trusts below).

- Some states also have no taxes on trusts with capital gains, or which accumulate income for future generations. Alaska has no income tax at all. Delaware has no income tax on capital gains or income accumulated for nonresident beneficiaries. Although some states will attempt to tax trusts based on the residence of the grantor of the trust, not the residence of the trustee, there may still be advantages in locating a trust in a state with favorable tax rules. Keep that point in mind; as noted below, even if you live in Florida, it may be possible to base your trust on Alaska's laws.

- A state may also be considered to be favorable to trust administration because the laws of the state may permit the trustee wide discretion in trust investments, permit the trustee to delegate investment decisions, provide liberal rules regarding trust accountings, or provide additional assurance of trust confidentiality.

In order to claim that a trust is a resident of a state that is different that the state in which you reside and that the trust should be subject to the laws of that other state, it is necessary (at a minimum) that the trustee of the trust be a resident of the other state. It may also be necessary to manage the trust investments within the state, or have other contacts between the trust and the state which you'd like to use.

Attempting to choose which laws of which state will apply to a trust, complying with the tax laws of different states, and resolving the possible conflicts between the laws of different states, are obviously tasks that are best left to a very experienced lawyer, and definitely should not be a "do-it-yourself" or "self-help" project.

Q. What is a "perpetual trust?"

A. A perpetual trust is one which has no statutory limit and can therefore legally last forever. Delaware, for example, has no rule against perpetuities for personal property held in a trust—and allows real property held in a trust to be held for 110 years.

Compare a perpetual trust with one limited by a state's rule against perpetuities which may last—at most—for a few generations before it is treated as owned for estate and gift tax purposes by someone—and therefore lose the benefit of the generation-skipping exemption allocated by the original transferor.

TRUSTS FOR HANDICAPPED CHILDREN

Chapter 19 explains:

• Special problems in planning trusts for handicapped children

• Options available to parents in planning for a handicapped child's financial future

• Advantages of trusts in planning financial security of handicapped children

• What a "special needs" trusts is

• What a "discretionary" trust is

• Medicaid trusts with "payback" language, the "pooled" trust, and trusts comprised of pension and social security benefits

• What a "spendthrift" trust is

• Limitations on the utility of a spendthrift trust

Q. Are there any special problems in planning trusts for handicapped children?

A. When planning trusts for handicapped children, parents must try to resolve these four major problems:

- • making certain that sufficient funds are available for the child's necessary care and treatment

- • providing the proper supervision, management, and distribution of the trust funds when the child is not in a position to handle and invest the funds

- • preserving the child's entitlement to governmental benefits, while planning for the child's future

- • attempting to treat your other children as equitably as possible while providing for your handicapped child

Q. What governmental benefits are available for handicapped children?

A. There are two major federal government support programs, known as Supplemental Security Income (SSI) and Medicaid. These are both need-based programs, under which benefits are paid only to persons with limited resources who meet welfare limitations on both income and assets. Because of these limitations, these programs, in effect, require a handicapped child to be almost destitute before he or she can qualify for benefits.

Moreover, the eligibility rules are constantly changing, and even when federal rules (such as the Omnibus Budget Reconciliation Act of 1993 (OBRA-93)) change eligibility status on a national level, the rules are still subject to different interpretation by the various states. Therefore, in determining eligibility and planning to maximize benefits for handicapped children, it is absolutely essential that you seek qualified legal assistance in your own state.

Q. What options are available to parents in planning for their handicapped child's financial future?

A. There are generally four options in planning for a handicapped child's financial future:

- distributing assets directly to the disabled child. Typically, this approach is not a realistic solution to the child's financial problems. The handicapped child may not be able to properly manage the assets and access and title to the assets will usually cause a forfeiture of any need-based government benefits.

- disinheriting the handicapped child. Assets left to a handicapped child may not really improve the child's quality of life. In fact, some mentally handicapped children may not even be able to see any difference between government-supported institutional care and the best care money can buy. So the inheritance may do nothing but disqualify the child from governmental benefits until the inheritance has been spent, which doesn't really do the child any good at all.

To avoid "wasting" assets in this way, parents can simply leave their assets to their other children. This will maximize the use of the family resources for their children and preserve all of the governmental benefits to which their handicapped child will be entitled. The problem with this approach is that there are no provisions for the handicapped child in the event that governmental benefits are not sufficient to cover all of the child's needs. This can be especially troublesome if the governmental funds are reduced or eliminated in the future.

- leaving property to another person and asking that person to use the money for the handicapped child. This is called the "morally obligated gift". Funds are left to a brother or sister or an uncle or aunt of the handicapped person with the understanding that the funds are to be used for the handicapped child if needed. The problems with this solution are that any income on the funds will be taxed to the person receiving it, and there will be no guarantee that whoever receives the assets would comply with the deceased parent's request that the funds be used for the handicapped child. Creditors of the morally obligated recipient might attach money you intended be used for the handicapped child. The funds could be squandered or embezzled by the morally obligated person—or could be the subject of a divorce settlement.

- setting up a trust for the handicapped child, either in the form of a "special needs" trust or a "discretionary" trust, both of which are described below.

Q. Are there advantages in using trusts in estate planning for the handicapped child?

A. Through the use of trusts, parents can ensure (1) proper management of trust assets, (2) supervision of the beneficiary, and (3) distribution of assets that will provide for the handicapped child's future, while at same time attempting to preserve the governmental benefits to which the child is entitled.

For example, Bill and Mary have three children—Dick, Jane, and Alice. Alice is mentally handicapped, is currently eligible for Medicaid, and is also eligible for and receiving SSI. Alice has been institutionalized many times during her lifetime.

Bill and Mary have been using their own funds to care for Alice and to give her the comforts and luxuries that the funds paid to the institution do not provide. Bill and Mary are worried about Alice's care after they both die or are no longer able to care for her.

What Bill and Mary would like to accomplish through estate planning is to have someone else take over their responsibilities when they are both no longer able to do so. They want someone to manage Alice's money, keep an eye on Alice to make sure that she is receiving the care, treatment, and benefits to which she is entitled, and to use the funds that they set aside for Alice to continue her care and to give her the comforts and luxuries not provided through government benefits. Of course, if the benefits programs change, Bill and Mary would like their funds to be used, if necessary, for the basic support that Alice will require. They would also like someone to monitor changes in the law to make certain that Alice is always provided for.

At Alice's death, any funds set aside for her that have not been used for her benefit can then be made payable to their other two children, Dick and Jane, or to Dick's and Jane's children if they are no longer alive. Bill and Mary can accomplish this goal by establishing a *special needs trust*, a *discretionary trust*, or a combination of the two.

Q. What is a special needs trust?

A. A *special needs trust* is a trust that parents establish to provide for the *supplemental* needs, and not for the basic support, of their handicapped child. You must make it very clear that your intention is to supplement rather than supplant public benefits the disabled child may be eligible to receive. The trust document might read as follows:

"My trustee's discretion as to the need, propriety, or amount of distributions to or for the use and benefit of my beneficiary shall be limited solely to providing only those comforts and luxuries not otherwise provided by the institution in which such child is living, or from other sources. It is not my (our) purpose to provide for maintenance or support where publicly funded benefits and programs are available to accomplish these purposes. So under no circumstances shall my trustee exercise its discretion to utilize funds for the payment of services that would otherwise be borne by any publicly or privately funded program or institution."

An example of the type of expenditures describe above is spending money for such small luxury items as toys, candy, shaving cream, and perfume that are for sale in the institution in which the child lives.

The special needs trust is designed so that the funds are not considered to be available to the beneficiary. Otherwise, the beneficiary could be ineligible for SSI and for Medicaid. (Court decisions in several states have held that a special needs trust will not disqualify the beneficiary for Medicaid. But we suggest that you consult with a knowledgeable lawyer to be certain that your trust complies with the court decisions in your state.)

Q. What is a discretionary trust?

A. Under the terms of a *discretionary trust*, the trustee is not required to make any payments or distributions on behalf of the beneficiary but can do so whenever, in the trustee's sole and unlimited discretion, payments or distributions are necessary. The purpose of a discretionary trust is to give the trustee flexibility to meet the beneficiary's needs and maintain the beneficiary's eligibility for benefits.

Because the beneficiary of a discretionary trust has no legal entitlement to trust assets, many states have held that the beneficiary is still entitled to receive governmental benefits inasmuch as it is the trustee—not the grantor or the beneficiary—who has the absolute discretion to distribute funds to meet the beneficiary's needs.

A discretionary trust can also provide for distributions to beneficiaries in addition to the handicapped child through the use of *sprinkling provisions*. Let's turn once again to the family we described earlier—Bill and Mary and their three children, Dick, Jane, and Alice, who is mentally handicapped, receives SSI, and is eligible for Medicaid. The survivor of Bill and Mary could establish a trust in his or her will that would leave the couple's entire estate in trust, with directions to the independent trustee

"to pay or apply the income and principal of the trust to or for the use of such one or more persons as the trustee may select out of a class of persons consisting of all three of our children, Dick, Jane, and Alice, giving the trustee the right to make payments, whether equal or unequal, and to the exclusion of any one or more of our children at such times as the trustee, in the trustee's sole and absolute discretion, shall deem desirable."

The trust could further stipulate that if a beneficiary is institutionalized,

> "the trustee's discretion as to the needs of the institutionalized beneficiary would be limited solely to providing only those comforts and luxuries not otherwise provided by the institution, and further that under no circumstance could the trustee use its discretion to utilize funds for the payment of services that would otherwise be borne by a publicly or privately funded program or institution of which the trustee had knowledge."

Under the above arrangement, the trustee would have even stronger justification to withhold distributions to or on behalf of Alice, the handicapped beneficiary, because of the trustee's fiduciary duty to consider the needs of the other beneficiaries. The trust might direct the trustee to assist the beneficiary in applying for governmental benefits and authorize the trustee to use trust assets in defending the beneficiary's claim for eligibility against an attack that trust assets constitute a disqualifying "available resource". We suggest that you provide at least one other beneficiary than the disabled child with a meaningful interest in the trust.

Q. Are there any other types of trusts that can be exempt for Medicaid purposes?

A. There are three additional types or trusts that are exempt for Medicaid purposes:

- trusts with payback language. Federal law dealing with trusts for disabled individuals under age 65 indicates that if a trust is established for that individual's benefit by a "parent, grandparent, legal guardian of the individual, or a court," the assets will be exempt for Medicaid purposes only if the trust specifically stipulates that upon the beneficiary's death, the balance in the trust must be used to reimburse the state for medical assistance paid on behalf of the beneficiary. Through the use of the payback provision, all of the trust assets can be available for the beneficiary's benefit, but they can eventually be lost to the other members of the grantor or beneficiary's family. (This could be made up through the purchase of life insurance on the life or lives of one or both parent(s) owned by and payable to the other children or to a trust on their behalf).

- the pooled trust. Trust assets can be exempt when the trust is established and managed by a nonprofit charitable association and upon the death of the handicapped person, the funds remain in the pooled trust for the benefit of other trust beneficiaries or they are applied to repay the state under the payback provisions discussed above.

- trusts composed of pension and social security benefits. There is also an exemption for trusts made up solely of pension, social security and other income payable to a handicapped person as long as the state is entitled to reimbursement upon the beneficiary's death.

Because the federal and state regulations governing these types of trusts are constantly changing, the regulations are subject to different interpretation by state courts. Reviewing your individual situation with a knowledgeable lawyer in your state is an absolute must before the preparation or execution of any such trust.

Q. What is a spendthrift trust?

A. A *spendthrift trust* is a trust that contains a provision that prohibits assigning any interest or distribution from the trust to creditors of the beneficiary or to reimburse any public or private agencies for benefits provided to the beneficiary. Estate planners almost always recommend including a spendthrift clause in an irrevocable trust, and many states consider the spendthrift provision a bar to a creditor's rights to attack the beneficiary's interest in the trust.

Q. Are there limits on the usefulness of a spendthrift trust?

A. There are limitations on the effectiveness of spendthrift provisions, particularly as they apply to trusts created for the grantor's own benefit or for the benefit of an individual that the grantor is legally obligated to support. In our opinion, every trust designed to protect a handicapped person should contain a spendthrift provision, although its use, standing alone, should not be relied on as a guarantee that creditors—including the state and federal government—will not be permitted to reach the trust assets.

Also remember that creditor issues are different than eligibility issues. Although a spendthrift trust is safe from many attacks by the beneficiary's creditors, it can still be considered a financial resource for determining eligibility for Medicaid and SSI (unless it also qualifies as one of the exempt forms of trusts discussed above). The mere fact that a trust is a spendthrift trust does not prevent the state from considering a trust to be a financial resource for the beneficiary.

HOW AND WHEN TO PUT YOUR HOUSE IN TRUST—THE HOUSE GRIT

Chapter 20 explains:

- What a GRIT (grantor retained interest trust) is

- Why the IRS allows a substantial valuation discount for transfers to a GRIT

- Advantages of a house GRIT

- Disadvantages of a house GRIT

- Estate tax implications of a house GRIT

- Gift tax implications of a house GRIT

- Personal residence trusts: How they differ from a house GRIT

- The distinction between a QPRT and a PRT

- Special provisions that must be in a house GRIT document

- What to do if you want to live in the house at the end of the trust term

- Why some authorities feel the house GRIT is one of the last great estate planning tools

Q. What is a GRIT?

A. A *GRIT* is a grantor-retained interest trust, often also called a QPRT (qualified personal residence trust). It is an irrevocable trust into which you place a personal residence but retain the right to live in the home for a fixed period of years. At the end of the specified term, the home will pass to the beneficiary or beneficiaries you name in the trust—typically a child, grandchild, or other family member or friend.

Through the GRIT, you are essentially retaining the right to live in the home but making a gift of the right to trust assets (your home) at the end of the specified term. In other words, you are making a gift to your trust's *remainderman* (the person or persons who will receive your home when the trust ends). Obtaining a large gift tax discount and saving a very large amount of federal estate tax are the *house GRIT's* major objectives.

Q. Why is there a substantial valuation discount for transferring a home to a house GRIT?

A. The gift tax discount is based on the economic reality that the beneficiary's right to receive money or other property X years from now isn't worth as much as the right to get it today.

Gift tax is based on the value of the gift—when it arrives in the donee's hands. In the case of a gift of a "future interest" (an interest the donee does not have the immediate, unfettered, and ascertainable right to use, possess, or enjoy), the gift's value must be discounted to take into account the time the beneficiary must wait to get the benefit of the gift. The longer your beneficiary must wait to receive legal title to your home, the larger the valuation discount and the lower the potential gift tax. This concept may make it possible to shift huge amounts of wealth to those you love at little, if any, out-of-pocket cost.

Let's look at an example. Wanda Widow, aged 60, inherited a $1,000,000 home on MalaBoo Island from her late husband. To remove the home—which is appreciating at about 8 percent per year—from her estate, she sets up a house GRIT. The terms of the trust state that Wanda can live in the home for 10 years. At the end of that period, ownership of the home will pass to Wanda's children.

Actuarially, the value of Wanda's house can be broken in two parts: (1) the value of the right to continue to live in the home for 10 years and (2) the value of the right to receive the home at the end of 10 years. In order to compute the future value of the house, you have to make an assumption about how much interest money could earn during that ten year period, and use that interest rate to discount the future value. For tax purposes, the allowable discount rate is determined by Section 7520 of the Internal Revenue Code, so the discount rate used to measure the value of future interests is called the *Section 7520 rate*.

Assuming a Section 7520 rate of 9 percent, the present value of Wanda's right to use the house (which is considered to be the same as the right to receive the income from an investment equal to the value of the house) is worth about $57.76 for every $100 of value she placed into the trust. Since she put a home worth $1,000,000 into the trust, the value of the income interest she retained is $577,600.

The present value of her gift to the children, the remainder interest (that is, the actuarial value of what Wanda gave to her children) is the difference between $1,000,000 and the $577,589 she retained, $422,411. In essence, if Wanda survives the 10 years, she will have removed the $1,000,000 from her estate based on a gift tax value of less than half of that amount.

Because none of the gift can be enjoyed until the 10-year period has expired, it is all a future interest gift and therefore ineligible for the gift tax annual exclusion. But Wanda can use her unified credit to offset any gift tax liability. Since the value of the gift ($422,411) is under the unified credit exclusion amount ($600,000 in 1997 and increasing by steps to $1,000,000 in 2006), Wanda will use up $422,411 of her unified credit exclusion amount, but she will pay absolutely no out-of-pocket gift tax.

If the home grows in value at the same 8 percent rate it has in the past, by the end of the 10-year term, it will be worth about $2,158,925! If Wanda survives the term of the trust, the entire value will be removed from her estate, so she will have given more than $2,000,000 to her children at a gift tax "cost" of only $422,000. (Remember, although she's had to use up $422,000 of her unified credit exclusion amount, she never paid a dollar of gift tax). The magnitude of the potential death tax savings on $2,158,925 at a 55 percent (or even 37 percent) estate tax bracket is obvious. (These computations and projections can be performed on the NumberCruncher program. For additional information, call 610-527-5216).

Q. *What are the advantages, other than significant gift and estate tax savings, of using a house GRIT?*

A. Aside from the tremendous estate tax savings potential and the extremely low gift tax cost, there are many reasons to set up a house GRIT, including these two:

- You can ensure succession. By setting up a house GRIT, you can be sure your home will go to one child rather than another, or you can ensure a child (or grandchild or any other selected beneficiary whether or not related to you) that he or she—and not your next spouse or a creditor—will receive your home. This can be particularly important in second marriages.

- You can avoid probate. Since title to your home will pass under the terms of your trust, your beneficiary avoids the potential costs, delays, and aggravation of probate.

Q. What are the costs or downsides of a house GRIT?

A. There are, of course, costs and disadvantages involved in putting your house in trust, as follows:

- You will incur set-up and administration costs. These costs include legal fees, appraisal fees, property titling costs, and trustee's fees. In some states, there may also be a real estate transfer tax.

- There is a loss of control. Once you place your home into the house GRIT, you have given up the right to dispose of your home in some other way or to some other person. If you no longer care for a named beneficiary or you want to change the proportion of ownership that beneficiary will receive, there is no way to do so once the trust is funded. The house GRIT is an irrevocable trust. Because the trust is irrevocable, once title to your home is placed into the trust, you are precluded from taking other planning measures with it.

- There is still a possibility that you will have to pay an estate tax on the home. If you die during the term of the trust, the IRS will include the value of the house in your estate. This would defeat the very purpose for which you set up the house GRIT. The longer the term of the trust, the greater the gift tax discount, but it is essential to select a period of time that you feel you are likely to outlive. Since there is no limit on how long the house GRIT must run (terms from 2 years to 20 years are common), we suggest that you ask your planner to make a reasonable projection of your life expectancy based on mortality tables, your family and personal health history, and your habits, occupation, and avocations. Then create a trust that can be expected to expire before you do.

Life insurance owned by a third-party beneficiary, such as an irrevocable trust or an adult child, can be used to "insure the death tax savings." What this means is that you could make gifts to your adult daughter, for instance, who could use that money to purchase term life insurance on your life in the amount of the projected federal estate tax savings. If you die during the term of the house GRIT, your daughter will have the cash to pay the estate tax or to make up for the federal and state death tax that would have been saved if you had survived the term of the trust.

- Your beneficiaries lose a "step-up" in basis. If you keep the home in your name until your death, the basis (cost) for purposes of determining the amount of gain on a sale is increased (or decreased) to the date of your death value of the house. In most cases, this reduces the taxable gain reportable by your heirs upon a later sale of the home. Of course, this increase in basis comes at a cost; the home must be included in your estate and subject to estate tax. With a house GRIT, if you survive the term of the trust, the value of the house is out of your estate, but your trust beneficiaries start with a basis carried over from you while you are alive.

- There may be insufficient growth in the home's value, or your home may decline in value. If the house doesn't appreciate substantially or drops below the value it had when you contributed it to the trust, you will fail to achieve the estate tax savings you had hoped for.

- You will face hidden costs and aggravations. Putting your house in trust entails changing title to your home from your name to the name of your trustee, who must then pay title insurance and homeowner's coverage. You must notify the local property-taxing authority. In some states, the change of title will trigger a real estate transfer tax, and since the house GRIT is an irrevocable trust, the odds of beating such a tax are slim—even if, for income tax purposes, the trust is considered a grantor trust. Some states might also impose a gift tax even if the federal government does not. Finally, if your property is a co-op or condo, the co-op board or condo managers will have to approve the transaction—before trust instruments can be drawn.

- You will lose the use of your home at the end of the term of the trust. Once the trust ends, your home is no longer yours and you will either have to move out or start paying rent to your children (or whoever becomes the owner under your trust). This is discussed in more detail below.

Of course, compared to the potential estate tax savings if your home appreciates substantially, these costs and aggravations are all relatively minor. Nevertheless, they must be considered.

Q. What are the estate tax implications in a house GRIT?

A. As we've noted above, if you outlive the term of trust, not one penny of the value of the home—no matter how valuable it becomes over that time—will be included in your estate for federal estate tax purposes. This is because you do not have any interest in the home once the trust ends.

However, the gift tax value of the gift you are making to the remainderman is called an *adjusted taxable gift*, which will push up the rate at which the assets left in your taxable estate will be taxed. (For example, if you have a $1,000,000 estate and make a $600,000 lifetime gift, the $600,000 is still included in the calculation of your estate tax to make sure that the $400,000 left in your estate is taxed at the rates for estates between $600,000 and $1,000,000, not the rates for estates between $0 and $400,000.)

On the other hand, if you die before the trust ends, the full date-of-death value of the home will be included in your gross estate for federal estate tax purposes.

Q. What are the gift tax implications in a house GRIT?

A. As we've also noted above, the gift you are making to the remainderman—the right to receive the house at the end of the term—will not qualify for the gift tax annual exclusion. Therefore, the entire discounted value of the home is subject to gift tax. (Of course, you won't pay any out-of-pocket tax unless the discounted value exceeds your unified credit exclusion amount.)

The value of the taxable gift is the value of the home minus the value of the right to live in the home for the term of the trust. Talk to your lawyer or accountant about how to calculate the income interest in the home in accordance with Section 7520.

If you live beyond the term of the trust, there will be no second gift tax when the home is paid over to your selected beneficiary, because the gift was complete upon your funding of the trust (the date you made the trust owner of the home).

Q. What is a personal residence trust, and how does it differ from a house GRIT?

A. Personal residence trusts (PRTs), and its close relation, qualified personal residence trusts (QPRTs), are merely other names for a house GRIT. However, there is a technical legal distinction between PRTs and QPRTs.

A PRT is allowed to hold only one residence, which must be your principal residence. Residence is defined not only as your home but also as the appurtenant structures and adjacent land reasonably appropriate for residence purposes; it does not, however, include personal property such as furnishings.

The home may not be used to provide transient lodging and substantial services (that is, it can't be used as a hotel or bed and breakfast establishment). The residence may not be occupied by anyone other than you, your spouse, or your dependent. It must be available at all times for your use and cannot be sold or used for any other purposes. A personal residence trust may include a home subject to a mortgage.

A PRT is not allowed to hold any asset other than your residence. It cannot, for example, hold any cash to pay mortgage or insurance expenses, all of which must be paid directly by the grantor. A PRT must not allow the sale of the residence during the term of the trust.

Q. What is a QPRT, and how does it differ from a PRT?

A. IRS regulations provide safe harbor to a second level of residence trust which is not as restrictive as a PRT. These regulations allow limited amounts of assets other than an interest in a personal residence to be held by the trust and further allow that interest in the house to be sold under certain circumstances. This type of house GRIT is called a QPRT (qualified personal residence trust).

A QPRT may have limited income. But if it does, that income must be distributed only to you, the grantor. Generally speaking, aside from limited assets related directly to the house (such as a homeowner's insurance policy or the proceeds of a sale of the house) the QPRT must specifically prohibit holding property other than the residence.

Q. Are there special provisions that I should place in my house GRIT document?

A. The IRS has imposed a number of highly technical requirements that house GRITs must meet. Obviously, only a lawyer who specializes in estate planning should create your trust document.

In addition to the technical provisions required for PRTs and QPRTs, there are some general estate and gift tax issues you may want to discuss with your lawyer to be sure that the following provisions are included in your trust instrument:

- You must surrender all dominion and control over trust assets.

- You must surrender any power to revoke the gift of the remainder (that is, you cannot change the ultimate recipient of the title to the home you place in the trust).

- The trust must prohibit any change in the beneficial interests of the trust.

- The trust must prohibit you from having any control over the manner or time in which the beneficiaries you selected will enjoy the home.

Q. What happens if I want to continue to live in the home at the end of the trust term?

A. You have a number of options if you'd like to continue living in the home you placed into the trust. The simplest (and the one we suggest) is to have the new owner—your child, for example—hire an independent qualified real estate appraiser to determine and document a fair rental value. You will then pay that amount to rent the home from the new owner. Be very careful with any agreement that restricts the rights of your beneficiaries (and could jeopardize the tax status of the trust). Never enter into any such agreement without the advice of a competent tax lawyer and CPA.

You are probably wondering why you can't continue to live in the house without paying rent to your own child. The answer is that the IRS could then treat the transaction as if you had never really ended your personal ownership of the home and thus include it in your estate at your death. By actually paying a fair rent to your child, you avoid that danger and you actually enhance the wealth-shifting opportunity of the house GRIT by removing more assets from your taxable estate.

Here's how: If you make gifts to your child, you'll have to pay gift taxes at your estate tax bracket. On the other hand, you'll pay no gift tax on your rental payments, so your rental payments are, in essence, gift-tax-free gifts to your child. (He or she, of course, will have to report your rental payments as income.)

Another alternative is to negotiate an arms' length sale and repurchase the home from your child for its value at the time the trust would otherwise pay it over to that child. For example, if your $1,000,000 home has appreciated to $2,000,000, you will pay $2,000,000 to your child to repurchase the home. That removes the $2,000,000 of cash from your estate and has yet another advantage: Even though the home will be included in your estate (because you now own it again), it will receive what tax practitioners call a *step-up-in-basis*. In other words, the heirs you have named in your will can sell the house for as much as $2,000,000 after your death and not pay any income tax since there will be no gain. That's because their basis (cost) for the home is its fair market value—$2,000,000, not $1,000,000—as of the date of your death.

In fact, if you arrange the sale while the trust still owns the home and the trust is set up so that you are treated for income tax purposes as the owner (tax practitioners call this a *grantor trust*), you can buy the home from the trust and neither you nor the trust will pay any income tax. (Of course, you must take as your income tax basis the same basis you had when you contributed the home to the trust.)

Alternatively, you can arrange for the repurchase of your residence through a repurchase option built into the trust itself. (If so, the trust must be a QPRT because, as we discussed earlier, a PRT is prohibited from selling the residence.) Assuming the trust is considered a grantor trust, no gain should be realized on the sale. You can even arrange that if you are incompetent at the time the trust ends, a trusted relative could use a power of attorney to exercise the repurchase option on your behalf. Once again, it is essential that there be a provision requiring third party independent valuation and terms.

Q. Why do some experts consider the house GRIT one of the last great estate planning tools?

A. Even if the home has relatively little appreciation, the house GRIT still works. Why? The main reason is that your estate is really being "defunded" rather than "refunded." Unlike alternatives such as the GRAT or GRUT (discussed in chapter 22), the house GRIT puts no income back into your estate. (As we all know, houses are cash drains, not money pumps—or if they are pumps, the money is pumped out, not in.) Therefore, the house GRIT does not have to outperform the Section 7520 rate to be a wealth shifting success. Unlike many other estate planning tools or techniques, it can save taxes at almost any age.

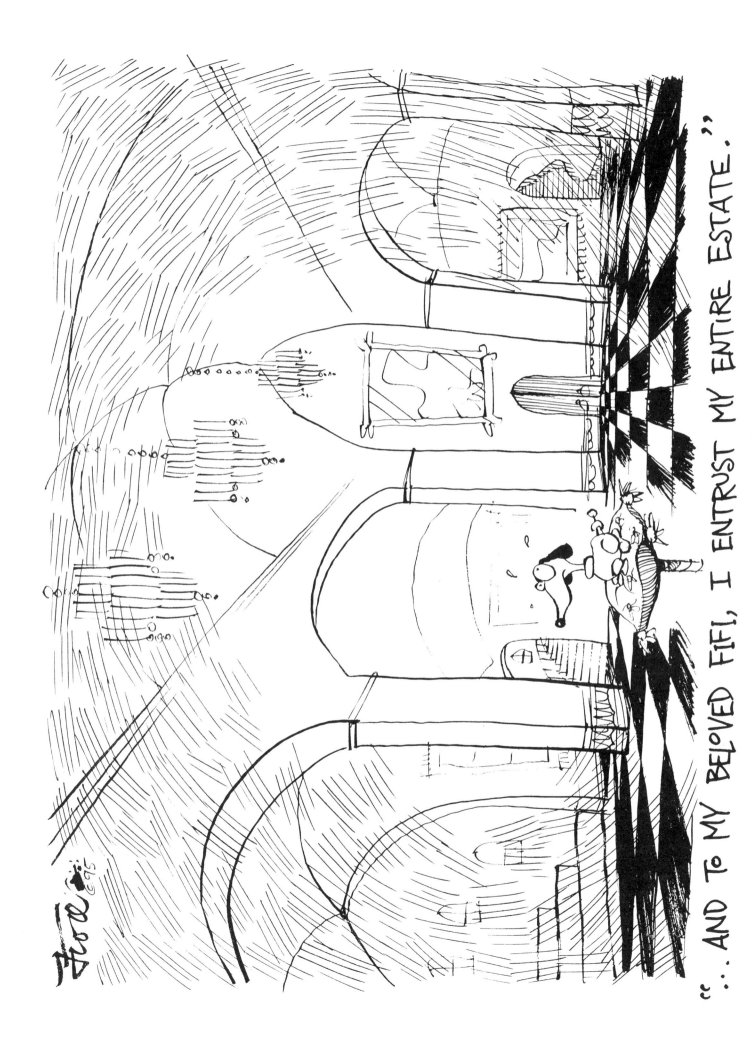

"... AND TO MY BELOVED FIFI, I ENTRUST MY ENTIRE ESTATE."

TRUSTS FOR UNIQUE AND DIFFICULT SITUATIONS

Chapter 21 explains:

- Why trusts are often the best way to provide for dependent parents

- How a trust can provide for a live-in companion

- How a trust can assure privacy

- Trusts for pets

- How to deal with beneficiaries who have drug, divorce, or other "difficult" problems

- How a trust can be used to handle large real estate tracts

- How a trust can be used to help assure that a buy-sell agreement with your business will be finalized

- How trusts can help you stay in control even after your death

> As we have stated many times in this book, the use of a trust to accomplish the grantor's wishes is restricted only by the grantor's imagination and the skill of the lawyer preparing the trust. In the other chapters of this book, we have discussed the most common uses for trusts, and we have also described many sophisticated trusts, the knowledge and use of which are often limited to estate planning specialists. In this chapter we will focus on some of the non-mainstream situations, where a trust can help resolve an otherwise difficult or delicate problem.

Q. Why are trusts often the best way to provide for dependent parents?

A. While much of this book deals with planning and tax savings for a spouse or descendants, what happens if you predecease a dependent parent? Suppose your mother has been living with you for 10 years following the death of your father. Her sole income is her social security pension. You have been giving her free room and board and enough cash to enable her to enjoy a comfortable standard of living. Although you are confident that your spouse would help care for your mother, you want to make sure that she is provided for financially if you predecease her.

You could leave her a specific amount of money in your will. But it might be too much or too little. If your gift is too little, your mother might outlive your gift and end her life with less financial support than she needs. If your gift is too much, it may be subject to death taxes (again) upon your mother's death. There is also another problem with a specific gift of money—the possibility that your mother might not be physically or mentally or emotionally able to manage the funds for her own benefit. Still another disadvantage is that if your mother is institutionalized and eligible for Medicaid, a lump sum bequest could disqualify her from benefits.

An excellent solution to these problems is to establish a trust for your mother's benefit. You could place a specific amount of money in the trust—say, $200,000. You could give your mother the right to the income from the trust, and if appropriate, you could give the trustee the right to use trust principal for your mother's health, maintenance, and support. At your mother's death, the balance in her trust could be distributed to your spouse or children and therefore avoid being taxed in your mother's estate.

Q. How can a trust provide for my live-in companion?

A. Trust and tax law are replete with benefits for a spouse, but in most cases, a "significant other" can be completely cut off from receiving any part of your estate unless you specifically provide otherwise.

By establishing a trust, you can make the necessary provisions for your companion—in effect, level the playing field—so that your companion can be provided for even though he or she is not your spouse. For example, you could establish a trust during your lifetime and place assets in the trust that can provide an income (with principal available) to meet your companion's needs. The trustee could be an individual or a corporate fiduciary, such as a bank with trust powers or a trust company or a combination. If the trust were irrevocable and established and funded during your lifetime, trust assets would not be included in your estate at your death.

The trust could also be funded with life insurance, and as discussed in chapter 17 (on irrevocable life insurance trusts), the insurance proceeds could be received by the trust, free of federal and state death taxes. This would place your companion on an equal footing with a surviving spouse, who is entitled to receive a deceased spouse's assets tax free due to the unlimited marital deduction (discussed in chapter 13). Furthermore, you could accomplish your objective in privacy because a trust, unlike a will, is not a public document and is unlikely to be challenged by a disgruntled heir.

Q. Can a trust ensure me of privacy?

A. Yes. For whatever reason, there may be circumstances where you would like to make gifts but avoid publicity. For example, you might have an illegitimate child whom you have supported and for whom you want to provide, but without making the relationship public. You might be charitably inclined and wish to pay for the education of a child or family in your community, but you prefer that your contribution and the provisions of your gift be kept confidential. You might also want to provide for someone for whom you care a great deal, but you do not wish that person to know from whom the gift came.

A trust could be the most appropriate way to deal with each of these situations. It could be established either during your lifetime or at death—separate and apart from your will or other estate planning documents—to make the necessary provisions for your beneficiaries.

Q. Can trusts provide for pets?

A. If you have a dog, cat, or any domesticated animal for whom you care a lot, you may be concerned about what will happen to your pet after your death. An "honorary" trust is an excellent solution—perhaps the only solution.

Through a trust you can leave a friend (or even a veterinarian or a home that cares for pets) a specific sum of money that is to be used for your pet's care, comfort and room and board during its lifetime and to pay for its burial when the animal dies. You can go into as much detail as you wish concerning the particulars of your pet's care. However, in establishing a trust for your pets—as in most trust situations—be sure to discuss your plans with the proposed trustee to be certain that the trustee will accept the responsibility of caring for your pet and complying with your trust provisions.

Q. How do I deal with beneficiaries who have drug, divorce, or other difficult problems?

A. Unfortunately, many of us face serious day-to-day problem situations. One of our greatest concerns is how these situations will be handled after our death. In chapter 19, we discuss some of the ways that trusts can help solve the problems of caring for handicapped children. Similar problems could arise in caring for children or other relatives who are dependent on drugs. You could have a brother or sister in serious financial difficulty to whom you have been giving financial assistance during your lifetime. You might have a child who has joined a religious or political cult that would confiscate any funds that you would give directly or bequeath to the child. You might have a child or other relative who has broken the law or may very well do so in the near future. You might have a son or daughter who is in the process of going through a second or third contested divorce with all of its inherent financial problems.

Although these problems will obviously not disappear after your death—and no trustee will be able to deal with them with the same knowledge and background that you have—a trust may be the only plan you can establish to handle the problem situation in the best possible way when you are no longer able to do so yourself. The reason a trust is the preferable solution is that only through a trust can you set money aside for the beneficiary, while at the same time give the trustee as much flexibility as possible to deal with whatever may arise.

In chapter 19 on handicapped children and chapter 23 on Medicaid, we discuss discretionary trusts—particularly appropriate for the problem beneficiary, because it gives the trustee flexibility to meet the beneficiary's needs as they arise. For example, the trustee can elect to pay funds for the beneficiary's care and maintenance or completely withhold funds from the beneficiary if, in the trustee's sole discretion, the funds will not be used properly or will not benefit the person for whom they are intended.

As a further precaution, your trust should contain a *spendthrift provision*, which prohibits the assignment of any interest or distributions from the trust to creditors of the beneficiary. That means a beneficiary could not go to Las Vegas and use his or interest in a trust as collateral. In most states, this will prevent creditors from reaching any of the trust assets, and it can bar a beneficiary's spouse from attacking the trust assets or claiming that they are marital property and therefore subject to the spouse's claim against the trust beneficiary's assets.

If the child in question has an alcohol or substance abuse problem, you might provide that only funds necessary for food, clothing, and shelter be disbursed—and that payments be made directly and only to the people providing the food, clothing, and shelter, not to the child. The trust can be set up to withhold trust assets until and unless two doctors are willing to certify that the child has been drug free for a specified period of time. Incentives could be provided in return for stated "drug free periods" or for other accomplishments you want to encourage.

In the case of an unsettled marriage, the trust could provide only income for your child and specify in the event of a divorce that all income is to be paid to or for the benefit of the couple's children or to another child. This would prevent the divorcing spouse from reaching trust principal.

The possible solutions to difficult problems are almost endless if your lawyer is creative.

Q. Can I use a trust to handle a large tract of real estate?

A. Yes. To illustrate, consider this example. Joe and Diane Farmer own 60 acres of real estate situated along a suburban highway. They want to keep all of the land in their family, and at the same time provide the means for having it eventually distributed to their children or grandchildren. They are concerned that if the ground is subdivided at this time, its value will be greatly diminished. They are also concerned that if they put all of their children's names on the property, it might become subject to the claims of their children's spouses in the event of a divorce and there will be no central management for the property.

The solution is to place the entire property in trust with a trustee (or several trustees) designated to manage the property after Joe and Diane's death for the benefit of their descendants. As long as there are sufficient other assets (or life insurance) to pay the death taxes that the land will generate in Joe and Diane's estate, the trust can be an effective mechanism for handling the real estate after the present owners' death.

Q. Can I use a trust for my family business?

A. Yes. Let's say you have a successful family business and want to keep it for the benefit of your children and grandchildren. In addition, you want to ensure that there is a central management for the business, an orderly disposition of its stock following your death, and few (if any) opportunities for disputes among your children.

You have several options. One option is to establish a business continuation ("buy-sell") agreement, under which you could set a price for the value of the business and draft an agreement with your children to purchase your interest in the business following your death. You could also make periodic gifts of your stock to your children to fully utilize your $10,000 annual exclusion and use life insurance to help provide the funds to purchase your shares of stock.

You may also want to consider a trust as one of the options available to you. A trust that is qualified to hold the company stock can have special provisions for voting the stock and for managing business affairs. (See our discussion in Chapter 11 on the potential problems when trusts own S corporation stock.) If your business is left to a trustee, management can be centralized in the trustee (or trustees), and you can make provisions for distribution of dividends or profits and continuity of ownership by leaving the stock to the next generation following the death of your children.

Furthermore, trusts can be used to guarantee the performance of business continuation agreements. Here's an example: Ben and Ian are brothers, and they have taken over control of the family business. They want to make an agreement that upon the death of one brother, the survivor must purchase, and the family of the deceased brother must sell, all of the deceased partner's interest. Their agreement is funded by life insurance so that at the first brother's death, the surviving brother will collect $500,000 in insurance proceeds and will pay the $500,000 to the executor (widow) of the deceased brother.

The brothers get along well; their wives do not. The husbands think that their arrangement is excellent. But their wives are worried that if the business is not doing well when the first brother dies, the surviving brother might put the $500,000 in his pocket and refuse to go along with the agreement. Although the agreement may be legally enforceable, the women want to have a firm guarantee that the wife of the deceased brother will indeed receive the full proceeds and not be forced to resort to litigation. To accomplish this objective, the families could agree on an independent trustee—a bank or trust company, for example— and then set up a trust that would be the owner and beneficiary of the life insurance. The trust would hold the business's stock in escrow, and it would stipulate that upon receipt of the proceeds, the independent trustee would collect the stock from the decedent's family, pay the insurance proceeds to them, and deliver the stock to the survivor.

Please be aware that there are serious potential tax issues that should be considered in connection with this plan. As with every suggestion in our book, you should implement the plan only on the advice of a qualified tax lawyer and CPA.

Q. Can trusts actually help me "rule from the grave"?

A. Our book is full with examples of ways we try to make sure that our loved ones are provided for after our death. We make specific provisions for the care of our children, our parents, and our favorite charities. We have the right to spell out in detail upon what terms and when our children will receive their money and who has the responsibility of making decisions for them. We can make a gift to charity and request that it be used to establish a scholarship for a specific class of individuals. We can even make provisions for payments to our grandchildren that will be effective many years following our death.

Some of us, however, have specific ideas and goals that go beyond these situations. Many of these ideas find their way into trusts, even though their enforcement may, in certain instances, be quite difficult. For example, you could leave money to children or grandchildren, providing they do not smoke or use drugs or leave money to persons depending on their marital status. Many people may want to provide for a son-in-law or daughter-in-law, for example, especially if there has been a long and happy marriage, but not if the son-in-law or daughter-in-law is not living with and married to their child at the time the gift becomes effective. In that case, a husband and wife could make a gift in trust to their daughter-in-law, providing that she is married to and living with their son when the second of them dies.

Be aware, however, that if you choose to include trust provisions that attempt to modify or control the lives of your intended beneficiaries, these gifts may not be legally enforceable, depending on the laws of the state, how the courts interpret public policy, and the degree of control you are attempting. Some questionable trust provisions include a gift to a public college to be used only for scholarships for a specific religious group; a gift to a child but only if he renounces all contact with the cult with which he is presently associated; and a gift in trust for a grandchild but only if she marries someone of the grantor's faith (compare that with a gift to a grandchild who is being raised in a different faith from that of the grantor, providing that the grandchild take at least one college course on the grantor's religion). If you have strong feelings about a particular provision that you would like to place in your trust, we strongly recommend that your lawyer research the question and advise you as to its validity and enforceability in your state.

GRATs AND GRUTs

Chapter 22 explains:

- What a GRAT is

- What a GRUT is

- Why a GRAT or GRUT might be a good estate planning tool

- Mechanically, how a GRAT works

- Mechanically, how a GRUT works

- Additional reasons you may want to set up a GRAT or GRUT

- Costs or downsides of a GRAT or GRUT

- The income tax implications of a GRAT or GRUT

- The gift tax implications of transferring assets to a GRAT or GRUT

- Tax implications if you buy back an asset held by your GRAT or GRUT

- Problems incurred when an asset subject to a loan is transferred to a GRAT or GRUT

- Problems when grandchildren are the beneficiaries of a GRAT or GRUT

- What a "rolling GRAT" is and why you may want to use one

Q. What is a GRAT?

A. A GRAT (grantor-retained annuity trust) is an irrevocable trust into which you can place cash, stocks, mutual funds, real estate, or other income-producing property. You are called the grantor (creator) of the trust. As its name implies, you retain the right to annual (or semiannual, quarterly, or monthly) payments of a *fixed amount* of principal and interest for a fixed period of years (i.e., you retain the right to a fixed *annuity* from the trust).

At the end of the period of time you specified when you set up the trust (which can be practically any amount of time from, say, 2 to 20 years), the asset will pass to the beneficiary you name— typically a child, grandchild, or other family member or friend.

Q. What is a GRUT?

A. A GRUT (grantor-retained unitrust) is also an irrevocable trust into which you can place cash, stocks, mutual funds, real estate, or other income-producing property. You retain the right to payments of a *fixed percentage* of the trust's value, as revalued each year, for a fixed period of years. For example, you could retain the right to receive 8% of the initial value of the trust each January 1st for 10 years.

At the end of the specified term, the asset will pass to the beneficiary you named in the trust—typically a child, grandchild, or other family member or friend.

Q. Why would I want to set up a GRAT or a GRUT?

A. In both types of trust, you are essentially making a gift of the right to trust assets at the end of the specified term (a gift of a *remainder interest* to the *remainderman*—your trust's ultimate beneficiaries). Saving gift and estate taxes are the two major objectives, although as you'll see below, there are many other auxiliary advantages.

In a nutshell, the GRAT and the GRUT allow you to transfer large amounts of wealth at a significant gift tax discount. Then, if you survive the term of the GRAT or GRUT—even by only one day—the value of the property in the trust at that time is removed from your estate and your family can save thousands— even millions—of dollars of federal and state death taxes.

The gift tax discount is based on this mathematical premise:

The beneficiary's right to receive money or other property X years from now isn't worth as much as the right to get it today.

Gift tax is based on the value of the remainder interest in the hands of the ultimate gift recipient. So you will obtain a "discount" for gift tax purposes since your gift is not measured by the current value of what you give but rather the much lower present value of the beneficiary's right to receive the trust assets at the end of the term of the trust. The longer the term of the trust (the longer the beneficiary must wait to receive the trust property), the greater the gift tax discount and the lower the gift tax. Using a GRAT or GRUT, it may even be possible to make a gift of property worth over $1,000,000—with no out-of-pocket gift tax cost.

Q. How does a GRAT work?

A. Here's an example of how a GRAT works: Johnson Wax is 60. He has an estate of about $10,000,000 and has $1,000,000 of stocks that are both appreciating (15 percent per year) and pay a reasonable dividend (about 4 percent). He'd like to remove both appreciation and principal from his estate but wants a steady and consistent income for at least the next 10 years. Because of the federal estate tax, if he does not remove the stocks from his estate, his heirs, Bea and Ella Quince, will lose more than 55 cents of every dollar Johnson Wax leaves them. He is in the same 55 percent bracket for federal gift tax purposes, so he is hesitant to make an outright gift of the stocks.

Wax sets up a GRAT. He puts $1,000,000 of income-producing assets in the trust. He retains the right to a fixed annuity from the stocks for 10 years. He decides he'd like an annuity with a steady payout equal to 7 percent of the initial $1,000,000 value of the trust and he wants that $70,000 annuity each year, regardless of how much income the trust actually produces during the 10 years.

Assuming a 9 percent federal discount rate (tax planners call this the Section 7520 rate), the actuarial factor for each dollar of the annual annuity Wax retains is 5.9641. Multiplied by the $70,000 a year, the interest he has retained (the right to $70,000 per year for 10 years) is worth $417,487. This means the value of the remainder interest, the gift he is making to the ultimate beneficiaries of the trust, his children, measured at the date the trust is funded, is only $582,513 ($1,000,000—$417,487).

Because none of the gift can be enjoyed until the 10-year period has expired, it is all a "future-interest" gift and therefore ineligible for the annual gift tax exclusion. Although that means the entire amount is taxable, it will qualify for Wax's unified credit. Since the $582,513 value of the gift is less than the unified credit exclusion amount ($600,000 in 1997 and increasing by steps to $1,000,000 in 2006), Wax will use up $582,513 of his unified credit exclusion amount but pay no out-of-pocket gift tax. Therefore, he's transferred property worth $1,000,000 today at a discounted gift tax cost of $582,513.

But if the property appreciates at 15 percent and produces income at 4 percent, it will be worth $4,084,490 at the end of 10 years, and none of it will be included in his estate if he survives that period. The estate tax savings will exceed $2,000,000. Wax has removed over $4,000,000 from his estate with no out-of-pocket gift tax cost.

Q. How does a GRUT work?

A. The GRUT works essentially the same way as a GRAT but with a slight twist: Assume Johnson Wax likes the idea of removing assets from his estate but wants to receive an annuity that pays according to the expected (and hoped for) growth in the value of assets he places into a trust. He sets up a GRUT and he retains the right to a fixed percentage of trust assets. He'll receive an annuity each year worth exactly 7 percent of the value of the assets in the trust, as revalued year by year.

If the trust is worth $1,000,000, he'll receive $70,000. If the trust is worth $2,000,000, he'll receive $140,000 (7 percent of $2,000,000). If the trust's value drops to $500,000, he'll receive only $35,000 (7 percent of $500,000). It's as if Wax had retained a variable annuity. Regardless of how much income the trust does or does not generate, Wax will receive 7 percent of the value of the annually revalued principal.

Assuming a 9 percent federal discount (Section 7520) rate, the actuarial factor for Wax's retained variable annuity interest is worth about 47.6 percent. That means that Wax has retained an interest worth roughly 48 percent of each dollar he places into the GRUT. Subtracting that from 100 percent shows that he has given away about 52 percent (.523946 precisely) of his interest. The taxable gift Wax has made, therefore, is $523,946.

Again, because none of the gift can be enjoyed until the 10-year period has expired, it is all a future-interest gift and therefore ineligible for the annual gift tax exclusion. All of that discounted amount is taxable, but it will qualify for Wax's unified credit. Since the value of the gift is less than the unified credit exclusion amount ($600,000 in 1997 and increasing by steps to $1,000,000 in 2006), Wax will use up $523,946 of his unified credit exclusion amount but pay no out-of-pocket gift tax. He'll receive an annuity that starts at $70,000 a year but grows year by year as the trust grows in value. Because he's received so much more income than he would have under a GRAT, his beneficiaries will receive only $2,855,631 and the estate tax savings at his 55 percent estate tax bracket will be much less—but still considerable—than under a GRAT.

In effect, a GRAT—and to a lesser extent, a GRUT—enables you to create what estate planners call an *estate freeze*. Your estate will either remain the same or decrease. A GRAT or GRUT makes it possible for the grantor to retain an asset within the family unit while its value is "frozen" for death tax purposes. This is particularly appealing during economic conditions in which asset values are depressed at the same time interest rates are relatively low.

We often recommend that a wealthy surviving spouse or divorced individual consider a GRAT or GRUT as a marital deduction substitute.

Q. What are some of the reasons, other than estate tax savings, to set up a GRAT or GRUT?

A. There are also many additional benefits to GRATs and GRUTs:

- You pay transfer taxes at a "discount." There are several levels of discount that you may obtain. First, in the valuation process, various discounts can and should be taken to assess the fair market value of the asset (including discounts for lack of marketability and lack of control, where appropriate). Valuation reduction techniques are particularly viable during times of economic slowdown, depressed business and real estate values and low interest rates.

  Second, as the grantor in either a GRAT or GRUT, you are making a current gift, but it is a gift of a "future interest" since your beneficiary has to wait a specified number of years to enjoy it. You pay gift tax, not on what your beneficiary might actually receive, but on the value of the asset today, discounted for the "money value of the time" the beneficiary has to wait.

  Since the actuarial value of the gift is measured by how long the recipient must wait, the longer the wait, the lower the value of the gift. In other words, you can lower the gift tax value of the gift by stretching out the period during which you retain an interest. In the earlier examples, instead of gift taxes based on the $1,000,000 value of the asset today, because the remaindermen will not receive their interests until the end of 10 years, the gift tax value is lowered to less than $600,000—more than a 40 percent reduction.

By changing from a 10-year GRAT to a 20-year GRAT, the value of the remainder interest drops to about $451,000. Stated another way, you can contribute even more without paying any additional out-of-pocket gift tax.

Compared to a current outright gift of the asset, GRATs and GRUTs are less expensive taxwise and should be particularly appealing if you are concerned about gift and estate tax savings and are willing to bet that you will outlive the term of the trust. The healthier you are personally and the longer your family's life expectancy, the more likely you are to survive the term of the trust and achieve the significant estate tax savings the GRAT or GRUT offers.

- You can ensure succession. If you want specific assets, such as stock in a closely held corporation or land or a family compound to go to one child rather than another, or you do not want a former spouse, creditor, or someone who contests your will to be able to obtain that asset, the GRAT or GRUT will help assure against such a contingency. In most states, since a GRAT and GRUT are both irrevocable trusts, it's much less likely that the property will be lost if your estate is embroiled in a will contest, election against the will, or a creditor-imposed lawsuit on your estate.

- You are able to unify assets. If you own income-producing property in more than one state and would like to unify the administration of those assets and save on probate costs, either the GRAT or GRUT will help avoid ancillary administration (probate of out-of-state property) and its consequent costs, delays, and aggravations.

- GRATs and GRUTs are age neutral. There is practically no cut-off age after which a GRAT or GRUT will no longer be mathematically feasible. These are "little to lose, lot to gain" tools that even people in their '80s may want to use.

For instance, a person who is 80 years old can transfer $1,000,000 of assets to a child at a gift tax value of about $757,000 through a 5-year GRAT and $652,000 through a 10-year GRAT. Life expectancy is about 9 years at age 80, but if you are healthy, it may pay to take the chance.

Staggered trust terms can be used if you have a lower risk-taking propensity. For instance, the 80-year-old can transfer some property into a 5-year GRAT or GRUT and some property into a 10-year GRAT or GRUT, or the octogenarian can create a series of 2-, 3-, 4-, 5-, 6-, 7-, 8-, 9-, and 10-year GRATs and GRUTs to hedge his or her bets.

- The trusts are an almost no-lose situation. Let's look at a worst-case scenario. Suppose you die during the term of the trust and, as a consequence, some or all of the assets are included in your estate. Because all the unified credit used during lifetime to eliminate taxes on the gift is restored and any tax actually paid can be used as a dollar-for-dollar credit against the estate tax, in essence you have "prepaid" your estate tax. You practically can't lose.

- Through a GRAT or GRUT you can leverage the unified credit. Compared to an outright gift, a GRAT uses up less of your unified credit. Stated another way, dollar for dollar, you can give more using the unified credit through a GRAT than through an outright gift. Since the GRAT typically will reduce the out-of-pocket cost to zero (or very close to zero), it is also psychologically superior to an outright gift (not to mention the fact that the pain of divestiture is eased by the ability to retain the annuity).

Q. What are the costs or downsides of a GRAT or GRUT?

A. As we've noted many times throughout this book, you should expect costs and downsides with every estate planning tool or technique no matter how exciting it is. GRATs and GRUTs are no exception. Here are some of the major ones:

- You will encounter set-up and administration costs. As is the case with most estate planing tools and techniques, there are out-of-pocket costs involved in GRATs and GRUTs. These include lawyer fees, appraisal fees, property titling costs (you have to make the trust the legal owner of the assets), accounting charges, and trustee's fees.

- You will experience a loss of control. You must be willing to give up the right to shift the income to someone else during the term of the trust. However, this income is roughly equivalent to what you would have had if you had done nothing. Furthermore, some of the income you receive can be given away or consumed. A more important cost is that you have also given up the right to dispose of the principal. Should you no longer care for a named beneficiary or you don't want that beneficiary to receive as much as you had originally intended, there is no way once the trust is funded to change the amount or proportion.

- You will also experience a loss of opportunity. Since both the GRAT and the GRUT are irrevocable trusts, once assets are placed into the trust, you are precluded from taking other planning measures with the property in the trust.

- There is the potential estate tax inclusion. If you die during the term of the trust, your executor may be liable for the tax on the includible assets. But your estate may not have the cash to pay this tax.

  The solution is for your planner to make a reasonable projection of your actual life expectancy, based on mortality tables, your family and personal health history, and your habits, occupation, and avocations. Then you can create one or more trusts that can be expected to expire before you do.

  Life insurance owned by a third-party beneficiary such as an irrevocable trust can be used to ensure death tax savings. You can also include a provision that returns all the assets in the trust to your estate rather than to the specified beneficiaries if you die during the term of the trust. This *reversion* to the your estate, and from there to your spouse through your will or through a marital deduction trust, can alleviate or eliminate the problem if it is set up so the marital deduction will eliminate the federal estate tax on the includible assets.

- Assets in the trusts may generate insufficient income. To produce the high annuity amounts required to reduce the value of the remainder interest to within unified credit protection limits, you must use assets that generate commensurably high income for the term of the trust. Most publicly held stocks are an inappropriate investment for a GRAT or GRUT because of their relatively low current yield. Few closely held stocks pay dividends high enough. S corporation stock may be an appropriate trust asset if it can be readily and cost effectively valued and if it produces income equal to or above the required annuity payment. A limited partnership or limited liability company that generates considerable income might be an even better choice.

To the extent that the investment doesn't pay income equal to or exceeding the annuity payout required, principal will have to be sold to make the required annuity payouts. If this is necessary, your remainderman (your child or other beneficiary) never receives wealth that you intended to shift to that person, and you never met your desired estate-tax-savings objectives.

If dividend income is insufficient to make the required payments, to whom can the GRAT or GRUT sell the closely held stock to raise the cash? At what price could a minority interest be sold? What would the (psychological and other) cost be—to shareholders and to the corporation itself—if the GRAT or GRUT sells the stock to someone outside the family unit? What if the buyer is a family member who, as a consequence of purchasing stock from the trust, now becomes a controlling shareholder?

Remember that a GRUT has the potential to pay you a higher income if and when trust assets rise in value. But this is not necessarily an estate-tax-planning advantage if your major goal is the "intentional defunding" of your estate. This is why many planners say that GRUTs are ineffective estate planning tools. As the GRUT grows in value, it pays more back to the party who was trying to get rid of it. On the other hand, if the value of trust assets falls, the size of the annuity payments paid to you drops as the value of the trust drops. This is not necessarily a disadvantage since the object is to reduce the size of your estate. Because of the uncertainty of asset value and annuity payments from a GRUT, most planners are currently recommending a GRAT over a GRUT because it is more likely in more cases to accomplish its wealth-shifting objectives.

- Trust assets may experience insufficient growth. If the combined earnings and appreciation are less than the federal discount (Section 7520) rate assumed in computing a GRAT or GRUT, any anticipated estate tax savings will be lost and reverse leveraging will occur.

- You may have valuation problems. Ideally, the best assets to place into a GRAT or GRUT are those that produce unusually high income, have a strong potential for significant growth, and are easily and inexpensively valued. Although there is now inexpensive business valuation software that you can use, in most cases, you will also need independent professional appraisals. Furthermore, there is also a high probability that the IRS will audit any valuation dealing with a closely held business. The GRUT, which must be revalued annually, leads to much more cost and aggravation than the GRAT, which needs to be valued only at inception.

Q. What are the income tax implications of a GRAT or GRUT?

A. Since you retain the right to trust income during the term specified in the trust, you will be taxed on all accounting income of the trust. You are not taxed on capital gains since they are added to the principal and will eventually go to your remainderman beneficiary. Once the term expires, the trust's remainderman beneficiary will be taxed on trust income, assuming it is paid out. Otherwise, it will be taxable to the trust itself.

You may be surprised to find that your estate planning team will try to have as much tax as possible taxable to you rather than to the trust itself or its beneficiary. Although this sounds counter-intuitive, think of each tax payment you make as a way to help your children or other beneficiary without the need for you to pay gift tax. Remember, the gift and estate tax rates start at 37 percent and proceed to 55 percent quite rapidly. These are much higher rates than the rates imposed on income taxes. This is why planners often try to have the grantor pay as much income tax as possible in order to create what is in essence a gift-tax-free gift from the grantor to the beneficiaries.

Q. What are the gift tax implications of transferring assets to a GRAT or GRUT?

A. The gift to the remainderman at the date the trust is funded (the date you put assets into the trust) is a gift of a future interest. This means it will not qualify for the annual gift tax exclusion. The value of the gift—the amount gifted—is found by subtracting the amount the grantor retains from the whole. If you live beyond the specified term, when the property is paid over or held in trust for the remaindermen beneficiaries, there will be no second gift tax since the gift was complete when you set up the trust and contributed cash or other assets to it.

Q. What are the tax implications if I want to buy back an asset held by my GRAT or GRUT?

A. If you have the right to remove and replace trust assets with other assets of equal value, the trust will be considered—for income tax purposes only—a *grantor trust*. This means you will be treated as the owner of each item of trust income, deduction, or credit. The implication, assuming you are treated as owner of the entire trust, is that the sale to you of trust assets in return for cash or other assets of equal value is not treated as a sale of trust assets for income tax purposes. (It's as if you "sold" something to yourself.) The trust, therefore, will not recognize gain on the sale of a trust asset to you. Nor will you have to report taxable income on the transaction.

Q. What problems, if any, do I face if I transfer property subject to a loan to my GRAT or GRUT?

A. In most cases, we advise against using mortgaged property as a gift to a GRAT or GRUT. Cash flow used by the trust to satisfy a loan against the property could be considered use of trust income for your benefit. Although this is not a major problem per se (since you expect to be taxed on trust income), if and when you make payments on the loan, the IRS could consider such payments as additions to the trust—an action impermissible in a GRAT but acceptable in a GRUT. In the case of a GRAT, therefore, you will have violated the trust requirements—with potentially disastrous gift tax consequences. The IRS could hold that the entire amount you put into the trust is a taxable gift.

Perhaps an even more serious problem is that additional payments of the mortgage may be viewed as taxable gifts. If the value of the original taxable gift is based on the net value of the property (that is, gross value less encumbrances), the IRS may treat each mortgage payment you make as an additional non-excludable gift.

Q. Are there special problems if I want my grandchild to receive property I place in my GRAT or GRUT?

A. The answer depends on the value of the property at the time your grandchild receives it. If the remainder person (the beneficiary who receives the principal of the trust when it ends) is a grandchild, the federal generation-skipping transfer tax (GSTT)— at the confiscatory level of 55 percent on every dollar (in excess of the $1,000,000 GST exemption) comes into play.

Does the GSTT apply when you set up a GRAT or GRUT and its assets appreciate and are later paid to a grandchild? The answer is that the transfer is deemed to be made for generation-skipping transfer tax purposes when there is an actual GSTT transfer during your lifetime or at your death.

For instance, say you transfer $1,000,000 to a GRAT. You retain an annuity of $70,000 a year for 10 years with the remainder to go to your grandchildren. If the value of the assets at the time they are transferred to your grandchildren is under $1,000,000 and you haven't used your generation-skipping transfer tax exemption, there probably will not be any such tax to pay. But assume the assets in the trust have grown to $3,000,000. You can apply your $1,000,000 GSTT exemption against the $3,000,000. $2,000,000 will be taxable. That means your grandchild will lose—and the IRS will gain—55 cents on every dollar.

Q. What is a "rolling GRAT"?

A. Rolling GRATs are short-term GRATs. The idea is that, rather than increasing the risk of the grantor's dying during the term of the GRAT, shortening the term decreases estate tax risk. This technique works best when you expect that the growth (aside from any income) in the funding property will significantly outpace the federal discount (Section 7520) rate during the short term specified. Although the taxable gift is higher for short-term GRATs (because the donee doesn't have to wait as long to get the assets), the amount that can be shifted to a child or other donee at relatively low risk and little cost is significant.

The younger you are, the more wealth you can shift. (The annuity is worth more for younger than older people because of the requirement that mortality must be considered even in a term-certain GRAT.) If you then take the annuity you receive and continue to create a series of short-term GRATs, the probability of death during the term is reduced. Therefore the value of the retained interest increases, lowering the value and therefore the tax impact of the taxable gift.

THE USE OF TRUSTS IN MEDICAID PLANNING

Chapter 23 explains:

- What Medicaid is

- What a Medicaid qualifying trust is meant to accomplish

- Trusts with some exemption from Medicaid

- How a "special needs" trust can meet the needs of a beneficiary and not disqualify the recipient from receiving Medicaid

- What a "discretionary" trust is and why it may provide for a beneficiary and yet not disqualify that person from Medicaid or SSI eligibility

- The possible dangers of ill-informed or overly-aggressive Medicaid planning.

Q. What is Medicaid?

A. Medicaid is a joint federal and state program of medical assistance to eligible needy persons. Medical services are provided by participating providers and reimbursed according to state formulas. People who are over age 65, blind, disabled or the parent of a dependent child, U.S. citizens, permanent resident-aliens, state residents, and financially needy are entitled to Medicaid.

Although Medicaid is administered by the states, and states have some flexibility in establishing rules for Medicaid eligibility, most of the important rules are established by federal, or the states are limited by federal law. For example, states *may* (but need not) deny eligibility for up to 36 months for any uncompensated transfer of assets. In fact, almost all states impose the strictest requirements allowed by federal law, and will deny eligibility during the period lasting 36 months after assets have been given away or transferred. For trusts, the period of ineligibility can be 60 months.

Q. What is a "Medicaid qualifying trust"?

A. A "Medicaid qualifying trust" is a trust or similar legal device established by an individual, or the spouse of an individual, under which the individual may be the beneficiary of all or a part of payments from the trust. A distribution of such payments is determined by one or more trustees who are permitted to exercise discretion regarding payments to the individual. Ironically, if a trust is considered to be a Medicaid qualifying trust, the amount distributable to the Medicaid applicant or recipient is considered an available asset for Medicaid purposes and can *disqualify* the trust beneficiary from eligibility for Medicaid.

"Medicaid qualifying trust" is therefore a misnomer and is not desirable from the standpoint of the trust beneficiary because the amount distributed to him or her will probably disqualify the trust beneficiary from eligibility for Medicaid.

Any uncompensated transfers of assets to a trust for a person who is institutionalized will affect his or her eligibility for Medicaid if the trust was established within 60 months of that person's eligibility for Medicaid. The exact effect of this provision on the establishment of irrevocable trusts to enable Medicaid recipients to continue Medicaid eligibility is not clear even to practitioners experienced in Medicaid planning. That is why we do not advise establishing such a trust in most instances, and certainly not without the express recommendation of, and preparation of the trust document by a highly qualified specialist in the area of Medicaid planning. In most cases we find that you can't have your cake and eat it too. You can't put your assets in a trust, retain rights to the income and principal of the trust, and still qualify for Medicaid.

Q. Are there trusts that can be exempt for Medicaid purposes?

A. As indicated in the chapter on handicapped children (see chapter 19), under the current federal and state regulations governing these types of trusts, certain types of trusts can be exempt for Medicaid purposes. However, the federal and state regulations governing these types of trusts are constantly changing and subject to different interpretation by state courts. A review of each individual situation with a knowledgeable lawyer, therefore, is an absolute must before the preparation of any of the following trusts:

- trusts with *payback* language. Federal law dealing with trusts for disabled individuals under age 65 indicates that if a trust is established for that individual's benefit by a "parent, grandparent, legal guardian of the individual, or a court," the assets will be exempt for Medicaid purposes only if the trust specifically provides that upon the beneficiary's death, the balance in the trust must be used to reimburse the state for medical assistance paid on behalf of the beneficiary. Through the use of this payback provision, all of the trust assets would be available for the beneficiary's benefit, but they could eventually be lost to the other members of the grantor's or beneficiary's family. (Life insurance owned by and payable to a separate trust for the other children could make up for the funds passing to the state).

- pooled trusts. Trust assets can be exempt if the trust is established and managed by a nonprofit association and it requires that upon the death of the handicapped person, the funds must remain in the pooled trust for the benefit of other trust beneficiaries or be applied to repay the state under the payback provisions discussed above.

- trusts composed of pension and social security benefits. There is also an exemption for trusts composed solely of pension, social security and other income payable to a handicapped person, providing that the state is entitled to reimbursement at the beneficiary's death.

- trusts established by third persons. Recent changes in the law seem to indicate that if an individual establishes a trust for himself or herself—a *self-settled trust*—the grantor/beneficiary will be disqualified from eligibility for Medicaid. However, when a trust is set up by a third party who is someone other than the Medicaid applicant or his or her spouse (e.g. a child or grandchild), the rules are more liberal. It may be possible to establish a *special needs trust*, a *discretionary trust*, or a combination of them to provide the necessary funds for the proposed Medicaid recipient's welfare and not disqualify him or her from receiving Medicaid or SSI (supplemental security income). This is an area in which decisions seem to vary significantly from state to state, so you will need to consult a knowledgeable lawyer in your state if you are concerned about Medicaid eligibility for your beneficiaries.

Q. How can a special needs trust meet the needs of a beneficiary and not disqualify him or her from receiving Medicaid?

A. A *special needs* trust established under the will of a parent for a child who is eligible for Medicaid might read:

"My trustee's discretion as to the need, propriety or amount of distributions to or for the use and benefit of my beneficiary shall be limited solely to providing only those comforts and luxuries not otherwise provided by the institution in which such child is living, or from other sources. It is my intention that the assets of this trust be used solely to supplement, and not replace, any benefits for which my beneficiary may be eligible under any private or governmental program, and I direct that my trustee shall not exercise its discretion to distribute or apply any funds for the payment of services that would otherwise be borne by any publicly or privately funded program or institution."

An example of the type of expenditures indicated by the trust language above is giving the beneficiary spending money for such small luxury items as toys, candy, shaving cream, and perfume. Because the special needs trust is designed so that the funds are not considered "available" to the beneficiary, the beneficiary is not disqualified from eligibility for SSI and Medicaid.

Q. How can a discretionary trust provide for a beneficiary and not disqualify him or her from eligibility for Medicaid or SSI?

A. Under the terms of a *discretionary trust,* the trustee is not required to make any payments or distributions on behalf of the beneficiary. A discretionary trust provides that distributions to or on behalf of the beneficiary are at the trustee's sole and unlimited discretion. The purpose of a discretionary trust is to give the trustee flexibility to meet the beneficiary's needs but, at the same time, to maintain the beneficiary's eligibility for benefits. Because the beneficiary of a discretionary trust has no legal entitlement to trust assets, a number of states have held that the beneficiary is still entitled to receive governmental benefits since it is the trustee, and not the beneficiary, who has the absolute discretion to distribute funds to meet the beneficiary's needs.

Through the use of *sprinkling provisions*, a discretionary trust can also provide for distributions to other beneficiaries in addition to the Medicaid recipient. Trust provisions can give the independent trustee the power to pay the income and principal of the trust to or for the use of one or more persons whom the trustee may select out of a class of persons, one of whom is the Medicaid recipient. The trust can further provide that if a beneficiary is institutionalized:

"My trustee's discretion as to the need, propriety or amount of distributions to or for the use and benefit of my beneficiary shall be limited solely to providing only those comforts and luxuries not otherwise provided by the institution in which such child is living, or from other sources. It is my intention that the assets of this trust be used solely to supplement, and not replace, any benefits for which my beneficiary may be eligible under any private or governmental program, and I direct that my trustee shall not exercise its discretion to distribute or apply any funds for the payment of services that would otherwise be borne by any publicly or privately funded program or institution."

Under this arrangement, the trustee would have even stronger justification to withhold distributions to or on behalf of the Medicaid recipient because of the trustee's fiduciary duty to consider the needs of the other beneficiaries. (See chapter 19, "Trusts for Handicapped Children.")

A discretionary trust established by a third person (someone who is neither a beneficiary nor trustee), which gives an independent trustee (or trustees) the right to make trust distributions as described above is probably the best method to preserve Medicaid and SSI benefits while providing for the beneficiary's needs.

Q. Are there any criminal penalties for trying to become eligible for Medicaid by giving away assets?

A. Yes. Under a new provision of federal law, added by the Health Insurance Portability and Accountability Act of 1996, anyone who "knowingly and willingly" disposes of assets in order to qualify for Medicaid can be fined up to $10,000 and imprisoned for up to one year.

What's even worse is that most lawyers who have studied the new law don't really understand how to tell what is—or is not—a violation of the law. The law refers to any transfer of assets which "results in the imposition of a period of ineligibility" for assistance. Most lawyers aren't sure if that means that a crime occurs only if you are foolish enough to file an application for benefits within the 36 month ineligibility period, or whether all transfers that result in eligibility are criminal, even if you wait the 36 months before applying for benefits.

Some lawyers believe that the criminal sanctions are only aimed at fraudulent conveyances. But because of the uncertainty in the law, you do not want to transfer assets in order to qualify for Medicaid without careful thought and sound legal advice. An ill-advised or overly-aggressive gift strategy could have criminal consequences.

TRUSTS FOR DISABILITY AND OLD AGE

Chapter 24 explains:

• Estate planning problems faced by senior citizens

• Impact of failure to plan for disability

• Options to provide security for older persons, including jointly held property, durable powers of attorney, standby trusts, self-trusted revocable living trust, and revocable living trusts with other trustees

• Problems in establishing a trust

• How the revocable living trust can provide for those you love after your death

---

Q. I've got my future all mapped out. My retirement looks comfortable, and my will is made. Why do I need any additional estate planning?

A. There are three things that an elderly person wants from his or her estate plan—security, security and security. If your own estate plan will give you personal security, enable you to have a comfortable retirement, and provide for any contingencies that might arise, then you have a good plan. If it doesn't accomplish all of the above, then this chapter should be especially valuable to you.

Let's take a look at an example. Could this happen to you? Sally is a retired school teacher. She worked for 35 years for the school system, did an excellent job, and the district rewarded her with a retirement income sufficient to enable her to maintain her pleasant lifestyle without having to cut corners or do without. Sally's husband died 10 years ago; they had no children. Her closest relatives are two nephews, both of whom live 3,000 miles away from Sally. Practically all of her close friends have moved away, and there is really no one nearby with whom Sally had a close personal relationship. Her estate planning consists of a will prepared by the law firm that represents the school district. That will leaves all of her assets to her two nephews in California, naming them co-executors.

In addition to Sally's pension, she has managed to accumulate $300,000, which she has conservatively invested in certificates of deposit. She has a savings and checking account at a local bank with which she has been doing business for the past 30 years.

Fortunately, when Sally retired, she still enjoyed good health, and planned to continue her practice of taking one big trip annually. One year, while traveling in Hawaii, she was hiking along a trail to get a close-up look at a volcano, and she tripped, receiving a severe head injury and a fractured hip. The tour director made certain Sally was properly hospitalized, but she had never told him whom to call in case she was injured. Sally was eligible for Medicare, and had her social security and Medicare card in her pocket, but there was no information in any of her belongings about anyone to contact in the event of an accident or illness. Furthermore, Sally's memory was seriously impaired, and she could not communicate well with her doctors. The hospital knew of no one to contact about Sally's condition or how to get money over and above her Medicare benefits to pay for Sally's treatment.

Unfortunately, since Sally had failed to take advantage of the various options available to her to plan for her own future security, she had unknowingly turned over the management of her affairs to the court system.

Q. What happens if I fail to plan—guardianship proceedings?

A. Sally's situation is an example of what can happen if you fail to plan. Since Sally didn't plan for her own future, it is now in the hands of the court system. Because she could not manage her own financial affairs, someone had to be formally appointed to handle them for her benefit.

The exact nature of the proceedings varies from state to state and sometimes from county to county, and even the title of the person or institution chosen to manage someone's affairs— sometimes called a "guardian," "conservator," or in some cases, "committee"—will differ depending on the state in which the legal proceeding is instituted. However, it is almost always a proceeding to be avoided if possible. The effect of appointing a guardian for a person who is not competent to handle his or her

Trusts/Leimberg Associates Books: 610-527-5216

own affairs is to transfer all power over the incompetent individual's life to a guardian who is appointed by a judge who may never have seen either you or your guardian before.

Although the procedure varies from state to state, the following is a general outline of what takes place when a guardian is appointed for an individual.

First, it is necessary for someone to bring the matter before the appropriate court. This is usually done by a close family member filing a petition with the court that has jurisdiction (the state in which the person lives or now resides). This can be called the probate court, orphans' court, or surrogate's court. Questions can arise over who has the authority to prepare the petition if no close relatives are available or in which court the petition should be filed. (For instance, should it be Pennsylvania where Sally was a permanent resident, or Hawaii where she is presently hospitalized? If it should be Pennsylvania, how does Sally get back to Pennsylvania for the hearing?)

Since the nature of the guardianship proceeding is—at least temporarily—to declare Sally incompetent and deprive her of her legal rights, she must be given the right to have her own counsel. Sally's physical and mental condition must be evaluated so that medical testimony can be presented and the court can be absolutely certain that Sally is not competent to handle her own affairs. A copy of the petition, with notice of the date of the proposed hearing, must be served upon and explained (to the greatest degree possible) to Sally. Notice must also be given to all other interested parties and relatives (her nephews) and to the institution in which Sally is currently residing. Usually, Sally must be physically present in the courtroom, unless the court is satisfied by medical testimony (or other proof) that her welfare would not be promoted by having her attend the hearing.

Assuming all of the above problems can be overcome and the guardianship proceeding takes place, the court must then decide who should be appointed as guardian for Sally. Her only relatives—her nephews—certainly do not seem to be appropriate, so the court has a very serious decision to make. The court might be allowed to appoint as guardian any qualified individual, a corporate fiduciary, a nonprofit corporation, a guardianship support agency, or a county agency. A family relationship might be preferable, or it might be a disqualification if the proposed guardian is an heir of the incompetent person and so might have a financial interest that is adverse to the incompetent person. A court may give preference to a nominee of the incapacitated person. In Sally's case, the ultimate choice will probably depend solely on the hearing judge's discretion.

Once Sally has been declared legally incompetent and a guardian appointed for her, she can lose her right to participate in and manage her own affairs—even to exercise her legal and civil political rights and privileges. Although there are circumstances in which the court will appoint a temporary or emergency guardian to serve only in a limited capacity for a limited amount of time, if the disabled individual's condition continues, the guardianship will be permanent—with the very serious consequences we just indicated above. While the purpose of the guardianship proceeding is to establish a system to meet the essential requirements for an incapacitated person's physical health and safety, protect his or her rights, and manage the person's financial resources until he or she regains ability to do so, the proceeding should certainly be avoided if there is an alternative.

Q. What options are available to provide security to elderly persons?

A. There are several estate planning methods that Sally could have used to protect herself. The decision as to which option you should choose depends on many factors, including your present financial situation, whether you have a relative or close friend available to lend support, your present physical and mental condition, and your personal feelings about managing your financial affairs. If you have a close relative or a very good friend in whom you have complete confidence and trust, you may want to put a few of your assets in joint names with that individual.

You could also give that person a power of attorney, either a "general durable power of attorney" or a "springing power of attorney" (both of which will be discussed below). If you want maximum flexibility, you could establish a trust.

Let's look at each of these alternatives!

Placing property in joint names. If you have a very close and comfortable relationship with someone you trust implicitly, one option is to place some of your property in joint names with that person. But there are inherent disadvantages under this option, including the possibility that the other person can take your money or that your money can be subject to the claims of the other person's divorcing spouse or creditors. If the other person dies before you, you may have to pay death taxes on your own money. Most joint-ownership arrangements call for the jointly owned property to pass to the surviving co-owner at death. This form of ownership of a bank account is called *joint tenancy with right of survivorship*, and we recommend it only when no other options are available and, even then, only for a small amount of money so that funds can be immediately available for the joint owner to use for you in the event of an emergency or disability.

Powers of attorney. If there is someone in whom you have complete trust and confidence, you could give that person a *durable power of attorney,* authorizing him or her to do almost anything that you could do. However, powers of attorney are usually presumed to terminate when the principal (the person granting the power of attorney) becomes incompetent. To make a power of attorney *durable*, the writing must usually contain these words:

"This power of attorney shall not be affected by my subsequent disability or incapacity" (or words with similar meaning).

Some states (Pennsylvania, for example) have reversed the presumption that a power of attorney terminates upon disability and now consider a written power of attorney to be durable unless the writing says it is *not* durable. (We suggest your lawyer use the word "durable" so that regardless of what state you are living in, the power continues beyond your disability.)

Returning to our example, if Sally had a daughter, Sally could have given her daughter a general durable power of attorney. Upon receiving notice of her mother's accident, her daughter could have taken the power of attorney to her mother's bank and then been able to use Sally's funds for Sally's care until she was capable of acting for herself again.

Most durable powers of attorney are *general* powers, so that the person you name has permission to perform just about any legal act that you could otherwise do for yourself. (If the power is *limited* or *special*, the person you name has permission to perform only the acts you describe in the power of attorney.) You can make your power of attorney as broad or as limited as you desire, so it is essential that it be prepared by an lawyer experienced in estate planning. A power of attorney can give your *attorney-in-fact* (the person to whom you give the power) rights as varied as withdrawing money from your checking account, selling securities, investing in new securities, entering into your safe deposit box, selling or renting real estate, instituting or defending lawsuits on your behalf, filing tax returns, making gifts on your behalf, authorizing your admission to a medical, nursing, residential or similar facility, and nominating someone to act as guardian of your estate.

A general durable power of attorney takes effect immediately upon your signing the power of attorney, and you can revoke it at any time. If you decide to revoke a power of attorney, you should give written notice to the person to whom you gave the power, as well as to any financial institutions which had received a copy of the power or had engaged in transactions with your attorney-in-fact.

Springing power of attorney. If you would like to give someone a power of attorney to act for you, and you don't want it to begin immediately but only upon your disability or inability to act for yourself, then you should consider a *springing power of attorney*. A springing power of attorney is available in most states and it can contain any of the provisions that could be included in a general power of attorney, except that it will spring into being and become effective only *after* your disability or incapacity.

How will a bank or other institution know you are disabled? In most states, you can specify in the springing power of attorney that you will be considered to be disabled if a physician (or two physicians) signs a written certification that the physician has examined you and that you are incapacitated mentally or physically and therefore incapable of attending to your business and personal affairs. The physician's certification can be attached to the springing power of attorney and presented to banks or other institutions who might need evidence that the springing power of attorney is effective.

(Many lawyers do not recommend springing powers of attorney because of the increased chances for a dispute with a bank or other financial institution over whether or not you are disabled and whether the power is effective. Their reasoning is that the purpose of a power of attorney is to eliminate delays and disputes, and anything that increases the chances of a delay or a dispute should be avoided. Besides, if you can't trust your attorney-in-fact not to act unless it is necessary, perhaps you shouldn't appoint that person.)

Living trust. The option that will give you the most security and flexibility is a living trust. There are several different types of trusts from which to choose. Your choice will depend on your present physical and mental health, your current financial condition, the availability of close friends or relatives upon whom you can rely, and your personal desires as to how much you want to remain in control of your financial affairs. The following are examples of the different types of trusts from which you can choose:

- *standby living trust.* If you'd like to remain in complete control of your financial affairs, but you want to have a trust available to take over and manage your assets if you are no longer be in a position to manage them yourself, you should consider setting up a standby trust. Here's how a standby trust works:

  Your lawyer prepares a trust document naming a trustee (a bank or trust company, for example) to take over the management of your affairs in the event of your disability. You put a minimum amount of money in the trust (perhaps $100) while you continue to manage the remainder of your assets yourself. You also sign a durable power of attorney that authorizes your trustee, as your attorney-in-fact, to transfer your assets into the trust in the event of your disability. When your disability ends, you can amend or revoke the trust and resume control of the management of your affairs.

  Your power of attorney (and trust) can be a "springing" power if you specify that the trustee is to transfer your assets to your trust only if two physicians certify that you are no longer able to manage your own affairs. Your trust can also provide for the standby trustee to step in and manage your affairs at your personal request. In other words, at such time as you feel that you can no longer (or do not wish to) handle your own affairs, you can activate your trust by written notice to the trustee.

  You should certainly contact the trustee prior to establishing a standby trust, and you should make sure that the trustee is regularly updated on your asset holdings in order to be in a position to step in and take over the management of your affairs if it becomes necessary. In addition to giving the standby trustee a list of your assets, you should establish a line of communication so that the trustee will be immediately aware of any changes in your health or in any circumstances that would warrant taking over for you. If there are no qualified individuals available to serve as trustee (as in Sally's case), a bank with trust powers or a trust company is a good choice to act as your standby trustee.

If Sally had had a standby trust or any trust (or even a power of attorney), she could have given the trustee (or her attorney in fact) information about her trip and arranged a way for them to communicate with each other. The trustee would have therefore been aware of Sally's accident, could have taken immediate steps to make sure that Sally was being properly cared for, and could have made her funds available for her use.

- *self-trusteed revocable living trust.* Instead of waiting for your disability to fund your trust, you can establish a revocable living trust for yourself that will become effective immediately. If you wish to maintain complete control of your assets, you can name yourself as the sole trustee of your revocable living trust. You will therefore be the grantor (the person establishing the trust), the initial trustee of the trust, and the current trust beneficiary. (For example, Sally's trust could be titled "Sally Jones, Trustee of the Sally Jones Trust, dated January 2, 1998, for the benefit of Sally Jones.) You can transfer assets to the trust by retitling the assets and listing them all on a schedule attached to your original trust document. Your trust can stipulate that if you become disabled—as certified by two physicians—the XYZ Bank, which you have named as successor trustee in your trust, will take over the management and control of the trust for your benefit. Because the trust is revocable and you retain the right to amend the trust at any time, you can always revoke the trust or change the trustee if you wish.

  By establishing the revocable living trust immediately, you will have organized all of your assets under the "umbrella" of your trust document. You will continue to pay your income taxes because you set up the trust for your benefit and all income will be paid to you; you can also provide for the disposition of your assets following your death. If all of your assets are in your trust at your death, they will be distributed to your beneficiaries in the way that you have selected through your trust, and the assets will completely avoid your state's probate process.

- *revocable living trust with separate trustee.* If you no longer want the responsibility of managing and investing your assets, you can transfer your property to a revocable living trust under which someone else—an individual, several individuals, or a corporate trustee—will act as trustee for you. If you wish, you can name yourself as a co-trustee.

Under this arrangement, the responsibility for the day-to-day management of your financial affairs shifts to your trustee. By choosing a professional trustee—such as a bank with trust powers or a trust company—you can ensure professional money management and continuity (individuals die, banks don't). You can also provide for the transfer of funds to your beneficiaries at your death. For example, if Sally had wanted the money she had left to her nephews to be held in trust for them until they were 30 or 35 years old, a bank or trust company might have been a better choice to act as trustee than one of Sally's equally elderly friends.

Q. What are the problems in establishing a trust?

A. There are basically three problems involved in setting up a trust. Two pertain to cost, and one to the selection of trustee, as follows:

- *initial cost.* The initial cost of setting up a trust can be anywhere from $1,000 to $2,500 (or even more) depending on the tax questions involved and the complexity of your personal situation. You should definitely use a qualified lawyer who can tailor your trust to meet your individual needs.

- *continuing expenses.* If you are the sole trustee of the trust, there are obviously no trustee fees. But a bank or trust company will properly require a fee to serve as trustee and may charge a fee even for serving as a "standby" trustee while you are still managing your own affairs. (Banks and trust companies usually having a minimum fee schedule, which you should demand to see and approve before agreeing to use that institution as your trustee.)

- *trustee problems.* There can be unforeseen problems that may prevent the individual (or individuals) you name from serving as your trustee. So always list at least two backup trustees in your trust instrument and specify how and when the successor trustees will begin to act as trustees.

There are different problems when a bank or trust company is trustee. Since trust assets are segregated from the bank's own assets, they should not be affected by a bank's financial condition. But there is still no guarantee of investment performance. Furthermore, your relationship with an institution is only as good as your relationship to the people who work at that institution with whom you come in contact. For these reasons, we recommend that when you select a corporate fiduciary (a bank or trust company) as trustee of a revocable trust, you retain the right to change the trustee for any reason. If a trust is to continue long after your death, you might want to give an individual co-trustee, the adult beneficiaries of the trust, or some other designated person or persons the right to change the corporate trustee to another corporate trustee of comparable size and investment experience.

Q. How can my revocable living trust provide for the people that I care about after my death?

A. After making provisions for yourself or your family or friends during your lifetime, your trust is an excellent and flexible vehicle for making provisions for those persons or institutions whom you wish to benefit following your death. If Sally has a trust, for example, it might provide that her trustee would hold 50 percent of the balance in Sally's trust for each of her nephews after her death. Her nephews could receive the entire income from their share of the trust each year, and the principal could be used for their education, to purchase a new home, or to enter into a new business venture. They could have the right to withdraw one third of the principal at age 25, an additional third at age 30, and the right to terminate the entire trust at age 35. As long as the trust remained in force for them, the assets in the trust could be protected from their creditors or their spouses. The nephews could also be given the option of continuing the trust past age 35 if they so desire.

Sally could have also provided for the money to be held in trust during her nephews' entire lives, and then paid to her nephews' children following their deaths. She could have further provided that a portion of her trust would be used to establish a scholarship at the university from which she graduated or used for other charitable purposes of Sally's choosing.

As we have emphasized throughout this book, the purposes for which a trust can be established are limited only by the needs and imagination of the grantor of the trust, as implemented by the lawyer preparing the trust document.

Charitable Remainder Trust

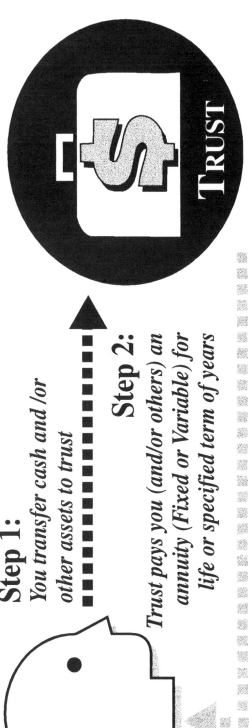

TRUST

Step 1:
You transfer cash and /or other assets to trust

Step 2:
Trust pays you (and/or others) an annuity (Fixed or Variable) for life or specified term of years

Step 3:
At death of non-charitable beneficiaries or end of term, assets pass to Charity

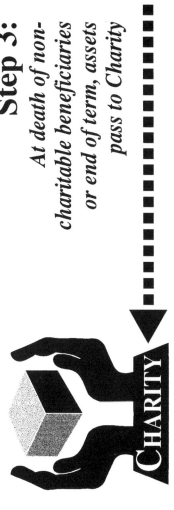

CHARITY

Charitable Remainder Trust
Coupled with Wealth Replacement Trust

TRUST

Step 1:
You transfer cash and/or other assets to trust

Step 2:
Trust pays you (and/or others) an annuity (Fixed or Variable) for life or specified term of years

Step 3:
At death of non-charitable beneficiaries or end of term, assets pass to Charity

CHARITY

Irrevocable Life Insurance Policy

Assets go to your beneficiaries to replace wealth passing to charity

Charitable Lead Trust

Step 1:
You transfer cash/other assets to trust

TRUST

Step 2:
Trust pays annuity for X years to the charity of your choice

CHARITY

Step 3:
Assets left to to beneficiaries of your choice

CHARITABLE GIFTS AND PRIVATE FOUNDATIONS

Chapter 25 explains:

- The advantages of making gifts to charity

- The tax consequences of gifts to charity

- The limits on tax deductions for gifts to charity

- The limits on the type of property that can be given to charity

- How to use life insurance to benefit charity

- What a private foundation is

- The advantages of a private foundation over a direct gift to an existing charity

- The advantages of trusts as private foundations

- Some limitations on charitable contributions to private foundations

- Why business interests cannot be controlled through a private foundation

- Other restrictions that exist for private foundations

- The costs of creating and operating a private foundation

Q. In general terms, what are the advantages of making gifts to charity?

A. Giving cash or other property to charity can accomplish many personal and financial planning objectives simultaneously. Among the many reasons are that charitable gifts can:

- enrich the lives of others

- increase your income tax deductions and lower your tax

- assist the charity of your choice (rather than some politician's)

- substantially reduce death taxes and probate expenses in your estate

- create a lasting tribute to you or a selected family member

Q. What are the tax implications of gifts to charity?

A. Congress has long recognized the need for public support of charities and religious organizations and has given favorable tax treatment to gifts to organizations that the Internal Revenue Service determines to be qualified charities, as follows:

- Lifetime gifts to qualified charities are completely free of federal gift tax—without limit.

- Testamentary gifts are deductible—without limit—in computing the federal estate tax. (Most states also allow an unlimited charitable deduction at death.)

- Gifts of money and other property, within specified limitations (discussed below), are tax deductible for federal income tax purposes.

Q. What the limits on how much I can deduct for gifts to charity?

A. There are no gift tax or estate tax limits on how much you can give to charity. If you decide to give your entire estate to charity, the entire estate will qualify for the federal gift tax or estate tax charitable deduction, and will not be subject to federal gift tax or estate tax. However, there are limits on how much you can deduct for federal income tax purposes.

- The general limit is that charitable deductions can not exceed 50 percent of "adjusted gross income" (or "AGI," which is gross income reduced by certain adjustments, such as IRA contributions and moving expenses, but before taking itemized deductions or personal exemptions). If you exceed this limit, the excess contribution can be carried forwarded and deducted the next year (but you cannot carry forward a deduction for more than 5 years).

- If the contribution is of tangible personal property (jewelry, furniture, works of art, books, rare coins, etc.)

that is unrelated to the functions of the charity (such as a gift of art to a college, or a gift of a rare book to an art museum), the deduction is limited to the cost basis of the property, not the fair market value of the property.

- If the contribution is of property which would have resulted in long-term capital gain if sold (other than tangible personal property unrelated to the functions of the charity), you are entitled to a deduction for the fair market value of the property, but your deduction is limited to 30 percent of AGI, not 50 percent of AGI. (You are still entitled to a 5 year carry-forward.) You also have the option of deducting your cost basis for the property, instead of the fair market value, and deducting up to 50 percent of AGI. (This option might be desirable if you made a large gift of property with a basis near fair market value.)

- If the contribution is of property that would have resulted in short-term capital gain or ordinary income if sold, the deduction is limited to your cost basis of the property, not the fair market value of the property.

- If the contribution is "for the use of" the charity and not "to" the charity (meaning that the charity gets the income from the contribution but not the contribution itself), the deduction is limited to 30 percent of AGI (with a possible carry-forward for 5 years). (This limitation really affects only charitable lead trusts, described in chapter 26 and life insurance premiums paid to the insurer rather than directly to the charity.)

There are also special limits (discussed below) on contributions to private foundations.

Several of these limitations were enacted to restrict the potential profit on charitable gifts of appreciated property. If you can claim a charitable deduction for gain that was never taxed, it may be better to give away the property than sell it. However, charities have lobbied for incentives for contributions, so Congress decided to limit charitable deductions to cost basis in some cases (so that the donor gets no benefit from the appreciation in the property) and to limit the charitable deduction to 30 percent of AGI in other cases (so that the donor gets a benefit from the untaxed appreciation, but not too much of a benefit in any one year). From 1986 to 1992, Congress tried another approach, which was to include the untaxed appreciation on charitable gifts in the donor's alternative minimum taxable income, so that the untaxed appreciation might result in some tax in some cases.

The rules regarding the deductibility of charitable contributions represent a rather complex political compromise between the needs of charities and the needs of the federal government for tax revenue. And it is a compromise that is being renegotiated all the time, which is why these rules change frequently and a knowledgeable tax advisor should be consulted before making a large charitable gift.

Q. What kind of property can I give to charity?

A. Most people think of gifts to charity as cash gifts, but you can also give property to charity. You can, for example:

- Give stocks, bonds, or real estate.

- Give tangible assets such as art, jewelry, antiques, or other collectibles.

- Give business inventory or crops.

The only limit on a cash gift to a church, school, hospital, community fund, or other public charity is that the deduction cannot exceed 50 percent of adjusted gross income (AGI), with carry-forwards of excess deductions for up to 5 years. The charitable deduction income tax rules will apply to these other types of property in the following ways:

- *gift of stocks, bonds, or real estate:* You are allowed a current income tax deduction of up to 30 percent of your adjusted gross income for a gift of appreciated securities or real estate. You can carry over any excess for up to 5 years. If you've held the asset for the requisite period of time to qualify the property as a long-term capital gain asset), your deduction will be based on the full fair market value of the gift. You can also elect to increase your current deduction from 30 percent to 50 percent of your adjusted gross income—if you are willing to reduce the amount of the deduction by the amount of appreciation.

  If the appreciated securities or real estate you contribute is considered "short term" or "mid-term", your deduction is limited to your *basis* (essentially, what you paid for the asset), rather than its fair market value. But you can take a deduction for up to 50 percent of your adjusted gross income and still carry over any excess deduction for up to 5 years.

- *gift of tangible assets:* If you make a charitable gift of a tangible asset such as art, jewelry, or antiques you have held for more than one year, your deduction depends on whether or not the use of the property by the charity is related to its charitable purposes or functions. A good example of a "use-related" gift is giving fine art photograph to an art museum to display to the public.

A property is "use unrelated" if the property is not used by the charity in its exempt function. For instance, if the same fine art Douglas Mellor photograph is given to the Philadelphia Museum of Art but the museum immediately sells it, the use is unrelated—even if the museum then used the proceeds of the sale to purchase additional fine art photographs or paintings. An even clearer example of a use-unrelated gift is giving the same Douglas Mellor fine art photograph to The American College in Bryn Mawr, Pennsylvania—a qualified public charity which almost always has a beautiful and interesting exhibition of art in its halls, but not an institution whose exempt purposes includes the display of fine art.

You are allowed a deduction for the full fair market value for your gift of use-related property. You can take that deduction in an amount up to 30 percent of your adjusted gross income and carry over any excess for up to 5 years.

If the property is not use-related, your deduction is limited to your basis (cost) in the property. But if this lower limit is imposed, you can currently deduct an amount up to 50 percent of your adjusted gross income. You may also carry over any excess (i.e. the amount not currently deductible) each year for up to 5 years.

When you make a gift of tangible personal property that does not qualify as "long-term" (for example, a recently purchased collectible stamp), your deduction—regardless of whether or not it is use related—is limited to your basis. The most you can deduct in any given year is 50 percent of your adjusted gross income, but you are allowed a 5-year carryover.

- *gift of business inventory or crops:* If you give property which, if sold, would have resulted in *ordinary income,* your deduction is limited to your cost basis of the property and cannot exceed 50 percent of your adjusted gross income—with a 5-year carryover of any excess. Examples of ordinary income property are a business owner's gift of inventory, a farmer's gift of wheat crops, or an artist's gift of a painting. (There are limited exceptions allowing larger deductions if a corporation makes a gift of inventory.)

Q. Which is better, lifetime gifts to charity or gifts by will?

A. For federal estate and gift tax purposes, it doesn't make any difference whether you make charitable gifts during your lifetime or at death. You may obtain a federal estate tax deduction for the entire fair market value of property you leave to charity in your will. There is no limit to the amount of this deduction. Conceivably, you can leave a charity $20,000,000 outright and pay no federal estate tax. In almost every state, you will also receive a charitable deduction for the same gift on your state inheritance tax return.

The advantage of lifetime gifts comes in the income tax deduction. By making gifts during your lifetime, instead of at death, you not only receive the honor and pleasure of seeing your gift used but also can get the advantage of the charitable income tax deduction and reduce your income taxes during your lifetime. This is a particular advantage of charitable remainder trusts, discussed in chapter 26, because you can get a charitable deduction for your gift to a trust even though you will receive distributions from the trust for the rest of your life. Through the combination of the charitable remainder trust and the charitable income tax deduction, you can actually have more income during your lifetime *after* making the charitable gift than you would have had *without* the charitable gift.

Q. What is a charitable bargain sale?

A. A charitable bargain sale is a sale of property to charity at less than its fair market value. When you make that kind of bargain sale, it is really part sale and part gift.

You are allowed a deduction for the difference between the fair market value of a long-term appreciated security or real estate you sell to a charity and its sales price. In essence, you are considered to have (1) sold part of the property and (2) made a gift of the other portion of the property. If you sell property worth $100,000 to a charity for $10,000, your charitable contribution is $90,000 ($100,000—$10,000).

Assume you bought the property for $10,000. That basis is allocated proportionately between the $90,000 gift portion and the $10,000 sale portion. Because you gave away nine tenths of the property, nine tenths of your basis must be allocated to that portion. Because you sold one tenth of the property, $1,000 (the remaining one tenth of your $10,000 basis) can be applied to reduce your gain on the sale. Your capital gain will therefore be $9,000 ($10,000 sale portion less $1,000 cost basis).

Note that a gift to charity of mortgaged property will be treated as a bargain sale. You will be considered to have sold the property for the amount of your mortgage.

Q. What is a charitable gift annuity?

A. A charitable gift annuity is something like a bargain sale to a charity, because it is partially a sale and partially a gift. However, unlike a bargain sale, in which the charity makes a single immediate payment in partial exchange for a property, in a charitable gift annuity the charity makes a promise to make a series of payments in the future. In exchange for a gift of cash or property, the charity agrees to pay an annuity to the donor.

The reasons for a charitable gift annuity are also similar to the reasons for a bargain sale to charity. A donor may wish to make a large gift of cash or give a valuable piece of property to charity and yet wish to obtain some money or some income in return. The charitable gift annuity allows the donor to make the gift to charity and yet retain an annuity that can never be outlived.

A charitable gift annuity may be an alternative to a charitable remainder trust, described in chapter 26.

Q. Are there ways to make gifts to charity through business organizations?

A. Yes. You can make charitable gifts through a partnership or limited liability company, or through a corporation.

- *gift through partnership or limited liability company:* You can take a deduction on your individual income tax return for gifts to charity that your partnership makes.

(No charitable deduction is allowed on the partnership return.) The same rules apply to a limited liability company that is treated like a partnership for federal income tax purposes.

- *gift through your corporation:* Your corporation can make a charitable gift and obtain a deduction up to 10 percent of its taxable income. Any excess may be carried over for up to 5 years. If your corporation uses an accrual basis of accounting, you can deduct the gift on this year's corporate tax return, even though the actual gift is not made until the following tax year if (1) payment is made within 2 and one-half months from the close of this tax year and (2) the gift is authorized by your board of directors.

Q. How can I use life insurance to benefit charity?

A. Life insurance is an excellent tool for making charitable gifts for many reasons:

- The death benefit is guaranteed as long as premiums are paid. This means that the charity will receive an amount that is fixed (or perhaps increasing) in value and not subject to the potential downside volatile market risks of securities.

- Life insurance provides an "amplified" gift that enables you to "purchase immortality on the installment plan." Through a relatively small annual cost (the premium), you can significantly benefit the charity of your choice. Moreover, you can make this sizable gift without impairing or diluting the control of a family business or other investments. Assets earmarked for your family can be kept intact. Think of the honor to your family of a $1,000,000 gift to your favorite charity—through the relatively low cost of life insurance premiums.

- Life insurance is a self-completing gift. If you live, cash values (which can be used currently by the charity for an emergency or opportunity) will grow constantly year after year. If you become disabled, the policy will remain in full force through the waiver-of-premium feature. This guarantees the ultimate death benefit to the charity as well, through the same cash values and dividend buildup that the policy would have earned if you had not become disabled. Even if you were to die after only one deposit, the charity is assured of your full gift.

- Your designated charity can receive life insurance death proceeds free of federal income and estate taxes, probate and administrative costs and delays, brokerage fees, or other transfer costs. Your charity therefore receives 100 cents on every dollar. Compare this prompt (and certain) payment with a gift to the same charity of the same amount under your will.

- Because of the contractual nature of the life insurance policy, large gifts to charity are not subject to attack by disgruntled heirs and arranged properly are virtually creditor-proof.

- You can make a substantial gift with no attending publicity. On the other hand, your amplified gift can bring you public honor and recognition if you desire.

You can apply your life insurance policy to the benefit of in a number of ways:

- Name a charity as the annual recipient of any dividends you receive from life insurance. As dividends are paid to the charity, you'll receive a current income tax deduction.

- Use dividends from an existing policy to purchase a new policy, and name the charity the owner and beneficiary of the new policy. You'll receive an income tax deduction for the premiums you've paid.

- Name a charity as contingent (backup) beneficiary or final beneficiary under a life insurance policy protecting your dependents.

- Name a charity as the beneficiary of life insurance you currently own or as beneficiary of a new life insurance policy. Although this will not give you a current income tax deduction, it will result in a federal estate tax deduction for the full amount of the proceeds payable to charity, regardless of how large the policy might be.

- Make an absolute assignment (gift) of a life insurance policy you currently own, or donate a new life insurance policy. This will give you a current income tax deduction. Your immediate deduction will be equal to the lower of (1) your cost (premiums paid less any dividends you've received) or (2) the value of the policy.

You'll also receive a deduction for amounts you pay to the charity in future years to help the charity pay premiums on the policy. Send your check directly to the charity, and have it pay the premiums. That way, you'll have proof of the date of your contribution and the amount of the gift, and you'll ensure yourself of receiving the largest possible deduction.

Note that neither deduction will be allowed unless you make the charity owner and beneficiary of the entire policy. You will lose the income tax deduction if you try to keep the cash values and name the charity as beneficiary, or if you give away the cash values but name a family member as beneficiary. You can also lose the charitable deduction for both the contribution of the policy and subsequent premium payments if the charity has no insurable interest.

- You can also use group term life insurance to meet your charitable objectives. By naming a charity as the (revocable) beneficiary of your group term life insurance for coverage over $50,000, not only can you make a significant gift to charity but you can also avoid any income tax on the economic benefit.

  For example, a 63-year-old executive with an average top tax bracket of 35 percent who had $140,000 of coverage would save $442.26 each year—35 percent of the $1,263.60 annual Table I cost (the amount reportable as income). The advantage of this technique was significantly enhanced by the introduction of higher group term rates for individuals over age 65 who receive group term insurance. You can save income taxes every year the charity is named as beneficiary. If you change your mind in a later year, you can change your beneficiary designation and name a new charity or even a personal beneficiary.

Q. Can I name a charity as the beneficiary of my retirement benefits or individual retirement account?

A. Yes, and that beneficiary designation can benefit your children or other non-charitable beneficiaries if you have both charitable and non-charitable beneficiaries for your estate. By paying your taxable retirement benefits to a charity (which is tax exempt and therefore pays no income tax on the benefits received), you can achieve your charitable goals and increase the non-taxable benefits for your non-charitable beneficiaries.

For example, suppose you have an individual retirement account (IRA) of $600,000 and other assets of $600,000. If you name your children as the beneficiaries of your IRA and leave the rest of your estate to charity, there will be no federal estate tax (because $600,000 is sheltered by the charitable deduction and the other $600,000 is sheltered by the federal estate tax unified credit). But your children will have to pay income tax on the IRA benefits received. Depending on their tax brackets and state income taxes, they could lose more than 40 percent of the IRA to income taxes, receiving only $360,000 net of taxes instead of $600,000.

However, if you reverse your estate plan and make the IRA payable to charity and the rest of your estate to your children, there will still be no federal estate tax but your children will now pay no income tax either, receiving the full $600,000 of other assets free of tax (and with a step-up in basis for any appreciated assets, so that there will be no taxable capital gains on the sale of any asset). The charity will receive the $600,000 of IRA benefits, but the charity is tax exempt and will pay no income tax, so the charity will also receive the full $600,000, for a net income tax saving of $240,000.

For similar reasons, it may be beneficial to name a charitable remainder trust as the beneficiary of your retirement benefits. Charitable remainder trusts and the tax benefits of those kinds of trusts are described in chapter 26.

Q. What types of charitable gifts can't be deducted? Can I make charitable contribution through a trust?

A. Most types of property can be given to charity. But in order to obtain a charitable deduction, your gift must almost always be of your *entire* interest in the property. If you retain some interests in the property, or give the property in trust so that the charity is only a beneficiary of the trust and does not receive the property directly, you will probably not be entitled to a charitable deduction.

There are only a few exceptions to this general "entire interest" rule:

- A gift of an *undivided fractional interest* in a property can qualify for a charitable deduction. However, the charity must have a present right to a proportionate part of the income or use of the property. For example, if you give one third of a painting to a museum, the museum must have the right to possession of the painting one third of the time. If you give a one half interest in real property to a charity, the charity must receive one half of the rental income of the property.

- You can get a current tax deduction for a gift of a *remainder interest in a personal residence or farm*. If you want a charity to receive your residence or farm after your death, you can make a present gift of the property, reserving the right to continue to occupy and use the property during your lifetime, and receive a current tax deduction for the present value of the charity's right to receive your property after your death. This might be excellent planning for a couple or single person with no children or other close relatives or friends.

- A *charitable remainder trust* can qualify for a current tax deduction, and provide other benefits, if the trust is in the form of a *charitable remainder annuity trust* or a *charitable remainder unitrust*. These trusts are described in chapter 26.

- A *charitable lead trust* can qualify for a current tax deduction if the income interest payable to charity is in the form of an *annuity* or a *unitrust* interest. Charitable lead trusts are also described in chapter 26.

- A gift to *pooled income fund* can also qualify for a current tax deduction, even though the donor retains a lifetime income interest in the fund. Pooled income funds are also described in chapter 26.

Q. What is a private foundation?

A. A private foundation is simply a charity that you create and control. You could, for example, create a trust dedicated entirely to charitable purposes, name yourself as trustee, and make a contribution to the trust, and your trust could be your private foundation. Typically, your charitable trust would collect and invest the contributions you make to the trust, and then make grants to other charities you select for charitable purposes or projects you select.

Like a public charity, a private foundation is exempt from federal income tax. Contributions to both public charities and private foundations are deductible for federal gift tax, estate tax, and income tax purposes.

However, there are a number of differences between private foundations and public charities:

- There are tighter limits on the income tax deduction for gifts to private foundations. Deductions for gifts to private foundations are limited to 30 percent of adjusted gross income (instead of the 50 percent limitation that applies to public charities). Deductions for gifts of appreciated property are limited to the donor's basis in the property (not the fair market value of the property) and 20 percent of AGI (instead of the 30 percent limitation that applies to public charities). (A special rule allowed a deduction for the fair market value of marketable securities given to a private foundation before 1995 or after July 1, 1996, but that rule is currently scheduled to expire on June 30, 1998.)

- Although a private foundation is exempt from income tax, it is nevertheless subject to a special 2 percent excise tax on its net investment income.

- Private foundations are subject to a number of very strict and very severe limitations on their operations, including rules and restrictions regarding the amounts of charitable distributions, the purposes of charitable distributions, transactions with contributors and trustees, and business holdings. (These rules are discussed in more detail below.)

- Private foundations are required to file longer and more detailed informational returns each year, and are required to make their returns available for public inspection.

Q. What are the advantages of a private foundation over a direct gift to an existing charity?

A. Despite the restrictions and limitations on private foundations, and the expenses of creating and maintaining them, a private foundation can be a very valuable part of a family's charitable planning.

- A private foundation can provide a way to convert a series of smaller gifts over many years into a few large gifts, with a commensurate increase in the public or private recognition appropriate to larger gifts. To take a fairly recent (and fairly extreme) example, publisher and philanthropist Walter H. Annenberg and his family created the Annenberg Foundation through a series of gifts over many years. Through the accumulation of those gifts (and the success of TV Guide magazine), the Annenberg Foundation eventually became a fund of more than *one billion dollars!* The multi-million dollar grants that have been announced by Mr. Annenberg in recent years have received much more publicity than the smaller individual gifts that created the foundation would have ever received.

  Although few people could create a private foundation as large as one billion dollars, many people could create private foundations of hundreds of thousands of dollars (or perhaps even millions of dollars) if they could accumulate the charitable gifts made by their families over many years.

- A private foundation can also provide a form of memorial or perpetual remembrance to your generosity. A one-time gift can result in a plaque or a building or scholarship fund in your name, but plaques tarnish, buildings can be renamed, and memories fade. A charitable foundation in your name provides new recognition for you and a new record of your generosity every time the foundation makes a charitable gift or grant. A private foundation that makes annual gifts receives annual recognition. The foundations that fund programs for public radio or television receive new recognition whenever a new program is broadcast. A gift can be forgotten, but a private foundation will be remembered because it continues to make new gifts each year.

- A private foundation can also provide a focus or common goal for your family. The administration of your private foundation can be a task that continues to bring your family together and join them together even after your death. Working together to select charitable beneficiaries can help your children or other successors to stay in touch with each other and get to know each other, and the administration of the foundation may also teach them some of your values and virtues of charity.

Q. *What are the advantages of a trust as a private foundation?*

A. A private foundation can be created as either a nonprofit corporation or a trust. There are a number of advantages to using a trust as your private foundation.

- Trusts can be easier and cheaper to establish than a corporation. A corporation requires both articles of incorporation and by-laws, filing fees for the articles, and the costs of public advertisements. A trust is usually a single document that is effective as soon as you sign it.

- Trusts provide greater flexibility than corporations. Nonprofit corporation statutes usually determine how the board of directors of a nonprofit corporation is elected, and the rights of the members (or stockholders) of the corporation. Nonprofit corporation statutes may also contain provisions for annual meetings, corporate records, and other formalities of corporate existence. To control your foundation the way you want, and provide for future control in the successors you select, it may be necessary for you to work within (or around) all of those statutes.

  However, when you create a trust, you create your own "laws" for the trust. You can designate the trustees by name, or provide a method of electing them. You can provide for majority votes of the trustees or any other system you choose. Subject only to a few restrictions imposed by the tax laws, the management provisions of your trust are limited only by your imagination and can be tailored to suit your particular goals and desires.

- Trusts are usually simpler to maintain than corporations. Nonprofit corporations are usually required to file annual reports with the state government (with annual filing fees), and are usually required to conduct annual meetings and keep records of those meetings. Failure to comply with those requirements can jeopardize the status of the corporation as a valid entity under state law. Most charitable trusts are not subject to any supervision by state governments or courts and are not required to make any annual reports beyond what is required by the Internal Revenue Service.

Given the advantages of trusts, why would anyone create a private foundation as a corporation? Corporations are usually created because of a concern about personal liability for directors or officers. State corporate law is usually clear that directors and officers are not liable for the debts or other liabilities of the corporation. Liability can be a concern if the foundation operates a library or museum that is open to the public, or has employees. People can fall or get hurt in many different ways, and employees can be negligent. Laws regarding trusts are often not as protective of trustees as corporate law is of directors and officers of a corporation.

Corporate law is often clearer and more developed than the laws relating to trusts. When you create a trust, you can create your own "law" for that trust, but there may be uncertainties or ambiguities in the areas in which you *don't* make any "law" and don't specify what is supposed to happen. By contrast, state corporate law usually provide enough rules to govern almost any situation. So if the articles of incorporation or by-laws are silent, there will be a statute or case decision that will tell you what to do. There is some benefit to avoiding uncertainty or confusion.

For most private foundations that do little more than receive contributions, invest funds, and make grants to public charities, a trust is an ideal form of organization. However, incorporating may be preferable in some cases.

Q. Can business interests be controlled through a private foundation?

A. No. One of the restrictions imposed on private foundations is that they cannot hold more than 2 percent of the stock or securities of a closely-held business. The receipt of any *excess business holding* can result in a severe penalty tax, and could even disqualify the foundation as a tax exempt charity.

Q. What other restrictions exist for private foundations?

A. There are a number of other restrictions imposed on private foundations, most of which were enacted to make sure that the tax-deductible contributions to the foundation are really used for charitable purposes and not for the private benefit of the contributors to the private foundation or the trustees (or "managers") of the foundation.

- *Excess business holdings.* As explained above, a private foundation cannot own stock or any other interest in a business

- *Minimum distributions.* A private must distribute at least 5 percent of its average asset values each year. So a private foundation can accumulate income only to the extent that its investment income exceeds the required 5 percent distribution.

- *Self-dealing.* A private foundation cannot engage in any sale or lease of property with any "disqualified person" (substantial contributors, foundation managers, members of their families, and certain government officials), lend money or extend credit to or from a disqualified person, or furnish goods, services, or facilities to or from a disqualified person. These restrictions apply whether the transaction is direct or indirect, and regardless of whether or not the transaction is "fair" to the foundation. For that reason, a bargain sale to a private foundation is *never* permissible, and even a gift of mortgaged property to a private foundation can result in severe penalties.

  There are exceptions to these self-dealing rules to permit private foundations to pay compensation to foundation managers and others for services which are reasonable and necessary to carry out the exempt purposes of the foundation, as long as the compensation is not "excessive." You can also lend or donate money, goods, services, or facilities to your foundation without charge.

- *Jeopardy investments.* A private foundation should not make any speculative or other investment that jeopardizes the ability of the foundation to carry out its exempt purposes.

- *Political activities.* A private foundation cannot carry on propaganda, attempt to influence legislation, or participate in any political campaign.

- *Grants to individuals.* A private foundation cannot give any of its assets to any individual as a scholarship or grant for travel, study, or other similar purposes unless the grant program has been approved *in advance* by the Internal Revenue Service.

- *Expenditure responsibility.* If a private foundation makes a grant to another private foundation, the managers of the granting foundation must make investigations, and keep records, to be certain that the grant is actually used for charitable purposes.

- *Taxable expenditures.* The use of any assets of a private foundation for any purpose other than the charitable purposes of the foundation is a "taxable expenditure" that can result in a penalty tax on the foundation and its managers.

- *Unrelated trade or business.* The foundation cannot be operated for the purpose of carrying on any unrelated trade or business.

These restrictions are enforced through a series of penalty taxes, usually imposed in two levels. If the foundation violates any of the rules described above, a "first tier" tax is imposed on the foundation and its managers. If the violation is not corrected within a certain time after the first tax is imposed, a "second tier" (and more severe) tax is imposed on the foundation and the responsible foundation managers. In extreme cases, involving repeated and serious abuses of the private foundation rules, the IRS can impose a tax equal to 100 percent of the value of the foundation. This "death penalty" terminates the foundation for all practical purposes.

Q. *What are the costs of creating and operating a private foundation?*

A. Although there are benefits to private foundations, creating and maintaining a private foundation is not without its costs.

- In order to qualify as a tax exempt organization, the trust you create as your private foundation will have to include a number of provisions required by the Internal Revenue Code and the Internal Revenue Service. An experienced lawyer should be able to create a simple "plain vanilla" private foundation for $500 to $1,000, but your special needs and special drafting considerations can push the costs considerably higher.

- In order for contributions to your private foundation to be tax deductible, you *must* apply to the IRS for tax exempt status within 18 months after the foundation is created. The application is long and complicated, and a lawyer or accountant will charge $2,000 to $5,000 to complete the application. And there is a filing fee to be

Trusts/Leimberg Associates Books: 610-527-5216

paid to the IRS. (The application fee is at least $150 for small foundations, but can be as large as $465.)

- A private foundation is required to pay an excise tax of 2 percent of its net investment income each year (and make quarterly estimated payments of that tax).

- A private foundation is also required to file an annual informational return with the IRS, reporting its investment income, its expenses, its charitable distributions, its asset values, the names of contributors and foundation managers, and other aspects of its operations of interest to the IRS. These informational returns are more complicated than most income tax returns, and so there can be significant costs in preparing the returns each year.

- Depending on state law, a foundation may also be required to file annual reports with the state attorney general or other state officials responsible for the oversight of charitable organizations in the state.

Fortunately, all of these costs can usually be paid by the foundation, which means that the costs can be paid by your tax-deductible contributions to the trust.

CHARITABLE SPLIT-INTEREST TRUSTS

Chapter 26 explains:

- The advantages of making split-interest gifts in trust to charity

- Why charitable gifts through split-interest trusts make sense

- What a CRAT (charitable remainder annuity trust) is

- How the deduction for a gift to a CRAT is computed

- What a CRUT (charitable remainder unitrust) is

- How the income tax deduction for a gift to a CRUT is computed

- What a net income unitrust (or a net income plus make-up unitrust) (NIM-CRUT) is

- Similarities between the CRAT and the CRUT

- How a CRUT differs from a CRAT

- What a "pooled income" fund is

- What a charitable lead trust (CLT) is

- How to "zero out" a CLT

- Estate tax savings opportunities with a CLT

- Generation-skipping transfer tax implications of a CLT

- Gift tax implications of a CLT

- Income tax implications of the CLT

- Factors in deciding if a CLT makes sense

- What wealth enhancement and wealth replacement trusts are

- How a charitable trust can benefit couples with no children

Q. In general terms, what are the advantages of making split-interest gifts in trust to charity?

A. Chapter 25 explained the advantages of outright gifts to charity. By making a gift in trust with both charitable and non-charitable beneficiaries, you can accomplish a number of personal and financial planning objectives simultaneously. In addition to the usual charitable objectives, charitable split-interest trusts can:

- enhance your own (and your family's) financial security

- increase your retirement income

- diversify and create a safer investment portfolio

- reduce investment management aggravation

- provide financial security for incompetent family members

- increase your income tax deductions and lower your tax

- substantially reduce death taxes and probate expenses in your estate

Q. Why do people use trusts for gifts to charity?

A. Many people want to give a portion of their estates to a charity during their lifetime but want to reserve some sort of income stream for themselves, their spouse, or someone else. For example, a woman may create a trust that provides that she will receive an annuity from the trust as long as she lives and that the principal of the trust will be paid over to a qualified public charity at her death. Another example is an elderly brother who wants to continue to support an equally elderly unmarried sister after his death, and would like to provide an annuity to her during her lifetime, with the remainder to charity at her death.

In each case, the charity gets only what's left—what remains of the property—when the interest of the donor (or other non-charitable beneficiary) ends. For this reason, planners call these trusts *charitable remainder trusts,* which can be made in one of these three ways:

Trusts/Leimberg Associates Books: 610-527-5216

- a charitable remainder annuity trust (CRAT)
- a charitable remainder unitrust (CRUT)
- a pooled income fund

Why do these kinds of charitable remainder trusts make sense? What are the advantages of the trust over outright gifts to charity?

- The obvious advantage is that it allows the donor to make sure that the beneficiary gets only what the beneficiary needs and that the charity gets the rest. For example, if a sister decides that a brother needs only an additional $20,000 per year (or a daughter decides that an elderly father needs only that much additional income), the sister (or daughter) can make sure that the brother (or father) gets only that amount during his lifetime, and the charity gets everything that is left after his death.

- A donor who creates a charitable remainder during lifetime is entitled to an income tax deduction for the present value of the projected charitable remainder. Similarly, someone who creates a charitable remainder trust at death is entitled to an estate tax charitable deduction. Those tax deductions can reduce the costs of establishing the trust, and can actually increase the amount of money going into the trust. The charitable deduction can therefore increase the size of the trust fund and the amount of annuity available to the beneficiary during his or her lifetime.

- A charitable remainder trust is tax-exempt so it pays no income taxes. Although taxable income earned by the trust is taxable to the beneficiaries when it is distributed to those beneficiaries, a charitable remainder trust can provide valuable tax deferral. For example, suppose a married couple owns stock or real property which has substantially increased in value and they now wish to sell the stock or property. The sale will result in substantial taxes on the capital gains. Only what's left after taxes can be invested. So the couple will have to live off of the investment earnings from the net proceeds of sale—after taxes. However, if they contribute the stock or property to a charitable remainder trust, reserving annuity payments from the trust for themselves for the rest of their lives, the trust can sell the stock or property without paying any federal income tax. The full proceeds of sale can be invested to produce an income to support the husband and wife during their lifetimes. Because of the value of tax deferral, it is quite possible that they will receive more from the trust than they could have earned without the trust.

Q. What is a charitable remainder annuity trust?

A. A *charitable remainder annuity trust* (CRAT) is an irrevocable trust you create. You put assets into it. The trust pays you (and one or more other beneficiaries if you wish) a fixed annuity for a term or years or for life. When you (and any other beneficiary) die, what remains is paid to the charity you have specified.

You cannot reclaim assets you put into the trust. Once it is established, you cannot change the terms or beneficiary of the trust.

As noted above, the CRAT will pay you a fixed dollar amount each year (or semi-annually, quarterly, or monthly) for the specified term or for as long as you (or you and your selected additional non-charitable beneficiary) live. The payments from the trust must be a fixed dollar amount, but it is common to describe the annuity as a percentage of the initial gift to the trust. For example, if you put $100,000 in the trust and reserve a 6 percent annuity payment, you would receive $6,000 each year, no matter if the trust earns more or less than the amount you are to be paid.

If the earnings of the trust are insufficient to pay you the promised fixed annuity, the trustee is authorized to invade principal. If the trust income is more than the fixed annuity you are to be paid, the excess is added to principal. It will eventually be paid to the charity.

In order to qualify as a charitable remainder annuity trust, the trust document must contain a number of very specific and complex provisions. The absence of any provision can "disqualify" the entire trust, meaning that there is no tax deduction for the trust. Furthermore, the trust would not be tax-exempt, regardless of how much the charity actually gets.

Among the more significant requirements are:

- The distributions to the non-charitable beneficiaries must be in the form of a fixed dollar annuity which cannot change during the term of the trust.

- The annuity must be at least 5 percent of the initial gift to the trust, but less than 50 percent of the initial gift. Also, the present value of the charitable remainder must be at least 10 percent of the value of the initial gift and there cannot be a greater than 5 percent probability that the charity will receive nothing. (See additional explanations below.)

- The trust must be for a fixed term (not to exceed 20 years) or for the lives of the non-charitable beneficiaries (all of whom must be living when the trust begins).

- The trust must be prohibited from receiving additional contributions. Once you fund the trust, that's it. Neither you nor anyone else can put additional amounts of cash or property into your Charitable Remainder Annuity Trust.

- At the end of the term you selected, everything in the trust must be distributed to charities recognized as tax exempt by the Internal Revenue Service. Furthermore, the trust must specify that no death taxes will be paid from the trust upon the death of the donor if the donor has retained an interest in the trust and the trust is included in the donor's taxable estate. (In order to get the maximum charitable deduction when the trust is formed, and avoid the limits on gifts to private foundations, the trust document should specify that the charitable beneficiaries must be not only tax exempt, but public charities and not private foundations.)

- The trust must be irrevocable. You can, however, reserve the right for you or your trustee to select other or additional "qualified" charities.

- The trust must contain many of the same prohibitions that apply to private foundations (see chapter 25), such as prohibitions against acts of self-dealing between the trust and the donor or the beneficiaries, "taxable expenditures" (expenditures for other than charitable purposes), "jeopardy investments" (investments that jeopardize the charitable purposes of the trust), and the retention of "excess business holdings" (interests in closely-held businesses).

Because of the many technical requirements for charitable remainder trusts, you should not attempt to create a charitable remainder trust without the advice of an experienced tax lawyer.

(A somewhat simpler alternative to a charitable remainder annuity trust is the charitable gift annuity, described in chapter 25, in which the charity agrees to pay the donor a fixed annuity for life in exchange for the charitable gift of the donor.)

Q. Is there a limit as to how large my annuity can be?

A. There is both a minimum and maximum. These apply to both CRATs and CRUTs. At a minimum, you must be paid an annuity of at least 5 percent of the initial value of the trust. The maximum annuity you can receive is restricted by three limits:

- The annuity must be less than 50 percent of the initial gift.

- The present value of the charitable remainder must be at least 10 percent of the value of the initial gift.

- If the initial annuity payout percentage is more than the assumed investment yield for the trust (i.e., the Section 7520 rate that is used to discount the future remainder to present value), so that the annuity must be paid at least in part from principal, there cannot be a greater than 5 percent probability that the charity will receive nothing.

The second two limits greatly restrict the annuities that can be paid out of CRATs when the trust is for a life (or lives). For example, if the Section 7520 rate is 7.6 percent, an annuity of 7.6 percent can be paid out of the assumed income of the trust, principal will not be invaded to make the annuity payments and will remain intact for charity, so the trust will satisfy the third test. However, the trust will generate a charitable deduction of only 9.98 percent for a grantor/beneficiary who is 38 years old, so the trust will flunk the second test if the grantor/beneficiary is 38 years of age or younger. If the grantor/beneficiary is 45 years old, an annuity of 8 percent of the initial trust value will produce a charitable deduction of 10.14 percent and satisfy the second limit. However, principal will have to be invaded to make the annuity payments because the trust is assumed to earn only 7.6 percent, and there is a probability of more than 5 percent that the grantor/beneficiary will live long enough to completely exhaust the trust principal, so the trust flunks the third test.

Q. *How is the deduction computed for a gift to a CRAT?*

A. When you make a gift to a charitable remainder annuity trust (CRAT), you receive an immediate income tax deduction for the gift the charity will someday receive. Your current deduction is measured by the present value (the worth today) of the charity's right to receive what remains in the trust (the remainder interest) at the end of the specified term of the trust or upon your death (or on the death of the specified annuity recipient). More specifically, the present value of the annuity payments is determined from actuarial tables published by the Internal Revenue Service. The value of the charitable remainder is the value of your gift to the trust less the present value of the annuity you have retained.

Here's an example of exactly how the charitable remainder annuity trust would work if you were 60 years old, decided to put $100,000 into a charitable trust, and retained a $6,000 annuity for the rest of your life, no matter how long you live. The present value of the annuity must be determined by using a mortality table based on the most recent U.S. census (to determine the probability of death each year during the term of the trust) and an assumed investment yield for the trust based upon average yields on federal securities for the month the trust is created (usually called the Section 7520 discount rate, and published monthly by the Internal Revenue Service).

For a Section 7520 discount rate of 9 percent, the present value of an annuity payable in one installment each year for the life of a person age 60 is the amount of the annuity times 8.3031. So the present value of the annuity that person retained would be $49,818.60 ($6,000 times 8.3031). The present value of the charity's interest, the deductible charitable remainder, would be $50,181.40 (the $100,000 gift to the trust less the $49,818.60 value of the annuity retained by the donor). [The actuarial factor for this calculation and the annuity and remainder interest were obtained through NumberCruncher, a software program available from Leimberg & LeClair Inc., 610-527-5216.]

Amazingly, the IRS allows you to select the federal discount (Section 7520) rate for the month of the transaction, or either of the 2 prior months' rate if one of those will result in a larger income tax deduction! That's right. You can select the discount rate for the month you fund your CRAT, or if a more favorable rate applied in either of the 2 prior months, you can use that rate. Higher federal discount rates result in higher deductions.

You can even get a 4-month look by waiting until the Section 7520 rate for the following month is issued (usually around the 22nd of each month for the next month) and then deciding whether to create the trust in that month or wait another 10 days for the next month (and the next discount rate). For instance, in the example above, the federal discount rate was 9 percent and the resulting deduction for a $100,000 contribution was $50,181. If the Section 7520 rate rose to 9.6 percent in the following month and you waited until then to fund your trust, the deduction for the same gift would increase to $52,286.80.

Q. What is a charitable remainder unitrust?

A. A charitable remainder unitrust (CRUT) is also an irrevocable trust. You cannot reclaim assets you put into it, and once it has been established you cannot change the terms or beneficiary of the trust. You put assets into the trust, but you retain the right to a percentage of the value of the trust (revalued annually) for a specified term of years—or, more commonly, for your life or for your life and one or more additional lives. For instance, the annuity can be paid for as long as you live and as long your spouse (or other designated beneficiary) lives.

The trust will pay you—for the specified term—or for as long as you (or you and your selected additional non-charitable beneficiary) live. But with a CRUT, instead of a fixed annuity, you will receive a fixed percentage (again, not less than 5 percent) of the value of the trust's principal (as revalued each year). In other words, the amount of payment you will receive in a CRUT will be determined by the total value of the trust assets, not upon the actual income of the trust, and the payments can increase or decrease, depending on whether the trust increases or decreases in value each year. The payout is therefore more like a variable annuity than a traditional fixed annuity.

For example, if you put $100,000 in the trust and reserve a 6 percent payout, you would receive $6,000 (6 percent of $100,000) in the first year. But if the trust increases in value to $110,000 in the second year, you'll be paid $6,600 (6 percent of $110,000). If the trust increased in value to $200,000 over the years, you could receive $12,000 (6 percent of $200,000) each year, rather than $6,000. However, if the value of the trust's assets dropped to $50,000, you would receive only $3,000 (6 percent of $50,000).

In order to qualify as a charitable remainder annuity trust, the trust document must contain a number of very specific and sometimes complex provisions. The absence of any provision can "disqualify" the entire trust. That would mean there is no tax deduction for the trust, and the trust is not tax-exempt, regardless of how much the charity actually gets.

Among the more significant requirements are:

- The distributions to the non-charitable beneficiaries must be a fixed percentage which cannot change during the term of the trust, and the trust must be revalued annually.

- The payout rate must be at least 5 percent of the annual value but less than 50 percent. Also, the present value of the charitable remainder must be at least 10 percent of the value of the gift. (See additional explanations below.)

- A complex formula must be used to adjust payments during a year if an error is discovered in the valuation of the trust assets.

- The trust must be for a fixed term (not to exceed 20 years) or the lives of the non-charitable beneficiaries (all of whom must be living when the trust begins).

- If the trust is allowed to receive additional contributions, then the trust must contain a complex formula for adjusting payments during the year for contributions received during that year.

- At the end of the trust, everything in the trust must be distributed to charities recognized as tax exempt by the Internal Revenue Service. Furthermore, the trust must specify that no death taxes will be paid from the trust upon the death of the donor if the donor has retained an interest in the trust and the trust is included in the donor's taxable estate. (In order to get the maximum charitable deduction when the trust is formed, and avoid the limits on gifts to private foundations, the trust document should specify that the charitable beneficiaries must be not only tax exempt, but public charities and not private foundations.)

- The trust must be irrevocable (although the identity of the charitable beneficiaries can be changed by the donor or the trustees).

- The trust must contain many of the same prohibitions that apply to private foundations (see chapter 25), such as prohibitions against acts of self-dealing between the trust and the donor or the beneficiaries, "taxable expenditures" (expenditures for other than charitable purposes), "jeopardy investments" (investments that jeopardize the charitable purposes of the trust), and the retention of "excess business holdings" (interests in closely-held businesses).

Because of the many technical requirements for charitable remainder trusts, you should not attempt to create a charitable remainder trust without the advice of an experienced tax lawyer.

Q. How is the income tax deduction computed for a gift to a CRUT?

A. When you make a gift to a charitable remainder unitrust (CRUT), you receive an immediate income tax deduction for the gift the charity will someday receive. As with a charitable remainder annuity trust (CRAT), that deduction is measured by the present value (the worth today) of the charity's right to receive what remains in the trust (the remainder interest) at the end of the specified term or upon the death of the non-charitable beneficiary. More specifically, the present value of the charitable remainder is determined from actuarial tables published by the Internal Revenue Service.

Here's an example of exactly how the charitable remainder unitrust would work if you were 60 years old, decided to put $100,000 into a charitable trust, but wanted a 6 percent variable payout from the trust for the rest of your life, no matter how long you might live. The present value of the charitable remainder must be determined by using a mortality table based on the most recent U.S. census (to determine the probability of death each year during the term of the trust). If payments are made more frequently than annually, or are made more than one month after the annual valuation date, then an adjustment must be made based on an average yield for federal securities for the month the trust is created (usually called the *Section 7520 discount rate*, and published monthly by the Internal Revenue Service).

For a unitrust with a payout of 6 percent in one installment each year for the life of a person age 60, the charitable remainder will be 34.824% of the gift to the trust, or $34,824.00 for a gift of $100,000. [This calculation was obtained through *NumberCruncher*, a software program available from Leimberg & LeClair Inc., 610-527-5216.]

Q. What is a net income unitrust? What is a net income plus make-up unitrust (NIM-CRUT)?

A. The Internal Revenue Code and regulations allow a trust to qualify as a charitable remainder unitrust even though the distributions from the trust are limited to the actual income earned by the trust. There are two major permissible variations on this theme:

A *net income unitrust* is one in which the annual payment is the lesser of (1) the specified fixed percentage of the value of the trust, and (2) the actual income of the trust as determined by state law or the governing instrument. If a distribution cannot be made in full because of a lack of income, the deficiency is lost forever and will never be made up.

A *net income make-up unitrust* (or NIM-CRUT) provides an annual payout equal to the lesser of (1) the fixed percentage of the value of the trust, and (2) the income of the trust as determined by state law or the governing instrument. However, if there is a deficiency in one year and the trust realizes income in excess of the fixed percentage in a later year, that excess income is paid out to the non-charitable beneficiaries to "make up" for the previous deficiency. In other words, the distribution of income in a year is not really limited by the percentage distribution for that year, but by the excess of (1) the aggregate amounts required to be distributed in all prior years over (2) the amounts actually distributed.

Net-income-only and net-income-make-up unitrusts have at least two important uses:

- If the unitrust will hold an asset which you do not want to be sold immediately, the net income provision will allow the trustee to hold the asset without being required to sell the asset in order to create the cash needed to make the distribution. (In the absence of a net income language, a CRUT is like a CRAT, in that the annual distributions must be made on schedule, without fail, even if there is no income and no cash to make the distributions. Without the net income provisions, a

CRUT would have to sell assets to make the required distributions, just like a CRAT.)

- The NIM-CRUT can be a powerful and flexible retirement planning vehicles. Here's how: Within reason, you can fund your trust with assets that are designed to achieve long-term growth with little current income. This means that during the build-up years, when you are still working and in a relatively high income tax bracket, the trust will distribute very little taxable income. Then, when you retire and your taxable income drops, the trust can gradually convert to assets producing a higher current income. By investing in high-growth assets initially, these two types of trusts will eventually give you the most income when you need it the most—at retirement.

In order to provide larger (and faster) make-up payments under a NIM-CRUT, many NIM-CRUTs state that capital gains are to be considered part of the income of the trust. So if your NIM-CRUT invests in long-term capital growth stocks before retirement, the trust would have very little income to distribute, but sales of the stocks after your retirement would produce not only larger current income, but capital gains that could be used to begin the "make-up" distributions for the past differences between the percentage payout and the actual income. The IRS currently appears to be willing to accept definitions of "income" that include capital gains, but proposed regulations in 1997 (not yet finalized) that would make certain that "income" could not include the gain attributable to appreciation that occurred *before* the asset was contributed to the trust. In other words, "income" that can be used for distributions in a NIM-CRUT can include capital gains beginning when the trust is created, but cannot include gains from *before* the trust was created.

In 1997, the IRS also proposed new regulations (not yet finalized when this book went to press) that would allow a new kind of CRUT, a "flip" CRUT. The proposed regulations would allow a unitrust to "flip" from net-income-make-up (distributions are limited to income) to a "standard" unitrust (with required distributions regardless of income). Under this proposal, a unitrust could be funded with real estate or other illiquid assets and distributions could be limited to income (which might be necessary if the trust had no cash other than the small amount of income earned by the asset and the asset itself were not easily sold). When the principal asset is sold, the trust could "flip" to a regular unitrust, with the required payments coming from both income or principal (if necessary). However, a trust could only "flip" once, and there could be no make-up for past income deficiencies after the flip.

We have already pointed out that the complexity of the rules regarding charitable remainder trusts make it essential to consult a competent tax lawyer. The continuing changes in the tax laws, regulations, and IRS rulings demonstrate the need for a tax lawyer who is constantly working with these kinds of trusts and so is aware of the most recent developments.

Q. In what ways are the CRAT and the CRUT similar?

A. Here are some of the important similarities between the charitable remainder annuity trust (CRAT) and the charitable remainder unitrust (CRUT):

- You receive an income tax charitable deduction (perhaps a sizable deduction) in the year you create the trust.

- The longer the trust is likely to last, the smaller the income tax deduction. Your deduction will generally increase if you retain income for only a few years, rather than for your lifetime, and your deduction will decrease if you retain income not only for your lifetime but also for the lifetime of a spouse or other selected beneficiary.

- The higher the payout from the trust (whether in the form of an annuity or a unitrust percentage payout), the smaller the income tax deduction.

- The tax deduction (value of the charitable remainder) must be at least 10 percent of the value of the gift to the trust.

- Your deduction for a gift of appreciated securities held for more than one year is based on the full fair market value, rather than on your basis (cost), if the charitable beneficiary is a public charity (not a private foundation). (See chapter 25 for additional information about the limits on gifts to private foundations.)

- The creation of the trust will not result in taxable gain or other income, even if you transfer appreciated assets to the trust.

- The trust is tax exempt. There is no federal income tax on any income or capital gains accumulated by the trust until the income (or capital gain) is distributed to the beneficiary (at which time it is taxable income or gain to the beneficiary).

- As a substitute for a gift to charity by your will, setting up a CRAT or CRUT during your lifetime can save both probate fees and estate taxes, because neither the CRAT nor the CRUT is subject to executor's fees or other probate costs in most states. Even if the assets transferred to a CRAT or CRUT are included in your taxable estate for federal estate tax purposes (because of the annuity or unitrust interest you retained during your lifetime), the amounts passing to charity at your death will qualify for the federal estate tax charitable deduction if the trust terminates at your death or, even if the trust continues after your death, the trust will qualify for the federal estate tax marital deduction (if your spouse is the sole remaining non-charitable beneficiary) or a partial charitable deduction (if there are other beneficiaries following your death). This may save significant amounts of federal estate tax.

- If you set up either a CRAT or a CRUT in your will, you can provide significant income for the life of one or more beneficiaries and still receive a charitable estate tax deduction that can actually increase the total amounts passing to your beneficiaries.

- You can use either a CRAT or a CRUT to increase your retirement income by giving low-income-yielding but highly appreciated stock or other investments to the trust. If you sell the asset personally, you'd only have the net after-tax proceeds to invest. But if you give the asset to the charitable trust (which will be paying you an annuity for a fixed term of years or for life), the trustee can sell the same asset but pay no income tax and then reinvest (all) the proceeds in higher-yielding investments. Deferring (or avoiding) tax on the capital gain means that there is more money to invest. That can increase your payout and give you a higher income than you would have enjoyed without the trust.

Trusts/Leimberg Associates Books: 610-527-5216

This technique also increases your financial security by diversifying your portfolio within the trust. For example, suppose that, instead of receiving the income from only one investment and taking the risk that the investment will in fact produce adequate income, you can give the asset to a CRUT or CRAT, which sells the investment, pays no income tax on the sale, and reinvests 100 percent of the proceeds in several mutual funds. The trust now pays you a fixed or variable annuity from a diversified portfolio, so declines in a single company or industry will have less of an impact on your income and financial security.

The net income unitrust adds flexibility to charitable gift planning, but it comes at a cost, the cost being that the income may never be sufficient to make up the past deficiencies and so the charity will receive more than it was really supposed to. And, although the charity is likely to benefit from net income option for unitrusts, there is no additional tax deduction for a net income unitrust. The tax deduction for a net income unitrust (with or without make-up provisions) is exactly the same as the tax deduction for a regular unitrust.

Q. How does a CRUT differ from a CRAT?

A. There are many ways in which a charitable remainder unitrust (CRUT) differs from a charitable remainder annuity trust (CRAT). Some of the most important are as follows:

- A CRUT is valued on the assumption that a percentage of both income and principal is paid out each year. A CRAT is valued on the assumption that the annuity could be paid solely out of the trust's income. For this reason, a CRAT with a percentage annuity rate that is close to the assumed income yield for the trust (the Section 7520 discount rate) will usually yield a larger charitable deduction than a CRUT with the same percentage payout rate. This reflects the reality that the economic value of the CRUT payout is higher than the economic value of the annuity from the CRAT.

- Because the annuity from a CRAT is fixed, the charitable deduction allowable for a CRAT is very much affected by the difference between the annuity percentage and the Section 7520 discount rate. If the annuity is less than the discount rate (so that the annuity could be paid from the assumed income of the trust), the charitable deduction can be sizable. As the annuity is increased to equal or exceed the discount rate (so that principal will have to be invaded to make the annuity payments), the charitable deduction rapidly declines, and then disappears. (You are not allowed any charitable deduction for a CRAT if there is a greater than 5 percent probability that the distributions will exhaust the trust fund before the death of the non-charitable beneficiary.)

Because a CRUT is based on a percentage of the trust fund as it is revalued each year, and reducing something by a percentage will never bring it entirely down to zero (although it can get very small), there will always be something left for charity and a CRUT will always produce some charitable deduction, even for relatively high payout rates. However, even a CRUT must create a charitable deduction of at least 10 percent of the gift to the trust in order to qualify as a CRUT.

- The amount paid to you (or your selected beneficiary) from a CRUT is directly affected by any increase in the value of a CRUT's assets, whether due to capital gains or accumulated income (income earned in excess of the amount required to be distributed). As the fund grows, so does your annuity. So if the fund's value grows year by year, the dollar amount of the payout you receive will increase over time. The CRUT, therefore, can serve as a hedge against inflation. On the other hand, because the CRAT's annuity payment to you is fixed, it is a relatively poor defense against inflation.

- Because the amount paid to you (or your selected beneficiary) from a CRUT can be reduced if the value of your CRUT's assets falls, you may be paid less than you anticipated or needed. Because the CRAT's income is fixed, you are more certain of receiving necessary income, even if the trustee must invade the charity's capital to do so.

- A CRUT is more difficult (and more expensive) to administer than a CRAT because the assets in a CRUT must be revalued each year. There are costs incurred in that annual valuation and, if the assets in the trust are not publicly traded, the appraiser's fee could be expensive.

- As explained above, a CRUT can be written so that distributions are made *only* out of the income of the trust. (The distributions are still limited to a percentage of the value of the trust, so the actual payments would be the lower of (1) the actual income of the trust or (2) the stated percentage.) This "net income" unitrust is unlike a CRAT, because a net income unitrust does not need to sell assets in a given year to make distributions if the income (cash) of the trust is less than is needed to make the required distributions. Further, a net income make-up unitrust (NIM-CRUT) can serve as a retirement planning vehicle, because the distributions from the trust can be controlled—within reasonable limits—through the investment policy of the trust. While you are working, the trustee can invest in high-growth, low-income securities (or real estate). Amounts required to be distributed to your would accumulate in a bookkeeping account like a debt from the trust to you. Once you retire, the trust can switch to high-income investments and begin distributing amounts from any excess current income to make-up for the missed annuity distributions from prior years. With a CRAT, there is much less planning flexibility.

- A CRUT can receive additional contributions after it is created, but a CRAT cannot. It is therefore possible for you or others to make additional lifetime gifts to a CRUT and also "pour over" future testamentary bequests by will into a CRUT.

These differences show that CRATs and CRUTs reflect very different charitable deductions, investment strategies, financial strategies, and retirement planning. These differences must be discussed with your estate planning team. Do you want the largest possible deduction, or do you want the largest possible annuity? Do you want an annuity that could rise, or do you want a fixed and certain stream of dollars? The choice is highly individual, and because there is no "right" answer, the proper decision of CRUT or CRAT, as well as the choices of beneficiaries, terms, and payouts, will differ in almost every case.

Q. What is a pooled income fund?

A. A *pooled income fund* is a trust established by a public charity. Individual donors may make contributions to that "pool" but retain an income interest for life. It is a form of charitable remainder trust with these key distinctions: First, a pooled income fund is created by the charity and not by the individual donors. Second, donors are entitled to a share of the income of the trust and do not receive an annuity or a percentage of the value of the trust. Third, in a pooled income fund, the remainder interest must pass to the named charity so donors cannot reserve the right to change the charitable beneficiary.

Assume you'd like to make a meaningful gift to charity, but you need to retain income, perhaps for as long as you and your spouse or some other relative lives. Maybe you don't have enough principal to make it worthwhile to establish and maintain your own charitable remainder annuity trust (CRAT) or charitable remainder unitrust (CRUT). Or perhaps you'd rather give more to charity and expend less on creating your own trust.

You can make a contribution to a fund (very much like a mutual fund) maintained in an irrevocable trust created by the charity you select. From this pooled income fund, you will receive your share of the fund's earnings (taxable as ordinary income) each year. In return for your contribution of assets to the pooled income fund, you'll be allowed to take a sizable current income tax deduction.

For example, say you contribute $100,000 to a pooled income fund with total assets of $1,000,000 after your gift. If the fund's rate of return this year is 9 percent, you'll receive $9,000 (your one tenth share of the fund's $90,000 earnings). Your charitable deduction is determined by IRS tables that compute the value of your charitable gift based on your life expectancy (or the life expectancies of you and your spouse or other beneficiary) and the highest investment yield of the fund during the three preceding years (not the usual Section 7520 discount rate).

There are two additional distinctions between a pooled income fund and the typical CRAT or CRUT: (1) Neither you nor any other donor or beneficiary can serve as the trustee of a pooled income fund, and (2) The pooled income fund can't accept or invest in tax-exempt securities. (Pooled income fund computations can be done on GPR (Gift Annuities, Pooled Income Fund, and Remainder Interest) Plus Software, which is available by calling 610-527-5216).

Q. What is a charitable lead trust?

A. A *charitable lead trust* (CLT) is an irrevocable trust that works exactly the opposite way from the charitable remainder trusts we've just explained. In a charitable remainder trust you keep a fixed annuity or variable (unitrust) annuity payout and the charity gets what remains when you die (or at the end of the period of time you specify). A charitable lead trust, on the other hand, pays an annuity to the charity for a set number of years (or for your life or the lifetime of some person you specify) and then pays what remains at the end of the specified term back to you (or more typically, to your specified beneficiary or beneficiaries, either directly or to another trust).

You can set up a CLT during your lifetime, or you can create one that takes effect at your death. Your will can pour over assets into the CLT, you can have your revocable or irrevocable living trust pour over assets into the CLT, and you can even have life insurance on your life and pension proceeds pass into a CLT established at your death.

A CLT can therefore serve as a receptacle for all or any portion of your estate's assets. To the extent that assets pass from a trust, from a pension or profit-sharing plan, or from life insurance into the CLT, those assets will avoid the delays, costs, and aggravations of probate. Your charitable gift can be as private (or public) as you'd like it to be.

When the CLT ends, the assets can—if you so choose when you set up the trust—return to you or the party you select. However, as we've noted, most CLTs pass trust property to one or more persons other than the creator of the trust. That's because the main reason most people set up CLTs in the first place is to shift wealth to family members at minimal gift tax cost and save estate taxes because the wealth is no longer in their (the donors') estates.

In design, the charitable lead trust is similar in many respects to the charitable remainder trust. The charity must be paid either a fixed annuity (a *charitable lead annuity trust*, or CLAT), or a fixed percentage of the value of the trust, revalued annually (a *charitable lead unitrust*, or CLUT).

If the annuity is fixed and you specify that the charity is to receive a 6 percent annuity and you put cash, securities, or other assets worth $100,000 into the trust, the charity will receive $6,000 a year, every year, for the number of years the trust is set to last. Whether the assets earn more or less than the 6 percent rate, the trustee will have to pay out $6,000 a year, even if the trustee must invade principal to do so.

If you create a charitable lead unitrust which is to pay the charity 6 percent per year, and you put $100,000 into the trust, the charity will receive $6,000 in the first year. If the trust assets appreciate in the second year to $200,000, the charity will still be paid 6 percent, but it will be 6 percent of $200,000, or $12,000. If the value of trust assets drops to only $50,000, the charity's 6 percent interest will yield $3,000. As the trust's principal increases, so will the size of the trust's payout to charity. As principal falls in value, so will the size of the charitable payout.

The calculation of the charitable deduction for a CLT is similar to the calculation of the charitable deduction for a CRT, except that the numbers are reversed. In a CRAT, the present value of the annuity is deducted from the value of the gift to the trust to determine the value of the charitable remainder. In a CLAT, it's just the opposite: the present value of the annuity is the charitable deduction, and that value is subtracted from the value of the gift to the trust to determine the value of the taxable remainder, the gift you are making to your children or other non charitable beneficiaries. In a CRUT, the value of the charitable remainder is determined, then subtracted from the value of the gift to the trust to determine the taxable gift (if any). In a CLUT, the value of the taxable remainder is determined, then subtracted from the value of the gift to the trust to determine the charitable deduction.

Although CLTs are similar to charitable remainder trusts (CRTs), there are some important differences:

- A CRT must pay an annuity or unitrust payout of at least 5 percent but less than 50 percent, and the present value of the charitable remainder must be at least 10 percent of the gift to the trust. (A charitable remainder annuity trust, or CRAT, also cannot pay an annuity so large that the charity is likely to receive nothing.) However, there are no floors or ceilings on the amounts paid to a charity from a CLT. So a CLT is much more flexible. Obviously, the more the charity is paid each year, the higher your charitable deduction and the lower the tax cost of shifting wealth to your ultimate beneficiaries.

- A CRT can be for a life (or lives) or a term of not more than 20 years. There is also no limit on the period of time the CLT can last. The longer the period over which the charity receives payments, the higher your gift tax deduction.

- Typically, there is no income tax deduction for a charitable lead trust. So the major tax savings are gift and estate tax savings, not income tax savings. (There are limited circumstances under which a CLT can qualify for an income tax deduction and these are discussed below.)

- A CRT is tax exempt, but a CLT is not. That means that a CLT may have to pay income taxes on income not distributed to charity. It also means that a gift of appreciated property to a CLT does not have the same benefits as the same gift to a CRT.

Q. What does "zeroing out" a CLT mean?

A. As we mentioned above, there is no floor or ceiling on the payments that can be made from a charitable lead trust (CLT). That means that you can set up a CLT that generates a charitable deduction that approaches the total value of the gift to the trust. Therefore, the charitable gift or estate tax charitable deduction for a CLT can substantially reduce federal gift or estate tax, regardless of how much you put into the CLT. This is the technique used by the late Jacquelyn Kennedy Onassis.

Some authorities have claimed that it is possible to structure the length of time the trust will run and the size of the annuity payout in such a way that the value of the charity's interest (that is, your gift tax deduction or your estate's estate tax deduction) will *equal* the full value of the assets that were transferred to the trust and eventually pass to your selected beneficiaries free of federal estate tax. This makes the CLT an alternative to—in some cases a replacement for—a marital deduction. The CLT may be the single person's "marital deduction."

Let's see how this is possible. The figures below are for a $1,000,000 gift to a charitable lead annuity trust that pays a 8.7 percent annuity to charity every year for 24 years. At the end of 24 years, whatever is in the trust will pass to the donor's children. What is the gift tax cost of removing $1,000,000 from your estate—as well as all the appreciation and income in excess of 8.7 percent for 24 years? As you can see from these numbers, practically nothing!

If the Section 7520 federal discount rate is 7.0%, the present value of an annuity of 8.7% payable for 24 years is 11.4693 times the value of the charity's 24 year annuity, or $997,829.10 (11.4693 times $87,000). This means that what would have been a $1,000,000 taxable transfer has been turned into a taxable gift (or taxable estate if the transfer occurs at death) of only $2,170.90 ($1,000,000—$997,829). This is an amazing 99.8%

reduction! [Calculation courtesy NumberCruncher software—610-527-5216]

In this example, almost 100 percent of a $1,000,000 estate passes free of federal estate tax. Only slightly more than $2,000 will be exposed to federal estate tax—out of $1,000,000. In fact, by increasing the time the beneficiaries have to wait or by increasing the payout to the charity, that small exposure can be reduced even further.

Of course, your designated charity (or charities) will receive $87,000 (8.7% of $1,000,000) each year for 24 years. If the investment in the trust earns less that the payout promised to the charity, capital must be invaded. This may reduce or even eliminate any remainder. This means there may be nothing left for the children at the end of the 24 years. However, if the trust can earn a return equal or greater than the payout you select, in this example 8.7% (or more), it can protect its principal against invasion and the children will be able to receive the full $1,000,000 (or more) at the end of the term of the trust. Therefore, the key to planning for a CLT is knowing whether the trust is likely to be able to earn more than the income assumed for the trust under Section 7520 and finding an investment that can perform that well over a long period of time.

Because the annuity from a charitable lead annuity trust (CLAT) is fixed, just like the annuity from a charitable remainder annuity trust (CRAT), the charitable deduction allowable for a CLAT is very much affected by the difference between the annuity percentage and the Section 7520 discount rate. As the annuity is increased to equal or exceed the discount rate (so that principal will have to be invaded to make the annuity payments), the charitable deduction rapidly increases, and the taxable remainder declines in value.

A charitable lead unitrust (CLUT), by comparison, can almost create a charitable deduction equal to the value of the gift to the trust, no matter how high the payout rate, because the payout is based on a percentage of the trust fund as it is revalued each year. Reducing something by a percentage will never bring it entirely down to zero (although it can get very small). The CLAT is therefore much more effective than a CLUT for "leveraging" the charitable deduction. This is why the CLTs used in estate and gift tax planning almost always are fixed annuity type trusts.

Q. *What are the estate tax implications of a charitable lead trust?*

A. The tremendous estate tax savings potential of a charitable lead trust (CLT) is the biggest reason why wealthy and super wealth individuals consider a CLT.

If you create a CLT during your lifetime, then the moment you put cash or other property into the CLT, it is no longer yours. You have made two gifts: (1) You have given the charity the right to an annuity or unitrust payout for the term of the trust, and (2) you have given the ultimate beneficiaries (your children or other specified individuals) the right to receive the principal in the trust when the charity's payments end.

Here are the estate tax implications in various situations:

- After your lifetime gift, the trust can't be taxed in your estate because the property is no longer yours (assuming the ultimate beneficiary is someone other than yourself). For instance, if you put $1,000,000 into a CLT and have "zeroed out" the CLT along the lines described above, then the trust property is no longer part of your estate and you have saved the $345,800 federal estate tax that the principal could have generated had you not given away the property.

- If you have retained the right to recover trust principal at the end of the trust, the present value of that right at the date of your death will be includible in your estate.

- If you create the CLT in your will, your estate will receive an estate tax charitable deduction. The charitable deduction will be equal to the present value of the charity's right to receive the promised annuity payments for the specified period of time. (When the charity's interest ends, there is no additional estate or gift tax and the assets in the trust will pass to your beneficiaries free of tax.)

Q. *What are the gift tax implications of a CLT?*

A. The value of your gift to a charity through a charitable lead trust (CLT) is, of course, fully deductible for gift tax purposes (assuming CLT rules are met). You will be allowed a federal gift tax deduction for the present value of the charity's *lead interest* when you set up the trust. Only the gift of the *remainder* (the gift to your children or other designated ultimate beneficiary) will generate gift tax. (If you specify that the principal in the trust is to return to you, there will be no taxable gift since you can't make a gift to yourself. But that, obviously, will not save any federal estate tax.)

Because your children must wait 10 or more years, in most cases, to receive whatever principal remains in the trust, your gift is only the discounted present value of what you put into the trust. In the case of a CLAT, this future remainder is discounted back to present value by using the Section 7520 discount rate. (The remainder for a CLUT is calculated in a slightly different way, that is largely independent of the Section 7520 discount rate.)

You are allowed to use the federal discount (Section 7520) rate for the month of the transaction or you may "look back" to the 2 prior months and select the most favorable of the three rates. In fact, by waiting until the IRS releases the next month's rate (somewhere between around the 22nd of the month) you can have your choice of four rates. The lowest discount rate will produce the largest allowable deduction for a CLAT. As we've noted above, it may even be possible, by combining (1) a low discount rate, (2) a long period of time during which the charity will be paid, and (3) a high charitable annuity, to lower the gift tax enough to allow almost the full value of the assets to pass gift tax free to your non-charitable beneficiary.

In some of the discussions above, we have demonstrated the possibility of making a gift to a CLAT with a charitable deduction almost equal to 100% of the gift to the trust. Let's now show a more modest example. Assume you've made no large gifts in the past and that you own assets with a strong growth potential that are producing income at a rate of only 5 percent. By using some or all of your unified credit, you can shelter your transfer from gift taxes by arranging the time period so that the remainder interest (the gift to your non-charitable beneficiaries) is just under the unified credit exclusion amount ($600,000 in 1997 and increasing by steps to $1,000,000 in 2006).

If the Section 7520 discount rate is as high as 9.0%, the present value of an annuity for 15 years is 8.0607 times the amount of the annuity. If the gift to the trust is $1,000,000 and the annuity paid to charity is only $50,000 each year (5% of the initial value of the trust), the trust will still generate a charitable gift tax deduction of $403,035 (the annuity of $50,000 times the factor of 8.0607). That means that the taxable gift is only

$596,965($1,000,000—$403,035). This taxable gift—$596,965—is less than the unified credit exclusion amount. (See chapter 13.) If the income produced by trust assets is sufficient to pay the annuity to charity, then you've transferred $1,000,000 of securities to your children at no out-of-pocket gift tax cost. And any appreciation in the value of the securities from the date you fund your CLT is also gift tax free.

Q. What are the income tax implications of a CLT?

A. Unlike a charitable remainder trust (CRT), which always qualifies for a charitable income tax deduction, a charitable lead trust (CLT) forces you to make a somewhat difficult "Hobson's choice" of income tax consequences:

- You can get a current income tax deduction for your gift to a CLT, but only if you are willing to report the future income of the trust (even though it is distributed to the charity rather than to you) as taxable income as it is earned by the trust). (That's right. The trade-off for a large income tax deduction the year you fund the CLT is that you must pay income taxes on income the trust generates in the following years—even though that money will be paid not to you but to charity)

- The CLT can be arranged so that you will never be taxable on trust income. If you are willing to give up any income tax deduction for your gift to a CLT, then the trust can be set up so that it is considered a separate taxpayer. So the trust (and not you) gets an income tax deduction for the income it distributes to charity.

If you prefer the type of trust that will allow you to take an immediate income tax deduction, you have to retain certain rights or powers over trust assets to cause you to be treated as the owner of the trust for income tax purposes. This is called a *grantor trust*. If you want to be considered the owner of the trust for income tax purposes but not estate tax purposes, this can get a little tricky, but it is possible. For example, you can retain an administrative power that you can exercise personally (but not as trustee) without the approval or consent of anyone else to reacquire trust assets, either by paying the trust cash or by replacing trust property with other assets of equal value.

So you can get an income tax deduction for a CLT, but it comes at a cost. The cost of your immediate, up-front income tax deduction is that each year, as the trust earns income, that income is taxable to you (even though it is payable to the charity). Why would anyone set up a trust that would provide a large immediate income tax deduction only to be taxed annually on the trust's income? There may be a number of reasons. For instance, this "deduct now, pay tax later" technique may make a great deal of sense if you receive a large windfall this taxable year. For example, suppose you win the lottery and take a lump-sum payment. Or perhaps you are a lawyer who earns an unusually high fee that you are not likely to earn in future years. Your accountant suggests that you maximize your deductions for the year to offset that income. If you anticipate that in the years ahead, you'll be in a much lower income tax bracket, it may pay to make a large contribution to a CLT, take a large up-front income tax deduction to offset your income, and in later years when you are in lower tax brackets, report a much smaller income.

Alternatively, you may know that you'll have large deductions in the coming years that you don't have now. Or you may anticipate a change in tax rates due to a change in the tax laws enacted by Congress.

The trustee may invest in tax-exempt securities to reduce the future tax costs to you. Then, even though you will be taxed on future years' trust income, there will be little, if any, taxable income to report.

The second choice is to set up your CLT so that you receive no income tax deduction but you can totally exclude any income the trust earns. The annual amounts paid by the trust to charity are completely nontaxable to you. You would probably choose this type of trust if you didn't have any unusual income in the current year and didn't expect any radical change in your income or deductions in future years.

Q. What are the generation-skipping transfer tax consequences of a CLT?

A. When the generation-skipping transfer (GST) tax was enacted in 1986, it was assumed by many lawyers that the $1,000,000 GST exemption could be effectively and profitably "leveraged" through a charitable lead trust (CLT). Suppose, for example, that a CLT could be established that paid the remainder to grandchildren and generated a charitable deduction equal to 80% of the gift to the trust, so that only 20% was taxable. A $5,000,000 trust would be a gift of only $1,000,000. That meant that the entire trust might be sheltered by the $1,000,000 GST exemption and the grandchildren could receive $5,000,000 at the end of the term of the trust, free of generation-skipping tax.

Congress later changed some of the definitions and technical provisions of the GST tax to reduce (if not eliminate) most of the tax advantages of CLATs for GST purposes. The way the law now works, the $1,000,000 GST exemption (which may be adjusted for inflation after 1998) is not applied until after the charitable annuity ends. The exemption is adjusted for the time (and assumed interest) between the creation of the trust and the termination of the charitable interests. In our example above, the $5,000,000 trust might have a value of only $1,000,000 for federal gift tax or estate tax purposes. But unfortunately, you can't apply your $1,000,000 GST exemption until the end of the term of the trust. If the term of the trust were ten years and the Section 7520 rate at the beginning of the trust were 7.0%, the adjusted GST exemption would be $1,967,151 (i.e., the same as $1,000,000 invested at 7.0%, compounded annually for ten years), not $1,000,000. However, if the trust were still worth $5,000,000 at the end, then only about 40% of the trust ($1,967,151 of the $5,000,000 trust) would be exempt from generation-skipping transfer tax.

Q. What factors should I consider in deciding whether or not a charitable lead trust makes sense?

A. It takes a significant amount of wealth and a strong charitable inclination to make any charitable trust work. In fact, in spite of what you may have heard or read elsewhere—or even in this book—about the significant tax advantages of charitable trusts, we usually recommend that you not set up any type of charitable plan—unless the satisfaction of giving to charity is very important to you.

Of course, you should not underestimate or ignore the significant collateral benefits of a charitable gift in trust. The larger your estate and the higher your potential estate tax, the more appealing the charitable lead trust may be. Typically, a lead trust is indicated if you are willing and able to personally give up income permanently or for a given period of time but would like the capital either to come back to you personally or to pass to a designated family member or others at the end of that time. Usually, to make the lead trust attractive, you'll need to have rapidly appreciating property that also pays income.

A charitable lead trust in your will might also make sense if you have charitable interests and beneficiaries (such as grandchildren) who are able to wait several years before receiving the remainder from the trust.

Q. *What are wealth enhancement and wealth replacement trusts?*

A. Many wealthy investors are able to make a charitable gift while they are alive, enjoy the benefits of a current tax deduction, as well as the pleasure of making a significant contribution to their cause, and replace the wealth their children would otherwise have received through a *wealth replacement* trust. In a few situations, this technique can actually serve as a *wealth enhancement* trust since the beneficiary may receive even more (net after taxes) than he or she would have had if you had made no gift to charity.

Using a program of gifts (often leveraged with life insurance), you can effectively transfer many of the tax benefits of your charitable gifts to your children or other beneficiaries, insuring that your charitable gifts do not reduce the inheritances or financial security of your children.

Suppose you are 60 years old. You are a widower with three children. You are in the top income tax bracket and in a 50 percent estate tax bracket—which means that half of every additional dollar you save or earn will go to the IRS rather than your three children. One of your assets is a $1,000,000 parcel of undeveloped land with a basis of $100,000. Assume you wanted to perpetuate the memory of your late wife though a memorial scholarship fund.

What problems do you face? First, you don't want to deprive your children of a sizable portion of your estate. So you hesitate to give the land to the charity. The charity, however, would like the gift up front, because it plans large capital expenditures in the near future. From the charity's viewpoint, as things stand now, the gift is "maybe someday" gift rather than a "right here, right now" gift.

But if you do nothing, your children will receive only half of the $1,000,000 parcel, since the other half will be lost in federal estate taxes, and the charity will receive nothing either during your lifetime or after your death. Doing nothing, therefore, is a "lose-lose" situation.

You have yet another problem: retirement income. You'd like to make the property income producing to supplement your income. But you don't want to sell the property because you know that tax on the gain will take a big chunk of the investible income.

A possible solution to your dilemma is as follows:

- You make an immediate gift of the land to the charity (or charities) of your choice. In return, you will receive a large and immediate income tax deduction.

- You use the benefit of that income tax deduction to offset other taxable income and that will result in a much lower-than-expected income tax bill. You can then make gift-tax-free gifts of up to $10,000 each year (with possible inflation adjustments after 1998) to each child from the income tax savings. That means you can give up to $30,000 a year ($10,000 a year to each of the three children) to a trust for your children every year without using any of your unified credit.

- Your children's trustee (or the children directly if they are financially mature adults) can use the cash gifts to purchase life insurance on your life, with the policies owned by and payable to the trust. At your death, none of the proceeds would be in your estate. The policy can be for as much as $1,000,000 (wealth enhancement) or as little as $500,000 (wealth replacement). (If you had made no charitable gift, your children would have received only $500,000 after estate tax. So it only takes a $500,000 policy to replace the net after-tax wealth your children would have received. If you give the trustee enough cash to purchase a $1,000,000 policy on your life, you have created a wealth enhancement trust because you are effectively doubling your children's after-tax wealth.)

This wealth replacement/enhancement concept often works with a charitable remainder trust as well as outright gifts to charity. If you need or would like additional income, you can leverage the classic wealth enhancement trust through a charitable remainder annuity or unitrust. Instead of an outright gift to the charity of your choice, you can transfer the land to a charitable remainder annuity trust (CRAT) or charitable remainder unitrust (CRUT) you create. (CRATs and CRUTs are discussed earlier in this chapter.) You'll receive a large immediate deduction for the now certain (but still future) gift to charity.

Note that money that you otherwise would have paid in income taxes can be given as gifts over a period of time at no gift or estate tax cost (or immediately under the shelter of the unified credit) to your children. If the trustee of the charitable trust sells the land and purchases income-producing property with the proceeds, your income will increase considerably, because in a charitable remainder annuity or unitrust, by definition, you keep the income from the trust for as long as you live.

Furthermore, because the trustee can reinvest the proceeds of the sale in a number of investments, trust principal will also increase. Yet you will pay no income tax on the gain, if any, that the charitable remainder trust realizes when it sells the asset you have contributed to it. Unlike the case in which you personally sell the asset and have only the after-tax sales proceeds to use for retirement income, using a CRAT or CRUT provides income based on 100 cents on the dollar for every dollar of value you've placed into the trust.

Q. We are married, have no children, and would like to make a meaningful charitable gift. How can trusts help?

A. If you have no children or other close relatives and are inclined to choose a charity as beneficiary, charitable trusts can be quite advantageous planning tools. Of course, you could leave all of your property to your spouse at your death through a simple will. Because of the unlimited marital deduction, there would be no federal estate tax (but there could be considerable state death) payable when you die. At your spouse's death, he or she could leave everything to charity. The problem is that there is no assurance that such a gift will be made.

An alternative is available. Instead of leaving property outright to your spouse, you could leave it to a *QTIP trust* (see chapter 9). This is a special type of trust that both qualifies for a federal estate tax marital deduction and allows you to select the ultimate recipient of the property in the trust at your spouse's death. This means, for example, that you could leave an estate of any size ($5,000,000, for example), pay no tax when you die (because of the estate tax marital deduction), and pay no tax when your spouse dies (because of the estate tax charitable deduction). This alternative guarantees a lifetime income for your spouse, an estate tax marital deduction, and the assurance that the charity you select will, in fact, receive the principal in the trust when your spouse dies.

You can create similar benefits for your spouse, and get an income tax deduction during your lifetime, through a charitable remainder annuity trust (CRAT) or charitable remainder unitrust (CRUT) that you create during your lifetime and that continues after your death for the benefit of your spouse. The CRAT or CRUT will qualify for the federal estate or gift tax marital deduction, just like a QTIP trust. At your spouse's death, the trust assets will be included in his or her taxable estate, but will qualify for the charitable deduction because the trust has ended and the assets will pass to charity under the terms of the trust.

TRUSTS THAT PROTECT ASSETS
FROM CREDITORS

Chapter 27 explains:

- Why creditor protection planning is important

- Alternatives to using trusts to avoid creditors

- Creditor-resistant forms of property ownership

- "Bullet-proof" ways to keep creditors from reaching property you want to go to your children

- How trusts can serve as asset protection devices

- How a *spendthrift trust* can protect beneficiaries from their creditors

- How a *discretionary trust* can protect beneficiaries from their creditors

- Limitations on the income you can receive from an irrevocable trust designed to provide asset protection

- The safest approach in using a trust to protect your assets

- Types of irrevocable trusts that can provide asset protection

- Offshore trusts: Advantages and disadvantages

- Income tax implications of an offshore trust

- What a fraudulent conveyance is

- More on Alaska and Delaware Trusts

Q. Why is it important to think about protecting my assets from creditors?

A. Protecting assets both during your lifetime and after your death is one of the major goals of estate planning. In other words, estate planning encompasses not only the accumulation and distribution of an estate, but also the conservation of both principal and income. Traditional estate planning concentrates on tax reduction and appropriate asset disposition techniques. We suggest, however, that your estate planning also consider the litigious society in which we live and the potential for the loss of a lifetime of effort because of an unanticipated (and underinsured or uninsurable) event. Beware of the financial devastation of a lawsuit and its impact on your estate, and actively seek competent estate planners' assistance in protecting your assets from such claims.

This chapter will focus first on the general means and extent to which an estate can be insulated from the claims of your potential creditors. You may want to think of it as "preservation planning." Many of the tools used in traditional estate planning—outright gifts, gifts in trust such as GRITs, GRATs, and GRUTs, marital property partitions, tenancy by the entireties ownership, tax-qualified retirement plans, general and limited partnerships, split charitable gifts such as CRATs and CRUTs, and deferred-compensation arrangements—offer such creditor protection, as do relatively new concepts such as family limited partnerships and limited liability corporations (LLCs).

Protection of assets through domestic and foreign situs asset-protection trusts will form the second portion of this chapter with emphasis on the opportunities and pitfalls of such devices. In this section, we will concentrate on practical considerations in the selection of a place to set up an offshore trust.

Vast and ever-increasing amounts of wealth are transferred through life insurance purchased by or transferred to irrevocable life insurance trusts. Be sure to reread chapters 16 and 17, and consider the creditor protection possibilities, as well as the tremendous tax-savings potential, of these devices.

Q. What are some of the alternatives to using trusts to avoid creditors?

A. Before considering the more esoteric forms of creditor protection, we suggest you focus on fundamental strategies to avoid personal liability. For instance, you could

- avoid or minimize high-risk business or personal activities

- increase the adequacy and scope of your homeowner's insurance

- check the limits of professional liability coverage

- check the amounts of umbrella coverage

- increase your own medical insurance coverage

- compartmentalize "dangerous assets" and place them into such "shielding vehicles" as business or professional corporations, limited liability corporations, or limited liability partnerships

- segregate creditor-attracting assets (for example, land that may have environmental problems)

Q. What are some of the more creditor-resistant forms of property ownership?

A. There are a number of ways to own property that discourage or legally prevent creditors from reaching it or establish practical barriers that make it more likely that creditors will give up or be willing to settle. The easiest of these to implement include the following:

- *tenancy by the entireties.* This is a form of joint tenancy that is based on very old common law principles, but is still recognized in many states. It is based on the old concept that a husband and wife are only one person in the eyes of the law. Therefore, the property cannot be sold or divided without the consent of both spouses, and the surviving spouse is automatically the owner of the entire property upon the death of the other spouse.

    Even property held as tenants by the entireties is subject to the joint debts of a husband and wife. If a husband and wife both sign a note, their entireties property can be attached to satisfy the note. However, there can be a different result if the debt is against only one of the spouses (as would be the case with most claims for negligence, professional malpractice, and business debts not co-signed by both spouses).

In some states, a creditor of one spouse cannot attach any part of entireties property; only when the debtor spouse becomes the sole owner of the property upon the death of the other spouse can creditors take any action with respect to the property. If the debtor spouse dies first, the non-debtor spouse owns the property free and clear of any debts. In other states, creditors of one spouse may be able to reach some interests of the debtor spouse even while the property continues to be owned by the entireties. (Note the distinction between spousal property held by the entirety, which is unseverable, and joint tenancy with right of survivorship, which is severable in many states and thus reachable by creditors despite the right of survivorship.)

In most states, only real property can be held as tenants by the entireties, but a few states also allow securities and other forms of personal to be held as tenants by the entireties, with the same protection from creditors.

- *homestead exemption.* Many states offer a special exemption from creditors' claims against a person's home. Two states, Florida and Texas, provide particularly liberal (perhaps downright astounding) exemptions for homes. This often prompts a change of domicile to one of these states. Note that the Taxpayer's Bill of Rights enacted by Congress provides significant exemption from federal tax levy for a personal residence, even though state law can't exempt property from levy by the federal government.

- *qualified retirement plans.* Generally, as long as funds remain inside a pension, profit-sharing, or other qualified retirement plan, they are not subject to claims of ordinary creditors. However, they may be subject to federal tax deficiencies and family support claims. Individual retirement accounts (IRAs) are not protected by federal law, although some states provide complete or partial protection for retirement benefits or retirement annuities.

- *life insurance and annuities.* Most states exempt life insurance proceeds from the claims of the creditors of the insured, and a few states even exempt cash surrender values owned by the insured (at least under some circumstances). Likewise, many states provide some protection for annuity contracts.

- *transfer restrictions on business interests.* Corporate by-laws, corporate buy-sell agreements, partnership agreements, and other business agreements can raise a number of legal and practical barriers to creditors.

  - Corporate by-laws and buy-sell agreements frequently restrict the transfer of stock of closely-held corporations. Although a by-law or buy-sell agreement usually cannot prevent a credit of a shareholder from attaching the stock of the shareholder, the by-laws or agreements can prevent the sale of the stock by the creditor, or can require the creditor to sell the stock back to the corporation or the other shareholders on favorable terms, greatly diminishing the value of the stock to the creditor and protecting the interests of family members who own stock in the corporation.

  - Partnership agreements and the operating agreements of limited liability companies can often go much further, leaving a creditor of a partner (or member) with little more than a right to future distributions from the partnership (or company), with no right to sell or assign the business interest, no say in the operation of the business, and no power to require any distributions.

  - For professional corporations or associations, state laws usually prohibit the transfers of stock or partnership interests to anyone other than licensed professionals, which creates other practical problems for creditors, because it limits salability and so narrows the number of potential purchasers for a creditor or a trustee in bankruptcy.

- *timely disclaimers.* A disclaimer (a refusal to accept a lifetime gift or a benefit from an estate) may help avoid your creditors by shifting a potential inheritance from you to a child or other relative. A disclaimer by a bankrupt or insolvent debtor will not be effective if it relates to property inherited within 180 days after a petition for bankruptcy is filed, and some states have held that a disclaimer may be a fraud on creditors if done with the intent to hinder the claims of creditors. But a refusal to accept property left to you in someone's will may protect that property from your creditors in some states or in some circumstances.

Q. Are there bullet-proof ways to keep creditors from reaching property I want to go to my children?

A. Subject to "fraudulent conveyance" rules discussed below, the most certain way to prevent creditors from reaching your property is to give away, sell, or never own that property. For example:

- If you are concerned about your personal creditors and you have wealthy parents, you might suggest that they leave their assets in a spendthrift trust for your benefit (as explained below) or directly to their grandchildren.

- If a parent has died and his or her will leaves assets to you or, if you not survive your parent, to your children, you should talk to your lawyer about a *disclaimer*—an unqualified refusal to accept the inheritance. If you are not already legally insolvent, that action can be effective in avoiding your creditors and assuring your children will receive your parent's wealth.

Once you own property, simple gifts of the property, either outright or in trust, is the most certain means of removing the property from the reach of your creditors. However, most states have enacted a version of the Fraudulent Conveyance Act or its more modern successor, the Uniform Fraudulent Transfers Act. Those acts allow creditors to reverse a transaction that was made with an actual or presumed intent of hindering or delaying creditors. There is also a federal bankruptcy law with similar rules. Fortunately, both state and federal laws are restricted by a statute of limitations that protects "old and cold" gifts—gifts you made before specified events or far enough back that they are not considered to have been made with the intent of defrauding your creditors. That means that time is of the essence in creditor-proofing your assets. The more quickly you act, the more likely you are to be successful.

Although lifetime gifts appear to be a simple means of avoiding creditors, be sure to talk to your planning team about the practical flaws often encountered with outright transfers. Children sometimes squander assets, attract their own creditors or predators, or take the money and run, leaving their parents with less control—as well as less cash and other assets. Children, like their parents, are subject to divorce and the consequent possible loss of the parent's gift. If a child dies, the parent's gift may end up in the hands of the child's spouse or the spouse's new spouse. For these reasons, and to improve asset management and investment opportunities, you may want to talk to your planners about a transfer to an entity such as an irrevocable trust, family limited partnership, or limited liability company.

Q. How can trusts serve as asset-protection devices?

A. By definition, a trust separates the benefits of the ownership of property from the management and control of the property. The trustee holds legal title to the assets of the trust and is responsible for the management of the trust, while the beneficiaries receive the income or other benefits of the trust. A trust is therefore an excellent device to enable you to control management and investment policies as trustee, yet insulate that same property from your creditors.

At first, it may appear that trusts are the perfect asset-protection vehicle. But there are costs that you must understand, including the following.

- Only *irrevocable* trusts will offer any creditor protection whatsoever. A revocable trust is an easily pierceable shell that offers no hope of defense. If you can reach the assets in your trust whenever you want, your creditors can too. You must be willing, therefore, to make an irrevocable transfer. That translates into a loss of control over the use of the property and its income.

- When you transfer assets to an irrevocable trust, you are making a taxable gift that may not qualify for the annual gift tax exclusion. This means that either a gift tax will be payable or you must use some or all of your unified credit to avoid an out-of-pocket gift tax cost.

- You cannot safely retain any interest in the trust's assets or income. As a general rule, any benefit you retain can be attached by your creditors. Certainly, they can reach an amount at least equal to any income or capital you might be paid by the trustee. (This general rule has apparently been changed by statutes in Alaska, Delaware, and Missouri, as discussed below.)

- There is a cost to create and maintain an irrevocable trust. The smaller the amount transferred to the trust, the larger these costs will appear. Stated another way, unless you transfer assets of considerable value to the trust, it may not be economically feasible to establish one.

Q. What is a spendthrift trust and can it protect beneficiaries from their creditors?

A. When a parent, grandparent, or other grantor creates a trust for a child, grandchild, or other beneficiary, the grantor of the trust can specify that the beneficiary cannot assign any of the beneficiary's interests in the trust and the creditors of the beneficiary shall not have any rights to any income or principal of the trust until *after* it has been distributed to the beneficiary. This kind of *spendthrift clause* is honored in almost all states, and allows grantors to create trusts that are safe from the creditors of the beneficiary.

As suggested above, if you are concerned about possible claims of present or future creditors, whether due to professional or business liabilities, lawsuits, or marital problems, you may wish to talk to your parents or other persons from whom you might inherit property about the possibility of creating a spendthrift trust for your benefit. If your spouse has separate assets, your spouse should also consider the advantages of a QTIP or other trust for your benefit (see chapter 13), because a trust can qualify for the federal estate tax marital deduction even with a spendthrift clause.

Although a spendthrift trust can protect gifts you receive from the claims of your creditors, in most states you cannot create a spendthrift trust for your own benefit, as explained below.

Q. What is a discretionary trust and can it protect beneficiaries from their creditors?

A. A few states do not recognize spendthrift clauses or limit their application. Even in states which recognize spendthrift clauses, the creditors of a beneficiary can attach income or principal after the beneficiary receives it. How do you stop creditors for seizing each income distribution as it is received?

  Leimberg Associates Books: 610-527-5216

One solution is to give the trustees the power to *apply* the income and principal of the trust for the benefit of the beneficiary, rather than distributing the income to the beneficiary. For example, the trustee might send a check directly to the beneficiary's landlord for the beneficiary's rent. The beneficiary never has possession of the check, and the landlord is owed the money under a contract, so there is nothing for the creditors to attach from either the beneficiary or the landlord, and the money in the possession of the trustee could be protected by the spendthrift clause. Similar arrangements could be made with the telephone company, the electric company, and even the beneficiary's grocer. The trustee may be able to provide for all of the basic living expenses of the beneficiary (and maybe even comforts beyond the basics) without any opportunity for any creditor to attach anything in the hands of the beneficiary.

The trustee can also be given the power to accumulate excess income, rather than being required to distribute all income. If it is within the discretion of the trustee to withhold income from the beneficiary, and the beneficiary has creditor problems, it is certainly a proper exercise of the trustee's discretion to accumulate income for the possible future benefit of the beneficiary, rather than allowing the income to go to creditors who are not related to the grantor of the trust and not within the grantor's generosity. Such a discretionary power can be effective even when a spendthrift clause is not, because the creditors cannot force the trustee to make distributions for their benefit.

A QTIP or other trust intended to qualify for the federal estate tax marital deduction (see chapter 13) cannot give the trustee the discretion to accumulate income, although the trustees can be empowered to apply income directly for the benefit of the surviving spouse. Similarly, charitable remainder trusts (see chapter 26) are prohibited from delaying distributions required to qualify the trusts as charitable remainder trusts, but the trustee can be authorized to apply distributions for the beneficiary.

The general rule is that a discretionary trust cannot protect the grantor of a trust from the grantor's own creditors, just as a spendthrift trust cannot protect the grantor of a trust from the grantor's own creditors, because the creditors of the grantor can almost always reach the interests of the grantor to the greatest extent of the discretion of the trustees.

Q. Can I safely keep the income from an irrevocable trust if I assign away the principal?

A. No. Trusts created by a grantor for the grantor's own benefit are afforded little, if any, protection against the grantor's creditors. For instance, a revocable trust or an irrevocable trust that provides income or capital to the person who creates the trust will be subject to the claims of his or her creditors. Likewise, even if you name an independent trustee, if that trustee has the power to distribute income or principal to you, your creditors will usually be entitled to anything the trustees *could* pay to you, even if that decision is solely in the discretion of the trustee, up to the maximum possible extent of the trustee's discretion. As a general rule, creditors can reach the maximum amount that *might* be paid to the creator of the trust, even if there are other potential beneficiaries.

This general rule has been changed in Missouri, and more recently in Alaska and Delaware in 1997, when those states changed their trust laws to permit a grantor to retain interests in a trust that are *not* subject to the claims of the grantor's creditors. However, the interests of the grantor must be purely discretionary (so that the grantor has no real **right** to demand any distributions unless the trustee agrees). The trust cannot have been created for the specific purpose of hindering existing creditors of the grantor. Even so, the changes in the laws in those states may encourage grantors who would otherwise be looking into foreign or "offshore" trusts to instead establish trusts in those states. And to establish a trust that is "resident" in those states and governed by the laws of those states, grantors will have to name a trustee in one of those states, preferably a bank or trust company in those states (and the encouragement of new trust business in those states is undoubtedly the reason these new laws were enacted).

These kinds of asset protect trusts will probably not work for those with existing creditor problems, because the formation of the trust may be seen as an attempt to hinder or defraud those creditors. However, for doctors, lawyers, entrepreneurs, and others who have accumulated wealth and who are concerned about with lawsuits from unhappy patients, clients, or business partners, these kinds of trusts could be an effective way of protecting a "nest egg" from future catastrophic losses.

Even under the traditional rules, not every retained interest will attract the rights of creditors. For instance, a parent can create an irrevocable trust for her children. If the parent retains no beneficial interest in either the income or principal of the trust but names herself as trustee with broad discretion over the timing of payouts and the selection of who will receive payments, the fact that the retained powers may trigger adverse income or estate tax consequences will not of itself also cause trust assets to be reachable by the parent's creditors.

Q. What is the safest approach in using a trust to protect assets?

A. Here's the bottom line: Trusts created for the benefit of others (such as children, grandchildren, nieces, nephews, or even unrelated individuals) in which you retain no interest are in almost all states a secure way to protect assets from your creditors' claims. Placing property in a trust that gives the trustee complete discretion over whether or when to distribute income or principal to the beneficiaries and contains a *spendthrift* provision (which bars beneficiaries from pledging or selling their interests before actual receipt of income or principal) offers the strongest protection in the greatest number of states. It will protect assets from the claims of bankruptcy creditors and even from the claims of a divorced spouse.

Some states now seem to allow you to protect assets by setting up a trust in which the trustee has discretion to give you back income or principal. How effective those new laws will be, and how they will be applied, is not yet certain.

Q. Specifically, what types of irrevocable trusts should I consider?

A. A number of common types of irrevocable trusts that we have covered throughout this book can serve multiple purposes and thus provide tax-saving benefits as well as a measure of creditor protection. Such trusts include irrevocable life insurance trusts, generation-skipping and dynasty trusts, Section 2503(b) trusts, Crummey trusts, QTIP trusts, GRATs, GRUTs, GRITs, CRUTs, and CRATs. (You'll find each of these terms defined in the Glossary, and the Table of Contents will help you locate extensive coverage on each of these concepts.)

Since flexibility is important, a provision in a family trust (see chapter 13) giving the trustee the discretion to "sprinkle income" or "spray principal" to beneficiaries who most need or deserve it is often appropriate. Arranged properly, these trusts will ensure financial security, along with investment and custodial management, for several generations.

Q. *What are offshore trusts?*

A. Trusts give your lawyer an opportunity to "forum shop" on your behalf, that is, to select the state's laws that are most advantageous to protecting your assets. Just as real estate is governed by the laws of the state in which it is situated, a trust is usually governed by the laws of its "home." (Lawyers call this the *law of situs* and frequently call the "home state" of a trust the *situs* of the trust.) You can even use a foreign country with laws more favorable to debtors.

A trust established in a foreign country is often called an *offshore trust.* Some foreign countries have a more protective (for the debtor) statute of fraudulent conveyances and a trust in one of those countries can place a substantial practical barrier to debt collection, because a creditor must first win in a United States court and then sue successfully in the foreign jurisdiction to be able to reach assets.

Nevertheless, offshore trusts have their own costs and limitations, which include the following:

- You personally remain within reach and jurisdiction of United States courts if you are a resident of the United States.

- If you name yourself as trustee, you retain control over the assets you've placed into the trust, but you lose the use of and income from the assets. A United States court that finds a debtor/trustee liable to a creditor may hold the trustee in contempt if the trustee doesn't exercise retained powers to distribute trust assets back to himself or herself—and therefore back to the hands of creditors. So you can't have the use of the money and protection too. (Typically, you would not be the trustee and the assets would not be in the same country where the trust is located. For example, you might have assets in Switzerland but locate the trust in the Cook Islands.)

- If you allow an independent foreign individual (a more common technique) to be trustee, you may be giving up control and incurring significant expense.

- Few lawyers or accountants fully understand offshore trusts and the tax complexities that surround them, so the costs of sound advice is high (and there is a great potential for poor advice, which can turn out to be more expensive than good advice).

- The political stability and the security of cash and other assets sent abroad is always a concern, even in the offshore sites that most encourage asset-protection trusts. These sites include the Bahamas, Bermuda, the Cayman Islands, the Cook Islands, and Gibraltar. The Isle of Man, Belize, Turks and Caicos, and Cyprus are also popular offshore trust sites. (Most experts in this field will be happy to accompany you to any of these typically warm and wonderful places for extended research.) It is a common practice to retain the power to change the location of the trust as well as the trustee so if there is a political change, you could quickly change the location of the trust. Note that you have a problem only if your assets and your trust are in the same country.

- Most offshore asset-protection trusts are grantor trusts for federal income tax purposes (a result that is difficult to avoid), so that you continue to be considered the owner of trust assets for income tax purposes and you will continue to be taxed on the trust income as it is produced. So offshore asset protection trusts are not income tax savings devices.

- Because most asset-protection trusts are structured to avoid a current gift tax (by having the grantor retain certain powers or interests strong enough to classify the transfer of assets to the trust as something less than a completed and therefore taxable gift), the trust assets will still be included in your gross estate for estate tax purposes. So offshore asset protection trusts are not estate or generation-skipping transfer tax savings devices.

- Several changes were made to the tax laws relating to foreign trusts in 1996.

As explained above, recent changes to Alaskan and Delaware trust law may make these states an attractive alternative to foreign jurisdictions for asset protection trusts.

Q. *In general terms, what are the income tax implications of an offshore trust?*

A. Tax law dealing with assets in offshore trusts is quite complex. If a United States citizen or resident creates a foreign trust, the trust is considered to be a "grantor trust," and the grantor is considered to be the owner of the trust assets and the income from those assets for federal income tax purposes, if any of the income of the trust is or *might* be distributed to a citizen or resident of the United States. Therefore, even if you have no interest or power over the trust, the trust is still considered to be a grantor trust if your children are present or future beneficiaries of the trust and your children are citizens or residents of the United States. **You will therefore realize no income tax savings from an offshore trust** because, as a U.S. citizen, you must report and pay taxes on all income you earn anyplace in the world.

There are also extremely complex rules enacted to discourage U.S. citizens and residents from even moving assets to an offshore trust (particularly appreciated assets):

- The 1997 Taxpayer's Relief Act mandates the recognition of gain (i.e., you must report as gain any growth) upon the transfer of appreciated property by a U.S. person to a foreign estate or trust. A transfer characterized as a contribution of capital to a foreign corporation or partnership will trigger the same treatment. However, a transfer to a trust in which the U.S. grantor is for income tax purposes treated as the owner of the trust will not trigger the gain on appreciation.

- There is also a requirement that (a) the creation of a foreign trust, or (b) the transfer of any property to a foreign trust, or (c) the death of the grantor of a foreign trust be reported to the Internal Revenue Service. The failure to report a transfer can result in a penalty tax of 35 percent of the amount involved.

If the income of the foreign trust is taxed to you, it will not be taxed again when distributed to a U.S. beneficiary. However, if the grantor trust rules have not applied to the trust (which would be true after your death), the distributions to your children (or other beneficiaries) may be taxed very harshly. For example, foreign capital gains will be considered to be part of distributable net income, but will be taxed as ordinary income to the beneficiaries. Furthermore, any accumulations of income or delays in the distribution of income can result in nondeductible interest charges on the taxes deferred.

Therefore, **while an offshore trust may have benefits in dealing with creditors, it will almost never result in any income <u>or</u> estate tax savings and could easily result in additional taxes and costs**.

Q. What is a fraudulent conveyance?

A. If you make a transfer to a trust with the intent of hindering, delaying, or defrauding creditors, it may be set aside (that is, ignored for legal purposes) by the courts. Each state has a statute of limitations—a time during which a transfer will be voidable by a creditor or bankruptcy trustee if the transfer is made with any of a number of "evil" intents. Of course, since it is difficult to prove intent, the law looks to certain *badges of fraud*—acts that are considered to evidence the intent to hinder, delay, or defraud creditors.

Badges of fraud include any transaction which does not change the economic position of the transferor, so that the transferor is in much the same position after the transfer as before the transfer, except for the change in legal title. Retention of control or possession of assets are common badges of fraud. For instance, if a parent transfers a business interest to a trust but retains the right to lease trust assets without paying a fair and reasonable rent, there is evidence of fraudulent intent. Likewise, when a transfer to a trust is concealed or a person transfers substantially all his or her assets to an irrevocable trust, fraud may be construed from that action.

The following are some other badges of fraud:

- continued control or management of assets

- possession or use of trust assets or income

- a transfer to the trust when you are already insolvent, have been sued, or have been threatened with suit

- a transfer made shortly before or shortly after you have incurred a large debt

Q. More Detail on Alaska and Delaware Trusts?

A. The Wall Street Journal (July 23, 1997) just ran an article on a new type of trust, the so called Alaska trust. Under the laws of Alaska as of April, 1997, you can set up a "self-settled" (See Chapter 28) perpetual trust (no rule against perpetuities limits the term of the trust and so it can conceivably run forever), have the assets in it protected against your "unknown future creditors", and still get assets you put in it back. (Under most states' laws, if you transfer assets to a trust you set up for your own benefit, the transfer can be ignored by both present and future creditors). Alaska law allows you to name yourself as a "discretionary beneficiary"—so you could request money or other property you put in trust if you need it. Some authorities are claiming that you can do this—and still keep the trust's assets out of your estate for federal estate tax purposes. They also claim it is possible to keep trust assets out of the estates of descendants and other trust beneficiaries. If they are right, the Alaska trust will become one of the most important planning tools of all for the highly successful.

Proponents claim that Alaska (and Delaware) trusts offer many of the same creditor protection opportunities available from the Cook Islands, Jersey (Channel Islands), Belize, or other noted offshore trust havens—at much less cost, without going offshore, and with the political and economic stability of the U.S. This places these two states high on the list as a good place to set up a trust designed mainly for favorable asset protection. They will be particularly useful where a client does not want to place the legal ownership of his or her assets in the hands of a person or entity that is offshore or if the size of the estate does not warrant the large expense of an offshore asset protection trust. Since Alaska has no income tax, income can accumulate on wealth free of state income tax upon the death of the trust's creator. This absence of income taxes on trust income not currently distributed to trust beneficiaries, vis a vis most other states, can make a dramatic impact upon the net amount received by heirs. (Consider also, that if a trust asset is about to be sold at a large state law capital gains tax, a move to an Alaska situs might be very beneficial). So peace of mind, reduced set-up costs, possible state income tax savings, and the freedom from the extensive IRS reports which are required of foreign trusts are all legitimate advantages of an Alaskan trust. (An Alaska trust will, of course, be exempt from the arcane and in some cases prohibitive foreign trust tax rules).

Proponents claim that "assets beyond creditor's claims are generally out of your taxable estate. Therefore, transferring assets to an Alaskan trust shelters them from estate tax. Yet these assets may be distributed to your loved ones—or even to you, the creator of the trust—at the trustee's discretion." "You can enjoy the estate tax savings available with discretionary irrevocable trusts even though you remain eligible to receive distributions from the trust." The authors of this book urge caution for the reasons noted above; the entire thrust of the estate tax Code is that the only way to remove assets from your taxable estate is to give up the right to control or use those assets as your own. The "discretion" granted to the trustee to return those assets to you—the creator of the trust—may be too much of a "string" for the IRS to ignore—and it may use that string to pull the assets back into the trust creator's estate. (At the very least, it will be necessary to assure no implied or express pre-arrangement with the trustee regarding the making of income and/or principal distributions back to the trust's creator).

Proponents further claim that the 55% generation-skipping transfer tax can be avoided—even though the trustee is allowed under state law in Alaska to distribute either trust income or principal or both to the trust's creator. They claim that—because it is at the trustee's discretion—and not on the demand of the creator—that the trust assets are available—that it is possible to remove all future appreciation from a couple's estate and avoid the GSTT—yet get the money back if they need it. Again, the authors are skeptical and urge caution on this almost "too good to be true" tax result.

Certainly, there are certain costs and guidelines that must be met for these trusts to achieve even the creditor protection that they promise:

- The trust must be irrevocable.
- The trust must be created well before there is a significant threat by creditors or potential known future creditors against assets or income of the creator. The longer the trust has been in existence before the creditor takes action, the safer the assets are. Clearly, as noted in the discussion above, a trust created to hinder or defraud creditors will fail to do so. This rationale applies to child support payments. Neither Alaska nor Delaware trusts will protect the creator from alimony or child support obligations.

- Some trust assets (Most authorities suggest at least $10,000 or more) must in fact be actually held in a bank account or brokerage account in Alaska or Delaware). The larger the amount of stocks, bonds, mutual funds, or bank accounts actually located in the protective state, the stronger the asset protection position. The trustee must be either a trust company with its principal place of business in Alaska or someone who lives in Alaska. Some or all of the trust's assets must be deposited in Alaska, the Alaska trustee must have the power to maintain trust records in the state and must have the power to file tax returns for the trust, and at least some of the trust administration must be performed in Alaska.

Some proponents also suggest that the trust provide that distributions can be made to the creator's spouse (and not to the creator) "as long as he (she) is alive and married to me" to provide further flexibility and asset protection and that the trust should be allowed to purchase a residence or summer compound for the use of family members (including the creator) to live in, rent free. A few proponents claim that the creator may retain the right to veto distributions to other beneficiaries or control the ultimate disposition of trust assets at death. Although this may provide creditor protection for several generations, the authors are again skeptical of the validity of proponents' claims that the homes or other assets will be beyond the reach of federal estate taxes because of the retention of rights by the trust's creator. The authors are most certain that the retention of a right to veto distributions or control the disposition of trust assets at the creator's death will trigger estate tax inclusion.

Of course, aside from the uncertainty of the federal tax results (the tax results claimed haven't been tested), the legal expenses will run between $10,000 and $15,000. And you can expect administration costs to run a low of about $3,000 a year up to as much as 1% of the assets in the trust. You may need to use Alaska counsel—along with your own attorney and CPA—and there are logistical problems when you conduct business—long distance.

The Alaska trust will not work to hide assets from existing or imminent creditors. So a doctor about to be sued for a botched operation or someone about to be divorced will not be able to protect his assets by setting up a trust tomorrow—that's a fraudulent conveyance. Such creditors will have up to four years from the date of transfer to the trust (or a year after discovery—or date when discovery was reasonable—of the transfer if longer) to file a fraudulent transfer claim. Compare this with some foreign jurisdictions which allow only a year to prove fraud. Furthermore, Alaska will respect the court judgments of other states. Compare this with the more bullet-proof creditor protection afforded by offshore countries; by going offshore creditors who argue that your transfers were made to defraud them must obtain a judgment against you—in that foreign jurisdiction. So the cost and aggravation incurred by creditors in the case of an Alaska trust is far less.

IRREVOCABLE "SELF-SETTLED" TRUSTS

Chapter 28 explains:

- What is an irrevocable self-settled trust

- Why an irrevocable self-settled trust will not save any income taxes

- Why an irrevocable self-settled trust will not save any gift or estate taxes

- Why an irrevocable self-settled trust will not avoid creditor problems

- Why an irrevocable self-settled trust may nevertheless serve important management goals

Q. *What is an irrevocable self-settled trust?*

A. Beneficiaries often receive benefits before they are ready for them. If a parent dies without a will, a child may receive an inheritance at age 18, the legal age of adulthood in most states. A child might drop out of school and, at age 18 or 21, become entitled to the entire amount of a Uniform Transfers to Minors Act account intended for college expenses. Even a beneficiary who inherits money in his or her thirties or forties may have problems investing and managing the money, may have trouble not spending it all, or may have problems with alcohol, drugs, gambling, or emotional issues. Sometimes, a beneficiary is able to recognize the problem and work with another family member to manage and protect the beneficiary's funds.

One solution is an irrevocable self-settled trust. The beneficiary would create a trust for his or her own benefit, naming a more responsible family member or other third party as trustee. The trustee would be responsible for investing and managing the assets, and would have the discretion to distribute as much money back to the beneficiary as the beneficiary might need from time to time, or even all of the trust fund if the beneficiary matures or recovers and the reason for the trust ends.

461

The purpose of an irrevocable self-settled trust, therefore, is to protect the beneficiary from himself or herself.

Q. Will an irrevocable self-settled trust avoid any income taxes?

A. No, the rights retained by the beneficiary will insure that the trust will be a *grantor trust* for federal income tax purposes, and all of the income of the trust will be included on the beneficiary's personal income tax return. The trust is therefore "invisible" for federal income tax purposes.

Q. Will an irrevocable self-settled trust avoid any death taxes?

A. If the trustee has broad discretion to distribute the funds back to the beneficiary, then the creation of the trust will not be a taxable gift, and the full value of the trust will be included in the beneficiary's estate for federal estate tax purposes. The trust is therefore meaningless for estate and gift tax purposes.

Having your cake and eating it too seems to be the goal that tax alchemists perpetually seek. To that end, some lawyers have claimed that an *irrevocable self-settled trust* can avoid estate tax. If the grantor makes large gifts to an irrevocable trust and retains the right to trust income or principal based only on a fixed (or ascertainable) standard to limit how much the grantor can receive, advocates of this approach feel that it is also possible to limit the portion of the trust's assets that will be included in the grantor's estate for estate tax purposes to the actuarial value of this limited right. The goal of an irrevocable self-settled trust is for the grantor to maintain access to significant income and principal placed in trust while avoiding estate tax on most of the trust's value.

Interest in estate tax planning with self-settled trusts was recently sparked again by changes in Alaskan and Delaware trust law. By a statutes enacted in 1997, Alaska and Delaware made it possible to create a trust in those states that would not be subject to the claims of the grantor's creditors even though the grantor is a beneficiary. A common grounds for including self-settled trusts in the grantor's taxable estate is that the trust is still subject to the claims of the grantor's creditors, and so is still subject to debts of the grantor's estate and can be considered to be part of his estate. If a grantor can create a trust from which she might receive benefits but which is not subject to the claims of her creditors, then some lawyers have speculated that it might be possible to make a gift to a trust for your own benefit and yet exclude the assets of the trust from your taxable estate.

The problem is that there is no tax statute, regulation, case, or ruling to support this exceptionally favorable result, and the claimed estate tax result conflicts with several very specific provisions of the Internal Revenue Code. It is therefore not something we can recommend without reservation. (At least one expert on tax planning has quipped that "You can always tell "pioneers" because they are lying face down with arrows in their backs.") When considering the possible rewards, you should also ponder the potential price of fame to become a tax pioneer in the area of self-settled trusts.

Q. Will the irrevocable self-settled trust avoid creditor problems? Is it really irrevocable?

A. As explained in chapter 27, a trust created for the primary benefit of the grantor is almost always subject to the claims of the creditors of the grantor, regardless of what the trust says.

The fact that the trust can be reached by the creditors of the beneficiary probably means that the beneficiary can assign his or her interests in the trust. And some courts have concluded that, if the creditors of the beneficiary can reach the trust and the beneficiary can assign the trust, what is the point of not allowing the beneficiary to terminate the trust? It is therefore likely that the trust is revocable both as a practical matter and a legal matter.

Q. If the trust saves no taxes, provides no creditor protection, and isn't really irrevocable, what is the point?

A. Although a self-settled trust saves no taxes and is not really irrevocable, it may nevertheless serve important management goals.

- While the trust exists, the trustee will be able to manage the investments of the trust, which was one of its principal purposes.

- Even though the trust is not safe from the claims of creditors, it may nevertheless discourage creditors. If the beneficiary applies for a new loan or line of credit, the potential creditor may not be aware of the trust assets and limit the credit of the beneficiary accordingly, limiting the total of the bills that the beneficiary can run up. Even if a potential creditor is aware of the trust funds, the existence of the trust may discourage creditors from lending too much money. And the existence of the trust may even discourage a creditor with a valid claim, allowing the trustee to work out a more favorable settlement.

- Finally, the existence of the trust will still allow the trustee to monitor the beneficiary's situation. The beneficiary cannot get money from the trust without asking the trustee, so the trustee may get enough warning of coming conflicts with the beneficiary to get counseling for the beneficiary or even initiate incompetency proceedings before the beneficiary wastes all of his or her funds. Similarly, inquiries from unhappy creditors may give some warning that the beneficiary is "off the wagon" before the beneficiary has done too much damage. The trust fund therefore puts the trustee into a position in the beneficiary's life where the trustee may be able to see problems arise and help the beneficiary before the problems get too bad.

"BUSINESS" TRUSTS

Chapter 29 explains:

- The differences between trusts used in business and other kinds of trusts

- What is a "Massachusetts trust" or "business trust"

- How a business trust is taxed

- When a business trust is (or is not) a good way to operate a business

- How employee benefits are provided through trusts

- How trusts (and life insurance) are used in buy-sell agreements

- What a "Rabbi trust" is

- How liquidation trusts are used by corporations

- Why a "trustee in bankruptcy" is not a trustee in the usual sense of the word

- What a common trust fund is

Q. The differences between trusts used in business and other kinds of trusts

A. Trusts can be used by corporations as well as individuals as part of business as well as estate planning. This chapter will explain some of the business uses of trusts. It is important, as you read, to note the differences between the commercial trusts described in this chapter and the personal trusts described in other chapters of this book.

- Commercial trusts are usually subject to very different laws than the personal trusts created by individuals for estate planning purposes. For example, "business trusts" (explained below) are usually defined by state statutes, while most other kinds of trusts are defined by common law (judge-made rules). Similarly, many aspects of the law relating to employee benefit trusts are governed by federal statutes, not state laws. Furthermore, litigation involving personal trusts is usually conducted in the probate courts along with estates. Lawsuits involving commercial trusts are usually heard in the regular civil courts. These seemingly legalistic distinctions can make significant differences in the outcome of real life situations.

- Trustees of personal trusts usually have a number of responsibilities, including the selection and management of investments. Trustees of commercial trusts usually have no investment powers and very few other responsibilities, often being merely nominees or agents with no authority other than to follow the directions of others.

- The tax rules that relate to personal trusts usually do not apply to commercial trusts. Commercial trusts may be taxed like corporations, like partnerships, have special rules under the Internal Revenue Code, or be treated as an agency and ignored altogether for tax purposes.

Q. What is a "Massachusetts trust" or "business trust"

A. Lawyers in Massachusetts have often used trusts as a substitute for corporations. Unlike the typical personal trust where a senior family member might create a trust for younger generation beneficiaries, in the Massachusetts Business Trust, it is the beneficiaries who create the trust. It works like this: The beneficiaries transfer cash or other property to the trustees and in turn receive "beneficial interests" proportionate to their contributions to the trust. These beneficial interests are freely transferable, like stock of a corporation. The beneficiaries often have the power to elect the trustees of the trust just like the shareholders of a corporation elect the board of directors of the corporation.

Delaware and at least 16 other states have enacted statutes that authorize the creation of "business trusts" (sometimes called "statutory trusts") intended to operate similar to Massachusetts trusts (although the trusts in Massachusetts are based on contract and case law, not statutory authority).

Q. How a business trust is taxed

A. Historically, business trusts established in Massachusetts and other states have been formed to operate as mutual funds or real estate investment trusts. They are therefore subject to the special provisions of the Internal Revenue Code relating to those kinds of entities. If a business trust does not qualify as a mutual fund, real estate investment trust, or other entity with special tax treatment, it has been classified as a corporation for federal income tax purposes. This means that there have been no tax advantages to a business trust, and a business trust was really nothing but an alternative to a corporation. In fact, in the past, business trusts have been considered inferior for most purposes to limited partnerships and limited liability companies, both of which could qualify as partnerships for federal income tax purposes and therefore avoid any federal income tax at the trust level.

This situation changed at the end of 1996, when the IRS adopted the so called "check-the-box" regulations. Before the adoption of those regulations, general partnerships were taxed as partnerships, corporations were taxed as corporations, and business trusts, limited partnerships, limited liability companies, limited liability partnerships and other entities were taxed either as partnerships or as corporations, depending on the number of "corporate characteristics" shown by the entity. These sometimes complex, and often-shifting rules about what was considered to be a corporate characteristic and what was not considered to be a corporate characteristic often created uncertainty and legal disputes with the IRS.

In 1996, the IRS gave up and announced that, if an organization was not a corporation or a partnership, it could choose ("check the box" on a form and decide for itself) whether the organization was to be taxed as a partnership or a corporation for federal tax purposes. In short, the IRS would accept whatever the decision the organization wanted to make about how it should be treated.

As a result of these new regulations, tax planners have shown new interest in business trusts as a tax planning device. A business trust may prove to be more flexible than a limited liability company, and provide many of the same opportunities for centralized management, restrictions on transfers of interests, and valuation discounts for estate and gift planning purposes as a family limited partnership.

However, the check-the-box technique is relatively new, the laws regarding business trusts vary greatly from state to state, and the tax consequences and legal consequences are not all certain. So it will probably be sometime before the estate and tax planning capabilities and potentials of business trusts are fully known.

Q. When might a business trust not be a good way to operate a business?

A. Despite the liberalization of federal tax rules regarding business trusts, there are reasons why a business trust might not be a good way to operate a business. Most of these reasons relate to the operations and liabilities of a trust when the trust is not simply holding and managing assets, but employing workers and operating an active business.

Business trusts are still recognized in a relatively few states. The operation of an active business, with sales or products in several states, could raise a number of questions regarding the liability of the business trust and its trustees in other states, and the taxation of the trust in other states. Corporate law is tested and relatively certain. All states recognize corporations for tax and other purposes. Shifting to a form of entity that might not be fully recognized in other states can create problems if the operations of the entity are not wholly local, or restricted to a single state.

Even in the state in which the business trust is created, there may be unresolved issues about the liability of trustees and beneficiaries for contracts of the trust, or injuries caused by the negligence of employees of the trust. Unless you and your legal advisors are sure that you know all the answers, it may be better to stick with tried and true methods, and not experiment with a legal technique that may be just a fad.

Q. How are employee benefits provided through trusts?

A. There are a number of different types of employee benefit plans that are administered through trusts. For example, the assets of qualified pension and profit-sharing plans are usually held in trusts. The sole duty of the pension, profit-sharing, or ESOP trustee is to follow the instructions of the plan administrator (i.e., the employer or a committee appointed by the employer) with respect to investments and distributions. Similarly, life insurance, medical insurance, and other forms of employee benefits are often administered through trusts.

Federal law governs most type of employee benefits, so the creation and operation of these trusts is usually governed by federal law, not state law. And special tax rules apply to these trusts, so they are not subject to the taxes that apply to personal trusts.

Q. How are trusts (and life insurance) used in buy-sell agreements?

A. Life insurance is commonly used to fund business cross-purchase agreements. But there are frequently concerns about the costs of multiple policies, and making sure that the insurance is used for what it was intended.

Suppose a corporation or partnership has three principals. Assume also that the business is worth $3,000,000 and the principals decide, for valid business reasons, to entire into a cross-purchase agreement rather than a redemption agreement. (That is, the principals will each individually purchase the interests of a deceased principal, rather than having the business purchase the interest.) In order to fund the cross-purchase obligations with life insurance, each of the three principals would have to buy $500,000 of insurance on the lives of the other two principals, so there are six life insurance policies, not three. (The formula for determining the number of required policies in a cross purchase plan is $N \times (N-1)$ with N being the number of owners). If there are four principals, then there are twelve policies, not four. As the number of principals increases, the complexity of the arrangement can become unmanageable and the costs and aggravation and potential for mistakes can become prohibitive.

Another problem is the question of the enforcement of the agreement upon the death of a principal. Upon the death of a principal, his family will be expecting $1,000,000 of cash for the one third business interest. Suppose that one of the other principals takes the cash and loses it in Las Vegas, or suppose the insurance proceeds are attached by their creditors?

The best solution to these problems may be a trust. The trustee can purchase the right amount of life insurance with one policy for each principal and, upon the death of a principal, the trustee will be required to purchase the interests of the deceased principal and divide that business interest among the remaining principals. The trust can similarly include provisions to handle adjustments if interests are sold or transferred during lifetime. However, with three or more owners, there is a potential deadly tax trap known as the "transfer-for-value" rule. We suggest you obtain one or more of the following books: *Tax Planning With Life Insurance*: *Financial Professional's Edition* (800-950-1210)*, The Corporate Buy-Sell Handbook* (800-982-2850), or *Tools and Techniques of Life Insurance Planning* (800-543-0874).

Q. What is a "rabbi trust"?

A. A "rabbi trust" (so-called because the first ruling by the IRS involved a Jewish rabbi) is a special kind of deferred compensation arrangement established by an employer for an employee. Under the usual tax rules regarding employee compensation, if the employer is entitled to a deduction, then the employee must report the same amount as income. And vice versa. If the employee has not received any income, then the employer is not entitled to a deduction.

Federal tax rules also require that an employee realize taxable income as soon as a deferred compensation plan is "funded," meaning that the funds are irrevocably committed to the employee. (The major exception to these rules is qualified pension and profit-sharing plans, because the employer can obtain a tax deduction for a contribution to a qualified plan even though the employee does not realize any taxable income until the benefits are actually distributed at retirement.) A "rabbi trust" is a way of deferring compensation even though the compensation is funded through a trust.

Under a rabbi trust, the employer sets up an irrevocable trust for the benefit of the covered employee (or employees). However, the rabbi trust is written so that it is subject to the claims of the employer's creditors (if the other assets of the employer are not sufficient to pay its creditors). As a result, the trust is a grantor trust for federal income tax purposes, and the employer's contributions to the trust are ignored for federal tax purposes. Therefore, there is no current tax deduction for the employer and no currently taxable income to the employee. The employee assumes a slight risk that the deferred compensation might be seized by a creditor of the employer, but is still somewhat better than an employee with deferred compensation that is a mere bookkeeping account and nothing but a debt of the employer. For more on rabbi trusts, see ***Tools and Techniques of Employee Benefit and Retirement Planning*** (800-543-0874).

Q. What is a "liquidation trust" and how is it used by a corporation?

A. In the past, it has often been necessary for a corporation which has begun to liquidate to complete the liquidation by a certain date to comply with tax or other regulations. For example, until 1986 it was necessary for a corporation to completely liquidate within one year of the beginning of the liquidation in order for the liquidation to enjoy favorable tax treatment.

When a corporation cannot complete a liquidation within the required time (usually because it has not yet converted all of its assets into the cash needed for the final distributions to the shareholders), the corporation can complete the liquidation by transferring all of its assets into a trust for the benefit of the shareholders. The sole purpose of this "liquidating trust" is to finish selling the assets and then distribute the net proceeds of sale to the shareholders. As a result, the trust is usually considered to be a grantor trust for federal income tax purposes, and all of the income is taxable to the shareholders in proportion to their interests in the trust, and not the trust itself. This kind of trust therefore allows a corporation to complete the liquidation within the time required by tax or other laws, even though the liquidation is not actually completed and can continue through the trust.

Q. Is a trustee in bankruptcy really a trustee?

A. Not in the usual sense of the word. A trustee in bankruptcy takes over all of the assets of the bankrupt individual or business and liquidates those assets for the benefit of the creditors, much like a liquidating trust sells assets for the benefit of the shareholders of the liquidating corporation. The duties and liabilities of a trustee in bankruptcy are determined by federal bankruptcy law, not state trust law. The taxation of a bankrupt's estate is also governed by special rules, not the rules that apply to decedent's estates and personal trusts.

Q. What is a common trust fund?

A. A common trust fund is a fund established by a bank to allow it to invest the funds of several estates or trusts together. The terms of the "trust" are governed by federal and state banking laws, and the income tax consequences are determined by a special section of the Internal Revenue Code. And so, like the other forms of trusts described in this chapter, the common trust fund is not governed by the same laws as personal trusts, or subject to the same tax laws as the trusts created by individuals for the benefit of their families.

Q. What is a Land Trust?

A. A land trust is a device by which real estate (including improvements) is conveyed to a trustee under an agreement which keeps for the beneficiaries of the trust the full managment and control of the property. The duty of the trustee, therefore, is to sign deed, mortgages, and other key documents and deal with the property at the direction of the beneficiaries. It is the beneficiaries who collect rents and operate the property. The beneficiaries exercise all rights of ownership—other than the legal holding or dealing with the legal title. In other words through a contract between the parties, the trustee holds both legal and equitale title to the property but the beneficiary has rights by virtue of that contract to possess, operate, maintain, control, and receive the proceeds of a sale from the trust's property.

Q. How is a Land Trust Created?

A. A land trust is created through the use of two instruments. One is a deed in trust which conveys the real estate to the trustee. At the same time, a trust agreement is signed by the parties giving the beneficiaries the power to change the ownership of the property, manage, and control it, and receive the proceeds if trust property is sold, mortgaged, or rented. So the trustee operates the property and issues "certificates of interest" to the beneficiaries.

Q. What are the advantages of a land trust?

A. There are a number of practical advantages of a land trust. These include

- privacy (the identity of the real owners, the beneficiaries, is not made public),

- protection against marital rights (a spouse does not have to join in signing documents with respect to a land trust and has no rights under law to property held inside it)

- protection against personal liability (nonrecourse mortgages or loans may be placed against the property itself without endangering the personal assets of the owners.)

- ease of transferability (an interest in a land trust is personal property and can easily be transferred by the execution of an assignment. Complex instruments of conveyance or title examinations are not necessary),

- use as collateral (since the beneficial ownership is personal property, it can be pledged as collateral for a loan).

Q. What are the federal tax implications of a land trust?

A. The interest of a beneficiary of a land trust will be included in his or her gross estate and taxed at its fair market value. When an interest in a land trust is irrevocably transferred to another person, the gift will be subject to the federal gift tax. For income tax purposes, the trust itself and the trustee are not taxabe entities. But the beneficiaries receive the trust's income and are therefore taxed on it. (Compexities may arise in this later area but often can now be solved through the "check-the-box" self-characterization for tax purposes as either a trust or a partnership).

TRUST FRAUDS, FANTASIES, AND ABUSES

Chapter 30 explains:

- How trusts can be used fraudulently, and the difference between tax avoidance and tax evasion

- The number and value of abusive trusts now in existence

- The truth about "Constitutional" or "pure" trusts

- Why future wages, salaries, or other earnings cannot be transferred to a trust

- How family residence trusts can be fraudulent or abusive

- How business trusts can be fraudulent or abusive

- How charitable trusts can be fraudulent or abusive

- Why "offshore" (foreign) trusts do not avoid taxes

- Why revocable living trusts and the other types of trusts recommended in this book are not abusive and not are subject to the same IRS attacks as abusive trusts

- Why promoters make extravagant claims about trusts (and how they break the law when they make those claims)

- The tax principles you should know to recognize when a trust might be a sham or a fraud

- Other warning signs to look for in order to avoid being cheated by a "trust mill" or abusive trust promoter

- Why things that sound too good to be true usually aren't

Q. Can a trust be used as a part of a fraud or sham?

> **A.** In this book, we have been careful to explain the benefits of trusts that are fully supported by the law. The tax benefits of trusts exist

because of specific provisions of the Internal Revenue Code or specific rulings of the Internal Revenue Service. The non-tax benefits of trusts are established by court decisions handed down in courts throughout the United States over many years. (Some aspects of trust law described in this book were established by court decisions in England before the American Revolution.) And we have been careful to describe the limitations and disadvantages of some trust arrangements, as well as the advantages.

Unfortunately, **the benefits of a trust can often seem so magical that it is only a small step from a valid application and interpretation of trust and tax law to a fantasy with no basis in law whatsoever**. Even more unfortunate is that **there are charlatans and con artists that would like to make a profit from selling their fantastic schemes at outrageous prices to a sometimes unsophisticated public**. The principles of trust law and tax law can be complex. Con artists can use that complexity (and subconscious greed or unrealistic hope) the same way that a street hustler can use rapid hand motions to hide the pea under the shell. By talking fast and making a lot of motions, a hustler can make the pea and your money both disappear, along with the truth.

And dishonest people can use trusts to obscure their financial dealings. We have all read about "shell corporations" and "dummy corporations" that are used to hide assets, create phony expenses, or create confusion regarding the true ownership of assets. Trusts can be "shams" and used the same way.

These outrageous frauds are, unfortunately, so prevalent that the Internal Revenue Service has issued a notice to the public. It announced that it is "aware" of what it terms "abusive trusts" and has undertaken a national program to recognize and address abusive trust practices, including the possibility of criminal prosecutions in appropriate cases. The invalid or fraudulent trust arrangements described in this chapter consider the types of trusts identified by the IRS as abusive. (The complete text of the IRS Notice can be found in the appendix.)

Courts often observe that everyone has the right to arrange his or her affairs to reduce his or her taxes to as little as possible. Tax avoidance is good tax planning in accordance with the law. But tax evasion is based on deception and is a crime. The difference is more than semantics, because it can mean a difference of up to $100,000 of your money and up to 5 years of your life.

Q. How may trusts be abusive?

A. The IRS has reported that it is investigating about 200,000 cases of potentially abusive trusts, affecting about $1 billion in assets held in those trusts. That may be just the tip of the iceberg.

The IRS will assess taxes and penalties against the taxpayers participating in these abusive trusts, as well as the promoters of abusive trusts. It has clearly announced that it will also seek criminal charges for evasion or fraud or other crimes "whenever warranted." Make no mistake: those charges can be levied not only against the promoters of trust schemes but also against those who underreport income or assets based on such abusive trusts.

Q. What is a "Constitutional" or "pure" trust and will it save taxes?

A. A description of a trust as a "Constitutional" trust or "pure" trust (or some other patriotic name) is almost always a warning that you are dealing with a slickly promoted scheme with no basis in law or fact.

The idea of the "Constitutional" trust seems to be that, because the words "common law" appear in the U.S. Constitution and because the law of trusts began in English common law (that is, the law that comes from the decisions of judges and not the enactments of legislatures), a trust may be entitled to some sort of Constitutional protection that makes it immune to the taxes that everyone else must pay. There also seems to be a theory that, because a trust is a form of contract and the Constitution forbids the "impairment" of contracts, a trust cannot be taxed or otherwise "impaired."

There is no valid legal basis for either theory. When presented to courts, these arguments have been described by judges as "ridiculous" and "frivolous." Anti-tax zealots who have insisted on raising these arguments have been heavily fined (repeatedly) by the courts for wasting judicial time and resources.

The fact of the matter is that the taxing powers of Congress under the Constitution are incredibly broad. A trust (or its grantor or beneficiary) will be subject to federal income tax unless a specific provision of the Internal Revenue Code can be found that exempts the trust. Claims to the contrary are nothing but fantasies.

Q. Can my future wages, salary, or other earnings be transferred to a trust?

A. You can transfer almost any property—or property interest—to a trust. But that transfer may not have any positive tax consequences. Numerous decisions of the U.S. Supreme Court and other federal courts have made it clear that wages, salaries, and other forms of earned income are *always* taxed to the person who earns the income. Such an "assignment of income" will be ignored for federal income tax purposes. Any attempt to assign future income to a trust is a complete waste of time if the goal is to save or shift the burden of income taxes. Anyone who makes any claim to the contrary is either incredibly ignorant or is not being honest with you.

In a similar way, the income from a property is taxed to the owner of the property. (This is sometimes known as the "fruit of the tree" doctrine since income, the fruit of property, is always taxed to the owner of the tree.) Many of the abusive trust arrangements described below are an attempt to disguise or hide the true ownership of property, and transfer the title to property without actually transferring the control or use of the property. Don't bother trying it since it just will not work (and will subject you to potential interest, penalty, and possibly criminal charges)!

Q. Can a family residence trust reduce my taxable income by allowing me to deduct the expenses of maintaining my residence?

A. In chapter 20, we described the gift and estate tax advantages of transferring a personal residence to a *grantor retained interest trust* (GRIT), also called the *qualified personal residence trust* (QPRT). This tax benefit is specifically authorized by the Internal Revenue Code. Used properly, it can provide a significant gift tax "discount". Why? Because your gift tax is based, not on today's value or on the potentially appreciated value of the house when the trust ends, but on the much reduced present value of your beneficiary's right to the residence at the end of the trust. When you set up a house GRIT, your gift is only the gift of a remainder interest in the residence. That can save hundreds of thousands of dollars in transfer taxes.

Not content with the generous gift tax benefits allowed by law, some people have tried to create income tax benefits by transferring a personal residence to a trust (other than a GRIT or QPRT) and then claiming income tax reductions as a result of the transfer. A common claim is that the residence generates deductible expenses after it has been transferred to the trust, as though it were a rental property and the expenses were incurred for the maintenance of the property. Some promoters have the gall to make this outrageous claim even though the residence actually generates no rental income and is still used as the personal home of the taxpayer. Sometimes the promoter of a trust scam will claim that the tax basis of the residence can be increased when the residence is transferred to the trust (even though no taxable gain or loss was reported by the transferor). This, the promoter will say, results in additional depreciation deductions.

A basic principle of tax law is that food, shelter, clothing, and other personal living expenses are not deductible. Scam artists will tell an unsuspecting potential purchaser of an abusive trust that by transferring a personal residence to a trust, he or she can convert a non-deductible personal expense to a deductible expense. As is the case with each of the tactics mentioned above, this claim borders on fraud.

Q. Can a business trust avoid income taxes?

A. As explained in chapter 29, a trust can be a valid alternative to a partnership or corporation for the operation of a business, and there are other valid business uses for trusts. However, a business can also be transferred to a trust as part of a scheme to evade taxes.

In an abusive business trust, the business owner might transfer a business to a trust in exchange for "certificates of beneficial interest" and then list on his trust's tax return "deductible business expenses for distributions to certificate holders or other trusts" so that the trust shows little or no taxable income. The business owner may then claim to owe neither employment (Social Security) tax nor self-employment tax, because no wages were paid and the trust had no income.

The business may generate income through the personal services of the original owner. Yet in an abusive trust, the income produced by that individual is distributed to the "beneficiaries" of the trust (the children of the business owner) and claimed to be their income taxable at their tax much lower rates. But of course, this trick can't work either. Remember, basic principles of tax law require that income be taxed to the person who earns it (the person who does the work or the original owner of the business).

A related scheme is to transfer equipment to a trust which then rents the equipment to the business trust, often at inflated rates. There are legitimate ways to transfer equipment to a trust and then lease the equipment back to the original owner. But these legitimate arrangements are based on fair market values and properly documented leases, and the lessor and lessee take consistent and reasonable positions on their tax returns. When equipment is transferred to an abusive trust, the trust might claim a new basis in the equipment and an increased depreciation deduction, even though the original owner of the equipment does not report any taxable gain on the transfer to the trust. This violates the basic principle that an increase in the tax basis of an asset only occurs when the asset is sold in a taxable transaction (or the owner dies). A taxable transaction must be a taxable transaction with respect to both parties (not just one). In the abusive trust arrangement, there may be other inconsistent tax treatments as well, so that tax deductions are claimed for payments upon which no one else reports any income.

Q. How can a charitable trust be fraudulent or abusive?

A. As explained in chapter 25, there are very specific requirements for charitable deductions and charitable trusts. In order for a trust to be tax-exempt and for contributions to a trust to be deductible for federal income tax purposes, the trust must be operated solely for charitable purposes and must serve public (and not private) interests.

Despite these clear rules, some grantors are creating trusts for which they claim charitable deductions. However, the abusive charitable trust does not serve any public purpose. Instead, it pays personal living expenses of the grantor and the grantor's family and makes the expenses appear to be charitable contributions. For example, the grantor might pay a child's college tuition from a "charitable trust" and then claim that the check to the college represented a deductible charitable donation and not a non-deductible personal expense.

Q. Can "offshore" (foreign) trusts be used to avoid income taxes?

A. As explained in chapter 27, even though offshore trusts have legitimate uses, Congress has enacted a number of measures to make the taxation of foreign trusts harsh and unattractive.

Trusts/Leimberg Associates Books: 610-527-5216

- If a United States citizen or resident creates a foreign trust, the trust is considered to be a "grantor trust." That means the grantor is taxable on all of the income earned by the trust—anywhere in the world—if any of the income of the trust is or *might* be distributed to a citizen or resident of the United States. We want to be very clear on this: You will realize no income tax savings from an offshore trust!

- The transfer of appreciated property to a foreign trust can result in an excise tax equal to 35 percent of the previously untaxed capital gain. (However, if the transferor of the property is considered to be the owner of the trust under the grantor trust rule described above, that tax may be deferred until the grantor is no longer considered to be the owner, such as upon death. If that's the case, then the capital gain at the owner's death will be added to federal and state death taxes and sometimes create a crushing tax and liquidity burden on the owner's estate).

- There is also a requirement that the creation of a foreign trust, the transfer of any property to a foreign trust, or the death of the grantor of a foreign trust be reported to the Internal Revenue Service. The failure to report a transfer can result in a penalty tax of 35 percent of the amount involved.

- If the income of the foreign trust is not taxed to you, the distributions to your children (or other beneficiaries) may be taxed very harshly. For example, foreign capital gains will be considered to be part of distributable net income, but will be taxed as ordinary income to the beneficiaries. Furthermore, any accumulations of income or delays in the distribution of income can result in nondeductible interest charges on the taxes deferred.

Claims that offshore trusts can save taxes are almost always founded upon a scheme involving multiple trusts, corporations, and other parties, such as the creation of a Panamanian corporation to create a Bahamian trust that will invest in Swiss bank accounts for the benefit of a Cayman Islands corporation that will be the beneficiary of the trust, the stock of the corporation to be held by another trust created by another corporation of which you or your family will be the beneficiaries. In other words, it is a shell game. The assumption is that the introduction of enough layers of trusts and corporations will keep the IRS from figuring out what is going on. This is fraud, not tax planning.

Q. Are revocable living trusts abusive?

A. No. All of the trust arrangements described in the other chapters of this book, including revocable trusts, are legitimate tax and personal financial planning techniques. They are based on full compliance with the rules and regulations under the Internal Revenue Code. The irrevocable life insurance trust, the credit shelter trust, the revocable living trust, trusts for minors, the QPRT (qualified personal residence trust), the GRAT (grantor retained annuity trust), the CRAT (charitable remainder annuity trust), and the CRUT (charitable remainder unitrust) are not abusive and can produce tax savings that can be amazing.

Although the IRS has announced a program to investigate abusive trusts, the IRS announcement clearly states that there should no concerns about the legitimate uses of trusts, including the proper use of trusts in estate planning.

The problem is often, not the trust itself, but the use to which the trust has been put or the tax treatment claimed for the trust. The abusive trusts identified by the IRS may be valid trusts under state law and still not produce the tax results claimed for the trust. Any of the trusts described in this book could be used as part of a fraudulent or abusive arrangement. That is why you need to understand what trusts can—and cannot—do.

Q. Who is promoting these trust abuses and why?

A. Selling trust packages to consumers has become a big business. People are concerned with high tax rates and creditors. So promoters who advertise "investment seminars" or "tax seminars" that promise to eliminate income, gift, and estate taxes—and at the same time provide complete creditor protection can draw large crowds. And promises of substantial tax savings can lure people into paying large sums of money for trust forms and instructions on how to create and operate trusts.

There are numerous reported decisions of taxpayers who have paid thousands of dollars for what amounted to nothing more than preprinted forms. The taxpayers who have been foolish enough to pay these inflated prices wind up being penalized twice. First, they pay large sums of money for forms and tax advice that is worthless. Then, they are audited by the Internal Revenue Service and are assessed with tax deficiencies, interest on unpaid or underpaid taxes, and penalties for negligence, substantial understatements of tax, and even civil (and possibly criminal) fraud. To add insult to tax injury, the Internal Revenue Service will not allow a tax deduction for the fees paid to the trust promoter, even though fees for tax advice are ordinarily deductible.

So the motivation for the trust promoter is often nothing less than pure greed. Some people are willing to allow themselves to believe in almost anything to avoid taxes or creditors. The trust promoter preys on that mindless willingness by telling taxpayers what they want to hear, and charging them dearly for the privilege.

Promoters of abusive trust arrangements may be subject to civil and criminal penalties, both for the violation of tax laws relating to abusive tax shelters and for simple consumer fraud, and the IRS (and the Federal Trade Commission) has already prosecuted many promoters of abusive trust arrangements.

Q. How can I recognize when a trust might be a sham or a fraud?

A. There are several common tax principles that are violated by abusive trust arrangements. These principles will help you recognize whether a trust arrangement is fraudulent or abusive, and not valid:

- In an abusive arrangment, deductions will be claimed for personal living expenses. In reality, you can't deduct personal expenses such as the costs of running your home, or depreciate your home or its furnishings.

- In an abusive arrangment, there is a claimed change in the taxation of income from property even though there is no meaningful change in the control or use of the property. In other words, the trust is used to disguise the true ownership of assets. Be suspicious any time it is claimed that you can have your cake and eat it too. In reality, you can not continue to use and control assets yet be exempt from income taxes on the income produced by those assets and estate taxes on that property at death.

- In an abusive arrangment, income is no longer taxed to the person who earns the income, and a person earning income is no longer required to pay Social Security or other employment taxes. In reality the opposite is true. If you earn income, you will be taxable regardless of how you disguise it. Likewise, you are subject to Social Security and other taxes on income you earn no matter how many layers of "fact" separate you from that income.

- In an abusive arrangment, a new tax basis is claimed for property even though there was no taxable gain or loss realized when the property was transferred to the trust. In reality, if there is no taxable event at the time of transfer, there will be no increase in basis available to either party.

- In an abusive arrangment, income is received that is not taxed to anyone. In reality a trust's income must be taxed to someone. The income of a trust must be taxed to the creator of the trust, the grantor (if the trust is a "grantor trust" because of rights or powers retained by the grantor), the beneficiaries of the trust (if distributed to them), or to the trust itself. And the trust must file a tax return showing how much income was received by the trust and how and to who that income will be taxed.

- In an abusive arrangment, charitable deductions are claimed for tuition or other payments benefiting family members. In reality only transfers to specified charities in specified manner will result in a charitable deduction.

Q. Other than tax principles, are there any other warning signs I can look for so that I am not cheated by a "trust mill" or abusive trust promoter?

A. Even if you have difficulty understanding the tax consequences or tax principles, there are several other "red flags" that should warn you that you are being sold an abusive trust scheme:

- Avoid trust promoters that describe their trusts using words like "Constitutional," "Fair," "Pure," "Equity," "Liberty," "Prime", or "Patriot." Those words have no legal or tax significance, and are often wrapped around illegal, impure, and fraudulent trusts the same way a wolf might wrap himself in sheep's clothing, in order to lull his prey into a false sense of security.

- Be wary of any trust promoter that claims "secret" or "insider" information known only to Kennedys, Congressmen, or other wealthy families. One promoter has sent out promotional materials that go so far as to claim proprietary rights in the will of Jacqueline Kennedy Onassis, implying that he wrote the former First Lady's will. What *baloney!* Mrs. Onassis's will was actually written by a well-known New York law firm and includes a charitable lead trust of the kind described in chapter 26 of this book.

There are no "great secrets" or conspiracies of concealment. The U.S. tax laws are all public documents and accessible information. You can find them on the World Wide Web. For instance, try:

http://www.irs.ustreas.gov/plain/forms_pubs/index.html

and you'll find connections to a wealth of free information on tax law. Lawyers in your state may also be providing useful (and free) Web Page information on trusts. For example, see http://www.netaxs.com/~evansdb/.

The bottom line is that there are very few tax techniques or "loopholes" that cannot be found in the books and magazines of any law library or from a legitimate (and often free or inexpensive) public source.

- In an abusive arrangment, multiple trusts are often required and the trusts are inter-related, with money or other assets flowing through labrynth funnels from trust to trust to trust. In reality, although it is sometimes necessary or useful to use two or more trusts to benefit different beneficiaries or to serve different estate and financial planning purposes, a number of trusts passing assets (or deductions) from trust to trust may be a sign that you are about to become part of a fraudulent "shell game."

- In an abusive arrangment, the trust is being sold by a promoter as part of a package. Typically, it's the only product or service sold by the promoter. Real tax and financial advisers provide a variety of services and are able to select the planning techniques (or combination) most suitable to the client from a number of possible tax and financial planning techniques. "One size fits all" rarely works for clothing, and it certainly doesn't work in estate and financial planning. Someone promoting a specific trust, and only that trust typically has the answer before you ask any questions and is probably a scam artist.

- In an abusive arrangment, the trust promoter suggests (or insists) that you not consult your lawyer, accountant, CLU, ChFC, CFP, a local bank, or the IRS. Legitimate tax planners have nothing to fear from a second opinion.

The harsh reality is that most things that sound too good to be true aren't true. If you receive promotional materials that claim tax benefits that seem too good to be true, check with a knowledgeable tax advisor (or with the IRS) before spending your money and risking not only additional taxes, interest, fines, and penalties, but perhaps your financial and personal freedom as well.

APPENDIX A

WARNING: THE APPENDIX SAMPLES ARE FOR EDUCATIONAL PURPOSES ONLY! WE STRONGLY ADVISE AGAINST THE USE OF THESE DOCUMENTS BY ANYONE NOT FORMALLY TRAINED AND PROPERLY LICENSED.

SAMPLE DEED PLACING REAL ESTATE IN TRUST

D E E D

M A D E   T H I S   day of   19 ,

B E T W E E N   JOHN DOE and MARY DOE, husband and wife of the Township of Upper Darby, County of Delaware and the State of Pennsylvania, (hereinafter called Grantors),

A N D

JOHN DOE and MARY DOE, husband and wife, Trustees as hereinafter set forth, of the Township of Upper Darby, County of Delaware, and State of Pennsylvania, (hereinafter called the Grantees),

W I T N E S S E T H   that in consideration of ONE DOLLAR ($1.00) in hand paid, the receipt whereof is hereby acknowledged, the said Grantors do hereby grant and convey unto the said Grantees, their beneficiaries, heirs and assigns,

A L L   T H A T   C E R T A I N   lot of piece of ground with the buildings and improvements thereon erected, Situate in the Township of Upper Darby, County of Delaware and State of Pennsylvania, as shown on Plan of Subdivision made for Benjamin F. Farrell by H. E. MacCombie, Jr., Consulting Engineer, dated March 4th, 1980, last revised July 7, 1980 and recorded in Plan Case 13, page 103, as more fully described as follows, to wit:

B E G I N N I N G   at a point of curve on the Southerly side of Aronimink Place FIFTY (50') FEET wide, said point also marking a corner of Lot #2 on said Plan, THENCE from said beginning point along the Southerly side of Aronimink Place, on the arc of a circle curving to the right having a radius of one thousand three hundred forty and eight one hundredths (1,340.08') feet, the arc distance of ONE HUNDRED THIRTY and THIRTEEN ONE HUNDREDTHS (130.13') FEET to a point; THENCE along Lot number 44 on said Plan, South fourteen degrees, fourteen minutes West, ONE HUNDRED THIRTEEN and THIRTY ONE HUNDREDTHS (113.30') FEET to a point on the Northeasterly side of Burmont Road FIFTY (50') FEET wide; THENCE along the same, North fifty-two (52) degrees, twenty-four minutes West, ONE HUNDRED THIRTY-TWO and SIXTY-EIGHT ONE HUNDREDTHS (132.68') FEET to a point; THENCE along Lot number 2 on said Plan, North fourteen degrees, fourteen minutes East, NINETY-SEVEN and FIFTY-TWO ONE HUNDREDTHS (97.52') FEET to the first mentioned point and place of beginning.

B E I N G   Lot number 3 on said plan and also known as House Number 822 Burmont Road.

THIRTEEN ONE HUNDREDTHS (130.13') FEET to a point; THENCE along Lot number 44 on said Plan, South fourteen degrees, fourteen minutes West, ONE HUNDRED THIRTEEN and THIRTY ONE HUNDREDTHS (113.30') FEET to a point on the Northeasterly side of Burmont Road FIFTY (50') FEET wide; THENCE along the same, North fifty-two (52) degrees, twenty-four minutes West, ONE HUNDRED THIRTY-TWO and SIXTY-EIGHT ONE HUNDREDTHS (132.68') FEET to a point; THENCE along Lot number 2 on said Plan, North fourteen degrees, fourteen minutes East, NINETY-SEVEN and FIFTY-TWO ONE HUNDREDTHS (97.52') FEET to the first mentioned point and place of beginning.

B E I N G   Lot number 3 on said plan and also known as House Number 822 Burmont Road.

B E I N G   F O L I O   N U M B E R   220066732.

B E I N G   the same premises which ROBERT A SMITH and JANE W. SMITH husband and wife, Indenture bearing date October 16, 1981 and recorded in the Office for the Recording of Deeds in and for the County of Delaware, at Media, Pennsylvania, on the 23th day of October, A.D. 1981 in Deed Book 1801, Page 444 &c., granted and conveyed unto JOHN DOE and MARY DOE, husband and wife, in fee, as Tenants by Entirety.

T H I S   C O N V E Y A N C E   is a transfer from husband and wife to husband wife, as Trustees and is exempt from realty transfer tax pursuant to 72 P.S., Section 91.193-(b-6).

U N D E R   A N D   S U B J E C T   to certain restrictions, agreements, and rights as now of record.

A L S O   U N D E R   A N D   S U B J E C T   to the payment of a certain mortgage debt or principal sum of THIRTY TWO THOUSAND DOLLARS ($32,000.00), (reduced to TWENTY ONE THOUSAND TWO HUNDRED FIFTY 00/100 DOLLARS (21,250.50) by payments on account), with interest thereon as the same may become due and payable.

REVOCABLE TRUST PROVISION

I N   T R U S T   N E V E R T H E L E S S   for the following uses and purposes and subject to the provisions, restrictions, limitations following:

T H A T   the said: JOHN DOE and MARY DOE, husband and wife, or the survivor of them, hereinafter called Trustees for the purpose of this provision, shall administer, manage and enjoy all of the benefits of the said realty and improvements during their lifetime.

A N D   upon the death of the said Trustees, the said premises shall vest in;

1. ROGER DOE, their son and

2. HAZEL PARKINGTON, (NEE DOE), their daughter,

equally, in fee as tenants in common, their heirs and assigns, forever, at which time said trust shall terminate and said premises shall be free and discharged from all trust limitations, restrictions, and powers whatsoever.

A N D , the said Trustee(s) as aforesaid, shall have the right, power and sole and absolute discretion to:

(a)   receive and consume all income, rents and profits from the granted premises for their own use or such other use as they desire,

(b)   to sell and dispose of the said premises hereby granted, or any part thereof, by deed, or other instruments of conveyance, and to grant, convey and assure the purchaser thereof and his, her, it or their heirs, successors and assigns, that the said premises be forever free, clear and discharged of and from all trust limitations whatsoever, and without any liability on part of the purchaser to see to the application of the purchase money;

(c)   and to lease for any lawful purposes for any period of time;

(d)   to improve, repair and alter the realty and buildings, to demolish, relocate, erect and construct all or any parts of said buildings;

(e)   to borrow money for any purpose from any person, firm or corporation on terms and conditions deemed appropriate, and to obligate, encumber, mortgage, and pledge said realty and execute any instrument whatsoever to accomplish same, and to replace, renew and extend any such encumbrance;

(f)   to sell at public or private sale;

(g)   and to alter, revoke or change all or any of the provisions declared herein, at any time by any written instrument, signed, sealed, and delivered as to all or any part of said trust;

(h)   and that the rights reserved to said Trustees shall not be exhausted by one or more exercise thereof, but shall continue to be effective as often as desired to exercise said rights;

(i)   and in the event of any sale or mortgage of said premises described and granted, the proceeds thereof shall be held by said Trustees for the same uses and purposes and under the same trust restrictions and limitations as set forth above, as the premises so sold, mortgaged, granted or conveyed;

(j)   and that the said Trustees as aforementioned, shall not be obliged or required at any time to account for the disposition, consumption or use of all or any part of said trust property or the income or proceeds thereof.

(k)   the Trustees shall have the right to nominate and appoint successor Trustees and to assign and transfer said trust property to such successor Trustees upon the same conditions and terms as set forth above.

No interest of any beneficiary or beneficiaries shall be transferable or assignable by such beneficiary or in any manner be liable for the debts or obligations of such beneficiary or beneficiaries while in possession of the Trustees.

In the event that the said beneficiary or beneficiaries hereunder are minors at the time the title could otherwise vest unto the aforementioned beneficiary or beneficiaries, title shall be held by the guardian of said minor's estate as appointed by the said Trustee's last will, or in default of such appointment,

ALBERT R. CUNNINGHAM, brother of MARY DOE, Trustee, is hereby appointed guardian of the minor's estate.

TRUSTEE'S ACCEPTANCE

THE UNDERSIGNED TRUSTEES, understand the terms of the herein trust agreement and accept and agree to the conditions as therein set forth.

_____(SEAL)

_____(SEAL)

A N D the said Grantors do hereby covenant to and with the said Grantees that, they, the said Grantors, their heirs and assigns, SHALL AND WILL, SUBJECT AS AFORESAID, Warrant and forever defend the hereinabove described premises with the hereditaments and appurtenances, unto the said Grantees, their beneficiaries, heirs and assigns, against the said Grantors and against every other person lawfully claiming or who shall hereafter claim the same or any part thereof, by, from or under, them or any of them.

IN WITNESS WHEREOF, the said Grantors have caused these present to be duly executed, the day and year above written.

SEALED AND DELIVERED
IN THE PRESENCE OF:

_____   _____(SEAL)

_____   _____(SEAL)

State of Pennsylvania, County of Delaware.

On this   day of   A.D., 19 , before me, the undersigned officer, personally appeared JOHN DOE and MARY DOE, husband and wife known to me (or satisfactorily proven) to be the persons whose names are subscribed to the within instrument, and acknowledged that they executed the same for the purposes therein contained.

I N W I T N E S S W H E R E O F I hereunto set my hand and official seal.

_____

NOTARY PUBLIC
My commission expires:

The address of the above named Grantee is:

621 Burmont Road, Drexel Hill, Pa. 19026
On behalf of the Grantee

RECORDED in the Office for the Recording of Deeds in and for the County of Delaware, State of Pennsylvania in Deed Book   page   .

WITNESS my hand and seal of Office, this   day of   , A.D., 19   .

_____

APPENDIX B

WARNING: THE APPENDIX SAMPLES ARE FOR EDUCATIONAL PURPOSES ONLY AND NOT MEANT TO BE COMPLETE AND "READY TO USE" DOCUMENTS! WE STRONGLY ADVISE AGAINST THE USE OF THESE MATERIALS BY ANYONE NOT FORMALLY TRAINED AND PROPERLY LICENSED.

HE WHO HAS SELF FOR ATTORNEY HAS A FOOL FOR A CLIENT!

SAMPLE REVOCABLE TRUST AGREEMENT

AND NOW, this 2nd day of January, 1999, I, SALLY JONES, of Montgomery County, Pennsylvania (hereinafter "Grantor"), grant, assign and set over to SALLY JONES, of Montgomery County, Pennsylvania (hereinafter "Trustee"), the property described in Schedule "A" attached hereto, and said property, together with all other property, real and personal, that may be added to the Trust (such property and additions being hereinafter called "principal") shall be held by Trustee, IN TRUST, as provided herein.

"This instrument shall be known as the Revocable Living Trust of Sally Jones, and assets transferred to the Trust shall be titled in the following manner: Sally Jones, Trustee U/D/T dated January 2, 1999, F/B/O Sally Jones."

FIRST: **LIFETIME PROVISIONS:** During Grantor's lifetime, Trustee shall manage all property comprising the principal of this Trust and shall collect the income therefrom and increments thereto and shall pay the net income and hold and distribute the principal of said Trust as follows:

A. All of the net income shall be paid to Grantor in such periodic installments as Trustee shall find convenient, but at least as often as quarter-annually.

B. The net income may be applied by Trustee for Grantor's support, should Grantor by reason of age, illness, or any other cause, in the opinion of Trustee, be incapable of disbursing it.

C. As much of the principal as Trustee may from time to time deem proper for Grantor's health, maintenance, and support shall be either paid to Grantor or applied directly for Grantor's benefit.

D. Grantor may withdraw as much principal as Grantor wishes from this Trust by a request made in writing to the Trustee signed by Grantor and delivered to the Trustee.

SECOND: DISTRIBUTION FOLLOWING GRANTOR'S DEATH: Upon Grantor's death, Trustee shall distribute Grantor's tangible personal property, together with any existing insurance thereon, and all of the then-remaining principal and income of this Trust to Grantor's nephew, TOM WILSON, if he is then living, or if he is not then living, to his then-living issue, per stirpes.

THIRD: DEATH TAXES: All federal, state and other death taxes payable because of Grantor's death on any property then held under this Trust or on any insurance proceeds or other death benefits payable directly to Trustee shall be paid out of the principal of this Trust.

FOURTH: PROTECTIVE PROVISION: All interests in this Trust, or in any Trust hereunder, are intended for the personal protection and welfare of Grantor's named beneficiaries, and no beneficiary shall be allowed to assign or anticipate his or her interest in the income or principal of this Trust or any Trust hereunder.

FIFTH: MANAGEMENT PROVISIONS: Grantor authorizes Trustee:

A. To retain and to invest in all forms of real and personal property, regardless of any limitations imposed by law on investments by Trustee;

B. To sell at public or private sale, to exchange or to lease for any period of time, any real or personal property, and to give options for sales or leases;

C. To allocate any property received or charge incurred to principal or income or partly to each, without regard to any law defining principal and income;

D. To distribute in kind and to allocate specific assets among the beneficiaries (including any Trust hereunder) in such proportions as Trustee may think best, so long as the total market value of any beneficiary's share is not affected by such allocation; and

E. If at any time there are Co-trustees serving, they are authorized to act either jointly or severally, and to delegate to any Co-trustee any power or discretion (including the power to sign checks). Notwithstanding the foregoing, no discretionary power may be delegated to a person who is otherwise prohibited from exercising such power under other provisions of this Trust.

SIXTH: INSURANCE POLICIES: Trustee shall have no duty to pay premiums on the

insurance policies payable to Trustee, and the companies issuing the policies shall have no responsibility for the application of the proceeds or the fulfillment of the Trusts.

EIGHTH: RIGHTS RESERVED: Grantor reserves the following rights, each of which may be exercised whenever and as often as Grantor may wish:

A. All rights vested in Grantor as the owner of the insurance policies payable to Trustee; and

B. The right by an instrument in writing—other than a Will—to revoke or amend part or all of this Revocable Living Trust.

NINTH: BENEFICIARIES UNDER TWENTY-ONE OR DISABLED: If any beneficiary becomes entitled to an outright distribution of income or principal and is (i) under the age of twenty-one (21) years, or (ii) in Trustee's opinion, disabled by illness or any other cause and unable to properly manage the funds:

A. As much of such income or principal as Trustee may from time to time think desirable for that beneficiary either shall be paid to him or her or shall be applied for his or her benefit; and

B. The balance of such income and principal—and the net income from those funds—shall be kept invested and managed as a separate Trust for that beneficiary, with the Trust funds paid to or for the beneficiary in accordance with the provisions of the preceding paragraphs. When the beneficiary reaches the age of twenty-one (21) years or, in Trustee's opinion, becomes free of disability, as the case may be, the balance shall be paid to the beneficiary. If he or she dies before that time, the balance shall be paid to his or her Executors or Administrators.

Any funds to be applied under this article either shall be applied directly by Trustee to a parent or guardian of the beneficiary or to any person or organization taking care of the beneficiary. Trustee shall have no further responsibility for any funds so paid or applied.

TENTH: PROVISIONS REGARDING SUCCESSOR TRUSTEES IN THE EVENT OF GRANTOR'S DISABILITY, INCAPACITY OR DEATH:

A. In the event of the disability or incapacity of Grantor, or if for any reason whatsoever, she ceases to serve as Trustee hereunder, Grantor's nephew, TOM WILSON, shall become Trustee of this Trust without Court approval upon his written acceptance of office. Grantor shall be deemed disabled or incapacitated upon the election of the successor Trustee to accept the written certification of a licensed physician, which states that such physician has examined Grantor and that Grantor is physically or mentally incapable of attending to Grantor's personal and financial affairs. The certificate of the physician shall be attached to the original of Grantor's Trust Agreement, but a copy of the certification attached to a copy of this Trust can be accepted and acted upon as if it was an original. The successor Trustee shall have all rights, powers, duties, authority, and responsibility conferred upon the Trustee originally named herein.

B. Upon Grantor's death, Grantor's nephew, TOM WILSON, shall become Trustee of this Trust without court approval upon his written acceptance of office.

C. Should Grantor's nephew, TOM WILSON, wish to resign, or be for any reason unable to serve or to continue to serve as Trustee, he shall have the right to appoint a successor Trustee to serve.

D. Grantor directs that:

1. The successor Trustee or Trustees shall have all rights, powers, duties, authority, and responsibility conferred upon the Trustee originally named herein.

2. The words "Trustee" or "Trustees" shall refer to all those acting as Trustees.

3. No successor Trustee shall be responsible for or required to inquire into the actions of a prior Trustee occurring before the successor's appointment.

4. No Trustee shall be required to give bond in any jurisdiction.

5. Each individual Trustee is entitled to reasonable compensation for services in administering this Trust and to reimbursement for expenses, and each corporate Trustee, if any is appointed, is entitled to compensation based on its published fee schedule in effect at the time services are rendered.

ELEVENTH: SITUS AND GOVERNING LAW: The situs of the Revocable Living Trust shall be in Pennsylvania. All questions as to the validity, effect, or interpretation of this Revocable Living Trust or the administration of the Trusts shall be governed by the law of Pennsylvania.

EXECUTED the day and year first above written.

Signed, sealed and delivered
in the presence of:

_____   _____(SEAL)
                                          SALLY JONES, Grantor

_____   _____(SEAL)
                                          SALLY JONES, Trustee

COMMONWEALTH OF PENNSYLVANIA)
) SS:

COUNTY OF MONTGOMERY)

On this 2nd day of January, 1999, before me, a Notary Public, in and for the Commonwealth of Pennsylvania, personally appeared SALLY JONES, and in due form of law, acknowledged the foregoing instrument to be her act and deed and desired the same to be recorded as such.

WITNESS my hand and notarial seal the day and year aforesaid.

                                          _____

                                          NOTARY PUBLIC
                                          My commission expires:

APPENDIX C

CHECKLIST OF TRUSTEE'S DUTIES FOLLOWING DEATH OF GRANTOR/BENEFICIARY[*]

ASSEMBLING THE ASSETS

- File claim for life insurance benefits for which the trust is the beneficiary (obtain Form 712 from each insurance company). Consider mode of payment.

- File claim for any pension or profit–sharing benefits from the employer and for any other work–related benefits payable to the trust: Consider mode of payment.

- File Notice of Fiduciary Relationship (Form 56) with the IRS. (If the trust does not have a tax identification number, file Form SS–4.)

- Write to banks for date–of–death value of any trust bank accounts.

- Analyze and review securities with emphasis on preserving trust assets, and value securities owned by the trust as of the date of death.

- Obtain appraisal of any real and personal property owned by the trust.

- Obtain last 3 years of fiduciary income tax returns and last 3 years of canceled checks of the trust.

- Review all accountings and distributions that have taken place for the last 5 years (or since the trust was established, if these records are available).

PAYMENT OF TAXES, DEBTS, AND EXPENSES

- Prepay state inheritance taxes to obtain a discount if available. Check state law to determine if it's permissible and advantageous, and if so, the applicable deadlines.

---

[*] Courtesy, *Tools and Techniques of Estate Planning,* 10th ed., National Underwriter Company, Cincinnati, OH 45203 (1–800–543–0874).

- File personal property tax returns, due February 15 of each year of trust.

- File U.S. Fiduciary Income–Tax Return (IRS Form 1041) and state income–tax returns, due April 15 of each year.

- Review and coordinate with executor the information necessary to prepare and file the state inheritance–tax return and the federal estate tax return.

- Obtain alternate–valuation–date values for federal estate–tax return.

- Pay U.S. estate tax return with flower bonds, due to any Federal Reserve bank with Form PD 1782 within 9 months of death.

- Consider election of extension of time to pay U.S. estate tax (Section 6161 or 6166), filed on or before due date of U.S. estate tax returns, including extensions.

- Consider election to defer payment of inheritance tax on remainder interests; where permitted, determine deadline for election.

- Consider election for special valuation of farm or business real estate owned by the trust under Code Section 2032A; must be made with timely filed U.S. estate tax return.

- Consider election for business interest exclusion under Code Section 2033A; must be made with timely filed U.S. estate tax return.

- Elect (or determine not to elect) to qualify certain terminable interest property (QTIP) for marital deduction.

- Elect (or determine not to elect) QDT (qualified domestic trust) treatment if spouse is not a U.S. citizen.

- Maximize GSTT (generation–skipping transfer tax) exemptions by making election or redistributing trust assets.

DISTRIBUTION

- Prepare an accounting of receipts and disbursements.

- Notify state attorney general if charitable gifts are involved. (Earlier notice may be required; check local requirements.)

- File accounting in court after proper notices to beneficiaries, *or*

- If informal distribution, give accounting to beneficiaries and obtain receipt and release from them.

- Transfer assets in accordance with distribution as indicated in trust.

- Establish and fund additional trusts if required.

WHAT ARE THE TRUSTEE'S DUTIES FOLLOWING THE DEATH OF THE GRANTOR/BENEFICIARY?*

While many of a trustee's duties in settling a trust are similar to those of an executor, certain formal requirements necessary to probate a will and handle an estate can be avoided. There are three main duties of the trustee:

(1) Assembling the assets of the trust;

(2) Paying debts, expenses and death taxes; and

(3) Distributing the assets to the beneficiaries.

ASSEMBLING THE TRUST ASSETS

In most cases, it is easier to assemble the assets of a revocable living trust than an estate, since all property held in trust must be clearly identified as such. For example, a bank account or stock held in trust by the grantor as trustee for himself could be titled "Stanley Jackson, Trustee, U/D/T dated April 2, 1999, F/O/B Stanley Jackson." If the grantor has named a different trustee, then the assets would be titled "Sally Johnson, Trustee, U/D/T dated April 2, 1999, F/B/O Stanley Jackson."

Some attorneys or institutions use different wording, but the main features are consistent: naming of the trustee, the date of the execution of the trust and the beneficiary. The designation F/B/O means "for the benefit of" (or "for and on behalf of"), and the U/D/T means "under deed of trust" (or "under declaration of trust").

There are trust assets that can be titled in an individual's name during his or her lifetime and at death are payable to a beneficiary. For example, Uncle Stan might have owned a $100,000 life insurance policy, payable to "Sally Johnson, Trustee, U/D/T of Stanley Jackson, dated April 2, 1999." Other assets paid to beneficiaries at a person's death can include IRAs, pension and

---

* Courtesy, *How to Settle an Estate*, LEIMBERG ASSOCIATES BOOKS, (610-527-5216).

profit-sharing plans and other work-related benefits. (But there are very important tax consequences which must be considered by tax counsel.)

It is possible that the trust records contain no information concerning these assets, so it is necessary for you to have access to the grantor's personal records and to work closely with the executor of the grantor's estate to make certain that the trust receives all of the benefits to which it and its beneficiaries are entitled.

You then file claims for all of the benefits and proceed to collect the other identifiable assets of the trust.

For accounting, and especially for tax purposes, you need a date-of-death balance sheet indicating the value of all trust assets at the grantor's death. You therefore have to contact banks and stockbrokers for a breakdown of the decedent's assets held with their institutions, including date-of-death balances for each bank account and security.

If the trust is the owner of real estate, obtain appraisals of any real property as well as any personal property in the trust at the decedent's death.

Also obtain all past checking accounts of the trust and copies of all fiduciary income tax returns filed by the trust during the grantor's lifetime. If any prior accountings had been made to the beneficiaries, you should have this information as well.

PAYMENT OF DEBTS, EXPENSES AND DEATH TAXES

Because the grantor had the right to revoke the trust at any time prior to death, the federal and state governments impose death taxes on the trust assets (See chapter 10). You must be familiar with the deadlines for filing these returns, and with the death tax laws of the trust's state (determine whether there are discounts for early payment).

You are also responsible for the payment of any outstanding obligations of the trust, including fees, commissions, and expenses incurred in the administration of the trust assets. It's also possible that trust assets will be needed to satisfy obligations of the decedent's estate. Therefore, coordinate your activities with those of the executor of the estate (of course, the trustee can be named as executor). (Also be aware of the many available options, which are set forth in the Trustee's Checklist.)

DISTRIBUTION

When you are satisfied that all of the assets of the trust have been identified, assembled and correctly inventoried, and all outstanding obligations have been satisfied, prepare an accounting of receipts and disbursements and then make distribution to the beneficiaries. This presents you with two major decisions: (1) How formal an account is necessary, and (2) should you file the account in court in order to be formally (and legally) discharged of your duties and responsibilities?

In a close family situation, where the composition of the trust is not complicated, the size of the trust is relatively small, and the relationship between the trustee and beneficiaries is a good one, an informal account and distribution on the signing of a release can be used. This simplifies the distribution process and avoids publicity.

However, if you have any concern about potential outstanding obligations of the trust (such as future income tax problems, a federal estate tax audit, or conflict with the trust's beneficiaries), then file a formal court accounting. Send notice of the accounting and the date it will be submitted to the court (certified mail, return receipt requested) to all beneficiaries and other interested parties (according to local court rules), so they will have the opportunity to appear in court and present any objections to the account and proposed distribution. (Some states require a more formal notice called *service*.)

Once the account and schedule of distribution have been approved by the court, you can be formally discharged from your duties. In many instances, it is advisable to hold a certain sum in the trust for a period of time after distribution, in the event of any additional claims against the trust following distribution (a future audit of income tax or estate tax returns might indicate a deficiency).

Instead of an outright distribution to beneficiaries, the trust may have provided for the trust to continue after the death of the grantor for a certain period of time (for example, until the beneficiaries reach their twenty-first birthday). It is then necessary for you to continue to hold the funds allocated to these trusts in further trust for the beneficiaries and continue to administer the trust until the indicated distribution date. At that time, you can make distribution to the beneficiaries in a manner consistent with the above provisions. For a complete guide to this topic, call 610-527-5216 and request our book, HOW TO SETTLE AN ESTATE.

IRS FORMS THAT MAY BE USEFUL IN PLANNING OR ADMINISTERING ESTATES OR TRUSTS*

Form	Title
PD 1782	Application for redemption at par of United States treasury bonds eligible for payment of federal estate tax
GPO 3565	Order blank for federal tax forms and publications
SS-4	Application for an employer identification number
W-9	Request for taxpayer identification number and certification
56	Notice of fiduciary relationship
231	Power of attorney by individual for the collection of checks drawn on the United States Treasury
706	United States estate (and generation-skipping transfer) tax return
706-A	United States additional estate tax return
706CE	Certificate of payment of foreign death tax
706GS(D)	Generation-skipping transfer tax return for distributions
706GS(D1)	Notification of distribution from a generation-skipping trust
706GS(T)	Generation-skipping transfer tax for terminations
706NA	United States estate (and generation-skipping transfer) tax return (for nonresident aliens)
709	United States gift (and generation-skipping transfer) tax return
709-A	United States short form gift tax return

* Courtesy, *Tools and Techniques of Estate Planning,* 10 ed., National Underwriter Company, Cincinnati, OH 45203 (1-800-543-0874).

712	Life insurance valuation statement
1040	United States individual income tax return
1040C	United States departing alien income tax return
1041	United States fiduciary income tax return
2848	Power of attorney and declaration of representative
4421	Declaration—executor's commissions and attorney's fees
4506	Request for copy of tax form
4768	Application for extension of time to file United States estate (and generation-skipping transfer) tax(es)
4808	Computation of credit for gift tax
4810	Request for prompt assessment under Internal Revenue Code Section 6501(d)
4970	Tax on accumulation distribution of trusts
4972	Tax on lump-sum distributions
5803	Explanation of tax return preparer penalty charges
6123	Verification of fiduciary's federal tax deposit
6166	Certification of filing a tax return
7990	United States estate tax certificate of discharge from personal liability
7990-A	United States gift tax certificate of discharge from personal liability

IRS ANNOUNCEMENT ON "ABUSIVE TRUSTS"

[IRS Notice 97-24, 1997-16 I.R.B. 6]

CERTAIN TRUST ARRANGEMENTS

NOTICE 97-24

This notice is intended to alert taxpayers about certain trust arrangements that purport to reduce or eliminate federal taxes in ways that are not permitted by federal tax law. (The notice refers to such arrangements as "abusive trust arrangements." See Section I. ABUSIVE TRUST ARRANGEMENTS—IN GENERAL, below.) The notice describes some typical abusive trust arrangements, as well as the tax benefits promised by promoters, and then explains the correct tax principles that apply to these trust arrangements. Taxpayers should be aware that abusive trust arrangements will not produce the tax benefits advertised by their promoters and that the Internal Revenue Service is actively examining these types of trust arrangements as part of the National Compliance Strategy, Fiduciary and Special Projects. Furthermore, in appropriate circumstances, taxpayers and/or the promoters of these trust arrangements may be subject to civil and/or criminal penalties.

This notice should not, however, create concerns about the legitimate uses of trusts. For example, trusts are frequently used properly in estate planning, to facilitate the genuine charitable transfer of property, and to hold property for minors and incompetents.

Under the federal tax laws, trusts generally are separate entities subject to income tax (except for certain charitable or pension trusts that are expressly exempted by the tax laws and certain grantor trusts described in sections 671-679 of the Internal Revenue Code). Under these laws and certain court developed doctrines, either the trust, the beneficiary, or the transferor, as applicable, must pay the tax on the income realized by the trust including the income generated by property held in trust.

I. ABUSIVE TRUST ARRANGEMENTS—IN GENERAL

Abusive trust arrangements typically are promoted by the promise of tax benefits with no meaningful change in the taxpayer's control over or benefit from the taxpayer's income or assets. The promised benefits may include reduction or elimination of income subject to tax; deductions for personal expenses paid by the trust; depreciation deductions of an owner's personal residence and furnishings; a stepped-up basis for property transferred to the trust; the reduction or elimination of self-employment taxes; and the reduction or elimination of gift and estate taxes. These promised benefits are inconsistent with the tax rules applicable to the abusive trust arrangements, as described below.

Abusive trust arrangements often use trusts to hide the true ownership of assets and income or to disguise the substance of transactions. These arrangements frequently involve more than one trust, each holding different assets of the taxpayer (for example, the taxpayer's business, business equipment, home, automobile, etc.), as well as interests in other trusts. Funds may flow from one trust to another trust by way of rental agreements, fees for services, purchase and sale agreements, and distributions. Some trusts purport to involve charitable purposes. In some situations, one or more foreign trusts also may be part of the arrangement.

II. EXAMPLES OF ABUSIVE TRUST ARRANGEMENTS

Described below are five examples of abusive trust arrangements that have come to the attention of the Internal Revenue Service. An abusive trust arrangement may involve some or all of the trusts described below. The type of trust arrangement selected is dependent on the particular tax benefit the arrangement purports to achieve. In each of the trusts described below, the original owner of the assets that are nominally subject to the trust effectively retains authority to cause the financial benefits of the trust to be directly or indirectly returned or made available to the owner. For example, the trustee may be the promoter, or a relative or friend of the owner who simply carries out the directions of the owner whether or not permitted by the terms of the trust. Often, the trustee gives the owner checks that are pre-signed by the trustee, checks that are accompanied by a rubber stamp of the trustee's signature, a credit card or a debit card with the intention of permitting the owner to obtain cash from the trust or otherwise to use the assets of the trust for the owner's benefit.

1. The Business Trust. The owner of a business transfers the business to a trust (sometimes described as an unincorporated business trust) in exchange for units or certificates of beneficial interest, sometimes described as units of beneficial interest or UBI's (trust units). The business trust makes payments to the trust unit holders or to other trusts created by the owner (characterized either as deductible business expenses or as deductible distributions) that purport to reduce the taxable income of the business trust to the point where little or no tax is due from the business trust. In addition, the owner claims the arrangement reduces or eliminates the owner's self-employment taxes on the theory that the owner is receiving reduced or no income from the operation of the business. In some cases, the trust units are supposed to be canceled at death or "sold" at a nominal price to the owner's children, leading to the contention by promoters that there is no estate tax liability.

2. The Equipment or Service Trust. The equipment trust is formed to hold equipment that is rented or leased to the business trust, often at inflated rates. The service trust is formed to provide services to the business trust, often for inflated fees. Under these abusive trust arrangements, the business trust may purport to reduce its income by making allegedly deductible payments to the equipment or service trust. Further, as to the

equipment trust, the equipment owner may claim that the transfer of equipment to the equipment trust in exchange for the trust units is a taxable exchange. The trust takes the position that the trust has "purchased" the equipment with a known value (its fair market value) and that the value is the tax basis of the equipment for purposes of claiming depreciation deductions. The owner, on the other hand, takes the inconsistent position that the value of the trust units received cannot be determined, resulting in no taxable gain to the owner on the exchange. The equipment or service trust also may attempt to reduce or eliminate its income by distributions to other trusts.

3. The Family Residence Trust. The owner of the family residence transfers the residence, including its furnishings, to a trust. The parties claim inconsistent tax treatment for the trust and the owner (similar to the equipment trust). The trust claims the exchange results in a stepped-up basis for the property, while the owner reports no gain. The trust claims to be in the rental business and purports to rent the residence back to the owner; however, in most cases, little or no rent is actually paid. Rather, the owner contends that the owner and family members are caretakers or provide services to the trust and, therefore, live in the residence for the benefit of the trust. Under some arrangements, the family residence trust receives funds from other trusts (such as a business trust) which are treated as the income of the trust. In order to reduce the tax which might be due with respect to such income (and any income from rent actually paid by the owner), the trust may attempt to deduct depreciation and the expenses of maintaining and operating the residence.

4. The Charitable Trust. The owner transfers assets to a purported charitable trust and claims either that the payments to the trust are deductible or that payments made by the trust are deductible charitable contributions. Payments are made to charitable organizations; however, in fact, the payments are principally for the personal educational, living, or recreational expenses of the owner or the owner's family. For example, the trust may pay for the college tuition of a child of the owner.

5. The Final Trust. In some multi-trust arrangements, the U.S. owner of one or more abusive trusts establishes a trust (the "final trust") that holds trust units of the owner's other trusts and is the final distributee of their income. A final trust often is formed in a foreign country that will impose little or no tax on the trust. In some arrangements, more than one foreign trust is used, with the cash flowing from one trust to another until the cash is ultimately distributed or made available to the U.S. owner, purportedly tax free.

III. LEGAL PRINCIPLES APPLICABLE TO TRUSTS

As noted above, when trusts are used for legitimate business, family or estate planning purposes, either the trust, the trust beneficiary, or the transferor to the trust, as appropriate under the tax laws, will pay the tax on the income generated by the trust property. When used in accordance with the tax laws, trusts will not transform a taxpayer's personal, living or educational expenses into deductible items, and will not seek to avoid tax liability by ignoring either the true ownership of income and assets or the true substance of transactions. Accordingly, the tax results that are promised by the promoters of abusive trust arrangements are not allowable under federal tax law. Contrary to promises made in promotional materials, several well-established tax principles control the proper tax treatment of these abusive trust arrangements.

1. Substance—not form—controls taxation. The Supreme Court of the United States has consistently stated that the substance rather than the form of the transaction is controlling for tax purposes. See, for example, *Gregory v. Helvering*, 293 U.S. 465 (1935), XIV-1 C.B. 193; *Helvering v. Clifford*, 309 U.S. 331 (1940), 1940-1 C.B. 105. Under this doctrine, the abusive trust arrangements may be viewed as sham transactions, and the IRS may ignore the trust and its transactions for federal tax purposes. See *Markosian v. Commissioner*, 73 T.C. 1235 (1980) (holding that the trust was a sham because the parties did not comply with the terms of the trust and the supporting documents and the relationship of the grantors to the property transferred did not differ in any material aspect after the creation of the trust); *Zmuda v. Commissioner*, 731 F.2d 1417 (9th Cir. 1984). Accordingly, the income and assets of the business trust, the equipment in the equipment trust, the residence in the family residence trust, and the assets in the foreign trust would all be treated as belonging directly to the owner.

2. Grantors may be treated as owners of trusts. The grantor trust rules provide that if the owner of property transferred to a trust retains an economic interest in, or control over, the trust, the owner is treated for income tax purposes as the owner of the trust property, and all transactions by the trust are treated as transactions of the owner. Sections 671-677. In addition, a U.S. person who directly or indirectly transfers property to a foreign trust is treated as the owner of that property if there is a U.S. beneficiary of the trust. Section 679. This means that all expenses and income of the trust would belong to and must be reported by the owner, and tax deductions and losses arising from transactions between the owner and the trust would be ignored. Furthermore, there would be no taxable "exchange" of property with the trust, and the tax basis of property transferred to the trust would not be stepped-up for depreciation purposes. See Rev. Rul. 85 13, 1985-1 C.B. 184.

3. Taxation of Non-Grantor Trusts. If the trust is not a sham and is not a grantor trust, the trust is taxable on its income, reduced by amounts distributed to beneficiaries. The trust must obtain a taxpayer identification number and file annual returns reporting its income. The trust must report distributions to beneficiaries on a Form K-1, and the beneficiary must include the distributed income on the beneficiary's tax return. Sections 641, 651, 652, 661 and 662.

4. Transfers to trusts may be subject to estate and gift taxes. Transfers to a trust may be recognized as completed gifts for federal gift tax purposes. Further, whether or not the gift tax applies, if the owner retains until the owner's death the use of, enjoyment of, or income from the property placed in a trust, the property will be subject to federal estate tax when the transferor dies. Section 2036(a).

5. Personal expenses are generally not deductible. Personal expenses such as those for home maintenance, education, and personal travel are not deductible unless expressly authorized by the tax laws. See section 262. The courts have consistently held that nondeductible personal expenses cannot be transformed into deductible expenses by the use of trusts. Furthermore, the costs of creating these trusts are not deductible. See, for example, *Schulz v. Commissioner*, 686 F.2d 490 (7th Cir. 1982); *Neely v. United States*, 775 F.2d 1092 (9th Cir. 1985); and *Zmuda*.

6. A genuine charity must benefit in order to claim a valid charitable deduction. Charitable trusts that are exempt from tax are carefully defined in the tax law. Arrangements are not exempt charitable trusts if they do not satisfy the requirements of the tax law, including the requirement that their true purpose is to benefit charity. Furthermore, supposed charitable payments made by a trust are not deductible charitable contributions where the payments are really for the benefit of the owner or the owner's family members. See, for example, *Fausner v. Commissioner*, 55 T.C. 620 (1971).

7. Special rules apply to foreign trusts. If an arrangement involves a foreign trust, taxpayers should be aware that a number of special provisions apply to foreign trusts with U.S. grantors or U.S. beneficiaries, including several provisions added in 1996. For example, a U.S. person that fails to report a transfer of property to a foreign trust or the receipt of a distribution from a foreign trust is subject to a tax penalty equal to 35 percent of the gross value of the transaction. Other examples of these provisions are the application of U.S. withholding taxes to payments to foreign trusts and the application of U.S. excise taxes to transfers of appreciated property to foreign trusts. See sections 6048, 6677, 1441, and 1491.

8. Civil and/or criminal penalties may apply. The participants in and promoters of abusive trust arrangements may be subject to civil and/or criminal penalties in appropriate cases. See, for example, *United States v. Buttorff*, 761 F.2d 1056 (5th Cir. 1985); *United States v. Krall*, 835 F.2d 711 (8th Cir. 1987); *Zmuda* and *Neely*.

IV. IRS ENFORCEMENT STRATEGY FOR ABUSIVE TRUSTS

The Internal Revenue Service has undertaken a nationally coordinated enforcement initiative to address abusive trust schemes—the National Compliance Strategy, Fiduciary and Special Projects. This initiative involves Service personnel from the Assistant Commissioner (Examination), Assistant Commissioner (Criminal Investigation), and the Office of Chief Counsel.

As part of this strategy, the Service seeks to encourage voluntary compliance with the tax law. Accordingly, taxpayers who have participated in abusive trust arrangements are encouraged to file correct tax returns for 1996, as well as amended tax returns for prior years, consistent with the explanation of the law set forth in this notice.

For information regarding issues addressed in this notice, taxpayers may call (202) 622-4512 (not a toll-free number).

GLOSSARY OF KEY TRUST PLANNING TERMS

A-B trusts: an estate plan under which the estate is divided between an "A" trust that qualifies for the federal estate tax marital deduction and a "B" trust, that uses up the decedent federal estate tax unified credit. See "credit-equivalent bypass trust," "marital deduction," "marital trust," and "unified credit," below.

Abatement: a reduction in the amount of a gift from a trust or estate because the assets of the trust or estate are not sufficient to satisfy the gift.   For example, if a trust directed that $100,000 be distributed to each of two beneficiaries, but the trust had only $150,000 left, both gifts would abate to $75,000 each.

Account: a statement by a trustee or other fiduciary, usually presented to a court, summarizing the receipts, disbursements, and other transactions of the fiduciary.

Ademption: a gift under your will of real or personal property that fails because you sold, lost, or for some other reason no longer had the item when you died.

Adjusted gross estate: gross estate less certain debts and expenses; an amount calculated for the purpose of determining your estate's qualification for a Section 6166 deferred payment of estate taxes.

Adjusted taxable estate: this is your taxable estate (less $60,000); it is the amount used to compute the federal credit allowed for the state death taxes your executor must pay in addition to federal estate taxes. The state death tax credit is computed by multiplying the state death tax credit rate by the adjusted taxable estate (taxable estate minus $60,000).

Adjusted taxable gifts: the taxable portion of lifetime gifts (total gifts less the charitable deduction, the marital deduction, and the $10,000 annual exclusion) you made after December 31, 1976—except for those gifts that for any reason were required to be included in the your gross estate.

Administration: the following three-step process of management of your estate: (1) the marshaling of assets, (2) the payment of expenses, debts, and charges, including taxes, (3) the payment or delivery of legacies, and the rendition of an accounting to the court of what came in, what was paid out, and proof that the terms of the will (or state intestacy law if there was no valid will) were met.

Administrator: a person appointed by the court to settle an estate. An administrator may be appointed (1) if you left no valid will, (2) if you left a valid will but failed to name an executor, (3) if the executors you named failed to qualify or refused to serve, or (4) if your executor, after having qualified, failed to settle the estate (for example, she died before the probate process was completed).

Advancement: money or property given by a parent to a child, other descendant, or heir (depending on the statute's wording), or expended by the former for the latter's benefit in anticipation of the share that the child, for example, will inherit in the parent's estate. This amount reduces the amount that would otherwise pass to the beneficiary at the testator's death.

Adverse party: anyone having a substantial beneficial interest in a trust or estate who would be adversely affected by another party's exercise of a power or by another party's taking under the trust or will.

After-born child: a child born after the execution of a parent's will.

Alternate value: for federal estate tax purposes, the value of the gross estate 6 months after the date of death, unless property is distributed, sold, exchanged, or otherwise disposed of within 6 months (In that case the value of such property is determined as of the date of such disposition.) The alternate valuation date can only be selected if the net effect of the selection is to reduce estate taxes.

Annual exclusion: for federal gift tax purposes, an exclusion of $10,000 (which may be adjusted for inflation after 1998) is allowed to the donor each year for each donee, provided the gift is one of a "present interest" (that is, the donee must be given an unfettered and immediate ascertainable right to use, possession, or enjoyment of the property interest).

Annuity: a periodic payment of a fixed amount of money until a particular date or the death (or deaths) of designated persons.

Anti-lapse statute: a law enacted to prevent bequests to certain relatives from lapsing (ending) if the relative predeceases the testator. Under a typical anti-lapse statute, a gift to a child under the parent's will should not lapse if the child predeceases the parent, but (unless the parent has directed otherwise in the will) the gift will pass instead to the child's children. An anti-lapse statute might or might not apply to a revocable living trust, which is one reason why trusts must be prepared carefully.

Apportionment: the allocation of receipts or disbursements among trusts, shares, or beneficiaries. Tax apportionment is commonly required when several different trusts or other kinds of property are included in the gross estate and the federal estate tax must be allocated among them.

Attestation clause: the paragraph appended to the will indicating that certain persons by their signatures thereto have heard the testator declare the instrument to be his or her will and have witnessed the signing of the will.

Attorney-in-fact: see "power of attorney."

Beneficiary: (a) one who inherits a share or part of a decedent's estate or (b) one who takes the beneficial interest under a trust, life insurance contact, or employee benefit or pension plan. (For "income beneficiary," see "life tenant.")

Bequest: technically, a gift of personal property left to someone through your will (as distinguished from a gift of real estate). However, the term is often used to cover a gift of either personal property or land, or both. Most people use the term "to bequeath" as the transfer of property of any kind by will. (See also devise and legacy.)

Bequests are classified as "specific" or "general." A specific bequest is a gift of a particular specified class or kind of property. For instance, you might make a specific bequest of your emerald ring to your daughter or a gift of General Motors stock to your grandson. Since a specific bequest designates a particular item of the estate that is to be given, if that item is not owned by the decedent at the time of death, the gift fails. See "ademption," above.

A general bequest is one that may be satisfied from the general assets of your estate. For example, you could make a bequest of $100,000 without reference to any particular fund from which it is to be paid.

Carryover basis property: the basis (the cost for purposes of determining gain or loss) of the donee (the recipient of a gift, either outright or in trust) when property is acquired by gift the donee's basis is "carried over" from the donor (in other words the donor's cost with certain adjustments for gift taxes paid on the built-in gain) and becomes the donee's basis.

Charitable deduction: a deduction allowed for income, estate, or gift tax purposes for a gift to a charitable organization. For federal tax purposes, a charitable deduction is allowed for a gift during lifetime or at death for religious, charitable, scientific, literary, or educational purposes.

Codicil: a document amending a will, typically making a relatively small change. A codicil must meet the same legal requirements regarding execution and validity as a will.

Collateral relations: uncles and aunts, cousins, and other relatives not in a direct ascending or descending line from you. Relatives such as grandparents or grandchildren who are in an up or down line from you are said to be your lineal relations. (If you die without a valid will, state law determines who receives your property.)

Community property: property acquired during marriage where the husband and wife are treated as each owning half. Because each is deemed to own half, not more than half can be disposed of by will by either spouse. Eight states (Arizona, California, Idaho, Louisiana, New Mexico, Nevada, Texas, and Washington) are community-property states. Wisconsin has quasi-community-property statutes.

Contingent interest: a possible future interest in real or personal property that is contingent upon the occurrence—or nonoccurrence—of a given event or stated condition.

Contingent remainder: a future interest in property that, as its name implies, is contingent on the occurrence (or nonoccurrence) of a given event or stated condition happening before a prior property interest ends. For instance, a husband might leave farmland to his second wife and corporate stock to his son from his first marriage in a trust. The trustee is required to pay the wife the income from the trust for as long as she lives. When the wife dies, the trustee is to transfer all the property in the trust to the husband's son from his first marriage if he is alive when the husband's current wife dies. If the son is not alive at that time, all the property in the trust is to pass to the children of the second wife. The son has been given a contingent remainder interest. If he fails to survive his mother (the condition), his estate and his children receive nothing. Likewise, the children of the second wife have a contingent remainder interest that requires that the son die before his mother dies for them to receive the property in the trust.

Corpus: the body of a trust—that is, the principal, as opposed to income.

Credit estate tax: a tax imposed by a state to take full advantage of the amount allowed as a credit against the federal estate tax (sometimes called a "pickup," "slack," "sponge," or "gap" tax).

Credit-equivalent bypass trust: a trust designed to receive an amount of property roughly equal to the unified credit equivalent (changing in increments from $600,000 in 1997 to $1,000,000 in 2006). Consideration must be given to the business interest exclusion if applicable. The advantage of a CEBT is that the assets that pass into it are sheltered from federal estate tax at the first spouse's death because of the unified credit and sheltered from estate tax at the death of the surviving spouse because of the limited interest the surviving spouse is given (enough to provide security and income but not enough to result in estate taxation at his or her death). So both assets placed into the CEBT at the first spouse's death and all appreciation from that moment until the second spouse's death bypass federal (and in most cases state) estate tax at both spouses' deaths. Typically, this is accomplished by giving the surviving spouse only an income interest but denying the carte blanche right to trust principal.

Crummey power: the right to make limited withdrawals from an irrevocable trust (generally an irrevocable life insurance trust) to obtain an annual gift tax exclusion of up to $10,000 adjusted for inflation ($20,000 if you are married) for gifts to the trust. Although beneficiaries are not expected actually to exercise their right to demand money from the trust, they must, in fact, have the right in order for your transfers to the trust to qualify for the annual exclusion. This can considerably reduce the gift tax cost of transferring enough cash to the trust to pay life insurance premiums on large policies used to provide federal estate tax liquidity and to pay taxes and other expenses as they fall due.

Custodian: A person appointed to hold property for a minor under the Uniform Gifts to Minors Act or Uniform Transfer to Minors Act.

Descent: the passing of real estate or other property to the heirs of someone who dies intestate (without a will).

Devise: a gift of real estate under a will.

Direct skip: a gift during lifetime or at death to a grandchild (or someone in the grandchild's generation) and skipping your child. Congress, concerned that in skipping your child, you were also making it possible to skip the estate tax at your child's death, passed a draconian levy called the generation-skipping transfer tax which is imposed on so-called generation skips. A direct skip could result in a tax of 55 percent on every dollar transferred—in addition to gift or estate taxes on the same transfer.

Disclaimer: a renunciation of your right to property. A disclaimer must be a complete and unqualified refusal to accept property or an interest to which you are entitled. A "qualified" disclaimer is one that meets certain requirements under federal law. It must be made without consideration or without directions as to what happens to the disclaimed property. The benefit of a qualified disclaimer is that you are treated as if you never received the property, and it went directly from the original owner to the party that did receive it. This can save gift taxes and, in some cases, significant federal estate tax.

Discretionary trust: a trust that gives the trustee the discretion to make or withhold payments or distributions for the beneficiary. Its purpose is to give the trustee flexibility to meet the beneficiary's needs and to maintain the beneficiary's eligibility for governmental benefits. A discretionary trust can also provide for distributions to various beneficiaries through the use of "sprinkling" provisions.

Distributable net income: essentially the taxable income of your estate or trust.

Distribution: the passing of personal property to the heirs of someone who dies without a will, or (more generally) the payment or delivery of cash or other property from an estate or trust to the beneficiaries of the estate or trust.

Domicile: your permanent legal residence, to which you intend to return whenever you are absent. You can have several residences, but only one domicile, and the establishment of a domicile is extremely important for people who have homes in more than one state. Failure to establish a clear domicile could lead to multiple state death taxation and many other problems.

Donee: the recipient of your gift.

Donor: the person who makes a gift.

Election: a choice. Often applied to tax decisions, such as whether to claim a federal estate tax marital deduction for a qualifying terminable interest property (i.e., "QTIP") trust. The term "election" is also used to describe the right of a surviving spouse to claim a share of the deceased spouse's estate determined by state law, instead of the decedent's will.

Estate: (a) the real and personal property owned by a decedent at death and subject to administration by an executor or administrator (i.e., the property passing under a will, sometimes called the "probate estate"), (b) the property subject to estate tax at death (which can include not only the probate estate but also life insurance, retirement benefits, jointly owned property, and other assets passing outside of a will, all of which is sometimes called the "gross estate"), or (c) a specific interest in property, such as a "life estate" (which is the right of a person to use or receive income from a property during his or her lifetime).

Estate tax: a tax imposed on the right to transfer property at death. The federal government imposes an estate tax, and all states impose a form of estate tax that is at least equal to the state death tax credit allowed for the federal estate tax. Some states also impose a death tax that is independent of the state death tax credit, and that tax may be called an estate tax, an inheritance tax, or a succession tax, depending on the state.

Executor: a person named in a will to carry out (or "execute) the terms of the will and settle the estate.

Family ("B") trust: the receptacle for assets that can be protected by the $600,000 (increasing to $1,000,000 in 2006) unified credit equivalent; also called the credit equivalent bypass trust (CEBT) or nonmarital trust. (Consideration must also be given to the business interest exclusion). Since your surviving spouse is given only an income interest in the assets of the family trust, none of the assets channeled to this trust will be taxable at your surviving spouse's death. Generally, the surviving spouse is given all the income plus the right to withdraw the greater of $5,000 or 5 percent of the trust's principal each year. At your surviving spouse's death, any remaining assets pass to your children or other designated beneficiary.

Fair market value: the hypothetical point at which property would change hands between a willing buyer and a willing seller, neither being under a compulsion to buy or sell and both having knowledge of the relevant facts. It is the value at which property (including a business interest) will be included in your gross estate for federal estate tax purposes.

Federal estate tax: a confiscatory tax on property transferred at death; rates start at 37 percent and rise to 55 percent, with a 5 percent surtax imposed on ultra-large estates.

Fee simple: the most complete right to property you can possess. The owner of a fee simple estate has the unconditional right to use the property and the conditional power to dispose of it either during lifetime or at death to anyone and in any way.

Fiduciary: a trustee, executor, administrator, or other person upon whom the law imposes certain responsibilities because of the position of trust afforded to him, her, or it.

Fiduciary income tax return: IRS Form 1041, which is an income tax return that must be filed each taxable year by the executor or administrator of an estate or trustee of a trust.

"5 and 5" power: a right to withdraw (or "power of appointment") from a trust that is limited to $5,000 or 5 percent of value of the trust, whichever is more. The lapse of a "5 and 5" power is not a taxable gift and has no estate tax consequences, so rights of withdrawal that might not be exercised (such as "crummey" powers) are frequently limited to $5,000 or 5 percent.

50-50 rule: a rule governing estate taxation of jointly held property between a husband and wife. Under this rule, only half the value of property owned by tenancies by the entirety or joint tenancies with rights of survivorship will be included in the gross estate of the first spouse to die, no matter how much or how little either spouse contributed. This is called the "50-50" rule.

Formula clause: a provision in a will or trust that channels property first to a CEBT (credit equivalent bypass trust) up to the amount of any remaining unified credit equivalent ($600,000 in 1997 and increasing to $1,000,000 by 2006) plus any allowable business interest exclusion and directs all property in excess of that amount either outright to a surviving spouse or into a marital trust. The purpose of the formula is typically to lower federal estate tax at both spouses' deaths to the lowest possible amount.

Fractional interest rule: one of two rules (see "50-50" rule above for a definition of the other rule) that govern the estate taxation of jointly held property; also called the percentage of contribution rule. Under this rule when jointly owned property with rights of survivorship is held between anyone other than spouses, it is all taxed in the estate of the first joint owner to die—except to the extent that the survivor can prove he or she contributed to it. (The burden of proof lies with the taxpayer.)

Funded insurance trust: an irrevocable life insurance trust, into which you put income-producing assets. The income is used to pay the premiums on the policies held in the trust.

Future interest: the postponement—even for a day—of a beneficiary's right to use, possess, or enjoy property you give. If a gift is a future interest, it will not qualify for the annual gift tax exclusion.

General power of appointment: the right you give to some other person to say who will receive property you put in trust. If that power is so extensive that the power holder can exercise it in favor of any person (including himself, his estate, his creditors, or the creditors of his estate), it is called a "general" power and the assets subject to that power, to appoint your assets will be included in the power holder's estate to the same extent as if he owned them outright at his death.

Generation-skipping transfer: a transfer that is subject to federal generation-skipping tax, including (a) a transfer to a grandchild or other "skip person," (b) a taxable termination (which happens when all of the grantor's children die or only grandchildren or other skip persons have any interest in a generation-skipping trust), or (c) a taxable distribution (which is a distribution from a generation-skipping trust to a grandchild or other skip person). There is a $1 million per transferor exemption (which may be adjusted for inflation after 1998) that can shield you from this 55 percent tax.

Generation-skipping trust: a trust which is not included in the taxable estates of the children of the grantor and is not subject to estate tax at their deaths, and so "skips" their generation for federal estate tax purposes. However, a generation-skipping trust may still be subject to the confiscatory generation-skipping transfer tax described above.

Gift: any gratuitous transfer of property or an interest in property made during lifetime.

Gift splitting: a married couple's agreement to treat a gift made by one of them to a third party as having been made one-half by each. This lowers the gift tax rate and in many cases, significantly reduces—or even eliminates—any gift tax.

Gift tax: a tax imposed on gratuitous transfers of property you make during your lifetime. Gift taxes are imposed at the same rates (37 percent to 55 percent) as estate tax rates, although there can be significant savings realized through intrafamily gifts.

Gift tax marital deduction: an unlimited deduction allowed for a gift made by one spouse to another during lifetime. This enables spouses to transfer wealth back and forth with federal tax impunity and to arrange their assets to minimize federal estate tax at death.

Grantor: the creator of a trust or other gift.

GRAT (grantor-retained annuity trust): an irrevocable trust into which you transfer cash, stocks, mutual funds, real estate, or other income producing property but retain the right to payments of a fixed amount (an annuity) for a fixed period of years. At the end of the specified term, the asset will pass to the beneficiary you have named in the trust, usually a child, grandchild, or other family member or friend.

GRIT (grantor-retained income trust): an irrevocable trust into which you place a personal residence (or tangible personal property such as art) but retain the right to live in the home (or enjoy the asset) for a fixed period of years. At the end of the specified term, the home (or art work) will pass to the beneficiary named in the trust, typically a child, grandchild, or other family member or friend.

GRUT (grantor-retained unitrust) an irrevocable trust into which you transfer cash, stocks, mutual funds, real estate, or other income-producing property but retain the right to payments of a fixed percentage of the trust's value, as revalued each year, for a fixed period of years. The percentage remains the same but the base against which the percentage applies will vary from year to year. At the end of the specified term, the asset will pass to the beneficiary named in the trust, usually a child, grandchild, or other family member or friend.

Gross estate: an amount determined by totaling the value of all property in which the decedent had an interest that was required to be included in the estate by the Internal Revenue Code.

Guardian: the person nominated by you in your will or appointed by a court to represent the interests of a minor. A "guardian of the person" of a minor child has legal custody of the child. A "guardian of the estate" of a minor child has is responsible for the child's property.

Heir: a person who will receive all or part of your estate if you die without a will. Sometimes also used to refer to someone who will receive all or part of your estate under your will.

Inheritance tax: a tax on the right to receive property from a deceased person. Unlike an estate tax, which is measured by the value of the property you own at death, an inheritance tax is one measured by the share actually passing to each beneficiary.

Insurance trust: a trust that owns and is the beneficiary of one or more life insurance policies on your life.

Intangible property: property that has no physical existence and cannot be touched, seen, or felt. Copyrights, patents, partnership interests, and corporate securities are all examples of intangible property. (In deciding whether property is tangible or intangible, you must consider whether the thing has intrinsic value or merely represents the something else. For example, a stock certificate may seem tangible, but it only represents the legal rights of the shareholder in the corporation. Similarly, a promissory note may seem tangible, but it is only the physical evidence of the maker's promise to pay, and it is the promise to pay that has value.)

Interest: entitlement to or being a permissible recipient of either the income or principal in a trust.

Interpolated terminal reserve: an interpolation between the last and the next reserve (a life insurance company must maintain a reserve to meet death claims) to measure the gift tax value of a policy on which future premiums remain to be paid.

Inter vivos trust: a living trust, one you create during your lifetime, which can be revocable or irrevocable. (If you create a trust under your will, it is called a testamentary trust.)

Intestacy laws: laws governing what happens and who receives your property if you die without a valid will.

Intestate: death without a valid will ("testament").

Irrevocable trust: a trust you cannot revoke or terminate—a trust to which you have given up the right to alter, amend, or in any other way change the terms or recover the assets you've placed into it. Its purpose is to save death taxes and protect against the claims of creditors.

Joint tenancy: a contract under which two or more parties hold property (such as real estate) that will pass entirely to the other(s) at the death of one of the parties.

Joint will: a single document that serves as the will of both a husband and wife and disposes of their property at their death (See also, "mutual wills.")

Lapse: the termination or failure of a right or privilege because of the expiration of time or some contingency. The lapse of a right to withdraw from a trust (or other power of appointment) is considered to be a gift for federal gift tax purposes if the amount that could have been withdrawn was more than $5,000 or 5 percent of the trust. (See "5 and 5 power," above.) A gift under a will may lapse if the intended beneficiary predeceases the testator. (See "anti-lapse statutes," above.)

Legacy: a gift of personal property by will.

Legatee: the person to whom a legacy is given.

Letters of administration: a document issued by a court or other state official authorizing the administrator of your estate to act on behalf of the estate when you die without a valid will.

Letters testamentary: a document issued by a court or other state official authorizing your executor to act on behalf of your estate.

Lien: an encumbrance on property for the payment of a debt.

Life estate or life interest: the right to live on property or enjoy its income for as long as you live, or for as long as the "measuring life" lives. The life tenant (see below) has no right to transfer property at death.

Life tenant: the person who enjoys the income from a life estate or from a trust fund during his or her own life or that of another person (income beneficiary).

Limited power of appointment: a power to appoint (say who receives someone else's money or other assets) but limited so that the holder of that power cannot take the property for himself, his creditors, his estate, or the creditors of his estate. Also called a "special" power, a limited power of appointment unlike general powers, will not cause the property subject to the power to be included in the power holder' estate. An example of a limited power would be if you gave your son Steven the right to distribute the property at his death to any of his children.

Liquid assets: cash or assets that can be readily converted into cash without significant cost within 9 months of the date of your death. Life insurance, cash, and money in a checking or savings account are considered liquid assets.

Living will: a document exercising a person's right to declare in advance which death-delaying medical treatments should be refused in the event of a terminal illness or injury.

Lump-sum distribution: a distribution or payment within one taxable year of the entire balance of an employee's interest in a qualified pension or profit-sharing plan on account of the employee's death or separation from service after age 59 1/2.

Marital deduction: the single most important deduction available to a married couple for reducing the tax on lifetime gifts or at-death transfers. There is no limit to the size of this deduction, and it can therefore eliminate the federal estate tax on any size of estate. It is allowed for the net value of the property passing to your surviving spouse either outright (or in a manner tantamount to outright) or in a form that meets rigid statutory rules.

Marital deduction trust: a trust designed to qualify property for the gift or estate tax marital deduction.

Marital deduction zero-tax formula: a provision your attorney builds into your trust to take full advantage of your unified credit and the estate tax marital deduction. It is designed to reduce taxes at both spouses' deaths to the lowest possible amount.

Medicaid: a joint federal and state program of medical assistance to eligible needy persons, under which medical services are provided by participating providers and reimbursed according to state formulas.

Medicaid qualifying trust: a trust under which the individual may be the beneficiary of all or a part of payments from the trust, a distribution of which would be considered an available asset for Medicaid purposes and could disqualify the trust beneficiary from eligibility for Medicaid.

Minor: a person who is less than eighteen (or, for some purposes or in some states, twenty-one) years of age.

Mutual wills: separate wills of two or more persons with reciprocal provisions in favor of the other person contained in each will.

Nonliquid assets: assets that are not readily convertible into cash without a serious loss. An example is investment real estate or a business interest where there is no buy-sell agreement between the owners.

Nonmarital trust: a trust designed to avoid federal estate tax at the death of the surviving spouse. See "credit exemption bypass trust," above.

Nonprobate property: property that does not become part of the probate estate and passes outside the ambit of probate court. Examples of nonprobate property include jointly held property, life insurance proceeds payable to a named beneficiary, and property in an inter vivos trust. Probate property consists of assets passing under the terms of your will or by your state's intestate laws if you have no valid will at death.

Payback language: a provision in a trust for a disabled individual under age 65 stipulating that upon the beneficiary's death; the trust balance will reimburse the state for medical assistance paid on behalf of the beneficiary. If a trust contains payback language, the beneficiary may still be eligible for Medicare.

Per stirpes: a distribution of property in which the children of a deceased beneficiary take the share which their parent would have received if living. Sometimes described as a distribution "by right of representation."

Personal property: any property that is not real property (i.e., land or buildings). Cash, cars, household furnishings, jewelry, shares of corporate stock, and interests in partnerships are all examples of personal property. All real property is tangible, but personal property can be either tangible or intangible.

Pooled trust: a trust whose assets can be exempt for Medicaid purposes because it is established and managed by a nonprofit association and provides that upon the death of the beneficiary, the funds must remain in the trust for the benefit of other trust beneficiaries or be applied to repay the state.

Pour-over: property passing under your will into a trust, which is said to "pour over" into the trust.

Power of appointment: the right to designate who receives property from a trust. For example, a marital trust might allow the surviving spouse to designate who will receive the principal of the trust at his or her death. A power of appointment can be a "lifetime" power, meaning that it can only be exercised during the power holder's lifetime, or it can be "testamentary," meaning that it can only be exercised at death through a will. A power of appointment can also be "special" or "limited," meaning that the trust property can only be appointed among a specified class of people (such as the grantor's children and grandchildren), or it can be "general," meaning that the trust property can be appointed to anyone. A general power of appointment is considered to be part of the power holder's gross estate for federal estate tax purposes.

Power of attorney: a power a person (the "principal") may grant to another (the "agent" or "attorney-in-fact") to act for the principal, which may include the power to sign deeds, contracts, and checks, and the power to make gifts. A "durable" power of attorney is one that is valid even if the principal becomes incompetent, and is often used with revocable living trusts to avoid guardianship or incompetency proceedings.

Precatory language: words in a will or trust document that express the wishes of the testator or grantor, but are not legally binding.

Present interest: the interest a donee receives when given the immediate, unfettered, and ascertainable right to use, possess, or enjoy property. A donee must be given a present (as opposed to a future) interest in order for you to obtain the $10,000 ($20,000 if you are married) annual gift tax exclusion. This amount may be adjusted for inflation after 1998.

Principal: the property first received by a trustee or other fiduciary, and the capital appreciation of that property, but not the income from the property. Sometimes described as "corpus." A person granting a power of attorney is also known as the "principal."

Probate: the process by which it is proven that a document is the valid last will of the decedent. After the will is probated, the court (or other official) issues letters testamentary to the executor, which empowers the executor to take possession the decedent's property in order to carry out the terms of the will. "Probate" is also sometimes applied to the entire court-supervised process by which that same personal representative is given authority to act on behalf of the estate and under which he or she assembles the decedent's assets, pays debts and taxes, and distributes what remains according to the terms of the decedent's will or under state intestacy laws. See our book, *How To Settle An Estate (610-527-5216)*.

Probate property: property you own in your own name at death or your half of community property that passes under the terms of your will or, if you leave no valid will, under your state's intestacy laws.

Prudent investor rule: a relatively recent (1990) rule, adopted by statute or judicial decision in some but not all states, that trustees, executors, and other fiduciaries must invest the funds entrusted to them with the same care that a prudent investor would use with his or her own investments. The rule looks to the risk and return of the entire portfolio, rather than individual investments, and recognizes the validity of some modern investment practices. The advantage of the prudent investor rule over earlier rules governing the investment responsibilities of trustees is that the trustee can delegate some investment decisions to professional investment managers and can have greater flexibility in maintaining a diversified portfolio.

Qualified domestic trust (QDT): a trust designed to delay the federal estate tax when the transfer is to a resident-alien-spouse.

Qualified terminable interest property (QTIP): property passing from the decedent to a spouse who is entitled to all income from the property for life, payable annually or more frequently. No person, including the spouse, can have the power to appoint any part of the property subject to the qualified income interest to any person other than the spouse during the spouse's life. This is property that qualifies for the estate tax marital deduction even though the surviving spouse can't specify the ultimate recipient of the principal, and it is often used in second marriages.

Real property: land, buildings, and things permanently attached to land or buildings. See also, personal property.

Remainder interest: the right to receive what remains after another party's interest ends. For instance, suppose you create a trust under your will in which income is paid to your daughter Lara for as long as she lives and at her death her daughter will receive the principal. Your grandchild then holds the remainder interest. Similarly, if you set up a GRIT and specify that you have the right to live in the house held by the GRIT for 15 years and then it passes to your daughter Charlee and her husband Rob, they have a remainder interest.

Remainderman: the person(s) or entity(ies) entitled to receive property (usually in trust) after the termination of the prior holder's interest. For example, Charlee and her husband Rob are each a remainderman of the trust in the example directly above.

Renunciation: a refusal to serve as an executor or an unqualified refusal to accept property or an interest in property. It can be the same as a disclaimer.

Reserve: the amount an insurance company is legally required to set aside to meet future claims. Technically, a reserve is the difference between the present value of future benefits (death claim and maturity value) and the present value of future net premiums for any life insurance policy. The term reserve is not synonymous with cash surrender value, although the cash surrender value ultimately equals the amount of the reserve after a policy (other than a term policy) has been in force for a number of years (in some companies this may be as long as 10 or 15 years).

Residuary estate: what is left of your estate after your executor has paid all debts, taxes, and expenses of administration, and has distributed any gifts of specific property or specific amounts. In order to make sure that everything the decedent owns is distributed, wills almost always have a clause disposing of the residuary estate (or "residue" of the estate).

Reversionary interest: an interest through which you can retain the ultimate right to recover property. For example, suppose you create a trust under which you give your mother the right to income from the trust for life but you keep the right to recover trust principal when your mother dies. Your property right is a reversionary interest.

Revocable trust: a trust under which you reserve the right to alter, amend, revoke, or terminate the trust or recover assets you've placed into it.

Rule against perpetuities: an old English rule, still in force in almost all states, that requires a trust to terminate (or "vest") within twenty-one years after the deaths of all the beneficiaries (or other persons named in the trust) who were living when the trust was created. The rule was intended to prevent the "dead hand rule" of grantors tying up property in perpetual trusts.

Shrinkage: the loss of assets your heirs will experience because of the normal (or abnormal) costs of probate, filing tax returns, and shifting property from one person to another. Sizable shrinkage often occurs because of the need to raise cash quickly to pay federal and state death taxes and to pay off or carry debts.

Situs: the location of a trust, usually considered to be the state in which the grantor was living when the trust was created, or where the trustee is located. The situs of a trust may determine which state has jurisdiction over disputes involving the trust, or to supervise the administration of the trust.

Special needs trust: a trust designed to care for a beneficiary's special needs so as not to disqualify the beneficiary from eligibility for SSI (supplementary security income) and Medicaid.

Spendthrift trust: a trust with a specific provision (sometimes called a "spendthrift clause") that prevents the beneficiaries from assigning their interests, and prevents the creditors of a beneficiary from taking the interest of the beneficiary. This kind of trust is intended to protect beneficiaries who would otherwise spend the trust's money too quickly, but it can also help protect beneficiaries from personal injury lawsuits, divorce disputes, catastrophic medical expenses, and other unforeseen debts.

Sprinkling or spray trust: trusts that contain a provision empowering your trustee to "sprinkle" income or "spray" capital in any manner and to any beneficiary deemed appropriate. For instance, you might give your trustee discretionary power to distribute any part or all of the trust's income among beneficiaries in equal or unequal shares and to accumulate any income not distributed.

Surcharge: a court-imposed award payable by a trustee, executor, or other fiduciary who has negligently or intentionally violated his or her duties to the beneficiaries of the trust or estate and so caused a loss to the beneficiaries. Such losses can be caused by a failure to invest the trust properly, by sales or other acts of self-dealing between the trustee and the trust, by improperly favoring one beneficiary over another, or by other violations of fiduciary duties.

Tangible property: any asset that has physical substance and may be touched, seen, or felt. A home, a car, a gold watch, and a computer are all tangible property.

Taxable estate: an amount determined by subtracting the allowable deductions from the gross estate.

Tenancy by the entirety: the holding of property by a husband and a wife in such a manner that, except with the consent of each, neither husband nor wife has a disposable interest in the property during the other's lifetime. Upon the death of either, the property passes automatically to the survivor. Technically, both spouses always own the entire tenancy.

Tenancy in common: the holding of property by two or more persons in such a manner that each has a separate but undivided interest in the property that can be sold during lifetime or passed through probate at death. The surviving tenant or tenants in common do *not* automatically own the interest of a deceased tenant.

Terminal reserve: the reserve on a life insurance policy at the end of any contract year; for policies on which premiums are still due, the amount of the reserve prior to the payment of the next premium.

Testament: a will.

Testamentary: of or by a will.

Testamentary trust: a trust created at death by the terms of the decedent's will.

Testate: having a valid will. (The opposite of "testate" is "intestate," meaning without a will.)

Testator: a person who has made a will.

Trust: a legal relationship under which one party, the grantor, transfers title to property to a second party, the trustee, for the benefit of one or more third parties, the beneficiary or beneficiaries. Legal title is held by the trustee, who is under a fiduciary duty to use and invest the property for the benefit of the beneficiaries. A trust can be created during lifetime by a written document (called a deed of trust, declaration of trust, or agreement of trust), at death by a will, or during lifetime by an oral agreement (without any written document). The word "trust" is also sometimes used to refer to the document creating the trust.

Trustee: the holder of legal title to property for the use or benefit of another.

Unfunded life insurance trust: an insurance trust that is not provided with cash and/or securities to pay the life insurance premium.

Unified credit: a credit against the federal estate and gift tax that is available to residents of the United States. The credit applies to taxable gifts during lifetime and, to the extent it is not used during lifetime, it reduces the federal estate tax at death. The unified credit exclusion amount (the amount that can pass free of federal estate and gift tax, assuming no previous taxable gifts) is $600,000 in 1997 and increases by steps until it is $1,000,000 in 2006.

Uniform Anatomical Gift Act (UAGA): legislation that enables the donation of body parts for the use of science, education, or for individuals needing particular organs.

Uniform Gifts to Minors Act (UGMA): a law adopted by almost every state that allows you to make gifts to minors without the need to create a trust but assures you of the gift tax annual exclusion. UGMA permits an adult to make a lifetime gift of specified types of property, such as securities, money, or a life insurance or annuity contract, to a minor by registering the property in the name of a custodian for the minor or by delivering it to an adult family member as custodian for the property placed in the minor's account.

The fundamental difference between a custodial account and a trust is that legally the child is the owner of the property under an UGMA, but in a trust the trustee is the legal owner of the property (although a trustee must use trust property exclusively for the trust's beneficiaries).

Uniform Transfers to Minors Act (UTMA): an act that is similar to the UGMA but is much more flexible because it allows *any* kind of property—real or personal, tangible or intangible—to be the subject of a custodial gift. Most states have replaced their UGMA laws with this much broader statute.

Vested interest: an immediate fixed interest in real or personal property that can't be lost or forfeited. A vested interest can delay the holder's right to possession until some future date or until the occurrence of a specified event. For example, suppose Ted leaves real property and securities to Dave as trustee. Dave is to pay income to Ted's wife, Alex, for as long as she lives. At Alex's death, Dave as trustee must transfer the trust's assets to "Pat and her heirs." The phrase ". . . and her heirs" makes Pat's interest vested. Alex has been given a vested life interest in the trust's income. Pat has been given a future vested interest in the right to the trust's principal. Pat takes what remains at Alex's death and therefore has a vested remainder interest.

Vested remainder: a fixed interest in property with the right of possession and enjoyment postponed until the termination of a prior property interest.

Will: a document by which you may direct how your property is disposed of at your death. A will may also be used to exercise other rights, such as your right to appoint guardians for your minor children, make anatomical gifts or other dispositions of your body, or exercise any powers of appointment you might have in existing trusts. Wills are defined by statute, and almost all states require that a will be in writing and signed by the testator in the presence of two (or three) witnesses, who must not be beneficiaries and who must also sign the will in the presence of the testator and each other. Unlike a trust, which usually does not need witnesses and does not even need to be in writing, a will must be signed and witnesses *exactly* as required by statute, or it is completely invalid. For example, if one of the witnesses does not see the other witness sign the will, the entire will may be invalid, even though 100 other people saw the will signed, or the signing was recorded on videotape.

INDEX

A

Accountability Act of 1996, *375*
Accountant's fees, *89*
Actuarial tables, *415*
Advertising, *84*
Alaska trusts, *42*
Alimony, *457*
Annuity *410*
Attorney
        durable power of, *107*, *380*
Automobile insurance premiums,
        52

B

Bankruptcy, *130*, *455*
Bankruptcy trustee, *455*
Belize, *453*, *456*
Big QDTs, *201*
Brokerage fees, *397*

C

Capital gains of trust, *264*
Cayman Islands corporation, *481*
Charitable Remainder Annuity
        Trust, *412*
Charitable remainder trust, *400*
Child support obligations, *457*
CLATs
        tax advantages of, *435*
Constitutional trust, *477*
Cook Islands, *452*, *453*
Corporate Buy-Sell Handbook,
        470
Corporate trustee, *40*
Credit equivalent by-pass trust,
        186
Credit Shelter Trust, *70*
CRT, *428*

Crummey power, *295*
Crummey trust, *238*

D

Debts
        decedent's, *154*
Deductible business expenses, *479*
Delaware trust law, *453*, *462*
Delaware trusts, *441*

E

Education
        college, *10*, *224*, *228*
Employer Identification Number,
        308
Entireties property, *443*, *444*
Estate,
        administration of, *81*
        assets of, *41*, *47*, *52*, *80*
        bankrupt's, *471*
        creditors of, *231*, *292*
        creditors of probate, *129*
        distribution of, *80*, *117*,
            442
        executor of, *99*, *120*, *134*
Estate administration, *90*, *91*, *112*
Estate administration expenses,
        168
Estate assets, *48*
        inventory of, *88*
Estate cash, *168*
Estate,
        probate, *96*
Estate freeze, *361*
Estate liquidity, *141*
Estate planning council, *70*
Estate planning lawyer, *67*, *77*,
        101

Estate planning methods, *380*

Estate planning objectives, *102*, *143*

Estate planning team, *70*

Estate planning technique, *99*

Estate planning tools, *75*, *101*, *102*,

Estate tax charitable deduction, *390*, *411*, *422*

Estate tax consequences of joint trusts, *214*

Estate tax cost of QTIP trust, *181*

Estate tax exclusion of life insurance federal, *290*

Estate tax implications of house GRIT, *339*

Estate tax inclusion of life insurance proceeds, *295*

Estate tax marital deduction, *182*

Estate tax return, *338*,

Estate tax value of assets federal, *149*

Estate trust, *181*, *197* Disadvantages of, *181*

Estate's creditors, *99*, *292*

Estate's executor, *90*

Estate's expenses, *142*

Estate's lawyer, *94*

Estate's tax year, *153*

Executor decedent's, *322*

Executor's fees, *90*

F

Fair market value, *220*

Fair market value of marketable securities, *401*

FDIC insurance, *129*

Federal Savings insurance protection of, *128*

Federal Trade Commission, *101*

Flat tax, *318*

Fraudulent Conveyance Act, *446*

G

Georgia Uniform Transfers, *229*

Gift tax annual exclusion, *299*

Gift tax charitable deduction, *144*

Gift tax discount, *340*, *358*

Gift tax exclusion, *283*

Gift tax implications of CLT, *409*, *431*

Gift tax implications of house GRIT, *339*

Gift tax implications of transfer of life insurance, *271*

Gift tax marital deduction, *144*, *202*, *214*, *439*

Gift tax value of life insurance, *273*

Gift taxes, *19*, *432*

GST tax, *434*

H

Health care provider, *144*

Health Insurance Portability, *375*

Homeowner's coverage, *343*

I

Income disbursements, *63*

Income tax implications of CLT, *409*

Income tax implications of GRAT, *357*

Income tax implications of irrevocable life insurance trust, *272*

Income tax reporting requirements federal, *147*

Income tax return, *145*, *147*, *462* fiduciary, *148*

Income tax treatment of revocable trusts, *220* Income, net, *265*, *409*, *455* make-up unitrust, *409*, *419*

Insurance, *8* casualty, *46*, *89* dollar-life, *313* FDIC, *129* Group, *311*

homeowner's, *443*
liability, *39*
medical, *469*
Split-dollar, *313*
Insurance application, *277*
Insurance contract, *309*
Insurance expenses, *345*
Insurance policies, life, *272*, *295*, *310*
Insurance premiums, *313*
Insurance proceeds, *98*
    management of, *167*
Insurance trusts
    revocable, *8*
Insurance, automobile
    premiums, *52*
Insurance, life, *98*
    contract, *309*
    Downsides of survivorship, *272*
    estate tax treatment of, *283*
    federal estate tax exclusion of, *290*
    Gift tax implications of transfer of, *271*
    gift tax value of, *273*
    premiums, *207*
    proceeds, *143*, *167*, *168*
    survivorship, *309*, *310*
    trust, *280*, *294*
Insurance, term, *272*
Insurance/irrevocable trust combination, *273*
Interest rates, *165, 361*
Intestacy, *133*
Inventory of assets, *110*
Inventory of joint accounts, *97*
Investing assets, *89*
Investment advisory fees, *89*
Investment diversification, *177*
Investment earnings, *227*
Investment experience, *39*
Investment fees, *150*, *265*
Investment income, *227*, *401*, *405*
Investment trust
    real estate, *467*

Investment yield, *414*
Investments, *48*, *177*, *463*
    fiduciary, *49*
    management of, *122*, *466*
    management of tax-free, *146*
    real estate, *46*
    statutory lists of fiduciary, *49*
IRS annuity tables, *184*

J
Jacquelyn Kennedy Onassis, *429*

L
Lawyer
    estate planning, *67*
    estate's, *94*
    executor's, *91*, *93*
Lawyer's fees, *91*
Liabilities of trustee, *471*
Liability partnerships, *467*
Life expectancy, *184*
Life insurance, *98*, *99*
    Downsides of survivorship, *272*
    estate tax treatment of, *283*
    federal estate tax exclusion of, *290*
    Gift tax implications of transfer of, *271*
    gift tax value of, *273*
    survivorship, *309*, *310*
Life insurance premiums, *207*
Life insurance proceeds, *143*, *167*, *168*
    estate tax inclusion of, *295*
Life insurance trust, *262*, *280*
    Income tax implications of irrevocable, *272*
    pourover, *8*
    trustees of irrevocable, *282*

M
Malpractice suits, *325*

Index

Marital assets, *200*
Marital deduction, *97*
 estate tax, *182*
 federal estate tax, *117*, *218*,
  264
 gift tax, *144*, *182*
Marital Deduction Estate Trust,
 198
Marital deduction formula, *85*
Marital deduction QTIP trust, *211*,
 255
Marital deductions
 gift tax, *202*
Marital difficulties, *9*
Massachusetts Business Trust,
 466
Medicaid, *371*, *372*
Medicaid eligibility, *371*
Megatrust, *325*
Mental illness, *121*
Minors Act, *21*, *22*
Minors Act account, *461*
 Mortgage, *108*, *129*, *165*
Mortgage interest, *145*
Mortgage of property, *108*
Mortgage payment, *368*
Mortgages, *472*, *473*
Mutual funds, *458*

P
Pension, *119*, *155*, *156*
 assets of qualified, *468*
Pension plan, *17*, *139*
 employee, *98*
Pension proceeds, *427*
Pension/profit-sharing
 distributions, *160*
Petroleum storage, *164*
Pourover life insurance trust, *8*
Power of Attorney, *21*
Powerholder, *305*
Powerholders
 Crummey, *303*
Probate assets
 Distribution of, *93*
Probate law, *142*

Profit-sharing plan, *155*, *159*
Property
 custodial, *225*, *226*
 income-producing, *277*
 non-residential, *165*
 possession of, *142*
Property taxes, *63*, *89*

Q
QDT law, *203*
QTIP election, *322*
QTIP property, *194*
QTIP trust, *195*, *197*

R
Real estate taxes, *145*
Rental income of property, *400*
Restatement of Trusts, *49*
Retirement funds, *119*
Retitling real estate, *95*
Revocable Living Trust, *166*

S
Schedule K-1, *267*
Settle Estate, *81*
Simplification of Fiduciary
 Security Transfers,
 162
Situs
 law of, *452*
Situs asset-protection trusts, *442*
Situs of trust, *452*
Social security benefits, *331*, *337*,
 373
Social Security number, *308*, *309*
Subchapter S, *156*
Supplemental Security Income,
 332
Survivorship life, *309*
 Downsides of, *310*

T
Tax
 federal generation-
  skipping, *316*

Tax benefits of dynasty trusts, *327*
Tax elections, *133*
Tax evasion, *475*, *476*
Tax, flat, *318*
Tax, gift, *7*, *168*, *212*
    annual exclusion, *313*
    charitable deduction, *144*
    consequences of gift of
        asset, *268*
    discount, *340*, *358*
    exclusion, *283*, *301*
    implications of CLT, *409*,
        431
    implications of house
        GRIT, *339*
    implications of transfer of
        life insurance, *271*
    marital deduction, *144*,
        182, *214*
    value of life insurance, *273*
Tax, income, *227*, *231*
    implications of CLT, *409*,
        433
    implications of GRAT,
        357, *366*
    implications of irrevocable
        life insurance trust,
        272
    liabilities, *116*
    reporting requirements,
        141
    return, *145*, *146*
    treatment of revocable
        trusts, *220*
Taxes, capital gains, *42*
    Taxes, estate, *183*, *211*
Taxes, gift, *19*, *327*
Taxes, income, *62*, *232*
Taxes, property, *63*, *89*
Taxes, real estate, *145*
Taxpayer Relief Act of 1997, *116*,
    145
Taxpayer's Bill of Rights, *444*

Techniques of Employee Benefit,
    471
Techniques of Estate Planning, *21*
Techniques of Life Insurance
        Planning, *470*
Term insurance, *272*
Terminable interest property trust,
    192, *193*, *195*
Totten trust, *171*, *172*
Trust agreement, *50*, *53*
Trust Company, *225*
Trust Division of American
        Bankers
        Association, *167*
Trust fund, *461*
Trust, charitable remainder, *394*
Trustee
        U.S., *201*
Trustees risk litigation, *49*

U
UGMA/UTMA, *223*
Uniform Fraudulent Transfers
        Act, *446*
Uniform Probate Code, *42*, *158*
Uniform Prudent Investor Act, *43*,
    49
Uniform State Laws, *49*
Uniform Transfers, *22*, *461*
Unitrust, *409*
    net income, *409*, *419*, *423*
    net income make-up, *409*,
        419
Unitrust payout, *428*

W
Wisconsin Marital Property
        Reform Act of
        1984, *221*

Z
Zoning regulations, *31*

The following pages illustrate in a hypothetical situation how the judicious use of trusts and careful planning can save thousands in taxes!

The illustrations are courtesy **ESTATE PLANNING QUICKVIEW** Software (610) 527 5216.

Estate Plan For:
Steve and Jo-Ann Smith

Prepared By: Howard Silverman

*One difference between death and taxes is
that death is frequently painless.*

Steve and Jo-Ann Smith

Input Values

	Husband	Wife	Joint
Net Assets:	$ 1,236,000	$ 800,000	$ 0
Life Insurance:	$ 100,000	$ 0	$ 0
Retirement Plans:	$ 200,000	$ 0	
Adj. Taxable Gifts:	$ 0	$ 0	

Years of Death :	1st-to-Die: 1997	Suvivor: 1997

Estate Growth

Domicile:	PA	0.0%

Nonmarital Taxable:	40.00%	50.00%

Steve and Jo-Ann Smith

	Taxes	Heirs
Steve Leaves All to Surviving Spouse	$ 767,120	$ 1,568,880
Steve's credit used for bypass trust; Balance to Jo-Ann outright	$ 489,938	$ 1,846,062
Steve's credit used for bypass trust; Balance to Jo-Ann's marital trust	$ 471,938	$ 1,864,062
Steve's credit used for bypass trust; Balance to Jo-Ann's marital trust; L.I. removed from estate	$ 434,093	$ 1,901,907
Steve Leaves None to Surviving Spouse	$ 486,856	$ 1,849,144
Jo-Ann Leaves All to Surviving Spouse	$ 752,640	$ 1,583,360
Jo-Ann's credit used for bypass trust; Balance to Steve outright	$ 475,459	$ 1,860,541
Jo-Ann's credit used for bypass trust; Balance to Steve's marital trust	$ 475,459	$ 1,860,541
Jo-Ann's credit used for bypass trust; Balance to Steve's marital trust; L.I. removed from estate	$ 437,608	$ 1,898,392
Jo-Ann Leaves None to Surviving Spouse	$ 486,856	$ 1,849,144

HSA Associates, Inc

Steve and Jo-Ann Smith

Steve Leaves All to Surviving Spouse

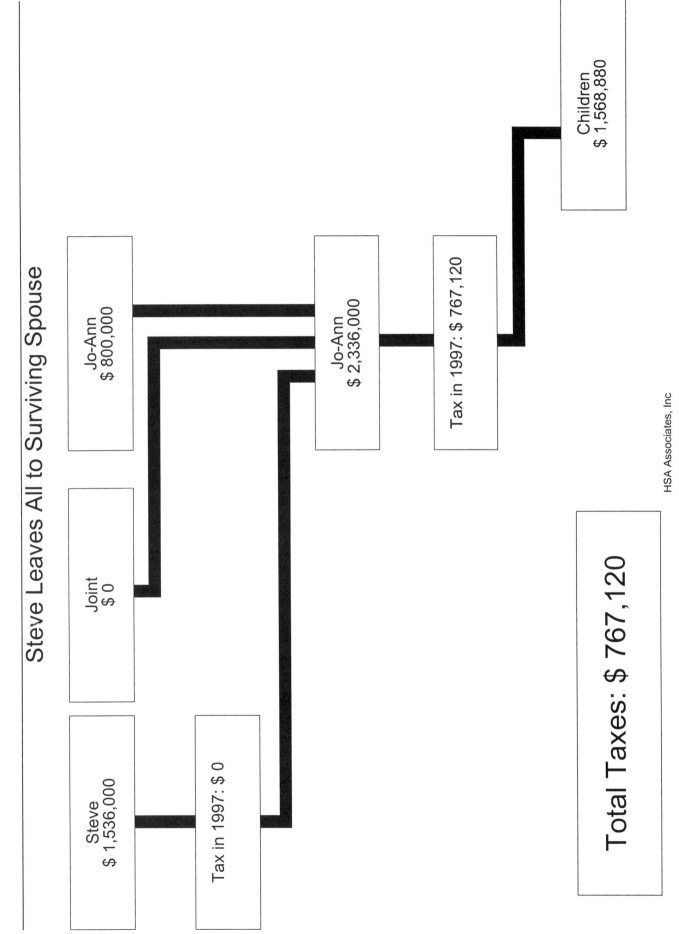

Steve
$ 1,536,000

Tax in 1997: $ 0

Joint
$ 0

Jo-Ann
$ 800,000

Jo-Ann
$ 2,336,000

Tax in 1997: $ 767,120

Children
$ 1,568,880

Total Taxes: $ 767,120

HSA Associates, Inc

Steve and Jo-Ann Smith

Steve's credit used for bypass trust; Balance to Jo-Ann outright

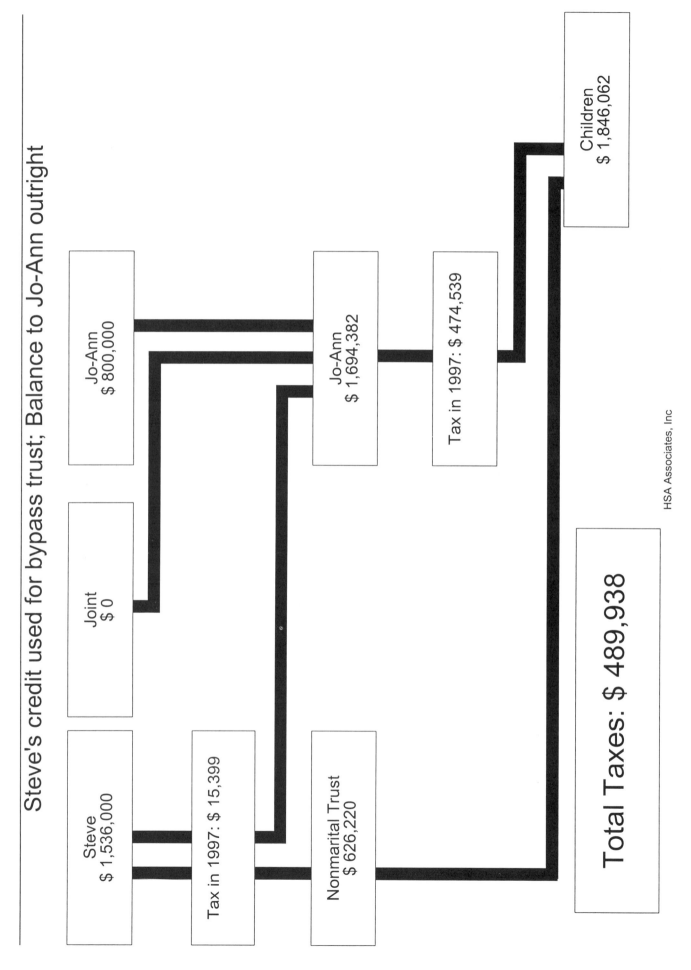

Steve
$ 1,536,000

Joint
$ 0

Jo-Ann
$ 800,000

Tax in 1997: $ 15,399

Nonmarital Trust
$ 626,220

Jo-Ann
$ 1,694,382

Tax in 1997: $ 474,539

Children
$ 1,846,062

Total Taxes: $ 489,938

HSA Associates, Inc

Steve and Jo-Ann Smith

Steve's credit used for bypass trust; Balance to Jo-Ann's marital trust

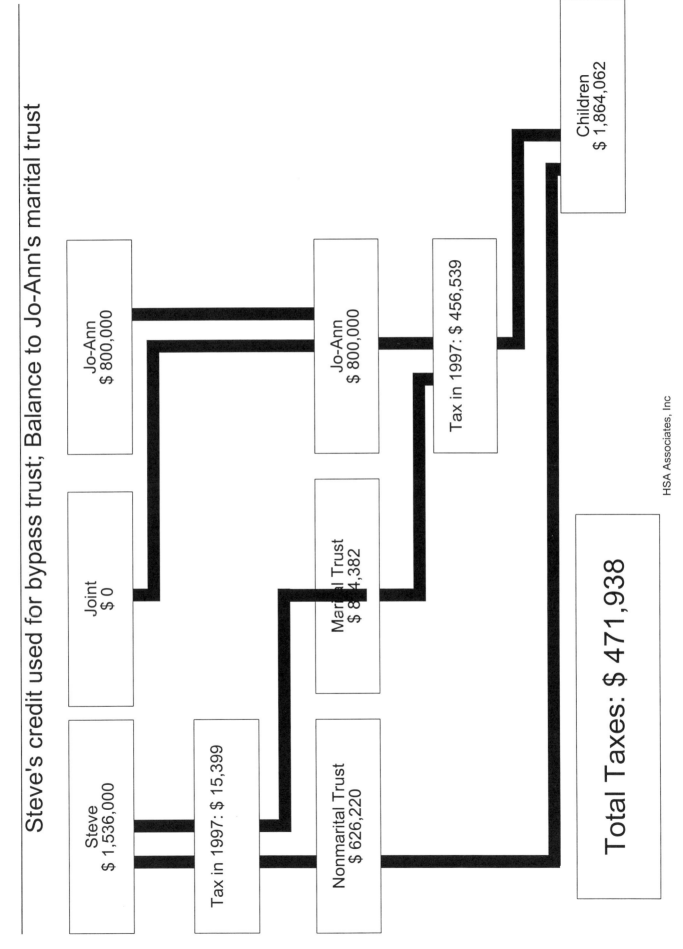

Steve
$ 1,536,000

Tax in 1997: $ 15,399

Nonmarital Trust
$ 626,220

Joint
$ 0

Jo-Ann
$ 800,000

Marital Trust
$ 874,382

Jo-Ann
$ 800,000

Tax in 1997: $ 456,539

Children
$ 1,864,062

Total Taxes: $ 471,938

HSA Associates, Inc

Steve and Jo-Ann Smith

Steve's credit used for bypass trust; Balance to Jo-Ann's marital trust; L.I. removed from estate

Life Ins. Trust $ 100,000	Life Ins. Trust $ 100,000	Children $ 1,901,907
Jo-Ann $ 800,000	Jo-Ann $ 800,000	Tax in 1997: $ 418,694
Joint $ 0	Marital Trust $ 7?4,382	
Steve $ 1,436,000	Nonmarital Trust $ 626,220	
Tax in 1997: $ 15,399		

Total Taxes: $ 434,093

HSA Associates, Inc

Steve and Jo-Ann Smith

Steve Leaves None to Surviving Spouse

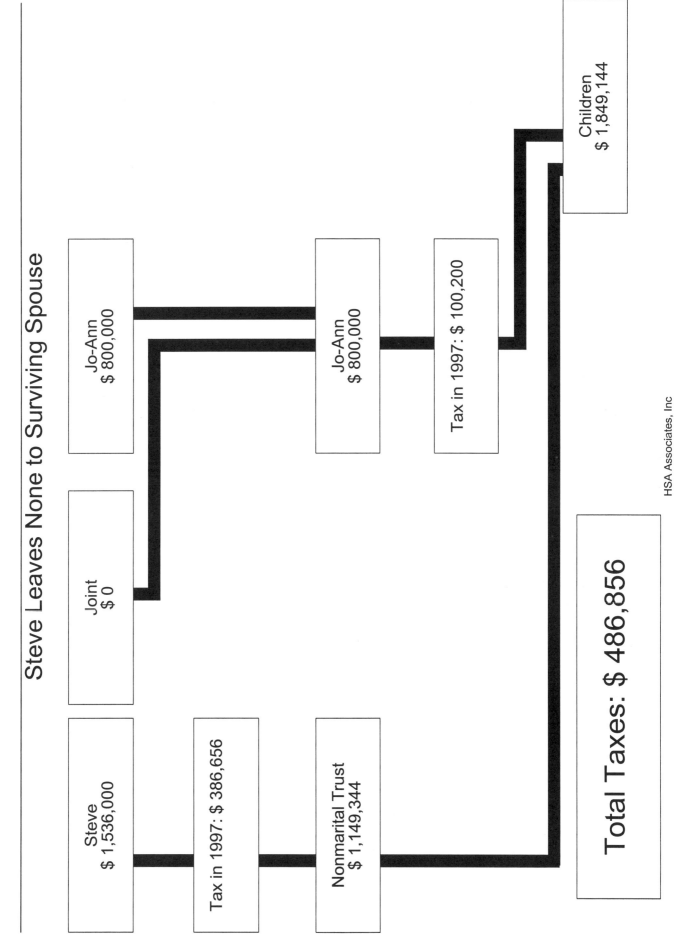

Steve
$ 1,536,000

Tax in 1997: $ 386,656

Nonmarital Trust
$ 1,149,344

Joint
$ 0

Jo-Ann
$ 800,000

Jo-Ann
$ 800,000

Tax in 1997: $ 100,200

Children
$ 1,849,144

Total Taxes: $ 486,856

Steve and Jo-Ann Smith

Jo-Ann Leaves All to Surviving Spouse

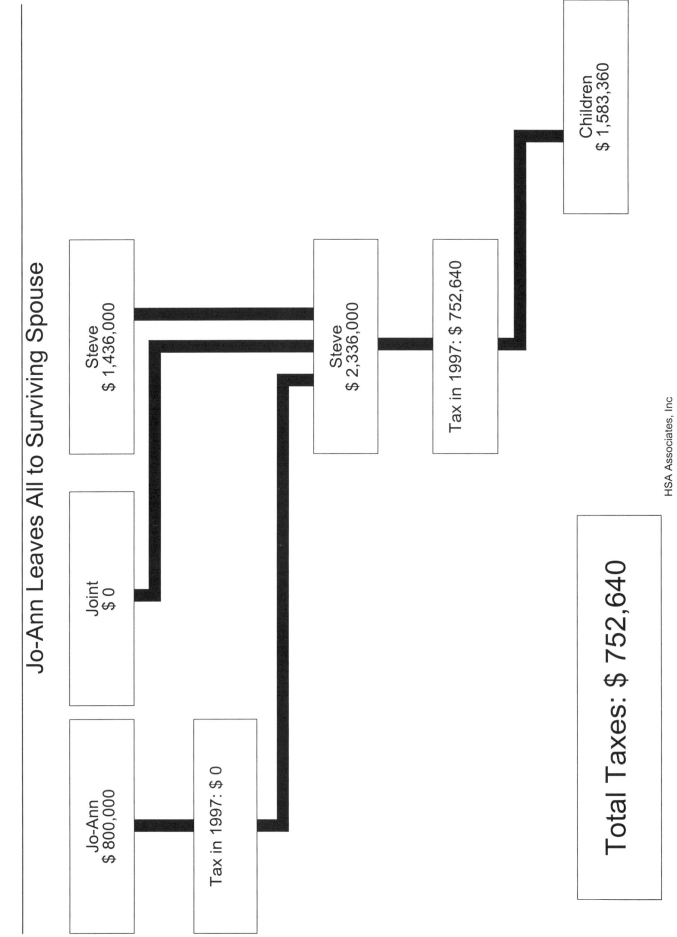

Jo-Ann
$ 800,000

Tax in 1997: $ 0

Joint
$ 0

Steve
$ 1,436,000

Steve
$ 2,336,000

Tax in 1997: $ 752,640

Children
$ 1,583,360

Total Taxes: $ 752,640

HSA Associates, Inc

Steve and Jo-Ann Smith

Jo-Ann's credit used for bypass trust; Balance to Steve outright

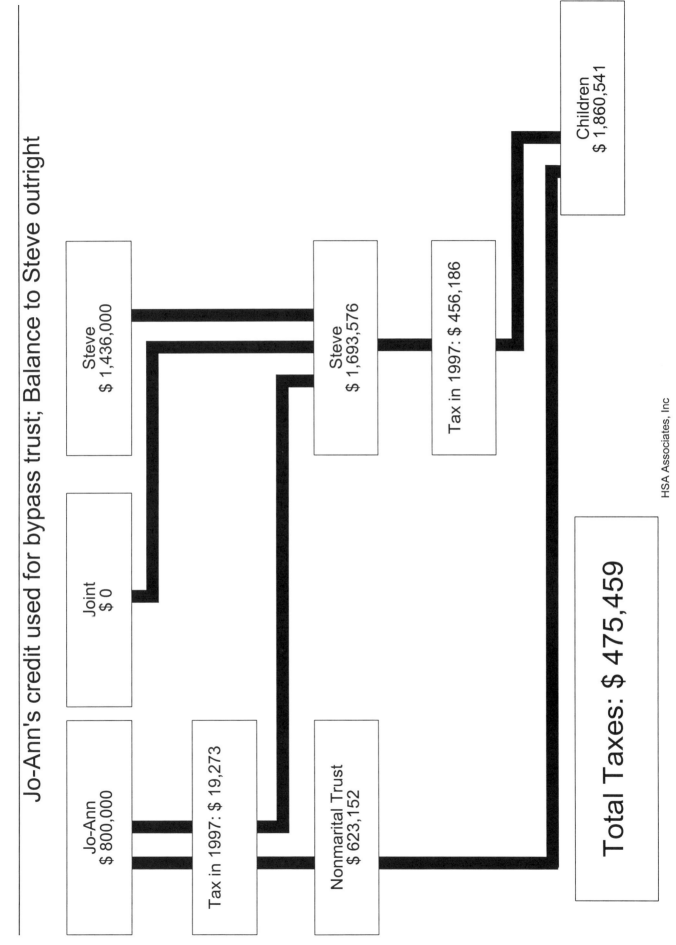

Jo-Ann
$ 800,000

Tax in 1997: $ 19,273

Nonmarital Trust
$ 623,152

Joint
$ 0

Steve
$ 1,436,000

Steve
$ 1,693,576

Tax in 1997: $ 456,186

Children
$ 1,860,541

Total Taxes: $ 475,459

HSA Associates, Inc

Steve and Jo-Ann Smith

Jo-Ann's credit used for bypass trust; Balance to Steve's marital trust

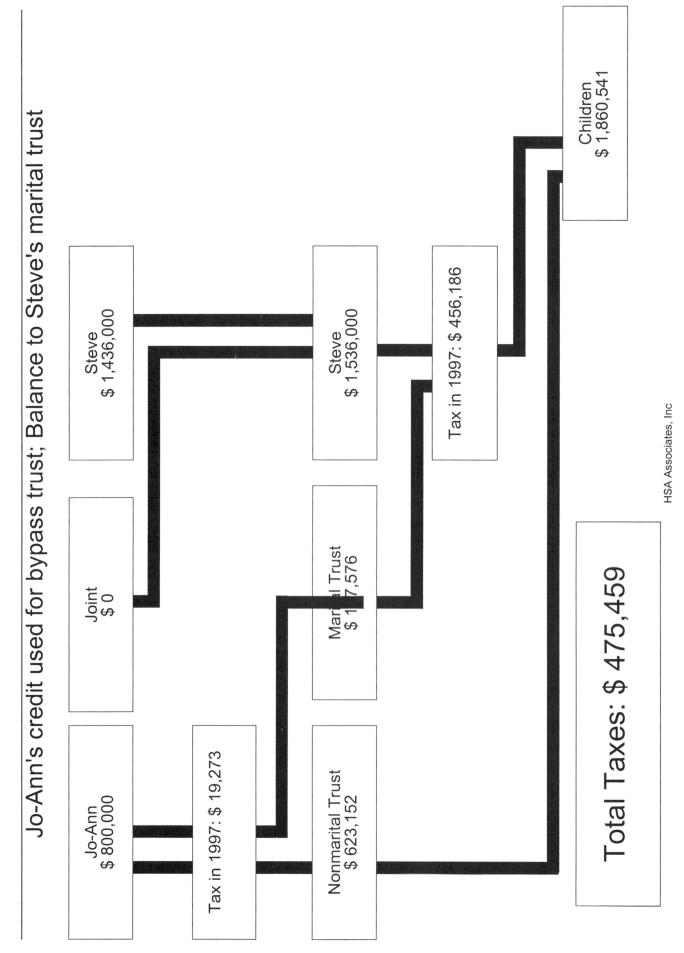

Jo-Ann
$ 800,000

Tax in 1997: $ 19,273

Nonmarital Trust
$ 623,152

Joint
$ 0

Marital Trust
$ 1,7,576

Steve
$ 1,436,000

Steve
$ 1,536,000

Tax in 1997: $ 456,186

Children
$ 1,860,541

Total Taxes: $ 475,459

HSA Associates, Inc

Steve and Jo-Ann Smith

Jo-Ann's credit used for bypass trust; Balance to Steve's marital trust; L.I. removed from estate

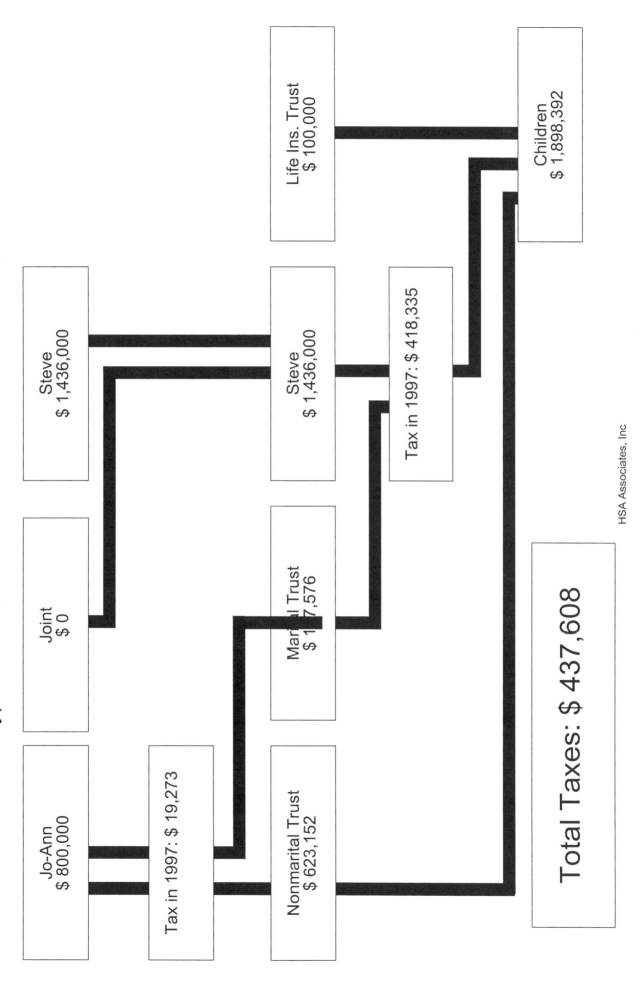

Life Ins. Trust
$ 100,000

Children
$ 1,898,392

Steve
$ 1,436,000

Steve
$ 1,436,000

Tax in 1997: $ 418,335

Joint
$ 0

Marital Trust
$ 1,7,576

Jo-Ann
$ 800,000

Tax in 1997: $ 19,273

Nonmarital Trust
$ 623,152

Total Taxes: $ 437,608

HSA Associates, Inc

Steve and Jo-Ann Smith

Jo-Ann Leaves None to Surviving Spouse

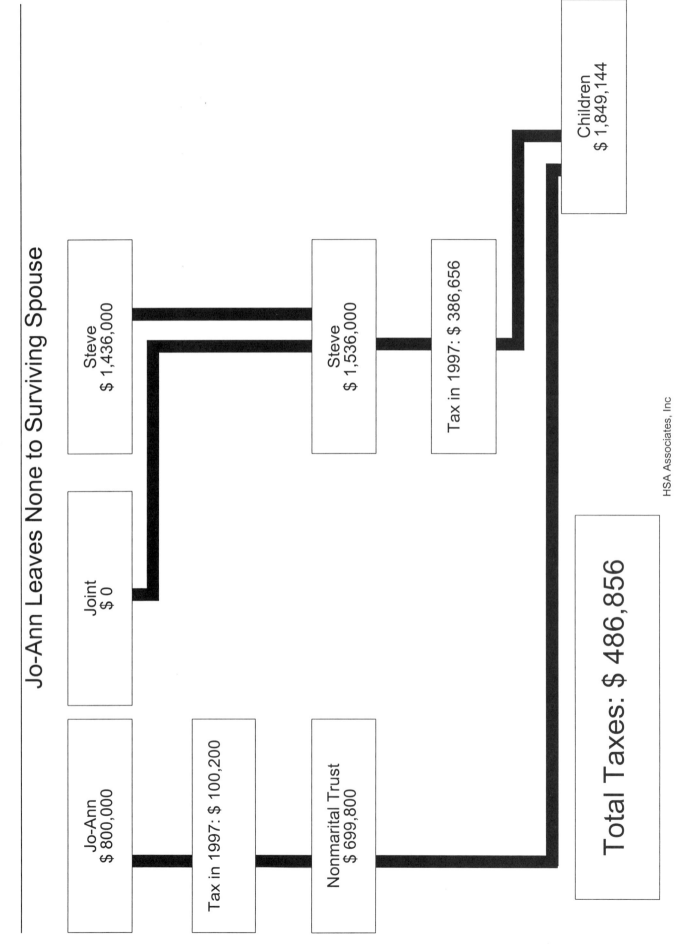

Jo-Ann
$ 800,000

Tax in 1997: $ 100,200

Nonmarital Trust
$ 699,800

Steve
$ 1,436,000

Joint
$ 0

Steve
$ 1,536,000

Tax in 1997: $ 386,656

Children
$ 1,849,144

Total Taxes: $ 486,856

HSA Associates, Inc

Net to Heirs

Steve and Jo-Ann Smith

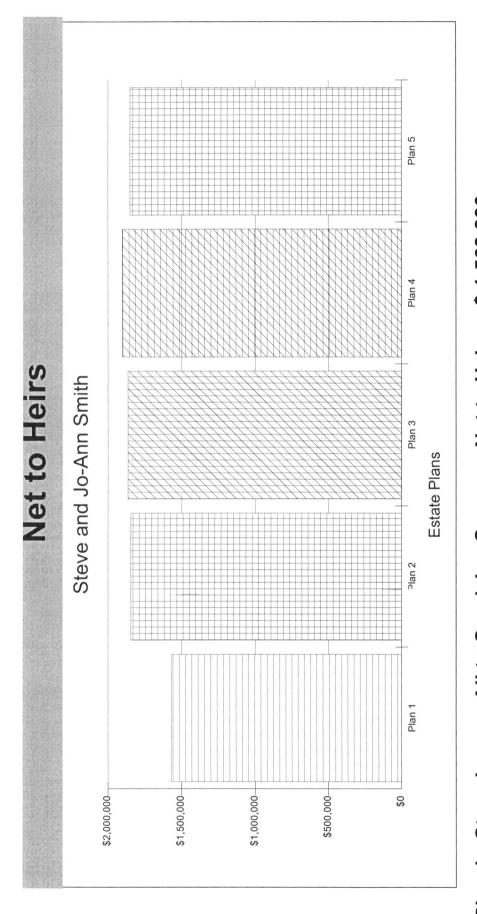

Estate Plans

Plan 1 - Steve Leaves All to Surviving Spouse : Net to Heirs = $ 1,568,880
Plan 2 - Steve's credit used for bypass trust; Balance to Jo-Ann outright : Net to Heirs = $ 1,846,062
Plan 3 - Steve's credit used for bypass trust; Balance to Jo-Ann's marital trust : Net to Heirs = $ 1,864,062
Plan 4 - Steve's credit used for bypass trust; Balance to Jo-Ann's marital trust; L.I. removed from estate : Net to Heirs = $ 1,901,907
Plan 5 - Steve Leaves None to Surviving Spouse : Net to Heirs = $ 1,849,144

HSA Associates, Inc

Total Taxes

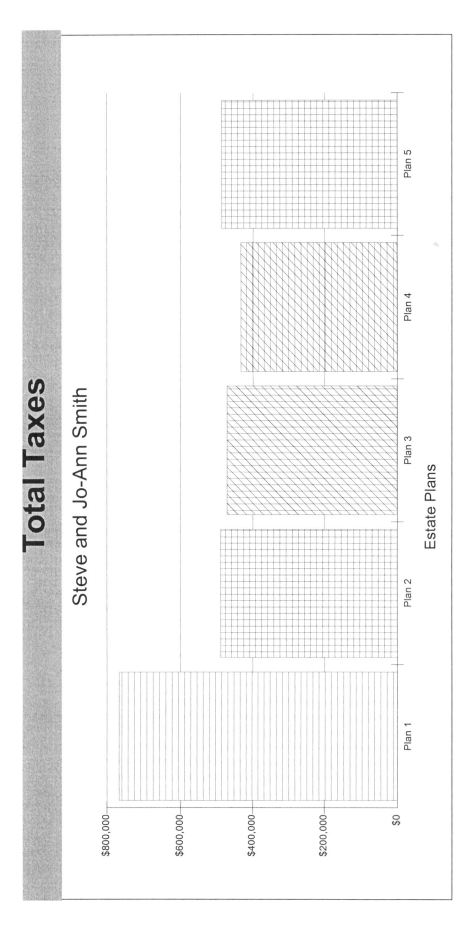

Steve and Jo-Ann Smith

Estate Plans

Plan 1 - Steve Leaves All to Surviving Spouse : Total Taxes = $ 767,120
Plan 2 - Steve's credit used for bypass trust; Balance to Jo-Ann outright : Total Taxes = $ 489,938
Plan 3 - Steve's credit used for bypass trust; Balance to Jo-Ann's marital trust : Total Taxes = $ 471,938
Plan 4 - Steve's credit used for bypass trust; Balance to Jo-Ann's marital trust; L.I. removed from estate : Total Taxes = $ 434,093
Plan 5 - Steve Leaves None to Surviving Spouse : Total Taxes = $ 486,856

HSA Associates, Inc

DEATH TAXES POST TRA '97: HOW MUCH WILL YOUR ESTATE PAY?*

Taxable	1997	1998	1999	2000	2001	2002	2003	2004	2005	2006
$625,000	$9,250	$0	$0	$0	$0	$0	$0	$0	$0	$0
$650,000	$18,500	$9,250	$0	$0	$0	$0	$0	$0	$0	$0
$675,000	$27,750	$18,500	$9,250	$0	$0	$0	$0	$0	$0	$0
$700,000	$37,000	$27,750	$18,500	$9,250	$9,250	$0	$0	$0	$0	$0
$850,000	$94,500	$85,250	$76,000	$66,750	$66,750	$57,500	$57,500	$0	$0	$0
$950,000	$133,500	$124,250	$115,000	$105,750	$105,750	$96,500	$96,500	$39,000	$0	$0
$1,000,000	$153,000	$143,750	$134,500	$125,250	$125,250	$116,000	$116,000	$58,500	$19,500	$0
$2,000,000	$588,000	$578,750	$569,500	$560,250	$560,250	$551,000	$551,000	$493,500	$454,500	$435,000
$5,000,000	$2,198,000	$2,188,750	$2,179,500	$2,170,250	$2,170,250	$2,161,000	$2,161,000	$2,103,500	$2,064,500	$2,045,000
10,000,000	4,948,000	4,938,750	4,929,500	4,920,250	4,920,250	4,911,000	4,911,000	4,853,500	4,814,500	4,795,000
20,000,000	10,948,000	10,938,750	10,929,500	10,920,250	10,920,250	10,911,000	10,911,000	10,853,500	10,814,500	10,795,000
50,000,000	27,500,000	27,500,000	27,500,000	27,500,000	27,500,000	27,500,000	27,500,000	27,500,000	27,500,000	27,500,000

Courtesy: NumberCruncher Estate Planning Software: (610) 527 5216. Figures include both federal and state death tax.

Warning: Actual cash-need tax total will exceed these amounts in some states. A number of states impose taxes significantly higher than the federal state death tax credit amount assumed! These numbers include only death taxes and do not include debts or administrative costs.

How to Obtain Steve Leimberg's

*Software: